Second Edition

*Learning
to Plan —
and
Planning
to
Learn*

Miles River Press

By Donald N. Michael

On Learning to Plan—and Planning to Learn:
The Social Psychology of Changing
Toward Future-Responsive Societal Learning

The Unprepared Society:
Planning for a Precarious Future

The Next Generation:
The Prospects Ahead for the Youth
of Today and Tomorrow

Cybernation:
The Silent Conquest

Proposed Studies on the Implications
of Peaceful Space Activities for Human Affairs

Second Edition

Learning
to Plan —
and
Planning
to
Learn

Donald N. Michael

Alexandria, Virginia

First Edition, 1973, Jossey-Bass, Inc.
Second Edition, 1997, Miles River Press

Ordering Information

Orders by U.S. trade bookstores and wholesalers:
Midpoint Trade Books
27 West 20th Street, Suite 1102
New York, New York 10011 .
Telephone: (212) 727-0190   *Fax:* (212) 727-0195

*Orders for individuals, organizations, quantity sales and
college course adoption:*
Miles River Press
400 Madison Street, #1309
Alexandria, Virginia 22314
Telephone: (703) 683-1500   (800) 767-1501
Fax: (703) 683-0827

Miles River Press Team

Peg Paul, Publisher
Sara Rau and Sandra Bisbey, Editorial
Weber Design, Cover
Julia Cade, Production

Library of Congress Cataloging-in-Publication Data:

Michael, Donald N.
    Learning to plan — and planning to learn / [by] Donald N. Michael. — 2nd ed.
    p.   cm.
    Rev. ed. of: On learning to plan & planning to learn. 1973.
    Includes bibliographical references and index.
    ISBN 0-917917-08-1 (Paperback)
    ISBN 0-917917-10-3 (Casebound)
    1. Social policy.   2. Planning.   3. Social psychology.
4. Organizational change......   I. Michael, Donald N.   Learning to plan &
planning to learn.   II. Title.
HN17.5.M5   1997
361.2'5—dc20   96-25477
                                                        CIP

Copyright © 1997 by Donald N. Michael

10 9 8 7 6 5 4 3 2

Dedication

*For
Geoffrey,
my son—
who
is
learning*

⋆ *Table of Contents* ⋆

Acknowledgments
First Edition

The work underlying this report was supported by the Center for Studies of Metropolitan Problems, National Institute of Mental Health, first through a Special Research Fellowship for me and later through a special research grant, #MH 14629. I am indebted to the Center for its support, and especially to its former Associate Director, Dr. Matthew Dumont, and its Executive Secretary, Richard Wakefield, for their enthusiasm and help.

Among other things, the Center grant made it possible to create a Work Group for the study. Its purposes are described in the Introduction. Here I want to thank its members for their conscientious, imaginative, and critical contributions to the study; their influence pervades the report. Work Group members were Raymond Bauer, Henry David, Robert Kahn, Matthew Dumont, Philburn Ratoosh, Donald Schon, Allan Westin, and Melvin Webber.

At various times James Crowfoot, Joseph DiMento, Alan Guskin, Robert Olson, and Meridith Spencer were project staff members. Crowfoot and Guskin, as Assistant Project Directors, were deeply involved through about the first half of the project. Olson, as Research Associate, came in part way through that period. Crowfoot made fundamental contributions to our theoretical understanding, especially concerning the role of planning as an organizational guidance system (Crowfoot, 1972). Guskin clarified our understanding of the social psychological implications of advocate planning, and initiated our advance into the murky area of personal time perspectives and their relation to felt needs for planning (Ross and Guskin, 1972). Olson enlarged our understanding of the social psychology of political processes as a property of social systems. I write "our" because at that time the project was very much a team creation. While much of the study was carried out after the team members departed, their influence contributed greatly to my understanding of what I was struggling with. It has remained strong in my thinking. Of course their contributions went well beyond the subjects singled out here: they accomplished difficult field interviews, wrote working papers that enlightened me and the Work Group, and provided a day-to-day intellectual atmosphere and supportive mood that were crucial for coalescing the directions of this study. It was a deeply rewarding time for me, and the study and I are much the better for it. Early in the study, Meridith Spencer undertook some very helpful literature searches on various meanings of planning and analyses of them. Toward the project's end, Joseph DiMento was invaluable as a literature reader, abstractor, and evaluator.

Melvin Webber arranged for one of his graduate students in planning to listen to the tapes of the Work Group meetings and abstract them, emphasizing the topics and arguments that most impressed him as new, useful, or important. The resulting report and critique, prepared by James Sundberg, were most helpful to further Work Group deliberations and most informative, thanks to his own interpolated comments on how, as a planner-to-be, he saw these issues and judged our approach to them. (Mr. Sundberg later became involved in community development and planning activities in the San Francisco Bay Area. His insights into those activities were especially valuable, in part because he and I had the material from his report as a shared basis for my questions and his answers.) I strongly recommend that others seek the benefits of such assessments when undertaking analogous studies.

Throughout, my students in the various versions of my seminar on technology and social change provided a supportive and responsive context for trying out ideas — theirs and mine, and who is to say which is which? All I can do is thank them for sharing and making productive so much ambiguity and uncertainty. John Krogman, James Pelikan, and Neil Tudiver have devoted many hours of effort and imagination to interviews and working papers that extended far beyond the period of their seminar involvement. Their interview-based examples and insights into structural and perceptual determinants of long range planning in some large corporations in the greater Detroit area have been especially helpful.

At the end of this report is a list of respondents who were willing to be identified. The trouble with such lists is that the very format washes out a sense of the uniqueness of each respondent as a busy but helpful person. The time, thought, and courtesy each gave to me, face-to-face or in a few cases, in correspondence, is nowhere evident in such a list. Yet their generosity was crucial to the development of the study.

Near the end of the study several people critically read a draft of this book. I have tried to be as responsive as I could to their many suggestions, and this version has greatly benefited from both their candor and support. In addition to members of the Work Group, draft readers were: Chris Argyris, Bayard Catron, C. West Churchman, Joseph DiMento, David Hertz, Alfred Kahn, Robert Olson, Richard Raymond, Geoffrey Vickers, and Dwight Waldo.

Of course I alone am responsible for what use I have made of the information, speculations, and advice offered by all those who have helped in this effort.

Throughout, Beverly Walter was the project administrative officer, comptroller, coordinator, caterer, note-taker, secretary, and overall integrator. She kept things together and going in the right direction at the right times in ways I only dimly understand but deeply appreciate. She comes close to having been *the* indispensable person in the project.

In turn, our activities were effectively facilitated by the many human and material resources of the Center for Research on Utilization of Scientific Knowledge and its parent organization, the Institute for Social Research, at the University of Michigan.

I am especially grateful for the time, resources, and ambiance needed to revise the manuscript, and to prepare it for copyediting and publication, which were generously and efficiently provided. These took the form of a Visiting Fellowship at the Institute of International Studies, University of California at Berkeley.

Permission to reprint extended passages from the following books and articles is gratefully acknowledged. Martin Rein, "Social

Planning: The Search for Legitimacy," reprinted by permission of the *Journal of the American Institute of Planners*, *35* (July 1969). Alfred J. Kahn, *Theory and Practice of Social Planning*, Chapter 2, Figure 1, and pp. 19-20, © 1969 by Russell Sage Foundation, New York. C. Argyris, "The Incompleteness of Social-Psychological Theory: Examples from Small Group, Cognitive Consistency, and Attribution Research," *American Psychologist*, *24* (1969) 10, copyright 1969 by the American Psychological Association and reproduced by permission. C. Argyris, "Resistance to Rational Management Systems," reprinted from *Innovation Magazine*, issue no. 10, 1970, by permission of *Business and Society Review/Innovation*. H. Wilensky, *Organizational Intelligence: Knowledge and Policy in Government and Industry* (New York: Basic Books, 1967), reprinted by permission of Basic Books, Inc. F. Emery, "The Next Thirty Years: Concepts, Methods, and Anticipations," reprinted from *Human Relations*, 1967, *20*, by permission of Plenum Publishing Corporation.

The seemingly endless editorial minutiae involved in preparing the manuscript for publisher and printer were accomplished, and the accompanying exasperation kept bearable, through the gracious assistance of my wife Margot. Indeed, during those last many months of writing, the most thankless tasks have been borne by her and by my son Geoffrey. All my bad moods and frustrations invariably came home to roost, but their moral support, good humor, and understanding prevented what could have been a miserable time for all of us and provided a setting in which I found refreshment and revitalization. Their caring was more important than I can say.

Berkeley, California   Donald N. Michael
February 1973

⋆ Foreword ⋆

A 1996 Reflection
on the Context and Conditions
for Learning

THEN AND NOW

In 1973 the arguments set forth in *On Learning to Plan — and Planning to Learn* seemed to speak more to theory, speculation, and desirable conduct than to imperative action in the face of undeniable fact. Now, chronic uncertainty is widely, if reluctantly, recognized. Indeed, scenario methodology — evolved in the 70's, even as *Learning to Plan* was being published — has made it rewarding, in some businesses and other entities, to make learning opportunities out of uncertainties. Nevertheless, I expect readers will be dismayed and fascinated to discover that the thinking and quotes in *Learning to Plan* still pretty well describe the current situation, and its caveats and injunctions are just as applicable today, if not more so. Surely the Epilogue could as well have been written today. Then, I urged readers to read it first; I do so again now, both as an overview of the rest of the book and as a benchmark for looking backwards — and forwards, too.

In this light, republication of *Learning to Plan* is intended, in part, to provide an historical baseline to compare now with then, when ideas about organizational and social learning were just emerging and the necessity for long-range social planning was a dubious societal imperative. In 1973 we had essentially no experience with meeting the social and psychological challenges involved in becoming learners, as persons and organizations, and none in practicing planning as a learning process. The current accumulating circumstances facing the world deepen my intention to continue to address these questions.

Today societal problems collide, pile up, and gridlock world-wide in ever more complex disarray. Bungled situations accumulate, "spin" substitutes for transparency, fractiousness is the order of the day, along with micro and macro violence. Drug dissemination remains uncontrollable, and international terrorist organizations grow — as do population, environmental threats, poverty, and endemic mal-education. In spite of ever more information, offered at ever higher rates, the world fumbles along with ever less-effective institutions. Many global analysts proclaim the market as *the* panacea — but let us not expect the market to solve this interlocked mess. To be sure, it is an effective instrument for implementing *some* policy purposes. It works very well indeed for *some* people, but very poorly for most. Most blatantly, it is by definition incapable of providing either the moral norms or long-term perspectives necessary for meaningful life ways. Today, nevertheless, long-range planning in the service of societal needs is not an idea in good currency. But in 1973, neither was learning.

Like it or not, *planning conducted as a learning process*, and *learning through planning*, are imperative. In this world driven by human rights, competitive markets, and technological innovation, planning becomes the consequential responsibility of those who insist on these freedoms. Social survival requires that we give self-conscious, systematic, reiterative attention to *learning* about where we want to go, how we might try getting there, what getting there means, and whether we still want to get there.

Traditional planning implies constraints. Planning by learning *reduces* constraints. Instead of being gratuitously blindsided by counterproductive consequences from short-term expedients, the process of ongoing learning reveals new options in the light of contexts illuminating longer time periods. The learning and planning emphasized here could be called, alternatively, "discovering," "exploring," "experimenting." Frankly, I would prefer to use "discovering," to differentiate learning as used here from the experiences most of us have associated with learning; usually we have been rewarded by getting the right answer, rather than by undertaking the challenge of discovering the useful questions. But "learning" is the word in good currency, so I shall stay with it.

I have not updated this work; for instance, I do not review or critique the literature on organizational change and management issues accumulated since 1973. I assume that readers are immersed in the current literature for the same reasons that bring them to this book. However, it has been edited to make for more user-friendly reading. To that end, some contents have been deleted as redundant (even by 1973 standards), and one chapter has been converted to an Appendix. But I have been careful to preserve the remaining contents as an expression of my ideas as of 1973 and of the historical context of associated ideas.

Finally, I want to be clear at the outset: The more I try to understand, the more I realize how much I don't understand. Nor do I believe other authors, and surely not leaders, understand. This is not to say that most authors and readers, leaders and followers, do not collude every day in their wanting to *feel* that they understand. But, for me, the compounding complexity of this world, fueled by the accumulating, anxious quests of multitudes for meaning in the face of such complexity, can birth only the vague semblance of understanding. In the words of Virginia Woolf, on matters such as I reflect on, "The truth is only to be had by laying together many varieties of error."

So saying, the reader should understand that this Reflection is not a focused essay, magisterially proffering linked and incisive conclusions; it is a collection of current reflections, musings, about aspects of planning, learning, and civil society, and the effects of boundaries and feedback on these circumstances. It is informed by and it is intended to inform the substance of *Learning To Plan*. The headings highlight topics — "varieties of error" — and using those, I search out paths, usually within sight of each other, that often intersect and sometimes converge. There are vast gaps, inconsistencies, and, surely, contradictions in these reflections. As a member of a civilization identically compromised — and as a learner — I cannot do other than be tentative and unraveled about these matters. My hope is that what I offer here will encourage others in *their* reflections, while further illuminating the ideas and topics explored in these chapters.

LEARNING, PLANNING, AND CIVIL SOCIETY

One cardinal reason we have not learned how to undertake long-range social planning is that efforts over the last 20 years or so have been devoted chiefly to learning how to help businesses learn. With regard to civil learning, we are where we were in 1973 with corporate learning. We are far from learning all there is to learn in this realm and we are at the very beginning of learning how to create learning norms and structures in government organizations. But these two settings are subsystems in the larger socio-political system; in a democracy, businesses and government organizations unavoidably depend — like it or not — on the support of the civil society. As I shall discuss later, one of the greatest contributions business can make to civil society, hence to its own future, is to take very deliberate steps to help civil society learn how to learn.

The future of complex democratic societies depends on the widespread practice of learning norms, so those experiments called "learning" within a business and within governments will need encouragement by the civil society, which must *also* experiment. Experiments they will always be, since the questions to be asked — the learning to be done — will be changing with each changing context. Yet, currently, most people who make up civil society are not self-conscious learners, and much conspires in the world to discourage or deny that capability. Undergirding this reflection, is preoccupation with the unmet challenge of how to change toward a civil society infused with the norms of learning in order to plan, and planning in order to learn how to become, in fact, *civil*.

The Influence Of Boundaries On Learning

Apparently, the most immediately appealing chapter in *Learning To Plan* has been the one that emphasizes the requirements for spanning boundaries, and the resistance to learning to do it. Today, engaging boundaries is even more demanding and complicated; it includes boundary maintenance and change, as well as boundary spanning. So I will devote especial attention to boundaries and their implications for learning to plan and planning to learn, especially for democratic civil societies.

But why should anyone attentive to this world of turmoil be especially attentive to boundaries, other than to span them and to expect the demise of those few remaining? This is the age of networks, not boundaries, right?

There is much more to it than that! A major cause and consequence of planet-wide social turmoil is increased efforts and demands to establish, change, or remove boundaries, and counter-efforts to preserve them. Networks may encourage boundaries to alter more rapidly, but boundaries are not disappearing. Perhaps more than in pre-network times, today's boundaries are built around concepts, convictions, relationships, and flows of information in the form of money or other symbols. But while flows of symbols may be unbounded in the abstract, they are absorbable only in the concrete — via organizational and personal interests, and actual operating modes. Ultimately, via individual human minds. All bounded. The mode and degree of absorption involve crucially important, mostly unmet, learning challenges, certainly in civil society. It is essential to have insight into the nature and functions of boundaries if we are to learn how to make the most felicitous use of extant ones and establish new ones. So a few rather heavy paragraphs are in order, to delineate the meaning of boundaries — acknowledging, as that splendid social philosopher and economist Kenneth Boulding observed, "All important distinctions are, ultimately, fuzzy."

Boundaries Discriminate Meanings

By boundaries, I mean those perceptual arrangements we use to separate or unite, differentiate and connect ourselves to the world. Our personally and culturally learned modes of conduct and expectations are reified, operationalized, expressed, and maintained by boundaries of many kinds — physical, temporal, ideological, territorial, factual, conceptual, procedural, relational, as well as organizational. They establish and maintain rules and expectations — hence behavior, rewards, sanctions, policies, and culturally-driven behavior.

Boundaries keep threats outside and give support inside. They determine access, power and legitimacy. Explicitly and implicitly, they define "me," "this," "us," and by contrast, "you," "that," and "them." While many attempt to shift or destroy one or another boundary, others are intent on boundary preservation. As the eminent social psychologist Marilynn Brewer says, "We need to belong to groups but more importantly, we need to have people not belong to our groups." Consequently, especially in our times, boundaries become the focus of feelings, claims, and actions.

Not being creatures of instinct, we survive by learning reliable, successful behavior — learning the answers, that is — which becomes habit. Once that success is attained, unlearning and relearning usually is not attractive to people. We are creatures of habit, and boundaries help us establish and maintain habits. Among our habits are those that determine where we set our boundaries for thinking, doing, responding, engaging, and disengaging. Boundaries enhance memory and recognition; boundary-setting is a means for categorizing and storing information so it is recognizable in the future. Of course, boundaries also reinforce the convictions and motives of those whose habits are different from ours, including those who have learned to believe that they would benefit from elimination or modification of current boundaries, or from the establishment of new boundaries.

Boundary-making is an act of discrimination. Boundaries are products of discrimination. The necessity and capability to discriminate are embedded in our genetic make-up and in our cultural endowment. We must discriminate, or everything would be a blooming, buzzing confusion. But *when, where,* and *how* we discriminate are crucial learning tasks as boundaries are challenged, changed, and redefined. As boundaries are challenged or blurred, or as new ones open new consequences, both sought and unsolicited, the comforts of known boundaries are threatened for some people and organizations. For others, such changes hold the promise of liberation from old boundaries. Whether boundary discrimination is socially positive or negative in its consequences depends on where boundaries are established, for what ends, and when the evaluation takes place. Of course, the nature of the evaluator's boundaries is of major importance.

The current social psychological context of boundary-shifting — the ambiguities, uncertainties, conflicts — exacerbates feelings of uncertainty and meaninglessness, of role conflict and role ambiguity. In turn, these engender still more efforts to change or to maintain boundaries in the search for meaning and certainty. This context of proliferating problematical boundaries contends with the meaning-giving comforts and discomforts of existing boundaries. Thereby learning risks are compounded and confounded and, if accepted, all the riskier. In the words of the Declaration of Independence: "All experience hath shown that man-kind are more disposed to suffer, while evils are sufferable, than to right themselves by abolishing the forms to which they are accustomed." Now, perhaps more so than then, learning which "forms" — that is, boundaries — to reject as insufferable, and which to "suffer," faces persons and organizations with mutually intense incentives to embrace and to resist change

Boundaries Become Operational
Through Feedback

Boundaries differ in their permeability, whether they discriminate a state's territory, a politically correct exchange, the perceptions of a visitor listening to a family's reminiscences, what a voter understands of a politically-motivated soundbyte, or a jargon-shaped conversation among experts.

A boundary operates as a feedback filter, and its permeability, for better and worse, is a consequence of the characteristics of the filter and of the feedback. In other words, I am using the term "feedback" in its original, broader cybernetic meaning: *those signals that effect boundary discrimination and maintenance.* This includes but is not limited to exchanges between persons, its conventional meaning in organizational and interpersonal psychology. Learning about the "other side" of a boundary depends on the characteristics and use of information fed back from that side of the boundary. The information that flows out from and in to those facing a boundary (on either "side") is what characterizes the fact of boundary. This is so whether one engages a border crossing, a partisan political position, an action advocacy group, a joint venture, a spouse, or a washing machine.

So, by definition, the information A intends to put out to define the boundary the way A wants it defined, may or may not be what B perceives on B's side. Inappropriate or indifferent feedback is experienced as frustrating and ambiguous; the boundary is experienced as a barrier. (Consider the chronic difficulties mere mortals experience when they try to interpret the information fed to them from the inside of their VCR, that is supposed to instruct them on how to feed information into it to record a program!) Increasingly this is the state of the world, and thereby the learning and planning tasks are compounded and confounded.

By contrast, when we say that a conversation or, say, an international commercial transaction flows smoothly, this does not mean there is no boundary; rather, it means that the feedback across the boundary, which is necessary to produce smooth functioning, has been carefully designed and maintained to meet those requirements. This is true whether the boundary has to do with laws, contracts, specific cross-cultural expectations, or accepting the obligations of personal candor or respect for the expressed desires of another person. So smooth functioning is evidence of well-discriminated boundaries, rather than their absence.

Therefore, boundaries should not necessarily be equated to barriers. Carefully designed feedback intended to define the boundary can reduce or eliminate barriers within the ambit of what the boundary is intended to discriminate and facilitate. A well-established boundary, then, is one where the signals that flow back and forth across the boundary are mutually understood and accepted. In this way reliability and "expectability" are maintained. Of course, what is understood and accepted may comprise collusive lies maintained so as not to disrupt relationships valued for, say, mutual self esteem.

Too often we assume that when we name a boundary, we have defined that boundary. Alas, this is where trouble begins. The learning challenge is to discover what information, fed back and forth, furthers the function the boundary is supposed to facilitate. The second challenge is learning how to establish the exchange of that information as the norm for boundary-related conduct. We need to learn which discriminations are productive under what feedback conditions. Since the information fed back and forth includes much more than rational "data," learning which discriminations really facilitate is a subtle and demanding task.

Contemplate, for example, that the boundary — as in the case of a policy that restricted my club's membership to males — may no longer be acceptable. These in turn have changed the boundaries that, for the wife, maintained a relationship to a spouse who had been a contented, exclusive member of the club. All this means that new learning is necessary among the members, and in the club's relations to the world beyond its boundaries, in order to use effectively the new filter characteristics that define, or bound, the club.

It is often observed that boundaries are fluid, and therefore people live with blurred boundaries — filling multiple roles, for example. And so what? Boundaries blur when there is inadequate discrimination, either because the person has not learned how, or because circumstances reward the costs of living with ambiguity, or because the culture deliberately obscures the distinctions. While there are obvious benefits to being able to shift focus across overlapping roles, there are also deep and destructive costs involved in struggling with role ambiguity and role conflict, as I describe in Chapter 7. Habitual ways of coping with blurred boundaries support beliefs and behaviors for one's way of life, for better and often for worse. But altering feedback across those boundaries creates new emotional and operational consequences, positive for some, for others not. Either way, learning anew what feedback is appropriate to establish more felicitous "overlapping boundaries" is increasingly imperative for the individuals involved, and for the civil society in which they act out their pleasures and pains.

Consider, for example, the increasingly vexing questions about the conflict between work and family obligations, boundaries that increasingly "overlap" in unfamiliar, non-habitual ways. Boundary discrimination tasks are exacerbated as work information is fed into what used to be the family environment — via the fax, the modem, the cellular phone — and into the work and family environments of two-career couples. There are no longer generally-agreed-upon feedback norms that establish what inflow of work information across the family boundary is appropriate. Or, for that matter, how to appropriately define the boundary called "family," or that of "married couple."

What becomes critical, then, is learning what information is needed to flow from inside the boundary to the outside and vice versa, so that the boundary can perform validly and productively its reasons for existence. Discovering feedback appropriate for the intended discrimination, and constructing the processes for interpreting the feedback accurately within an appropriate time frame, become major tasks for all involved in a specific discriminated realm. In some business organizations, and here and there in civil society, learning how to do this is well begun. Overall, it is a major unmet challenge.

In sum, boundaries are acts of discrimination. They contribute to felicitous human intercourse, or disrupt it, according to how well the feedback flows back and forth across them. Learning what feedback is useful, and learning to design and maintain that feedback, is a major and ongoing planning task. As such, it is a crucial prerequisite for a society that must learn how to be civil.

Implications for Planning and Learning

In light of the above, the tasks of interpreting and designing new boundaries, or maintaining old ones, requires unprecedented attention to the nature of information flow (feedback) across boundaries. We shall have to learn over time how to attend to and design these flows. As I emphasize in *Learning To Plan*, feedback information is essential for learning via the method of error embracing. Learning how to reduce error can be done by learning what to change in expectancies. Or learning what to change in the nature of the information to be attended to in the feedback. Or learning what to change in the signals fed into the world so that, in turn, they create response signals that become better feedback for evaluating error. Any or all these options can result in learning. Learning how to do these things — learning to learn — is also part of the learning process.

However, no feedback system can be infinitely responsive; the consequences of information overload are not only psychological. Useful feedback in cybernetic systems depends on the interplay among the amount of information fed back; the rate at which it flows through the error detecting system; the error-reduction precision the feedback is intended to accomplish; and the degree of match between the feedback return rate and the response rate of the system it is intended to adjust. In the nature of cybernetic systems, tradeoffs are unavoidable between rate of information flow, speed of response, precision, and stability.

An essential task, then, is learning to design boundaries so that the feedback across them is appropriate for the purposes the boundary is intended to serve. This is an enormous task indeed! How to move society so that the multiple bounded entities it comprises can learn how to become a learning society? Since boundaries both create and remove obstructions to learning, the question becomes how to add or subtract bounded entities to this end? For example, if the feedback should be richer than it was with the old boundary conditions, then there will need to be more time for interpretation. If the feedback is to be more elaborate, and the response to it made more precise, we must understand that within a given period of time, the signal range of precise responses must be narrowed, or the response time will have to be extended. We can't have it all at once!

The current presumption is that more and more information can be stuffed into less and less time, with greater and greater precision of response. Instead, this causes more and more overload in the system, with increasing pressures, leading to chronic fear and exhaustion — numbing — or traumatic burnout of the humans involved. (Of course people differ in their tolerance for overload. However, a tacit discriminating of people according to this criterion presents yet another difficult challenge for democratic civil society.) Currently, these interacting feedback variables manage complex social systems poorly; the ethical, cultural, and operational tradeoffs among them have not been adequately recognized as inherent in information processing.

A dismaying example of this is the enthusiastically asserted, sloppy-minded presumption that because most everyone can see the same output at the same time on TV screens, we are rapidly becoming a "global village." But that same TV output is filtered through differing boundaries of ideas, sociality, language, culture, and ideology, resulting in different consequences at different time periods, shaped or bounded by different norms that in turn evoke action. In terms of the anthropological meaning of "village" as a group of people mutually reflecting and sharing a set of boundaries (i.e., a set of feedback experiences), nothing approaching a "global village" exists.

To presume otherwise is to grossly misunderstand the feedback norms and their implications — including resentment by other cultures, and the dangerous belief, at least in the United States, that what we see on, say, CNN, tells us what is really happening, and that "we" and "they" are experiencing it in the same way. (If we were truly a global village, the feedback arrangements for sharing ideas would be well established; but, ironically, the whole question of "intellectual property rights," indeed the very meaning of that concept, is in contention everywhere.)

Nevertheless, the industrialized world, obsessively intent on increasing the amount of information, and increasing the rate of flow of that information, apparently presumes that both will result in more precise responses to ever more-complex situations, in ever shorter time periods.

The question, then, is: Given the proliferation of boundary changes, and continuing attempts to make such changes, what generic feedback characteristics need to be established in order that, on both sides of a boundary, mutual learning can occur? I am talking about mutual learning appropriate for democratic conduct in a world whose complex requirements might be met only by including among its primary modes of conduct long-range social planning. Again, long-range, because *ad hoc*, bits and pieces, on-and-off attempts will not do it; they are what have led us to the present condition.

What are some of the generic discriminating feedback requirements? Surely, all those urged in this book; and as noted earlier, much more awareness and sensitivity to the design of trade-off conditions that will make for useful feedback in specific situations. Too little effort to learn how to build shared signals will result in the degeneration of diversity into mere noise, or worse.

More awareness is imperative about how unconscious needs and motives undergirding so-called rational behavior influence conscious responses to feedback. This is a semi-taboo subject in the organizational world. The benefits of applied intuition have become recognized, but it is hardly acceptable to draw to attention that both rationality and intuition also serve our unconscious needs for denial, domination, aggrandizement, compensation for childhood traumas, and the expression of deep reservoirs of fear and rage. Of course, there are unconscious needs for giving and receiving love, spiritual fulfillment, nurturing, and other positive drives that are also expressed through intuitions and rational actions. We eagerly turn to these positive expressions from the unconscious; but to believe these can carry the day, that the only unconscious motives acting are those in the service of reason and good will, is to invite disappointment, and worse. This is why *Learning To Plan* puts emphasis on recognizing the sources of resistance to becoming learners. And this is why *Learning To Plan* emphasizes that interpersonal skills are prerequisite for the personal and organizational risk-taking that unavoidably accompanies acknowledging uncertainty, error embracing, and boundary spanning.

INFORMATION, UNCERTAINTY, AND THE SEARCH FOR MEANING

For some, increased boundary shifting and boundary challenging often results in more uncertainty and meaninglessness; for others, depending on which boundaries are changed, increased certainty and meaning. Overall, however, interacting consequences from boundary shifting amplifies complexity, and intensifies the search for certainty and meaning, which results in still more boundary shifting and defending. This increases the uncertainties with which planning as a learning process must deal, and, in turn, deepens difficulties for the processes of governance. For, as *Learning To Plan* emphasizes, it is the acknowledgment of specific uncertainties that makes learning possible.

Information and Uncertainty

According to conventional wisdom, more information makes learning new answers easier, and decision-making more decisive. Ironically, just the opposite usually happens; the human condition is such that more information generally leads to more uncertainty. Usually, more information tells us that we need still more information to interpret the information we have, whether it pertains to toxic substances, sustainable futures, economic projections, welfare policy, the social impact of global warming, or the consequences of changes in public or private decision-making procedures. The feedback from the social and natural environment is not adequate to definitively shape the outflow of information from a person or office or agency. More information simply increases uncertainty regarding where boundaries should be set. (Needless to say, most well established bounded entities feed out information intended to show that he/she/they have more than enough information to justify doing what they are doing.)

Another type of information, increasingly pervasive, encourages doubts about the validity, reliability, or integrity of information sources. At best, non-natural science "data-bases" cannot reliably be "mapped" on to one another. Therefore, the consequences flowing from the application of feedback from one or another data source are not reliably predictable. (An example is the multiple, contending predictions forwarded by economists, derived from their preferred economic information selected to fit their preferred theory. And theory, of course, is just another bounded set of criteria for making sense.) Many feel that this state of affairs, exacerbated by lying and "spin," is all the more "reason" to look elsewhere than data-based criteria, to other criterial boundaries for discriminating, choosing, and acting. All this adds to the uncertainty.

Persons and organizations view information from within their personal and peer-shared boundaries. More information provides an ever-larger pool from which interested parties can fish differing positions on the history of what has led to current circumstances, on what is now happening, on what needs to be done, and on what the consequences will be. And more information often stimulates the creation of more options. As a result, still more information is generated, including more information about the information, and so on, around and around the self-amplifying "information" loop.

Deconstructing Language

In Chapter 1 and again in the Epilogue, I emphasize how the recognition that we *construct* social reality opens possibilities for major changes in our beliefs about the feasibility of apparently unlikely changes, such as future-responsive societal learning. Since the 1970s, under the rubric of deconstructionism, this way of understanding the way we use language has become a major intellectual position, with its own esoteric jargon, writing styles, in-fights and alliances. The claim is that ordered words — books, research reports, encyclopedias, speeches, whatever — are only narratives, ungrounded in anything else but narrative. There never was or is permanent meaning or certainty; there are only stories, and stories about stories. There is no place to stand — except to assert and demonstrate this "fact" about what others call "reality." (It is informative to note that, as ordered words, deconstructionist tracts are also deconstructable, are also just another story. But this doesn't seem to discourage deconstructionists from making their claim at great length.)

What I write in this Reflection is a story, or is a story about stories. Boundaries, learning, planning, multicultural identity, complexity, the future —even stories, and stories about stories — are all social constructs, stories explaining and prescribing how humans do or could or should behave. Stories are the ineluctable context and stimuli to thinking and acting, for changing and for maintaining boundaries.

Deconstructionist boundary-demolition is important and very useful. It encourages learning by demonstrating that positions are socially constructed, and, as such, are potentially mutable. It encourages the creative use of language to construct social realities other than the conventional. It can help discourage fundamentalisms for the same reason. It emphasizes that reason is always accompanied by passion and often masks the urge to power. It encourages the tolerance of relativism. It encourages thoughtful choosing among stories as the basis for action. In this way it encourages acknowledging uncertainty, and thereby opens otherwise-unnoticed options and alternatives. In sum, it can help encourage a decent, moderate, creative, collaborative, ironic approach to life.

But the deconstructionist story is insufficient to undergird society. It overlooks the majority of humans whose lives, in one way or another, are too nasty, brutish, and short to indulge in this generous way of thinking. It overlooks the powerful role of unconscious fears, rages, needs, that drive so much of what most of us *are* most of the time (Even when we try to be learners. Even the deconstructionists!). Of profound importance, it leaves out politics. ("Your policy proposal is just a story?! Well, you wimp, mine is truth!") Therefore, it has little to offer those multitudes who seek or know some truth or another so that life will be more certain and meaningful for them.

Discovering how and when deconstructionist theory and practice can help construct a *civil* civil society is a major learning challenge. Currently the difficulty is vividly demonstrated via conflicts over what language and behavioral feedback is acceptable

to groups that have embraced reconstructed stories that establish
or change their boundaries as cultural and minority groups. Again,
the yearning for certainty and meaning too often results in the new
story proclaimed as the truth.

The Function of Metaphors

Before leaving this topic, let us dwell on the crucial role of
metaphor in the construction of social reality. We construct our
realities for ourselves and each other chiefly through language. And
language derives much of its influence from its metaphoric content.
Here is how George Lakoff and Mark Johnson describe metaphor's
essential function:

*What is real for an individual as a member of a culture, is a product
both of his social reality and the way in which that shapes his
experience of the physical world. Since much of our social reality is
understood in metaphorical terms, and since our conception of the
physical world is partly metaphorical, metaphors play a very
significant role in determining what is real for us.*

*Because so many of the concepts that are important to us are either
abstract or not clearly delineated in our experience (emotions, ideas,
time, etc.), we need to grasp them by means of other concepts that
we understand more clearly (spatial orientations, objects, etc.). This
leads to metaphorical definitions in our conceptual system.*

Metaphors are, in my metaphorical terminology, boundary
discriminators. They are words (and images) that both designate
boundaries, and inform the feedback that flows across them.
Therefore, they are a powerful means by which we maintain, span,
and change boundaries. If felicitously chosen, they can change the
atmosphere in which issues are debated, and actions selected,
implemented, and evaluated. In other words, metaphors can
profoundly motivate or discourage learning, and the content of
planning. Throughout this Reflection, then — indeed, as you read
Learning To Plan — never forget that the occasions for learning to
plan and planning to learn will be grasped, detoured, or blocked

completely by the metaphors that are self-consciously applied, or unconsciously or indifferently accepted, to draw attention to the nature, function, and processes involved.

In the Western construction of reality, war-time language provides pervasive metaphors for describing peace-time activities and goals: "target" audience, "victorious" political "allies," "defeat" or "shoot down" the opponent's proposal, "attack" and "destroy" the causes of the problem, "capture" a share of the market. (Note that sport, the other popular source of metaphors for describing civil society, also uses many war metaphors.) These metaphors explicitly and (perhaps more importantly) tacitly emphasize we/they, before/after, winner/loser, beginning/ending — fixed boundaries in time, space, and relationship. Such metaphors, used deliberately or thoughtlessly, reinforce the persistence of inappropriately discriminated boundaries that are maintained by feedback norms hopelessly inadequate for a world of learning and planning. Learning requires metaphors that are compatible with its purposes and experiences in a fluid, amorphous world. Discovering which metaphors serve learning will itself be a learning task for civil society.

As of now, it is usually through the conventional metaphors (data never stand alone) that activists and policy makers present their proposals, and the media disseminate them — most of the time unquestioningly. Consequently, much of what the media convey, maintains beliefs based on boundaries that are metaphorically reinforced by a now-inadequate construction of social reality.

Slowing Down

Time — enough time — is essential to engage the feedback onslaught. As I have described above, the more complex the changing boundary situation — the feedback — the more time is necessary to understand, and to plan and to act. But as of now the technological/financial world hurtles on, ever faster, ignorantly forcing endless boundary changes that in turn engender still more boundary changes. The result is a world increasingly enmeshed, eroded, and nagged by ever more uncertainty and complexity, compounded by *ad hoc*, quick-fix, inappropriate feedback. Consequently, learning norms that sustain slowing down parts of "the system" are necessary. Is this possible? Perhaps.

The advancing pace of tech-economic market activities encourages a growing likelihood of all sorts of disasters, if only because there is a decline in shared and committed sense of where we are, where we are going, and how to keep matters coherent, whichever way we are going. As I described earlier, more information results in divergent uncertainties and responses — in a word, incoherence. Disasters are incoherent contexts; familiar boundaries disintegrate. In the Epilogue I examine disasters as a source of change encouraging moves toward future-responsive societal learning. Here I would add that the disorder and friction engendered by disasters could brake (and break) the headlong drive of ambitions and markets that depend on a reasonably reliable context for expansion.

In addition, there could also be a slowing down by significant numbers of members of the work force, who feel themselves pushed too hard by technology and competitive requirements — too tired, too stretched out, too deprived of the rest of living, and "for what?" Disenchanted workers could be replaced by others, initially innocent of or otherwise able to withstand the pace; but the economic and social costs of repeated replacements rise. The combination of burnout and denouement could lead to political action for a better, slower-paced life. Moreover, my sense is that a non-trivial number of managers and business leaders also feel much too overworked. But they fear admitting it, in the face of the public statements by some leaders enthusiastically upping the pace (cheered on by their trendy associates, the authors who live a reasonably-paced life *as* authors). Rejection of an overpaced work-life provides a potential for action built around different norms.

Another incentive to slow down the system is the time requirement for civil-society participation in what Daniel Yankelovich calls "coming to judgment;" the time-consuming group process of deliberating about the concepts and actions entailed in specific civil choices and commitments. And there are precedents, as in the time it takes for environmental impact statements to be constructed and responded to. Or the time it took to obtain approval for the construction of a nuclear energy plant. The time it takes to determine the safety and efficacy of a new pharmaceutical. Or the time the Japanese invest to attain consensus before undertaking major activities. Of course some developers, entrepreneurs, and activists object to such delays. We shall have to learn under which conditions which objections are valid. We shall have to learn what and when slowing down adds meaning and satisfaction, and when not.

No amount of information alone, no matter how elaborately available in depth, is sufficient for deciding. If it were, we could leave it to the computers. Indices and other such data-combining procedures, designed to shorten the time needed to understand and act, do not obviate the need to slow down the system. Such procedures by their very nature *lose* information. Time is needed to understand and respond to the changing boundary complexity we live in; time to learn how to judge the value of more and different information that characterizes, or should characterize, the feedback across those boundaries.

Judgments *must* lie at the basis of action and policy; those discrimination criteria called "values" are central. There is no value-free information. All information is the consequence of money, motivation, and effort to create, disseminate, and use it. So it must be of value to those who do so. Values determine what to pay attention to, and what to do about it. But values are increasingly diverse and in contention — at least as to *which* take priority under what conditions. And what passes for information is also dependent on the choice of, the valuing of, the human boundary filters participating in decisions and interpretations. Indeed, who decides who decides? What more value-laden question can be asked of those inside a boundary, or those outside of it?

Making sense of a world where much that gives it meaning is non-quantitative, occurs within *individual* human minds. And if we hope to maintain a democratic *civil* society, answers to important questions must go through many human minds. Obviously, those minds vary in their absorptive and interpretive abilities and capabilities, and their commitment. And all this takes far more time to do well than we currently acknowledge.

Slowing down would require radical restructuring of those activities increasingly overloaded with information, and of the requirements for ever more-complex judgments about the meaning of the information, and the consequences of actions based that information. It would require compelling evidence that the approaches currently used are not working, and that disasters loom; or that extant disasters derive significantly from the pace. To be sure, the psychodynamics of denial will discourage recognizing this; that's why a knowledgeable civil learning society is necessary to override such denial by business and government — and vice versa.

Note, however, that not everybody, every group, every government will respond at the same time to this need to slow down. As a result, governments incompetent to plan ahead; ignorant and angry civil societies caught in the present and looking for or subscribing to something they deem more promising than bumbling democracy; and businesses fearful of losing profits and customers, promise a nasty time of it. But if none try to learn how to slow down, I expect disasters will do it for us.

LEARNING IN A CIVIL SOCIETY OF CHANGING BOUNDARIES

Civil society subsumes all those bounded realms of activity, and collective and special interests, that at a given time are not preempted by government or business — from neighborhood betterment groups to grass-roots activist organizations, through philanthropies, to non-governmental organizations devoted to global issues.

This book emphasizes that a learning approach is essential for government and business, and I also strongly imply throughout that a learning approach is essential for civil society. However, long-range social planning is not essential for *all* government offices, businesses, or civil activities. Some are appropriately preoccupied with and designed to deal with the present. Part of the vitality and function of civil society arises from *ad hoc* or short-term preoccupations. And part of the vitality and function of government and business is rapid responsiveness. What *is* essential is that all be *learning* systems. Because their current context will always be changing, processes that undergird long-range social planning apply in the short run as well.

Other components of civil society do indeed require the long range, integrated perspective for which planning as learning is the appropriate mode of conduct. But today too few are using learning systems. Instead, for the most part, habitual beliefs, ignorance, and emotion expressed (and obsessively reported) as "opinion" prevail. The slow, deliberate, thoughtful approach of "coming to judgment" is not the norm. And persistent monitoring of the *consequences* of those judgments, practiced as long-range social planning, is rare at best.

It is imperative that all components of civil society understand, approve of, and in fact *insist* that some civil activities perform in this mode. Absent these norms, vast realms of civil society, and surely of business and government, will continue to be deceptive and opaque in those arenas of "privileged information." Operating according to conventional definitions of competence, it is very much in their interest *not* to publicly acknowledge uncertainty, embrace error, and operate by the other norms and conditions I set out here.

On the other hand, if, in their quest for immediate, narrow-interest changes, civil-society entities reject the inevitable experimental and time-consuming processes entailed in social learning and long range social planning, then government, business, and other civil-society entities will be blocked and undermined in their imperative efforts to learn how to cope humanely with this complex world. To persist in experimenting under such inhospitable circumstances, they would have to do so clandestinely, which would undermine the very requirements for learning — and learning how to learn.

We must learn which entities would benefit society by performing according to the norms of long-range social planning, and how to manage their mutual boundaries in order to do so felicitously. At the least, we must learn how to convert into learning organizations, a substantial portion of the participants in the civil society — a formidable and unprecedented task.

The Undergirding Societal Morass

The circumstances that make it imperative that civil society become what I term a learning society have been described by many others as well as myself. I draw these observations from my current experience in the United States, but what is so in the U.S. is also evident or nascent elsewhere. I summarize here in order to emphasize the enormity (and enormousness!) of the learning challenge.

There is no agreement on basic definitions for describing and interpreting the human condition. There is no agreement on which values take priority under which conditions, or how these values should be expressed in behavior. Environmental sustainability, how much poverty is acceptable, population stabilization, group rights vs. individual rights, public interest vs. private interest, "quick fixes" vs. long-term prudence, the limits of national sovereignty, and the conduct of the media, are chronic, festering examples of disagreements over what values pertain under what circumstances.

As a basis for action. there is no accepted, reliable, encompassing theory of social change under turbulent conditions. Human behavior is always over-determined; there are unnumbered ways of explaining why we do what we do — we cannot even make reliable economic forecasts beyond a few months, if that. Given the incomprehensibly-complex social world humans have accumulated, we do not understand where we are, hence where we are going.

Leaders, at whatever level, cannot acknowledge publicly, or often even to themselves, either their ignorance or impotence. And if they should do so, citizens would act to replace them with others who claim they can do what needs to be done.

Everyday language and its semantic baggage imputes a "reality" that does not match the complex "reality" we must deal with. It is hardly possible to use that language to describe what is wrong with that very language. Examine closely an idea, a description, a definition, and each gradually evaporates into metaphors and meta-metaphors. Meanings branch interminably and disappear into the gloom. (This Reflection suffers the same distortions.)

Most humans are insufficiently educated, skilled, and motivated for reasoning systemically, cybernetically, in multivariable terms, and in terms of both/and, rather than either/or. They are unskilled at bringing together rational reasoning, emotions, and feelings in the service of solving problems and living with predicaments.

These dismaying and desperate circumstances would surely seem sufficient to turn all parties toward learning how to overcome them. Given the imperatives for undertaking social programs to deal with this morass over the long term, how is it that we do so little planning with regard to them, and that we learn so little?

In part, important ideas and processes discriminated in *Learning to Plan* have yet to be fully engaged because the intimate relationship between learning and planning — planning as the pedagogy for learning — is still not well understood or appreciated, or accepted.

In part our only-modest progress, even in the corporate world, results from inattention to — one might even hazard denial of — deep social-psychological resistances to learning in the emerging societal context. Trying to become learners is fraught with profound social and psychological risks. Ironically, as I have earlier observed, the more disrupting the world becomes, the more tightly most of us grasp what we already have learned. As the saying goes, "Better the devil we know." It is no wonder that the process is slow and fitful, and mostly yet to be undertaken.

Learning to Plan delineates the social-psychological resistances that would discourage persons and groups that are trying to become learners — such as fear, distrust, denial; protecting the habits of learned successful behavior comprising our unconsciously held sense of self; and meeting deep needs for continuity and invulnerability. From the grass roots through the formal organizational world, denying the uncertainties that accompany *any* interpretation, policy, or action in this turbulent world, or the having the skill to deny errors successfully, rather than to embrace them, are still all too often the measures of a competent manager/leader. These resistances are alive and well! Indeed, there are new resistances to learning, even as there are new imperatives for learning. So long as we overlook the deep-lying sources of resistance to learning, we will underestimate the truly daunting challenges facing us.

For example, an important and vexing circumstance that adds to these learning difficulties in civil society is the proliferation of current efforts to enhance meaning in an uncertain world, by establishing group-identity boundaries that recognize as correct only that feedback defined by the member boundary-setters. The identity criteria that provide the basis for a comforting and protective boundary — along with the collateral outflow and inflow of information that determines what merits attention — are as various as the conditions that can be created, around which a group can coalesce: ethnic identity, self-help, spiritual and religious practice, ideologies, thought patterns, liberation aspirations, civil causes, whatever.

Of the many reasons many groups currently claim the virtues of diversity and differentiate themselves from others, surely one is the opportunity it offers to reduce uncertainty and meaninglessness for those within the boundary. It may also well be that those *outside* a boundary hope *their* uncertainty will be reduced as well, because previous, mutually-unclear claims may now be clarified by the new boundary separating "us" from "them." Separation rather than multiculturalism looks easier; and sometimes it is, at least for the time being. But the feedback characteristics defining the bounded groups may result in new difficulties.

When a group establishes its boundaries by insisting on its exclusive rights to set criteria for what is acceptable for others to "say" about it, real multicultural accommodation cannot occur. Instead an ambiguous and frustrating situation ensues, wherein the *acceptable* feedback across the boundary blurs the very boundary its creators intended to establish. Recall, an important function of boundaries is to distinguish A from B. But this function fails, if A cannot know B well because A establishes the boundary in such a way that B is unable to feed to A information that tells A who B is. In turn, the feedback A provides in response to B, cannot provide B with information B needs in order to know A. Proscribing uncomfortable feedback is a form of withdrawal, making genuine exchanges among the bounded groups impossible. It reduces uncertainty and meaninglessness for A, but the cost is misinformation or the absence of information about the other. These results frustrate and detour civil learning.

The extreme and most dangerous form of boundary preservation obstructing civil learning is fundamentalism. This anti-learning mode can reinforce any source of group identity, whether it be spiritual, ideological, conservative, or New Age. In this form group identity/belief boundaries are so impermeable to disconfirming feedback, that they provide their members with complete certainty and meaning. Sometimes the advantages provided to its members by such a boundary are so absolute, that what is fed out through their boundary is insistence that those defining themselves according to other boundary criteria are deluded, damned, and even merit destruction.

There is another way the need for meaning and the frustrations with existing boundaries expresses itself; a kind of inverse fundamentalism. I refer to the efforts of those seeking spiritual realization, to transcend the secular costs of boundaries by including *everything* within the comfort of an all encompassing boundary; all is one, and nothing is put outside this boundary — except, for some seekers, evil. But note that even here, at the quotidian level of verbal life, discriminations operate.

Those who believe in the virtues of diversity shall have to learn how to deal with those who do not, or who wish to obscure the differences inherent in diversity. This surely will be a central and daunting learning task for civil society, including among its profound challenges, learning how much and what kinds of diversity merit encouragement and acceptance.

Is a Learning-Mode Civil Society Possible?

There are many *small* bounded efforts at community development and these hold a promising potential as proto-learning experiments. In a like manner to the commune experiments in earlier American history, they manage to be insulated, to some degree, from the ongoing morass of the big system. That is, they are insulated enough, they have enough control over what passes through their boundaries, to succeed in shaping their community. Outside, those concerned with civil society's role in governance closely attend to these innovations, studying their processes and group norms. Communitarian enthusiasms and ongoing efforts of community development could subscribe to norms and skills for long range-social planning. And their practice could encourage more experiments using a learning mode.

But operating according to the norms of a learning system is not the prevalent mode of conduct within and between *large* civil enterprises. Rather, the facts of life listed earlier pertain. And like governments and businesses, civil enterprises are caught up in protecting and extending their operational and ideological boundaries. What then might move one or another species of civil organization to take the risks of becoming learning systems? Pressures to shift their boundaries defining their missions and modes of pursuing them might well come from other civil entities.

Women's-health advocacy groups dramatically shifted the preoccupations of more than one foundation supporting population limitation. Indeed, competition among foundations might encourage some to become serious about learning by planning.

And growing preoccupation with future threats of disaster could encourage long range social planning, as I explain in later chapters. However, disasters also result in retrenchment into previously-learned successful behavior. (After the 1906 San Francisco earthquake, building codes were ignored in order to quickly revive the commercial fortunes of the city.)

Business: An Important Contributor to Civil Learning?

Self-supported, self-initiated citizen-group actions to become learning systems are not impossible. But from beyond the boundaries that define the civil society, there could and should be a singular source of encouragement and support for civil learning systems: enlightened businesses.

Let me be clear. I fully recognize that for many, probably the majority of businesses — especially multinational corporations, the conventional perspective is, "The last thing we need is an informed civil society that is learning how to constrain our private interests, in order to further *their* ideas of the public interest!" However, there is a minority that recognizes from their own learning that acting from that perspective will destroy truly viable democratic societies; and, while others with power may be indifferent to this demise as long as they retain their perquisites, that isn't what life is all about. What is more, given the rising number of unavoidable social traumas, a business attitude intent on maintaining a world of passive consumers rather than active citizens, will be unable to continue unchallenged and unabated.

It makes sense, then, to look to business to encourage civil learning, and to be a major resource for learning how to learn. It is chiefly within business contexts that techniques and cultural norms for learning, and planning as learning, are being developed and applied. So it should be a strategy for some businesses and some entities in the civil society to search each other out, as a matter of mutual, long-term self-interest.

For the purposes of civil society, this boundary-changing approach to learning how to learn is fraught with its own learning challenges. The current flow of feedback across government, civil society, and business boundaries is intense, increasing, and increasingly ambiguous. Clarifying the feedback criteria necessary to enhance the societal value of each kind of activity, is a growing operational challenge and ethical obligation. It is made all the more difficult by the power of those businesses, civil groups, government offices, and politicians committed to the usual parochial payoffs.

Moreover, one group's admirable civil activity may sometimes be another group's anathema — or worse.

Be that as it may, some businesses pursue extra-business functions in the civil society — providing sabbaticals for members so they can devote time to civil-society activities; funding community education, recreation, and the arts; etc. While these business contributions are not disinterested, neither are those of civil society activists pursuing their causes.

NO SIMPLE CHALLENGE

The current possibilities for shifting the boundaries between enlightened business, government, and civil society in order to sustain learning-system norms, are probably limited to the post-industrialized societies, working out from the conventional boundaries that are the historical products of democratic and industrial experience. There remains the enormous challenge of jointly creating a sustainable, humane planet that includes the majority of humans who live outside the boundaries of post-industrial thought, policy, and action. And there are increasing numbers *within* post-industrial societies who dwell in misery, alienation, and violence, outside the boundaries of democratic and industrial experience. Learning how to incorporate all these into a viable civil world will depend on the understanding acquired through long-range social planning.

Learning for a Civil Society

At a minimum, to do this will surely require boundary spanning, boundary respecting, and boundary designing *with* civil, political, and commercial entities from the non-post-industrial world. The learning task is learning how to design boundaries so they reduce the disorganizing consequences of feedback that amplifies uncertainty and meaninglessness. Absent such reductions, anger, fear, efforts to dominate, and the consequent behavior of violence, denial, rigidity, withdrawal, and cynicism will continue to undermine civil and open society.

Business would need to shift its ethical and conceptual boundaries from maximizing current return for its stockholders, to maximizing long-run returns from societal civility. But just as it is in the interest of business to make important contributions to upgrading formal education, so too, it is in its interest to share its skills and resources so that citizens can learn how to learn to be contributors to long range social learning. At the least, business could subsidize the services of learning-system designers who sell those services to business, and who would be eager to apply their skills to civil organizations.

Laws, norms, and value boundaries would require alteration to allow such changes. This is not impossible; research demonstrates that the norms of relationships between business and civil society differ in different cultures. Today, organizational learning is an idea in good currency in the business community, as amply evidenced by Peter Senge's best-seller status. And the whole realm of thinking about learning has been enhanced by the contribution of the idea of organizational, especially corporate, culture as conceptualized especially by Edgar Schein. So the changes necessary to facilitate significant business contributions to civil learning might not be impossible. How soon, and how much, is something we shall have to learn.

Changing laws and regulations that bound business, government, and civil-society relationships require government involvement, government learning. It is not quite a hopeless ambition to change at least components of governments toward becoming learning systems. We are only beginning to learn about how this might be done. In the United States (until recently) the Congressionally-mandated Office of Technology Assessment; in Europe the Organization of Economic Cooperation and Development (OECD); and in Canada, an ongoing working group of high-level government administrators systematically deliberating on "governing in an information society," all use sophisticated scenarios for thinking through alternative policies and actions extending into the future.

Willy nilly, a normative rationale for long-range social planning is beginning to emerge in the guise of arguments, policies, and programs intended over time to protect the environment, educate and provide meaningful work for a structurally changed economic world, reduce population growth, manage proliferating megacities, allocate water, and so forth. But the conditions required for translating the emerging normative rationale into a *learning* process that is future-responsive and persists through time, have only begun to be recognized, let alone established.

Another crucial challenge involves learning how to insulate such efforts from shredding by the media and politicians. The degree to which the media and the politicians respect and facilitate a learning mode will vary with the societies and cultures involved and with their historical, current, and anticipated circumstances. Therefore, it is precisely the civil society, augmented by principled business and government-agency allies, engaged in genuine efforts at long-range social planning, that hold the best hope to influence these two formidable holdouts. After all, it is citizen and business groups that, for better and worse, currently influence the media and the politicians. The question is: Can they learn how to persuade the media and politicians to support long-range social planning via learning, and to cease sabotaging learning in furtherance of their own pursuit of profits, organization dominance, ego aggrandizement, market share, and reelection? It won't be easy!

Recommendations about what should be done, however laudable, chronically overlook the more-difficult task of learning how to *activate* such recommendations; they beg fundamental questions. The proposer usually ends with a rousing, "After all, all humans value the same fundamental things." Or, "All we need is leadership." Or, "The only thing lacking is the political will." *Why* these lacks are chronic and pervasive, and *how* to learn to remove these impediments to alleged paths to salvation, is left to some other problem solver.

To say we need leadership, or political will, or an enlightened public, are all true. But *what we do not know is how to get them.* Why don't we have them? The short answer is the morass I have briefly sketched above. Given these conditions, I am not optimistic that we can find our way out. The depth of learning to be

done grows ever more daunting. Whether that learning can be
accomplished remains to be seen. But, since we don't
understand the dynamics of complex social change under
turbulent conditions, there is no reason not to *hope* — hence to try.
First and foremost, we must accept our ignorance — accept that we
must learn how to learn, and plan in order to do so.

San Francisco, California   Donald N. Michael
November, 1996

REFERENCES

Virginia Woolf, "A Room Of One's Own." New York: Harcourt Brace, 1979, p.109.

Marilynn Brewer, quoted in *The Monitor*, American Psychological Association,
    Nov. 1993, p. 22

Lakoff, G. and M. Johnson, "Metaphors We Live By." Chicago: University of Chicago
    Press, 1980.

Acknowledgments
Second Edition

I want to acknowledge gratefully help from my friends and
colleagues Napier Collyns, Gerard Fairtlough, Art Kleiner,
Martin Krasney, Michael Lerner, Stephen Rosell, Edgar Schein, and
Brewster Smith. All read early drafts of this Reflection.
I hope I have made good use of their invaluable suggestions; but
that, of course, is my responsibility.

Mark it well, the communication of new ideas, new conceptions, new understandings, inventions, new ways of doing things, between individuals fixed in their ways and intent upon their separate objectives is difficult and rare. The intent to communicate is the exception rather than the rule; the more common motivation, indeed, is to hide and obscure. Nor need there be a common language. If there is a common language, it is likely to be inadequate for the task of conveying what is intended, for the very novelty of an idea sets it outside the common points of reference by which communication occurs. Even if the inventor wants to communicate and has the language that explains, others need not want to listen nor have the time and will to attend. These are the difficulties of communicating a new idea even between individuals, face to face, man to man. In fact the problem is far more difficult, for the communication of invention is rarely from man to man, from inventor to innovator, from source to destination directly. Rather it is a transmission of an idea "through channels," infiltrating, drifting, passed along through the layers upon layers of organization. Beyond the barriers that separate individual from individual, it must cross those which set apart groups and communities.

Robert A. Solo
*Economic Organizations and
Social Systems*

⋆ Part One ⋆

The Problem

1

Overview and Context

For more than one hundred years we as a society have been learning how to conduct an industrial democracy. Now we must expand the process to learn as a society how to conduct long-range social planning. But much more so than in the past, in order to accomplish this, we shall have to be self-conscious and committed to the learning process and the learning experience.

In his extraordinary delineation of the nature of and need for societal learning, Edgar Dunn observes:

The principal problem of social organization that confronts advanced societies . . . can best be seen by contrasting the organizational consequences of normal problem solving and paradigm shifts. In normal problem solving, system reorganization is purposive, anticipatory, and controlled. In contrast, paradigm shifts have historically been primarily reactive, unanticipated, and uncontrolled. They tend to arise out of a reaction to exogenously and endogenously generated boundary crises. They are frequently unanticipated by the management elite of the system. The reorganization is often defensive in character — that is, it is directed toward preserving and extending the life of the system in the face of change rather than taking the form of a directed, self-transformation in pursuit of some higher order goal.

We appear to have arrived at a point in social history where this kind of uncontrolled social reorganization is taking on a rate and form that seem to threaten the viability of the social process itself. The reason for the special nature of the threat in advanced societies is the fact that we have formalized and mastered the process of normal problem solving in the physical sciences and in the design of physical systems to the point that this very process is generating an accelerated and escalating series of boundary crises for established social systems.[1]

If Dunn is right, and I believe he is, we must seek means for "directed self-transformation," or abandon ourselves to the consequences of drifting and muddling. Accepting this latter alternative as the dominant mode of response, it seems to me, would mean abdicating the essential human obligation to take responsibility for self and others, for today and tomorrow. The means for directed self-transformation that we will be concerned with is *long-range social planning.* But it will not be in the spirit or form usually associated with the term "normal problem-solving." Normal problem-solving won't work during "paradigm shifts," or whatever one prefers to call the turbulent and radical process of social change we seem caught up in. The very circumstances that lead to defensive behavior under such conditions, strongly discourage the kinds of purposive and anticipatory performance appropriate to the situation.

There is an alternative meaning for the term *long-range social planning:* it can be understood as a procedure for accomplishing *future-responsive societal learning.* This is the meaning I intend long-range social planning to convey: purposes and procedures for learning how to cope constructively with the changing society; for learning what can be anticipated, chosen, regulated; for learning how to overcome defensive behavior that either tries to use long-range social planning for social engineering, or avoids it altogether — hoping to get through "as we always have."

By "social engineering," I am referring to an attitude, as much as a method; an attitude held by the planners, toward planning and society — an elitist, top-down planning that assumes that those doing the planning hold a monopoly on expertise. Planners engaged in social engineering are impatient with and resistant to any feedback from the environment that might upset their plans or the means used to implement them. Their goals tend to be set rigidly, with emphasis placed on means for reaching them. Social engineering is a "can-do" attitude in which the problem is assumed to be a given, and the task is to devise efficient means to "overcome," "break through," or "war on" the problem. Careful assessment of what *is* the problem is usually bypassed on grounds of expediency, or because no one acceptable to the planners questions the definition of the problem. "Everybody knows what delinquency is; the trick is to get rid of it." Or, "Everybody knows what causes delinquency; the task is to remove the causes." (Note that at various times over the years, "everybody" knew delinquency was caused by inheritance, family, peer group, and lack of access to society's goodies, among other things.) The *definition* of the problem tends to remain unexamined during the life of the engineering project. Too many expert reputations are at stake, and, because the public has been assured that the means used will work, too much is at stake politically.[2]

My concept of long-range social planning is as *a societal learning process for learning how to do long-range social planning*. It could be a means — perhaps the only means — for accomplishing future-responsive societal learning. Certainly the intention to accomplish future-responsive societal learning will be necessary to permit the development of norms and organizational arrangements needed to learn how to do long-range social planning.

As I see it, most of the activities that constitute long-range social planning would be located in organizations, but they would be dependent on an environment that believes and participates in learning to be a future-responsive learning society. This will be a dialectical process that evolves as we learn how to change toward long-range social planning, and learn to be a society that values future-responsive societal learning. To emphasize this interdependence, which in many ways amounts to an identity of activities and intentions; and especially to emphasize that long-range social planning is treated here as a learning procedure, I will sometimes use the terms "long-range social planning" and "future-responsive societal learning" interchangeably. The reader should understand that whichever term is used here, the other will probably fit just as well.

WHAT WILL BE REQUIRED TO CHANGE TOWARD LONG-RANGE SOCIAL PLANNING?

In the chapters ahead I will try to demonstrate that changing toward future-responsive societal learning would require that people working in organizations, and in the social and natural environments linked to them, find it rewarding to learn how to do the following things:

- Live with and acknowledge great uncertainty;
- Embrace error;
- Seek and accept the ethical responsibility and the conflict-laden interpersonal circumstances that attend goal-setting;
- Evaluate the present in the light of the anticipated future, and commit themselves to actions that respond to such long-range anticipations;
- Live with role stress and forego the satisfactions of stable, on-the-job social-group relationships; and
- Be open to changes in commitment and direction suggested by changes in the conjectured pictures of the future, and by evaluations of ongoing activities.

To be able to learn these things will require basic changes in the ways people view themselves and others, as well as basic changes in the organizational norms and structures that facilitate and reward some behaviors, and punish others. It will also require changes in the way members of the environment view themselves and the organizations that serve them.

Changing people, organizations, and environments to meet these requirements can succeed only if it is done in a spirit that treats all aspects of the changeover to long-range social planning as a learning process, rather than as a social engineering technology.

Everything that follows in this book rests on understanding why this is true. And whatever feasibility there may be for such change will rest on the availability of circumstances that encourage such learning. It is thus appropriate to include in this overview a summary of my position on why long-range social planning must be a learning process.

First, the social technologies for facilitating this learning process are underdeveloped, because social science theories and the data needed to refine and test them are inadequate for understanding and delineating complex and changing social systems. Indeed, it is not clear how much systematic and useful information about societal dynamics can be developed. We face a long period of learning how to create theories and technologies applicable to long-range social planning.

Secondly, we will have to learn how to introduce the prerequisites for long-range social planning into organizations in ways that will not result in their rejection, or their distortion into ritual or into rigid, dehumanizing social-engineering exercises. We have to learn *how* to change toward long-range social planning. We need to learn what organizations and their members need to do in order to function effectively as part of a future-responsive societal learning arrangement, and we will need to learn how organizations and their members can best change over to functioning in those ways. Our theory and methods for organizational development, for felicitously relating the needs of humans to the techniques and structures of an organization, need much research and development. The development of personnel must be articulated with the development of organizational structures willing and able to redesign themselves continually. And both personnel and organizational structures must be able to incorporate the evolving technology of long-range social planning. A long period of lies ahead, of learning how to apply organizational development techniques for introducing long-range social planning into organizations.

Third, a particularly difficult research and development activity will have to do with learning how to incorporate members of the environment into the process of long-range social planning. But this incorporation is mandatory, because members of the environment share norms and expectancies that reinforce the very organizational norms, structures, and self-images that produce resistance to the introduction of long-range social planning. Shifting these environmental norms and expectations so that people will permit or encourage organizations to experiment with learning how to meet the requirements for long-range social planning, requires that members of the environment become part of the planning process. Just as importantly, there will be need at all stages of planning for ideas, arguments, perceptions, and information from those in the environment, who presumably stand to gain and lose from the unfolding of particular activities guided by long-range social planning. We do not yet know how to incorporate input from the environment into the process; what constitutes competence, relevance, and effective procedure has yet to be discovered, especially as we move into a time of partisanship and confrontation politics.

Finally, we shall have to learn which aspects of a turbulent world can be guided and regulated, and which aspects it is necessary or desirable to regulate. There are no ready-made, tested "solutions" — nor, usually, even humane coping procedures — for dealing with the major societal tasks. Even when a wide-ranging "solution" can be proposed, candid examination usually reveals that there are no available political, fiscal, and organizational means for implementing the proposal. These remain to be invented and developed through the processes of future-responsive societal learning. We shall have to learn what it is that we can try to manage through long-range social planning, as well as learning how to manage it.

In light of these learning requirements, long-range social planning is needed to develop society's capability to meet needs and opportunities that cannot be quickly accomplished, but must work themselves out over a period of ten to twenty years. Whatever approaches we develop will be developed in the future, and applied still later. Consequently, the very goals for which social research and development are undertaken, as well as the means to be used to move toward them, will have to be chosen with an appreciation for what alternative aspects of the longer-range future seem worth achieving, and possible to achieve.

Even if an organization's relevant future is so close that it appears to harbor no new sources of uncertainty, or requirements to rethink and re-feel the value bases for the organization's activities, responding to the requirements for long-range social planning still seems to be a prerequisite for responsible organizational performance in the public interest. Many sub-units in large government agencies are necessarily oriented in time and practice toward the near term — essentially the next few years. Nevertheless, they should be operating as part of a larger organizational perspective, with a longer-term orientation. If the overarching units are to be effective in their long-range social planning, they will need knowledgeable interpretations and data from these sub-units about what is happening in the present. It would seem, then, that even if a government organization's short-term perspective is appropriate, it will have to shift its style of assessing purpose and procedure from looking at where it has been, to looking at where it is going. Decisions will have to be based on an appreciation of what needs to be done in a functional and temporal context that is more comprehensive than the disjointed incremental approach. The incrementalist policy-maker, "typically a partisan, often acknowledging no responsibility to his society as a whole, frankly pursuing his own segmental interests,"[3] has no place in such a setting. While I emphasize changing toward long-range social planning, because that is what we desperately need to do, the same social psychological sources of resistance would seem to apply whether the subject is changing over to long-range social planning, or changing over to social planning with short-term perspectives.

The necessary learning task will be enormous and terrifying, as learning tends to be in threatening and confusing situations. We will look at only two facets of the task: first, the nature of the social psychological resistance to making the organizational changes required if long-range social planning is to be a societal learning procedure; and second, what might help overcome such resistance. One of the most difficult aspects of this learning task will be to discover when it may actually be appropriate to *resist* changes in the direction of long-range social planning. In Geoffrey Vickers's words,

the heritage we enjoy owes just as much to stout-hearted defenders as to fluid-minded innovators. . . . The slowing of change is one of our normal, as well as one of our pathological, responses and it is widely practiced for good, as well as bad reasons.[4]

The determination of what is normal or pathological, good or bad, resistance to change toward long-range social planning will depend on the context. Then too, the appropriateness of resistance to this change will be complicated by questions of ideological compatibility. As C. West Churchman has pointed out to me, some will argue that before planning can be humane, each member of humankind must learn to obey the command, "Know thyself;" or that the proper way to deal with social issues is through politics, not planning; or that planning is just another way to deny or put off the allocation of resources to the dispossessed and deprived. To some extent I share these positions, at least when I am apprehensive about the possible misuse of planning. On the whole, though, I believe future-responsive societal learning can further the ideological concerns of those who at first might consider long-range social planning antithetical to their interests. I will not, however, argue that here; I simply acknowledge that such concerns will be among the sources of resistance to long-range social planning, and we will have to learn to value them when they arise in particular situations.

Of course, there will be enormous obstructions to learning to change toward long-range social planning: limited funds, technology, time constraints, and manpower; contradictory and constricting laws, legislative prerogatives, and conventional political aspirations; an obscene number of overlapping, competitive, and obstructionist municipalities, jurisdictions, commissions, authorities, and so on; all will stand in the way. Some would say that if the legal, political, jurisdictional, and power issues could be resolved, and if we were not plagued with the politics of confrontation, then the social psychological matters would take care of themselves. But these aspects and the social psychological matters comprise a self-reinforcing system. We are, in John Platt's term, "locked in;" [5] if interventions in one "part" of the system are likely to be successful, it will be because attention was given to anticipating their impact on the other "parts." If there is to be system change there must be interventions — at least if we want to feel that changes in the system are deliberate, rather than simply the product of "historical forces." Present arrangements were created by people — though not always with deliberation, and not necessarily with the intention to produce the consequences that have occurred; and they persist because changing them would confront people with the private and public costs of coping with innovation. Thus, if changes are to be made in the direction of long-range social planning, they will have to be made by people choosing to do so, by people choosing not to resist innovations that may it at the time seem natural or right to resist.

As a contribution, then, to overall understanding of what is required to change toward long-range social planning, I will examine here the social psychological level of reactions that can be anticipated to such efforts at change. This level of description and analysis is not now part of the planning literature. Its usefulness lies in the fact that, in other settings involving other innovations, understanding and overcoming resistance to change has been amply demonstrated to be in significant part a social psychological matter, whatever other factors also operate.

I will try to show that resistance to changing toward long-range social planning derives from images of man and his purposes, and from the organizational means accomplishing these purposes, that are incompatible with the requirements for long-range social planning. Historically, it is these images of man that have brought us to where we are: they have resulted in ways of expressing and organizing human behavior that are characterized by hierarchical organizational structures; public organizations that try to minimize or avoid open contact with their relevant environment if that environment threatens them; and a host of negotiating procedures that reward secrecy, resource and power preemption, ambiguity, disjointed incrementalism, deceit, error-denial, distrust, interpersonal distance, pseudo interpersonal collaboration, and pseudo emotional support. They have resulted in setting organizational and sub-organizational survival above the anticipatory responses to the future appropriate for environmental development; in seeking to attain and maintain power through aggressive and possessive actions; in encouraging personal and organizational amorality; in avoiding feedback from the environment; and in waffling about serious future-responsive goal setting. In other words, we reward forms of organizational life that at best discourage effective societal learning, and at worst make it impossible. Instead, people are rewarded for behaving in ways that are producing an ungovernable and unsatisfying world, which is made the more so because efforts to counteract this situation move in the very directions that exacerbate it — more novelty, distraction, image-making, security-seeking; more "nowness," more separatist "individuality;" and splintering autonomy.[6]

I will also show that images of man and the good life are now developing that seem compatible with the social-psychological requirements for future-responsive societal learning — most notably the definition of man that derives from human-potential explorations in psychology, philosophy, and theology; and that there are circumstances developing in our society that might make feasible serious movement toward long-range social planning. While the likelihood seems very small that this shift in definition of man, and collateral changes in the structure of organizations, will become dominant in the foreseeable future, we know far too little of what it takes to bring about massive social change to be sure that change cannot occur. We do not even know whether massive social change per se is necessary. This perspective rests in turn on the position I accept regarding the nature of human nature, and its expression in the way men organize themselves to compete or collaborate.

SOCIETAL EXPRESSION OF HUMAN NATURE: ONE PERSPECTIVE

We are, after all, dealing with something we call "human nature" when we examine the way people resist or respond favorably to change. Why and how people resist the changes associated with the requirements of long-range social planning seems to be "natural," given the way people "are," and organizations "are." If so, it would seem that delineating why people resist is an idle exercise; seeking to change people and their institutions so that they are able to meet the requirements of long-range social planning will seem an attempt to make people or organizations act "unnaturally." To appreciate why this is not an idle exercise, it is necessary to understand that I accept the well-supported but poorly-understood position that we human beings make our own social reality. This reality seems natural to us because we are part of it, subject to the same reality-shaping process as the people we shall be examining. As Geoffrey Vickers has observed:

It is clearly true that both science and philosophy, by the concepts of human nature that they use and propagate, can powerfully affect men's views of themselves, their possibilities and their limitations, and may thus alter what human nature effectively is. A mistaken view of planetary motion, though held for centuries, had no effect on the motion of the planets. They continued on their elliptical way, undisturbed by human preference for circular motion; and even when men discovered their mistake, they had no means to bring the course of nature into line with their aesthetic predilections. A too restricted view of human nature, on the other hand, even though only briefly ascendant, can significantly alter the expectations and hence the behavior of men and societies and may thus provide its own bogus validation.[7]

I am not arguing that man is infinitely plastic, unlimited by his biological nature. Doubtless there are limits on what he might be, in himself and in his relation to others. But we do not know what these limits are, or where they are; whereas we do know that, through time and across cultures, the demonstrated plasticity of man is far greater than any one culture has made use of.

A study published by Richard Titmuss notes that in Britain, blood is given without compensation, while in the United States, people are paid for their blood; yet blood donated in Britain is more readily available, and generally of better quality, than here. In a review of this study, R. Claiborne observes:

Set up a social framework in which men are encouraged to be generous and most of them will rise to the occasion; set up one which encourages them to be selfish and most of them will sink to it. . . . Thus the assumption that man is motivated only by immediate self-interest . . . turns out to be merely another of the self-fulfilling hypotheses of social and political "science." . . . The utilitarian, having helped create a world in which human relationships have increasingly been brought — forced — into the marketplace, finds in it superb confirmation of his initial dogma; that man is governed by marketplace motives.[8]

Chris Argyris makes a similar observation in arguing for research on interpersonal behavior that is more open, trusting, supportive, and feeling — for what he calls Pattern B behavior, in contrast to Pattern A, the conventional mode of organizational behavior.

If one does not study the Pattern B world, one runs the risk of developing a conception of man in which the "natural" behavior is hiding feelings, not taking risks, showing little concern, individuality, and trust. This will tend to occur naturally because individuals will turn to the descriptive research to develop their views about man. What is becomes what ought to be. Existing theory is used to explain existing behavior. Thus black militants have defended their aggressive behavior by citing psychological research that "proves" aggression is an expected response to frustration. The covert and silent analyzing of other people and unilaterally attributing motives to them can be shown to follow from present conceptions of attribution theory.[9]

Two other authors, Peter Berger and Thomas Luckmann, put it in more abstract but more general terms:

It is important to keep in mind that the objectivity of the institutional world, however massive it may appear to the individual, is a humanly produced, constructed objectivity. . . . Despite the objectivity that marks the social world in human experience, it does not thereby acquire an ontological status apart from the human activity that produced it. . . . It is important to emphasize that the relationship between man, the producer, and the social world, his product, is and remains a dialectical one. That is, man (not, of course, in isolation but in his collectivities) and his social world interact with each other. The product acts back upon the producer.[10]

The objectivity of the social world means that it confronts man as something outside of himself. The decisive question is whether he still retains the awareness that, however objectivated, the social world was made by men — and, therefore, can be remade by them. . . . Typically, the real relationship between man and his world is reversed in consciousness. Man, the producer of a world, is apprehended as its product, and human activity as an epiphenomenon of non-human processes. Human meanings are no longer understood as world-producing but as being, in their turn, products of the "nature of things." It must be emphasized that reification is a modality of consciousness, more precisely, a modality of man's objectification of the human world. Even while apprehending the world in reified terms, man continues to produce it. That is, man is capable paradoxically of producing a reality that denies him.[11]

In reading and responding to this book, it is critically important to appreciate that what we call the nature of man is only the nature he shows in a particular kind of man-made social structure that rewards or punishes him for behaving in certain ways, for seeing himself and his society in certain ways, and for expecting kinds of reciprocal behavior from others. In this regard, Clyde Kluckhohn and William Kelly write:

A culture is not only a reticulum of patterned means for satisfying needs but equally a network of stylized goals for individual and group achievement. Almost no human situations are viewed in ways which are altogether a consequence of the individual's experience. Culture is — among other things — a set of ready-made definitions of the situation which each participant only slightly retailors in his own idiomatic way; Cultures create needs as well as provide a means of fulfilling them; cultures create problems as well as solving them.[12]

If the reader even tentatively accepts this position, it will be easier to see behavior as a product of culture, and subject to change. If the reader persists in viewing typical organizational behavior as "natural," then what is called for in the following chapters will seem to counsel saintliness, or perfection. By conventional standards it would be asking for that; but alternative ways of being and doing, suggested along the way, need not be judged for acceptability according to some presumed standard of "naturalness." There are perceptual changes afoot not only with regard to planning but also with regard to the nature of human nature, and to the events that people attend to and consider important.[13]

Perhaps moves toward future-responsive societal learning can be facilitated if individuals try to accept and encourage as potentially "natural," certain arrangements of people and their activities that are different from those that seem so natural to us now. Even if the establishment of new norms and structures seems highly problematic, if we see more clearly what needs to be done, and what added knowledge is needed to attempt it, we should at the very least enlarge the moral and intellectual setting in which to choose whether to accept the clear risks of drowning in our own social disorder, or whether to take the new risks of social learning that might lead to a new social order.

To see *what* human nature may need to become, and what organizational norms and structures would be needed to sustain and reward it, it is first necessary to understand how and why the presently legitimated, hence rewarded, definition of human nature operates to resist changing over to long-range social planning. Since it is people who have to design and make the transition to living in new structures that sustain a different human nature, we need to know more about people who are asked to change from their conventional structures. People will have to change themselves and other people, sometimes through less-personal interventions in the forms of organizational arrangements and social programs. We need to understand why people act as they do in such situations of change; hence this social psychological exploration.

ENVIRONMENTAL TURBULENCE AS THE CONTEXT FOR LONG-RANGE SOCIAL PLANNING

Ironically, appreciation of the need to cope with social turbulence has produced not only the beginnings of a technology for coping, but also one which on every hand brings would-be planners information emphasizing that things are much more complicated, interlocked, intractable, and unpredictable than was appreciated before these evolving means were available for probing societal processes. This information emphasizes the pathetic limits of our theory and methodology for understanding what is going on "out there," for coping with societal turbulence.

Throughout this book, we will struggle with the question: Is there really any reason to believe that society *can* be contained, smoothed-out, anticipated, and studied, so that we can learn enough through long-range social planning to find our way to a preferred future? An examination of the idea of the "turbulent environment" will help us cope with this question.

Two seminal papers — one by Fred Emery and Eric Trist,[14] the other by Emery alone,[15] have differentiated among four types of environments in terms of the kinds of transactions a system or organization must arrange in order to attain or avoid what the environment contains.[16] These transactions depend on whether the relevant elements of the environment are randomly or non-randomly distributed, and whether they are active or passive in their response to the intervening system. What Trist and Emery refer to as Type 3 and Type 4 environments are important here.

The Type 3 environment is one within which organizations have operated for approximately the last two hundred years. For effective transactions within it, its members have developed the familiar, hierarchically-structured organizations and the corresponding supportive and legitimizing definitions of man. In the Type 3 environment,

each system does not simply have to take account of the other when they meet at random, but it has to consider that what it knows about the environment can be known by another. That part of the environment to which it wishes to move is probably, for the same reason, the part to which the other wants to move. Knowing this, they will wish to improve their own chances by hindering the other, and they will know that the other will not only wish to do likewise, but will know that they know this. In a word, the presence of others will imbricate some of the causal strands in the environment. The causal texture of the environment will, through the reactions of others, be partly determined by the intentions of the acting organization. However, the environment at large still provides a relatively stable ground for the arenas of organizational conflict.[17]

The Type 4 environment is "the turbulent environment," which Emery and Trist argue now exists in our kind of society; it differs from Type 3 in having the profoundly important characteristic of, in Emery's words, "dynamic properties that arise not simply from the interaction of the systems [organizations], but also from the field itself."

There are undoubtedly important instances in which these dynamic field properties arise quite independently of the system in the field. . . . [However,] most significance attaches to the case where the dynamic field processes emerge as an unplanned consequence of the actions of the component systems. . . . We have recently become more aware of these processes through the intervention of the ecologists in problems of environmental pollution. . . . The emergence of active field forces (forces other than those stemming from the individual organizations or the similar organizations competing with it) means that the effects will not tend to fall off . . . but may at any point be amplified beyond all expectation. . . . Similarly, lines of action that are strongly pursued may find themselves unexpectedly attenuated by emergent field forces.[18]

This perception of what the world is like is what is intended when I refer to "turbulence" or the "turbulent environment." The Type 4 environment has evolved from Type 3, and is exemplified by societal conditions familiar to readers of this book. Such is their momentum and pervasiveness, and "these fields are so complex, so richly joined, that it is difficult to see how individual organizations can, by their own efforts, successfully adapt to them."[19]

Emery and Trist look at two modes of adaptation, the first of which "downgrade[s] complexity" by processes of "segmentation," "fractionation," or "dissociation." I will not use these terms, but later on we shall recognize these processes among the means for avoiding facing up to the requirements for changing over to long-range social planning. Emery's estimate of the utility of these processes for coping with a turbulent environment merits quoting:

(a) they are mutually facilitating defenses, not mutually exclusive; (b) they all tend to fragment the spatial and temporal connectedness of the larger social systems and focus further adaptive efforts on the localized here and now;

(c) they all tend to sap the energies that are available to and can be mobilized by the larger systems and otherwise to reduce their adaptiveness. [20]

Emery's second approach to a solution for coping with our Type 4 environment is to transform the environment by transforming the value system that defines it.[21] He proposes the redesign of social organizations as the most likely means of doing this comparatively quickly, on the following grounds:

It is in the design of their social organization that men can make the biggest impact upon those environmental forces that mould their values (that make some ends more attractive, some assumptions about oneself and one's world more viable); further, it assumes that if these changes are made in the leading part, the socio-technical organizations, the effects will be more likely to spread more quickly than if made elsewhere. . . . We are suggesting that adults be the educators and that they educate themselves in the process of realizing their chosen organizational designs. This confronts us with the question of what values, and we are suggesting that the first decisions about values for the future control of our turbulent environments are the decisions that go into choosing our basic organizational designs. If we can spell out the possible choices in design we can see what alternative values are involved and perhaps hazard a guess at what values will be pursued by western societies. [22]

Reasoning from cybernetic principles, Emery and Trist deduce that organizational redesign that emphasizes redundancy in an organization's response repertory has the most chance of succeeding in coping with turbulence, and that such redundancy is facilitated by non-hierarchical, multiple-participation organizational design. As we shall see, there is evidence that supports their hypotheses.

Emery and Trist do not claim that their analysis is complete or that their proposals for coping are sufficient; they simply think they are pointing in the right direction, and so do I. Their analysis is important because it tells us about a general and crucial characteristic of information from the environment with which organizations and members of the environment seeking to change toward long-range social planning will have to contend. And it is important because it raises a question about potential individual and organizational effectiveness that is bound to affect the social psychological context of those seeking to move toward or to avoid long-range social planning: Is it reasonable to expect that our Type 4 environment is so autonomous and unanticipatable that there is very little reason to hope that actions taken in the present can be guided and revised through what we learn about the environment through long-range social planning?

To go through all the troublesome changes involved in moving to long-range social planning, members of organizations would have to believe their relationship to the environment is such that actions undertaken in the present, aimed at attaining a chosen future, have enough likelihood of success to make the burden of trying worthwhile. Perhaps there is a tenable basis for hope, if we can believe that the turbulent environment comprises these three components:

1. Those aspects that we believe are well enough understood in terms of present theory, that positions can be taken and acted on with some sense of the probability of outcomes, but which require, for the development of such positions, data that have not yet been collected and analyzed;

2. Those aspects that we believe are hypothetically understandable, but for which no theory has yet been created; such aspects must wait both for data and experiment to provide the basis for their conceptualization; and

3. Those aspects of the environment that we believe are not understandable, controllable, or predictable by scientific means because they cannot be conceptualized within the ways of thinking available through science. These aspects would include emergent phenomena such as the "creation" of new social theory and images, and phenomena that are important in their singularity but for which scientific methods supply only average or aggregate results.

An example may be helpful here. Scientific reasoning can predict with great precision what percentage of a sample of radioactive material will disintegrate within a given time. But the model that allows this prediction can say nothing at all about *which* atoms will disintegrate in that time period, much less which one atom will be the next to do so. For humans, what we want to anticipate in many situations is precisely the outcome of a *specific* interaction among, say, eight committee members. Yet, except for certain classes of Newtonian relationships, scientific method can only supply theory with representations of aggregate or average outcomes of interacting events. What is more, the properties of a *system* of interactions cannot be predicted from the properties of the components. To describe these "emergent" properties seems to require a state of being or conceptualizing that is outside the system of components that comprise it.[23]

Understanding human beings and their organizations would seem to be, to some important degree, not possible for those who are part of the social system they want to understand. These methodological and conceptual difficulties, and their significance for the problems of anticipating the future, are perhaps best symbolized by the perennial argument about the "great man" as maker or product of history. Although there is a strong counter-argument, it often seems as if a single event or person precipitates turbulence or tranquillity; these seem to be the unexpected, the unanticipated developments that make previous predictions or expectations obsolete. (A superb introduction to the question of the extent to which individuals make history, or history makes individuals, is found in Isaiah Berlin's classic *The Hedgehog and the Fox*.)[24]

To the extent that our beliefs about components 1 and 2 can be made to work, changing toward long-range social planning could enhance our ability to reduce turbulence. Future-responsive societal learning could be a means for inventing and then coming to believe in a social reality in which people and organizations behave in such a manner that significant amounts of the turbulence they now generate could be understood, and could be regulated or eliminated. As Geoffrey Vickers says,

Men in their dealings with men create and recognize another kind of regularity — rules of their own devising, imposed and accepted consciously and unconsciously. The only reason men are by and large more predictable than the weather is that they are concerned to be predictable; concerned to meet each other's expectations by accepting common self-expectations.[25]

As I have emphasized earlier, our social reality operates as it does because we have created it that way, by our actions in response to the expectations we hold out about what constitutes "natural" modes of operation. We act out our own theory of reality. In time, we could hope that people and institutions will learn to define themselves in new ways, and to expect responses from each other that would lead them to increasingly behave so as to make future-responsive societal learning possible. Berger and Luckmann write:

The social processes involved in both the formation and the maintenance of identity are determined by the social structure. Conversely, the identities produced by the interplay of organism, individual consciousness, and social structure react upon the given social structure, maintaining it, modifying it, or even reshaping it. Societies have histories in the course of which specific identities emerge; these histories are, however, made by men with specific identities.[26]

We are beginning to be self-conscious about this process of creating reality by believing it "really" is thus and such. For example, we apply fiscal and monetary theory in the light of a self-conscious effort to anticipate likely behavioral responses to its application. Many well-educated people define themselves in psychoanalytic terms and respond to others in terms of the psychoanalytic attributes they ascribe to them, such as "paranoid," "repressed," "defensive," "compulsive," "neurotic," and so on. And recently, anti-racist and anti-sexist individuals have, with growing effect, shed light on the usually unconscious beliefs, behaviors, and institutional arrangements that have resulted in a reality that guides blacks, women, homosexuals, and others into ways of being that reflect self-fulfilling prophecies about them.

The third component of a turbulent environment would remain outside the direct purview of long-range social planning, but trying to cope with it would involve two kinds of behavior facilitated by future-responsive societal learning. First, a variation of "management by exception," but with the important difference that there are more resources for coping with the exception because not so much would be frittered away in trying to manage by *ad hoc* or incremental means, societal circumstances that could be better managed through long-range social planning. And second, an expanded capacity for and supportive sensitivity to long-range social planning would enable us to recognize and avoid actions that would be likely to have serious unanticipated or unregulatable consequences. (Precursors of such avoidance actions can be seen in the decisions to abandon nuclear testing in the atmosphere, and to forgo the supersonic transport project.)

The societal rewards from learning through long-range social planning should encourage the development of values that improve the setting for societal learning and enhance sensitivity to and discouragement of the production of unregulatable turbulence.

Of course the unregulatable, unanticipatable component of turbulence may turn out to be overwhelming rather than residual. If so, we have produced for ourselves an environment in which our civilization, or at least our present society, cannot survive. (There are, after all, more dead societies than live ones, and many apparently died as a result of conditions they themselves produced.) But we are a very long way from knowing that our turbulence is so intractable; we have not instituted long-range social planning, or even the efforts to change over toward it, that would allow us to learn the extent to which we can understand, transform, control, and cope with the turbulent environment that makes planning necessary in the first place.

Some Sources of Turbulence and Their Implications

Those involved in changing over to long-range social planning must be able to deal with several often-simultaneous contributions from the overall turbulent environment. If organizations are going to try to discover to what extent and in what ways long-range social planning can enable us to cope with turbulence, they will have to begin by facing turbulence openly, rather than avoiding its manifestations or refusing to recognize our finite ability to regulate it. But we have almost no tested organizational forms appropriate for engaging domestic turbulence. (Military organizations, on the other hand, have developed such forms under some combat conditions. It would be fruitful to compare both the conditions of turbulence in combat, and the means for responding to it — including the moral imperatives — with the domestic situation.)

To an important extent, organizational leadership has defined its competence by its ability to reduce or remove turbulence from the organizational setting, or, under conditions of its choice, to introduce turbulence for special change-inducing purposes. One of the most powerful psychological rewards an organization can provide its members is protection from turbulence; at the least, the organization specifies the kinds and sources of turbulence with which its members are expected to cope, as well as how to cope through performance of an assigned role. William McWhinney describes this practice:

> One of the functions which formal organizations perform is to buffer the individual member from the impact of the chaotic interrelation of everything to everything. Ideally, organizations free the member effectively to deal with just so much of the environment as his intellect and psyche permit. The organization, through compartmentalization of tasks and responsibilities, circumscribes for each member the domain of environmental factors with which he must be concerned, and permits a match to be established between the complexity of the environment, the type of role and the modalities of decision-making which are appropriate in the functions performed by the members.[27]

Much of our cultural emphasis on control probably stems from a desire for a stable and predictable, hence nonthreatening, life setting. Traditionally, the most-approved models of behavior have been those individuals who are able to control themselves, others, and nature. So deep is the satisfaction of feeling in control, that rather than risk loss of control by becoming involved with turbulence, many people live on the edge of becoming what I have elsewhere called "petit Eichman;" they avoid, and are encouraged to avoid, reflection about the moral consequences of their role performance by believing that "that's not my job." [28] For them, somebody else in the organization, or some other organization, has responsibility for the larger ethical issues underlying what they do. Most people avoid examining the ethical bases for their performance, partly because doing so exposes the ambiguous consequences of their actions; this in turn exposes the questionable extent to which they really control their world. If turbulence invades the organization, these arrangements will no longer be adequate to protect individuals from facing the ethical implications of their actions. As a result, some individuals resist any movement toward long-range social planning, because the openness to turbulence implicit in such a move pressures them to reexamine themselves, which they want to avoid.

Information feedback from the environment will be mandatory for long-range social planning; it will also become a generator of turbulence within the organization, because it provides continuing evidence of the turbulence outside. To some degree, this internal turbulence will mirror external turbulence, because many organization members, particularly those professionals in human welfare areas, are also members of various contentious groups in the environment. (Recall the civil servants who joined protests against the Vietnam war in defiance of the Hatch Act, and the many leaks of organizationally-embarrassing government reports.) In part, internal turbulence will result from members' reactions to efforts to change toward long-range social planning — the very change needed in order to respond creatively to information about the external environment. While evaluations of the usefulness of public agencies are admittedly difficult to design and interpret, it is clear that the rarity of such evaluations is at least as much because the organizations prefer it that way, as because the methodology is weak. Instead of seeking more feedback for better decision making and evaluation, organizations use many defenses against feedback in order to avoid the disruption that it inevitably generates. (See Chapters 13 and 14.)

In the future, more voluntary organizations will provide consumer advocates, environmentalists, protesters, and advocate planners to serve special needs and interests.[29] There will also be more circumstances, value shifts, and voluntary organizations to incite and train members of the environment to marshal their data and force their feedback upon other organizations. Social-indicator data and more-sophisticated models of societal processes will make more information available to support differing interpretations of the feedback; these interpretations will in turn become part of the feedback forced upon organizations. To the degree that internal and external interpretations differ, internal turbulence will increase, especially when interpretations are based on different and strongly-held value priorities.

Attending seriously to feedback from the future — future studies — will also contribute to turbulence. Future studies inevitably will raise questions about the longer-term utility of present activities; in doing so they also confront those involved in such studies with disturbing questions about their usefulness and commitments. Since conjectures about the future must change over time, and since they cannot be proven correct or incorrect before the fact, their contribution to organizational turbulence will be repetitive, as well as self-imposed.

In situations where turbulence is high, and its repression would be counterproductive, people in organizations will have to learn anew how to demonstrate competence, and those in the environment will have to learn how to assess it. They will have to learn how to respond to turbulence without overreacting or underreacting. Conventional reactions include avoiding feedback, tightening-up, firing the bearer of bad news, obfuscation, repression, and "fire-fighting," which is usually a consequence of actions previously taken to protect an organization (especially a government organization) from turbulence-generating feedback. Fire-fighting aims at getting things under control as fast as possible with little or no attention to the impact on any plans, much less long-range plans. It is disjointedly incremental in style and philosophy; indeed, it has often been lamented that organizations use so much of their resources in fire-fighting that they have none left with which to plan. It should also be noted that one of the great rewards of fire-fighting is that it removes one's sense of uncertainly and indecision — quite the opposite of the state of mind needed for long-range planning. Since fire-fighting is compatible with the reward structures of conventional organizations, it seems much easier to maintain the relationship with the environment that eventually results in fire-fights, than to take on the social psychological burdens of changing over to arrangements that would reward long-range planning.

Instead of resorting to conventional reactions to turbulence, leaders will need to see themselves, and to be seen by their organizations and their environments, as competent precisely *because* they seek out environmental turbulence instead of trying to avoid or repress it. Of course this approach poses formidable problems for the conventional politician, political appointee, or administrator, who expects to reduce turbulence, not seek it out, and believes that this is what his superiors and constituents expect of him. And those in the environment will have to forego seeking a leader who, by conventional definition, is able to protect them from turbulence. As Erich Fromm observes in his book *Escape from Freedom*, we know that it is difficult to accept the burden of freedom, of personal responsibility.

In all, making an individual or an organization accessible to turbulent input means living with larger overloads of information, and more confusion about who one is and what one is supposed to do. In conventional organizations, with conventional norms and rewards, planning doesn't happen under conditions of overload and ambiguity; instead, tempers shorten, people and organizations play it safe and defensively close to the chest, values either surface irritatingly or are repressed dangerously, and management leans toward hierarchical command philosophies (i.e., "When the crunch comes, you do what you know works — and no nonsense."). Yet it is societal turbulence that makes long-range social planning necessary; and if it is to be tried, it will be necessary to be open to turbulence. Organizational structures and the behavior of the organization's members must be redesigned so that information overload and existential ambiguity do not produce resistance to long-range planning.

Before undertaking a detailed examination of the social-psychological nature of such resistance, and what might be done to reduce or remove it when appropriate, we need to be clear on the characteristics of long-range social planning. For it is these specific characteristics, set against the background of a turbulent social and natural environment, that give us clues as to which social-psychological factors to focus on within organizations, and among their members.

1. Dunn, E. Economic and Social Development: A Process of Social Learning. Baltimore: Johns Hopkins, 1971, pp. 214-215.

2. For a knowledgeable and incisive summary of the weaknesses in the social engineering approach to social planning see Rittel, H. and M. Webber. "Dilemmas in a General Theory of Planning." Institute of Urban and Regional Development. University of California Working Paper No. 194. Berkeley: 1972.

3. Hirschman, A. and C. Lindblom. "Economic Development, Research and Development. Policy Making: Some Converging Views." Behavioral Science, 7(2) (1962), p. 220.

4. Vickers, G., in personal correspondence.

5. Platt, J. "What We Must Do." Science, 149 (1969). See also Platt, J., "Hierarchical Restructuring," University of Michigan Mental Health Research Institute Communication 269. Ann Arbor: 1970. See also Hoffer, E. The Ordeal of Change. New York: Harper and Row, 1963.

6. See Slater, P. The Pursuit of Loneliness. Boston: Beacon Press, 1970.

7. Vickers, G. The Art of Judgment. New York: Basic Books, 1965. p.17. For a discussion of how psychological theory and psychiatry derive from and culturally reinforce given definitions of human nature, see Bart, "The Myth of a Value-Free Psychiatry," The Sociology of the Future, eds. W. Bell and J. Mau. New York: Russell Sage Foundation, 1971. See also Kantor, R. "Psychological Theories and Social Groupings." Stanford Research Institute Research Memorandum EPRC-6747-5. Menlo Park, Calif.: 1969.

8. Claiborne, R. Book review of R. Titmuss, The Gift Relationship. "Book World." The Washington Post (May 9, 1971), p. 4.

9. Argyris, C. "The Incompleteness of Social-Psychological Theory: Examples from Small Group, Cognitive Consistency, and Attribution Research." American Psychologist, 24(10) (1969), p. 901.

10. Berger, P. and T. Luckmann. The Social Construction of Reality. Garden City, N.Y.: Anchor Books, 1966, p. 60.

11. Ibid. p. 89.

12. Kluckhohn. C. and W. Kelly. "The Concept of Culture." The Science of Man in the World Crisis. ed. R. Linton. New York: Columbia University Press. 1945. pp. 78-106.

13. Such shifts in definition *have* happened before in what we call Western culture; Robert Heilbroner has described in a clear and fascinating manner the shift to market-economy man from the definition of man that sustained and was sustained by the feudal culture of the Middle Ages. *See* Heilbroner. R. The Making of Economic Society. Englewood Cliffs. N. J.: Prentice-Hall (1962) *See also* Brinton. C. Shaping of the Modern Mind. New York: Mentor Books. 1953. *See also* Mumford. L. The Transformation of Man. New York: Harper Bros.. 1956. *See also* Drews. E. and L. Lipson. Values and Humanity. New York: St. Martin's Press. 1971. *See also* Arendt. H. The Human Condition. Chicago: University of Chicago Press. 1958.

14. Emery. F. and E. Trist. "The Causal Texture of Organizational Environments." Human Relations. 18 (1965).

15. Emery. F. "The Next Thirty Years: Concepts. Methods. and Anticipations." Human Relations. 20 (1967).

16. *See also* Terreberry. S. "The Evolution of Organizational Environments." Administrative Science Quarterly. 12(4) (1968).

17. Emery. op. cit.. p. 221.

18. Ibid. p. 223.

19. Ibid.

20. Ibid. p. 228.

21. It is possible that error-embracing and the open acknowledgement of uncertainty. as explored in later chapters. may represent such value system changes.

22. *See* Emery. op. cit.. pp. 229-30.

23. Polanyi. M. *The Tacit Dimension.* New York: Doubleday. 1966.

24. Berlin. I. *The Hedgehog and the Fox.* New York: New American Library. 1957. *See also* Hook. S. The Hero in History. Boston: Beacon Press. 1943.

25. Vickers. G. *Freedom in a Rocking Boat.* Middlesex. England: Penguin Books. 1970. p. 101.

26. Berger and Luckmann. op.cit.. p. 173.

27. McWhinney. W. "Organizational Form. Decision Modalities. and the Environment." Human Relations. 21(3) (1968). p. 269.

28. *See* Arendt. op. cit.. p. 253. *See also* Vandiver. K. "The Aircraft Brake Scandal." Harpers Magazine. 244. (1972). See also Terkel. S. "Servants of the State." Harpers Magazine. 244 (1972).

29. *See* Chapman. J. "Voluntary Association and the Political Theory of Pluralism." Voluntary Associations: Nomos XI. eds. J. Pennock and J. Chapman. New York: Atherton. 1968.

2

The Meaning and Purposes of Long-Range Social Planning

This chapter has three tasks: first, to establish an understanding of exactly what I mean by long-range social planning; second, to demonstrate why, from the technological standpoint, long-range social planning can operate only as a means for societal learning, rather than as a means for social engineering; and third, to explore in a general way certain terms and activities that will pervade later chapters.

WHAT IS MEANT BY LONG-RANGE SOCIAL PLANNING?

The concept of long-range social planning grows out of a variety of hopes, motivations, perceptions, and ambivalences. The evolving idea of long-range social planning is very much a product of the times, but it is also a product of the history of planning *per se*. For many people, it carries with it the semantic freight of earlier, essentially elitist meanings: planning in which middle-class "city-beautiful" or land-use criteria were established by experts working with those in power. People were "planned for." If this old approach continues to be the standard supported by professionals and laymen, it will present a formidable source of resistance to the societal learning approach espoused here.

Among those quoted here, there is broad consensus about the normative and operational requirements for long-range social planning; but the political consequences of what is being proposed are not clear. Given the real-world context in which attempts to change over to future-responsive societal learning would take place, Bertram Gross' "friendly fascism" looms. If it were to regress, as it easily might, into efforts at social engineering, long-range social planning could indeed contribute to the arrival of fascism.[1]

One motive for trying to do long-range social planning could be to maintain the present distribution of power. In the mixed motives behind the thrust to introduce long-range planning, there is a real risk that alterations in organizational behavior could be corrupted in the direction of social engineering; but learning how to avoid that eventuality is one of the risks involved in learning how to accomplish future-responsive societal learning. To not attempt this kind of learning, and to continue to try to muddle through, carries a far higher risk of societal disaster — quite possibly, of "friendly fascism," increasing disruption, and decay.

I begin, then, with an attempt to strip away misleading semantic freight and to suggest how I envision long-range social planning, by quoting some individuals who are struggling to invent purposes and activities appropriate to it, both now and in the kind of world we think we would like to attain.

Hasan Ozbekhan has contrasted the "mechanistic" or "social engineering" planning concept with what he calls a "human action" model.[2] The chart on the following page organizes his ideas.

John Friedmann, in an elegant summary of the inadequacies of the traditional concept of urban comprehensive planning, expresses the mood of this book's intentions regarding long-range social planning in the quote at the bottom of page 65.

Contrasting Planning Concepts

Mechanistic Model	Human Action Model
Goals given from outside	Selects values, invents objectives, defines goals
Designed to solve specific class of problems	Seeks norms, defines purpose
Internal organization independent of purpose	Higher order organization defined by purpose
Controlled by external policy	Self-regulating and self-adaptive
Programmed actions toward given outcome	Regulation of steady-state dynamic through change and governance of meta-system's self-adaptive and self-regulatory tendencies, through policy formation

*If knowledge about metropolis is revealed to us only in fragments and sequentially, a **flow concept** must come to replace the now outdated notion of learning as a fixed stock of knowledge. The policy analyst, accordingly, is not a man having a superior knowledge in some field, but a superior ability to learn. To be a rapid learner, he will need new tools for exploring complex problem situations, a facility at concept formulation, and a background of relevant theory that will help him integrate new observational data into ad hoc models useful for strategic intervention. But capability for rapid learning is not enough. Unless potential client groups can be taken along on this learning trip, the expert's models will . . . simply remain models. Expert and client must share in the learning experience so that a joint reconceptualization of problems can occur and the possibilities for concerted action be discovered. The policy analyst must thus be able also to structure the learning experience of others, to be a teacher and learner at the same time.*

Mutual learning involves a symbiosis of policy analysis and client group that should go beyond a single interaction and extend to a continuing relationship. It is not a limited deficiency that has to be made up. The metropolitan age imposes upon all organizations a requirement of continuous adjustment, of exploration, discovery, and learning.

. . . In a situation of accelerated change and only limited autonomy, this will require a tightening of the feedback loops of information about change in both internal and environmental states, a general attitude of openness towards the future, and a quickening of the response times to new learning.

. . . A willingness to explore alternative futures in the search for new possibilities of action is an important part of the learning orientation here proposed.[3]

Erik Jantsch summarizes the contrasts between the old mechanistic, or social-engineering, concept of planning and those concepts we will attend to:

Three essential features of the "new" planning make it radically different from the "old" (non-creative) planning: (1) The general introduction of normative thinking and valuation into planning, make it nondeterministic and futures-creative, and places emphasis on invention through forecasting; (2) the recognition of system design as the central subject of planning, making it non-linear (i.e., acting upon structures rather than variables of systems) and simultaneous in its general approach; and, following from the two preceding points, (3) the conception of three levels — normative or policy planning (the "ought"), strategic planning (the "can"), and tactical or operational planning (the "will") — in whose interaction the "new," futures-creative planning unfolds.

Planning deals with system design at the levels of total system dynamics, system structures (goals), and changes of variables in given system structures. Planning provides the information basis, in dynamic terms, for decision-making.[4]

J. Friend and William Jessop of the Tavistock Institute argue:

In public planning . . . it is exceptionally difficult to formulate strategies in advance which are sufficient to cope with all conceivable contingencies; the complexity of the community system, and the imperfect understanding of it in the governmental system, combine to prevent any complete enumeration of the situations which the former might be expected to present. In these circumstances, planning must become in some degree an adaptive process. Although firm commitments may from time to time be required in particular sectors of a complex decision field, it may also become particularly important to retain an element of flexibility in other sectors in the expectation that, by the time commitment in these sectors becomes inevitable, the state of knowledge of the environment may be very different and the whole context of decision may have changed. This does not necessarily mean that the process has reverted from one of planning to one of uncoordinated short-term response: by adopting a strategic approach, involving formulation and comparison of possible solutions over a wide decision field embracing anticipated as well as current situations, the governmental system may find that it is led to select a very different set of immediate actions than would otherwise have been the case.[5]

Amitai Etzioni's concept of "mixed-scanning" seems entirely compatible with the approach proposed here. His point is:

What is needed for active decision-making is a strategy that is less exacting than the rationalistic one but not as constricting in its perspective as the incremental approach, not as utopian as rationalism but not as conservative as incrementalism, not so unrealistic a model that it cannot be followed but not one that legitimatizes myopic, self-oriented, non-innovative decision-making.[6]

Alfred Kahn has written the most searching examination of social planning.[7] Consequently, an extensive quotation from his work will help reinforce the concept of long-range social planning proposed here and also provide a sense of the scope of human welfare subsumed by the word "social":

The central goal of planning is not a blueprint but a series of generalized guides to future decisions and actions. It demands: (a) selection of objectives in the light of assessment of interests, trends or problems, social goals or values, and awareness of their broader implications; (b) a willingness to act in foresight, based on more or less faith and rigorous projections; (c) constant translation of policies into implications for specific objectives and for programs and action; (d) constant evaluation and feedback.

Kahn's diagram — essentially a normative expression — of the "steps" or "phases" in long-range social planning summarizes the tasks to be accomplished, and emphasizes the unavoidably cyclic and interactive nature of these activities.[8] See page 69.

Edgar Dunn provides some observations that fuse the previous quotations and point toward individual and societal behavior, the social-psychological sources of which will be the subject of later chapters:

> Prediction takes the form of a developmental hypothesis, which may be expressed as follows: "We hypothecate that if we undertake a certain course of action; the performance of the social system will be modified in such a way as to improve its efficiency in satisfying the goals or objectives of the system." This is not known to be true on the basis of established deterministic laws. It is not an exercise in simple engineering design. Planning takes the form of conducting an experiment by embodying the new modes of behavior in the performance of the system. It can be viewed as testing the developmental hypothesis in action. If the developmental hypothesis is not falsified by the results of the experiment (i.e., if the performance of the system with reference to its goals is improved), the novel mode of behavior will be reinforced and persist. If the results call the hypothesis into question, a new or modified one will take its place and a new experiment in social action carried out.

> It is not implied that social learning is always the product of a consciously designed and carried out social action experiment. During much of social history to date this has not been so. . . . Even where free from self-deception, those who are engaged in initiating a change in behavior often feel it necessary to represent the change proposal as a certified cure for social ills or a certified instrument of social gain. . . . As a consequence, the implementation of social action is rarely viewed as a test. Indeed, it is often carried out in such a way as to obscure the results of the test and render difficult, if not impossible, dispassionate evaluation.[9]

Many of these intentions and descriptions converge in Melvin Webber's incisive description of activities that should constitute social planning.

> 1. The explication of goals, objectives, and targets for each subsystem under consideration including, in the public sphere, each of the publics that will be touched by the planned actions.

Planning in Action

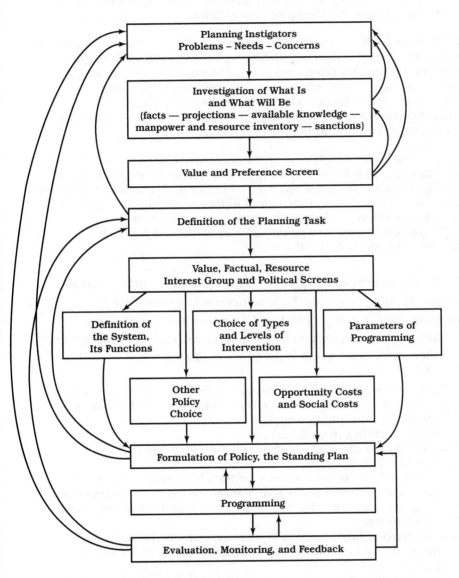

Interlocking Circles and Spirals: Planning in Action. From Alfred Kahn, *Theory and Practice in Social Planning*, Chapter Two.

2. The continuous forecasting of both qualitative and quantitative changes that lie outside the planners' control.

3. The continuous forecasting of likely chains of consequences, within and especially among subsystems, resulting from each set of alternatively hypothesized planned actions.

4. The appraisal of investment costs and welfare payoffs attached to each alternatively projected history. If a reasonable fit is found between an hypothesized course of action and the value sets, a time-sequenced action strategy is synthesized, comprising shorter-run action tactics, each with its time targets. Each shorter-run tactic is carefully appraised for its likely net return, and is then expressed in the language of fiscal budgets.

5. The continuous monitoring of the systems being planned. A constant flow of information on actual outcomes is fed back into the planning system to signal forecasting errors and to actuate corrective steps. In addition, early warning of imminent danger or opportunity can alert deciders and, most important, the effectiveness of goal-directed actions can be empirically evaluated for each subsystem and each public.[10]

Since the phrasing in the above passage tends to stress budgetary and fiscal criteria, it unnecessarily constricts our meaning here. Webber's reformulation provides a simplified summary of the requirements for long-range social planning which will serve us well as a quick-reference checklist:

1. Conjectures about future settings *(differentiating exogenous and endogenous factors) for which the working out of the plan over time is relevant and desirable.*
2. Analysis leading to goal setting.
3. Evaluation of the costs and benefits *of alternative plans for goal seeking.*
4. Tracing out the consequences *for the chosen plan, of pertinent circumstances outside the plan's direct operating environment.*
5. Laying out and carrying out sequenced chains of actions *that define the plan.*
6. Evaluation *of how the plan is working out,* on the basis of environmental feedback *that permits recycling of the above steps.*[11]

Carrying out bits and pieces of the list is not of itself long-range social planning — though succeeding with bits and pieces may create a supportive atmosphere for further attempts to change over to it. Emphasizing the bits and pieces without appreciating what else is required, encourages overlooking two crucial consequences inherent in the multiple requirements that characterize long-range social planning: First, in the context of the *set* of activities comprising long-range social planning, the social-psychological implications for the people involved will always extend beyond those associated with a particular activity. Second, to be meaningful in the sense of long-range social planning, the implementing any one procedure requires that the other activities be implemented as well. All requirements need not be implemented by the same people, or even by the same organization, but those involved in any given activity must know and understand why their activities are integrated into a deliberately designed set of activities intended to lead toward future-responsive societal learning. During the period of changing toward long-range social planning it is particularly important that people understand that the intention is to fold their activities, over time and across and within organizations, into a long-range social planning "package." Accordingly, then:

It will not be long-range social planning if a systematic examination of relevant futures is not part of the basis for choosing goals and programs. Merely projecting or extrapolating from the past or present is not a systematic analysis of alternative futures. As an example, it is now the fashion for colleges and universities to plan for their futures. Almost invariably the issues examined have to do with new capital investments and faculty additions to service a projected future population of students. It is seldom considered that in the university of the future, faculties may be smaller, with students dispersed geographically, possibly linked electronically (and through cheap and easy transportation) into several universities (or learning centers) rather than only one.

It will not be long-range social planning if future-responsive goals are not spelled out and priorities assigned as a basis for program design and resource allocation. This includes explication of both the social costs and benefits expected to be attached to a given goal, since all goals, if described so that progress toward their attainment can be evaluated, embody undesirable consequences as well. At present no such goal explications are made in areas such as power, pollution, education, employment, or transportation. For example, city planners typically set as a goal the capacity to accommodate a certain number of private automobiles ten to twenty years from now. They almost never expose the anticipated costs in public health that could result from the increased automobile pollution, nor do they examine the possibility that in the future, staggered work hours or much smaller commuting vehicles could relieve peak road capacity demands. (In the federal government the activities closest to the explication of goals and their consequences are often those undertaken by Presidential Commissions; yet for all their careful analyses and qualified recommendations, the trivial destiny of Presidential Commission studies is too well known to merit further comment.)

It will not be long-range social planning if requirements 2 and 3 — analysis leading to goal setting, and evaluation of the costs and benefits of alternative plans for goal seeking — are not met. PPBS (planning, programming, budgeting systems) and related methods are a beginning; but so far, not only are the techniques inadequate, but there is also a strong tendency to use PPBS to bolster the preferences of superiors, rather than as a deliberate method for evaluating costs and benefits and then acting in conjunction with other agencies in the light of the requirements for long-range social planning. (Passage of the Environmental Protection Act, requiring the preparation of environmental impact statements, bodes well; but the attempts to amend the Act into impotence, and the Secretary of Commerce's rejection of the findings on likely adverse impacts of the Alaskan pipeline, make it clear that this move toward a philosophy of long-range social planning will be strongly resisted.)

It will not be long-range social planning unless the plan includes procedures intended to accomplish the plan. Typically, plans omit this requirement either because it has not been thought through, or because of fear that explicating the procedures will also raise intransigent political, ideological, organizational, and goal-priority problems. But avoiding requirement (5) — carrying out a sequence of actions that define the plan — vitiates most of the usefulness of the other requirements. Implementation planning is of the essence for assessing goals and program feasibility, and in the case of future-responsive societal learning it is crucial for exposing the areas where learning will be necessary in order to discover implementation procedures. We do this phase of planning very well when scheduling the development of hardware, whether it be buildings, dams, or spacecraft. Indeed, much of the feasibility evaluation for the manned moon-landing program revolved around the question of sequencing the research and development and creating documentation procedures, so that learning could and would occur. (Thus when three astronauts died in a space capsule fire, it was possible to pinpoint precisely what had gone wrong and what needed to be done to avoid another such tragedy.) In social planning, however, the strong tendency is to avoid exposing the implementation requirements for fear the plan will be rejected before it begins to be implemented. One reason that "plans" evaporate is because those involved have not tried to anticipate "what they are getting into," and shared this in advance with others who would be in it with them, to get their understanding and commitment.

It will not be long-range social planning if evaluation of both goals and means is absent. Evaluation, when it is conducted, is usually done in an adversary spirit, because organizations are reluctant to discover whether their preferred and publicized goals are meaningful and their programs effective; this is so because evaluation is perceived as a threat. If long-range social planning were the norm, however, negative findings would not need to be threatening. Nor would organizational efforts need to be represented in ways that result in negative findings being a threat. Instead, untried programs and goals would be treated as experiments. If the findings were negative they would be treated as they are in the laboratory; as hypotheses that were not verified. Through the increased understanding thereby provided, a new program or goal would be introduced. The resistance to evaluation under present norms emphasizes the second requirement for evaluation to meet its requirements within the context of long-range social planning: organizations must be designed so that the evaluations do in fact systematically influence changes in program content and conduct, and in the choice of goals. As of now, there is no certainty that evaluation results will be influential. Indeed, at one time it was highly unlikely that evaluations would be undertaken.

Finally, *it will not be long-range social planning*, in the spirit intended here, unless actions in fulfillment of these requirements are undertaken self-consciously for the specific purpose of facilitating future-responsive societal learning. In this, there is a precedent and perhaps a model in the self-conscious efforts of the writers of the Constitution to build in mechanisms to regulate the use and abuse of power.

That none of these requirements are in themselves long-range social planning, and that seldom is any one of them understood to further the development of future-responsive societal learning, does not mean that they cannot further that development. The very fact that there are more efforts to implement some of the requirements, and increasing recognition that they are interdependent, suggests that a cumulative positive thrust may develop. The problem is, of course, that because the requirements are tied together, the difficulties of implementing them (in part, social-psychological difficulties) will increase enormously. The strong incentive, therefore, will usually be to meet these requirements in piecemeal fashion and hope that will be enough. These difficulties and negative incentives are what this book is about.

What I have listed here are characteristics I would expect future forms of long-range social planning to include. But let me reemphasize, it is unknown what forms long-range social planning would take if were to become the norm; the whole societal setting would be different. Characterizing such a culture presents us with culture-bound conceptual limitations analogous to those that might have faced a feudal lord asked to describe the future characteristics of society based on a market economy. Thus, when I write here "changing toward long-range social planning," let the reader beware of reifying "long-range social planning" (or "future-responsive societal learning"). I do not mean either term to signify a thing, a dogma, or a rigid program. Long-range social planning would be a societal condition characterized, I imagine, by these listed attributes, the meaning of which would partake of what are now their familiar meanings, and whatever new meanings they may come to have in the very process of trying and learning how to apply them.

THE STATE OF THE TECHNOLOGY

Changing toward future-responsive societal learning will depend on willingness and ability to do so; on the capabilities of planning technology to aid that human will and skill; and on a data base that is appropriate for humane development aided by planning technique. Most people think planning technology and a data base are the necessary and sufficient conditions for long-range social planning. Very little attention has been directed to the human condition that must be created if the technology is to be developed and applied fruitfully. Since attention is first directed to technologies, and expectations are based on their potential, we will first look at the present and anticipated state of the art; and since technique and data are so interdependent I will treat them together.

For the purposes of our exploration, it is not necessary to describe the methods and means now being developed to assess the condition of society, and to make estimates of the future as a basis for present action. There is a large literature on these matters[12]; it is sufficient here merely to name some of these methods and means:
- computer-based information systems (such as data banks and management information systems);
- social indicators;
- PPBS [Planning, Programming, Budgeting Systems];
- economic and social modeling;
- simulation;

- gaming;
- future-conjecture methods (such as Delphi, cross-impact, and technology assessment);
- heuristic, linear, and dynamic programming;
- the systems approach;
- operations research;
- planned social change techniques;
- program evaluation methods.

Throughout, I shall use "technology" as a catch-all word for this mixture of analytical modes, data systems, and techniques. What is important is to have a sense of how useful and valid we can expect such technologies to be over the next couple of decades, and particularly in the near future.

The trustworthiness and utility of the technologies will influence the degree to which most public organizations will be willing to accept the pain and the long periods involved in changing over to arrangements that can use these technologies effectively for future-responsive societal learning. Less prudent organizations that succumb to fad or fancy and try to go beyond the capabilities of the technologies, will face gratuitous frustrations and costs that will further discourage change-over efforts — not only in those organizations, but in others that learn of their experiences. Withdrawal from changeover efforts would be a rational response; technological limitations will provide an excellent rationalization for avoiding changing toward long-range social planning. But this would further inhibit refinement of the technologies, since, as I shall argue later, for the most part these technologies can only be refined in the laboratory of the real world.

What, then, is the state of planning technology? It is rudimentary, in the light of what is needed — though certainly the components represent improvements over what we could do and understand before they existed. In a report commissioned by the Conference Board in 1972, several authors examined the implications and state of information technology (a catch-all term for much of long-range social planning technology) over the next two decades.[13] In my chapter, I summarized the mood of the report as follows:

Information technology, as a monitoring and guidance system, will be unavoidably immature during much of the next two decades. A crucial inhibitor will be the inadequate social technology needed to develop organizations humanely so that they can make use of information technology proportionate to its potential. Also, much of the needed data base and theory for interpreting it will still be insufficient for many applications of information technology, especially in the public interest area. Necessarily, at least the 'seventies will be a time for fundamental information technology— pertinent research and development on manpower, legislation, organizational design, education, ethics, as well as on information technology hardware and software per se.

For organizations and for society as a whole, the impact of information technology during these decades will be sporadic, uncertain, and uneven. Information technology's development and application will be aided and obstructed by the turbulent state of the society and by the felicitous and disrupting consequences of applying immature information technology when the laws and ethics pertaining thereto are only partially developed. That is, the turbulent society will both encourage the use of information technology to understand and guide it, and interfere with its rapid development because it will make difficult the simultaneous development of all the necessary parts of the organizational-data- hardware-legal-ethical-information-decision-making system. The resultant likelihood of undesirable consequences from using only a partially developed information technology system will also discourage its application and inhibit further development if it is misapplied.[14]

A few examples will illustrate the interdependence and immaturity of these techniques, hence the need to plan for their simultaneous development.

The primitive state of social-change theory is almost common knowledge; it is exemplified by our continuing inability to predict changes in birth rates.[15] In the words of the distinguished sociologist and pioneer in social-indicator theory Wilbert E. Moore, "We don't know what is the sequence of modernization: we do know history is no guide." [16]

Our ignorance of the dynamics of change is more profound than is commonly realized. We are quick to acknowledge that we cannot predict the future and we are prepared to argue about how the present is unfolding, but we usually overlook the fact that "the past is unpredictable" also.[17] Historians know that, starting at any point in the past with all the information available on the situation up to that time, it is not possible to predict what happened "next." The same branching tree of plausible but unpredictable alternatives faces the historian, just as it faces the futurist. Henry David writes:

The history of human experience is not singular. It is plural, and the histories of human experience may be viewed as competitive and complementary. The burden and meaning of the past that establishes the present or initial state for the futures researcher is not given; it is a function of his choice. That choice will depend first upon how he perceives and defines his own task and, second, upon bodies of historical knowledge — within which are included angles of vision and assignments of meaning as well as 'hard' data created by others.[18]

According to Bell and Mau,

Nearly every generation of literate peoples has some who desire to shape the world to suit themselves by rewriting their history. Even if intentional falsification does not take place, facts can be mustered to support different interpretations. No one would deny this who has read E. Wilson or A. Cobban on the historians' conflicting versions of the French Revolution or who has compared the different scenarios that portray American history.

Nevertheless, we act as if we knew how the past got from then to now, as if we really understood the dynamics of social change.

The inadequacies of economic theory are hidden behind a well-perpetuated mythology that acclaims its potency. Only occasionally do prominent economists assert its inadequacies in public places. One of these, Robert Solo, has written:

It comes down to this: The Establishment economics that is taught in the universities, proliferated in the journals, regurgitated in the councils of government, with all its mountains of published outputs, has not advanced our capacity to control our economy beyond what it was in the late 1930's.

. . . The real complexities of real economies elude us. Establishment economics provides no conceptual approach to measure and comprehend industrial performance, nor to reform, restructure, or control industry. The multifaceted dynamics of technological advance and industrial transformation — the underpinnings of increased productivity — are almost wholly excluded from the normal purview of Establishment economics. Nor does it offer any guide to a control of price that reflects a rational policy for allocation of resources, for the distribution of income, or for incentives for efficiency and technological progress.[19]

In view of these limitations in economic and social theory, the well-publicized procedure of technology assessment is completely inadequate when the future social and economic context must be attended to as a necessary part of that assessment. Dr. Albert Olenzak, manager of technical planning for Sun Oil, points out:

Although much effort has been expended on technological forecasting, few people are satisfied with the results achieved relative to the effort expended. Many programs bog down in overcomplicated systems with excessive data handling and failure to communicate results to management in a meaningful way. The state of the art leaves a lot to be desired.

Dr. Olenzak adds that changes in public attitudes toward technology, and the increasing interdependence of technological change with the rest of the social and physical environment "have added new dimensions of difficulty and uncertainty to the fundamentals of technological forecasting."

As of now, technological assessment is at best a method for choosing a likely path to success in research and development on a technology *per se*, rather than a method for assessing the social consequences of the development of the technology.

Since, ostensibly, a chief reason for doing technological assessments is to detect second-order and third-order consequences, it should be emphasized here that the very concept of "second-order and third-order consequences" is snarled in epistemological dilemmas and semantic traps. The phrase has a kind of intuitive meaning probably based on an essentially linear rather than cybernetic imagery of causal processes. But when the matter is looked at systematically, it turns out to be inordinately difficult to get either a conceptual or an operational fix on it.[20] Suffice it to say that this crucial reason for technological assessment is seldom dealt with at more than a metaphoric level, even though the methods for describing such impacts give an impression of rigor.

The conceptual and utilitarian limitations of cost and benefit analysis, which is also a major method used in PPBS, are well documented.[21] These limitations derive from lack of appropriate data for calculating costs and benefits of alternative approaches within a program; from the unavailability of other than economic criteria for measuring social value; and from incommensurables when costs and benefits are compared among different activities. In this regard, Alice Rivlin has written:

While the income and economic growth benefits of social action programs will probably become less important and less interesting to decision makers over the next few years, this does not mean that it will be impossible to compare the benefits of social action programs. Ingenious analysts will be able to place shadow prices on the non-income benefits of social action programs. But these estimates are likely to be shaky and highly judgmental.

Once we leave the fairly firm ground of income we move into a kind of never-never land where we must set values on self-reliance, freedom from fear, the joys of outdoor recreation, the pleasures of clean air, and so forth. The result may not be worth the effort.

Even if we could compare the benefits of social action programs in commensurable terms, we would be left with the problem that different programs benefit different people. Social action programs typically produce both private and public benefits. The first accrue to individuals, who are, for example, cured of cancer or enjoy the better life a literate society provides.

The private benefits of different types of social action programs may go to entirely different groups of people. People who have cancer are not the people who cannot read. Even if we knew that the benefit-cost ratio was higher for reading programs than for cancer programs, we would not necessarily choose to devote more resources to reading. The decision would depend in part on the values attached to benefiting cancer victims and illiterates.[22]

As for the utility of the mix of operations research and system design and analysis methods subsumed under the term "management science," the assessment of David Hertz, one of the founders and most distinguished contributors to that field, merits repeating:

We have begun to see all around us the kinds of limitations on the techniques of management science. . . . The limitations show up most often as uncertainties and our inability to effectively sort out conflicting objectives. At the moment they appear to be quite unyielding. We need to discover better ways of dealing with uncertainty of all kinds and, in particular, with the complexities and interconnections of organized human behavior and the goals of institutions.[23]

Inadequate data bases for choosing among programmatic means, and for program evaluation, fuel the search for social indicators. Not only are the data lacking, but the experts are quite clear on how enormously difficult it will be to design valid social indicators and to interpret them, especially for the purposes of coping with or conjecturing about social change.[24]

There are two special difficulties in this area. Understanding social change will depend on time series data, which for the most part we presently do not have. In addition, time series data inherently contain an assumed model of social change; otherwise there is no way to decide what it is important to collect data about. This situation has led Moore to observe that, in spite of sophisticated data-collecting and data-processing techniques, as of now "our refinement in quantifiable data about society does not help us with understanding social change."[25]

Dunn puts the task of generating relevant information for future-responsive societal learning this way:

Those forms and sources of information that have been traditionally exploited by social science do not adequately serve the study and practice of social learning.

*What is needed is information about social system goals and
controls that will reveal the degree to which the system's response to
environmental signals is goal satisfying. The identification and
definition of social problems requires the ability to judge the
consistency of social system goals and controls. Once the problem
areas are identified and the need for boundary revisions
established, information is needed about the behavioral options that
are candidates for formulating a developmental hypothesis. This
requires a means for becoming informed about the goals and controls
and technologies employed by other systems that might be borrowed
as well as inventive imagination. Once a developmental hypothesis
is formed, one needs political information concerning the system's
human constituents necessary to the formulation of a consensus.
One needs a technology of organization for change. Once the social
experiment is performed, one needs information that measures goal
convergence and, hence, is necessary for reality testing.*

*Here we are talking about information about social system goals, the
goals and attitudes of human components, machine technologies,
organizational or control technologies, and similar matters. None of
these are forms of information provided by the classical information
systems of social system management or social science. The
conventional internal accounting and reporting systems of
management and the traditional general-purpose, general-parameter
information systems conventionally employed by social science do
not generate information of these kinds.*[26]

Thus the development of valid social indicator data will take
much research, development, and revision. It will take years to test
theory against data. This testing itself will have to be planned even
while the available data are used. Hopefully, the data will be used
with a tentativeness appropriate to the limited understanding of
their meaning. Whether they are used in this way will depend in
part on how successfully organizations come to cope with the
requirements for future-responsive societal learning.

The absence of data, and of criteria for selecting or using
that data, are some reasons why data banks, which have played
such a large role in the imagery of urban planning over the last
few years, are presently inadequate for that task. As Alan Westin
has written,

Scores of handsomely printed long-range plans and feasibility studies speak confidently of affecting higher decision-making levels by producing information geared to program evaluation, alternative policy formulation and testing, and information systems for top management. But no data bank has been found in civilian agencies of city, county, state, or federal government that is in fact delivering on such promises. . . . Most of the systems remaining in existence are geared to automation of existing program operations or of similar programs mandated to new legislation.[27]

Westin's observations and my interviews indicate that the situation has hardly improved since O. Dial's 1968 survey, of which he reported:

the author visited a number of the cities which had the largest experience in developing urban information systems. In none of them did he find a computerized based urban information system in being. Furthermore, after conferring by telephone with officials in selected other cities, and after attending a conference on the present "state of the art," it could only be concluded that there are no such systems in existence today.[28]

Future studies — including this book, to the degree that it is a future study — suffer the conceptual and informational weaknesses of these methods and theory. Even though methodologically-ingenious and operationally-rigorous techniques are being developed, the simple fact is that logic and procedure cannot make up for ignorance about the present processes of society, or for unanticipated developments whose interactions with the rest of society will follow dynamics whose properties we hardly understand at all. In the words of J. Salomen, "The art of conjecture, however strict the scientific apparatus on which it rests, remains an art." [29]

If the technologies are so rudimentary, why even bother trying to change toward long-range social planning? In the first place the technologies, crude as they are, are marginally and narrowly useful, even now. Sometimes they help us know more about the present, and they surely provide more detailed images of the future than before. They have helped clarify social program options and some of the economic costs and benefits associated with the options. Future studies have influenced corporate actions. The technologies have produced new data and new concepts about what is happening in society, and these have influenced the recommendations of government commissions and committees. Complex simulations of social and ecological processes have stimulated international discussion and apparently broadened appreciation of the substance of the issues. Even these rudimentary technologies have aided the legitimization of a long-range perspective, and furthered the expectancy that long-range planning can be done; here and there, they have even made possible more rational and informed decisions and allocations.

Again I caution that using some of these technologies does not of itself constitute planning, much less long-range social planning.[30] Much of the imagery that suggests that long-range planning is underway, results from using the technologies for scheduling, administration, public relations, and the like, and then equating these uses with planning. There is a strong tendency for organizations to encourage others to believe, and often to believe themselves, that by doing a future study they are planning, or that by installing a computerized management information system or data bank, they are planning. Neither activity constitutes planning, though such activities could deliberately or inadvertently facilitate a changeover to planning. So far, however, such activities usually become encapsulated or die.

Changing toward long-range social planning need not depend on fully-developed and validated technologies. The human requirements for beginning to change, as we shall see later, are independent of the state of the technology. Essentially, long-range social planning is a philosophy, with operational consequences, for going about *learning* how to act in the present, in light of continuously-revised anticipations about the future. It is a philosophy of responsible, strategic decision-making in a complex and changing society; it is inherently open and tentative, but strongly committed to acting in terms of chosen futures. However, the legitimation and application of these technologies can be expected to provide a pedagogy, a discipline, for thinking and acting in ways that are compatible with future-responsive societal learning. Thereby they will help undermine belief in the naturalness and sufficiency of disjointed, incremental, and *ad hoc* responses. These technologies can encourage belief in the need to think systematically about the longer-range future as a basis for present action; to look for many more options than arise when decisions are based on unexamined expectations about the future; to recognize that value issues inhere in facts and must be faced openly; and to know that assumptions about the dynamics of society always need examination, and that models and data can assist in that examination. By their very existence, the technologies can be another source of moral and rational obligation to be much more deliberative, systematic, and strategic about getting from here to there — and to be more knowledgeable about what constitutes "here" and "there."

There is another argument for trying to change toward long-range social planning even though the technologies are weak: it is only through attempts at change that there will be occasions to strengthen the technologies. As Donald Campbell writes:

Let us accept the fact that man's deeply ingrained concept of cause is a product of biology, psychology, and evolution rather than a pure analytic concept. If so, it reflects the adaptive advantage of being able to intervene in the world, to deliberately change the relationship of objects. From among all the observable correlations in the environment, man and his predecessors focused upon those few which were, for him, manipulatable correlations. From this emerged man's predilection for discovering "causes," rather than mere correlations. In laboratory science, this search is represented in the experiment, with its willful, deliberate intrusion into ongoing processes. Similarly for the ameliorative social scientist: Of all of the correlations observable in the social environment, we are interested in those few which represent manipulable relationships, in which by intervening and changing one variable we can affect another. No amount of passive description of the correlations in the social environment can sort out which are "causal" in this sense. To learn about the manipulability of relationships one must try out manipulation. The scientific, problem-solving, self-healing society must be an experimenting society.[31]

Ultimately these technologies can only be tested in the real world and revised in the light of those tests: the only way they can be developed and refined is by going "back to the drawing board;" but there has to be a place where the drawing board can be. Less metaphorically, research and development of technology for long-range social planning will itself be a long-range planning task, a future-responsive learning activity. The research and development effort must be part of those relationships the organization has with its environment, where it is intended that long-range social planning will become the operative method for effective responses to the environment's needs and wants. The financial, moral, social, and psychological support for developing the technology will come only from those who need the technology. But the technology will remain feeble if organizations avoid recognizing their need for long-range social planning technology, or if they recognize the need for it but nevertheless resist using it because it is weak. Not using the technology because it is weak will complete a vicious circle, and keep the technology feeble.

To reduce whatever impressions might remain about inherent elitism or rigidness, it is necessary to comment further on some characteristics of the long-range social planning philosophy.

THE RELATIONSHIP BETWEEN THE ORGANIZATION AND ITS ENVIRONMENT

In the Introduction, I explained that the term "environment" as used here refers to the environment of people and other organizations that are associated with a particular organization. (When reference to the natural environment is intended, I will so specify.) It will be helpful to be a bit more explicit about the content of the "surround" of a given organization — for example an agency, department, bureau, mayor's office, or planning commission. (Each could have a capability or requirement for long-range planning at a given time, and if the change to long-range social planning were ultimately successful, most or all of them would.) The surround includes formally-linked superior and subordinate organizations; organizations that supply resources; groups that are beneficiaries of the organization, and groups that suffer adverse consequences from it; groups it controls or regulates; and organizations and groups that are at times allies, competitors, or enemies. Some components of the environment are essentially stable and permanent; others arise or disappear in response to the organization's actions or inactions, or to other happenings in the environment that, rightly or not, implicate the organization. The "environment," then, would be the interdependent cluster of persons, groups, organizations, political parties, and so forth, to which the organization must respond.

The set of requirements for long-range social planning represents a cybernetic system. These requirements take signals from two sources — from the planning activities (the planning organization), and the plan-using activities (the planning-using environment) — and relates the signals to each other, so that differences between what is intended and what is happening can be detected and serve as a basis for adjusting the relationship between the sources, and any mismatch can be minimized. Meeting these requirements becomes problematic when they are translated into human behavior, because this cybernetic scheme requires that people articulate the goals they seek, in such ways that the nature and extent of error in pursuit of these goals can be detected. It requires persons and organizations to seek out their own errors and reward their detection, rather than repressing errors in the hope of avoiding punishment for "failure." It requires that the activities involved in responding to the environment have the "requisite variety" built into them to make the needed responses. And this requires that organizations be designed with a large internal capability for modification. Thus, long-range social planning has two areas of application: the first is in reorganizing and controlling the internal structure and processes of an organization; the second is in responding to and influencing the relevant environment in order to aid society in moving from "here" to "there," in time and content. For the second to occur at all, some substantial accomplishments must occur with regard to the first.

Planning (whatever was meant by that word) was a much more comfortable activity for planners when it was assumed that the environment did the altering while the planning organization, which produced the conditions for alteration, stayed the same. When performed this way, planning inevitably was seen as elitist, and often as manipulative and antidemocratic. The assumption of a passively responding environment was also comfortably compatible with a belief in the naturalness of a hierarchical model of human relations. This perspective has been abetted by our language structure, which implicitly assigns cause and effect, subject and predicate, and thereby treats social systems as if they were "naturally" linear rather than circular in process. [32] Throughout this book the reader should keep in mind that both syntax and brevity carry with them a linear, "we-they" hierarchical implication that is explicitly rejected here. Instead, a circular relationship between an organization and a potentially *active* environment is assumed here.[33]

Rather than conceive of long-range social planning as differing, in an almost geographic sense, between a planning activity and the environment that absorbs it, it is more useful to think of sequences of information and activity that tend to get processed and used by various persons or groups at different times. Some individuals and groups will functionally fill the same processing and utilization roles all or most of the time; others will fill these roles some of the time. At any given time, the distinction between planning-doers and planning-users would to some degree refer to what are in principle temporary allocations of functions. Note, however, that in the process of changing over to long-range social planning, endowing the environment with active, error-responding characteristics also imposes on the environment many of the same obligations that are required of the organization in its part of the process. But social-psychological sources of resistance to efforts to change over to long-range social planning will operate in the environment as well as in the organization; thus, if the requirements for long-range social planning are to be met, relearning must characterize *all* parts of the system.

As Kahn has noted, long-range social planning will involve many more kinds of people than the conventionally-defined "planner:"

Planner, community organizer, and administrator are . . . in closely interrelated and interacting roles. The social policy analyst or policy scientist (an American variation) is sometimes a scholar of social policy, often a planner or administrator. All are interested in and draw upon the work of students of social change theory and organization theory. And, because the roles not only interrelate but also have unclear boundaries, each is readily found functioning in the domain of the other and defining it as his own.[34]

Because of the kinds of requirements that must be met, changing toward long-range social planning would involve all levels and functions in an organization. The means and organizational structures for selecting goals; for conducting, revising, or eliminating programs; for generating and applying information from the present and the future, will all have to be created. Some of this work could be done better by the "line," some by the "staff;" some by the organization, and some by parts of its environment, depending on the competencies needed and the setting required to use them. Here the point is that long-range social planning must be a normative and operational characteristic of a *system* that includes the environment. Changing toward long-range social planning could not be the exclusive responsibility or perspective of planners, or a "planning staff," or management, or a consumer group, and still be a means for future-responsive societal learning. At the same time, the performance of changeover activities and the impact of these performances would be distributed differently according to function and competencies.

Since we are concerned here not with the final form of an organization and environment *doing* long-range social planning, but rather with the *changeover* situation, it is important to add that the incentive to change over could come from anywhere in the organization or environment where resources and rationale provide means to push for such changes. However, it does seem clear that, at least when changeover efforts are initiated within an organization, sophisticated, enduring, and participative support from the highest level will be required.[35]

In addition, means must be invented for effectively utilizing environmental participation in the process of long-range social planning. Appropriate forms do not now exist for using different competencies, perspectives, representations, jurisdictions, and so forth. Research and development of such inventions will be a major and continuing task during the changeover to future-responsive societal learning.

On Incrementalism and "Satisficing"

A major contribution to the disjointed incrementalist philosophy is Herman Simon's argument that in the nature of things men are constrained to use what he calls "bounded rationality." Limitations of time, resources, access knowledge, and wits mean that we settle for less than what perfect rationality, and perfect conditions for obtaining and using knowledge, would lead us to; in Simon's term, we "satisfice," or settle for a "good enough" solution to the problem. He proposes that this is a reflection of limitations in human wits.[36] Others argue that it is not wits but will that sets the level at which satisficing occurs.[37] The important point for this exploration is that, barring some absolute limit on conceptual abilities in the individual, or in some augmented arrangement involving other people or machines, the degree to which a situation is examined and alternatives explored is culturally determined; what constitutes a satisficed solution or action is determined by what the society will settle for. If the demand goes up for more-comprehensive searches, and deliberations of a wider-ranging set of alternatives, then satisficing conditions won't be met at the same old level that previously served. This is what Yehezkel Dror means when he writes,

The main weakness of the [satisficing] model is that it takes the satisfactory quality as given, and so ignores a main question it should be answering, namely, what the variables shaping the satisfactory quality are, and how much they can be consciously directed.[38]

Thus long-range social planning is quite compatible with the satisficing model of human behavior; it simply requires that the standards be set much higher.

From place to place in this book the requirements for future-responsive societal learning will be contrasted with those ascribed to incrementalism. When I refer to incrementalism, I mean the disjointed incrementalism that is associated with what Alan Schick calls "process politics" and "process budgeting," [39] and which has been most articulately espoused in the writings of Charles Lindblom and Aaron Wildavsky. [40] The learning approach described and promoted in *Learning to Plan* is of course incremental in the sense that experiments, and program and goal alterations, proceed in steps. But the philosophy and the consequences of its application are the antithesis of what is called for and follows from disjointed incrementalism, as conventionally described and justified. The "increments" involved in long-range social planning are defined by deliberate choices of goals; they are future-oriented, innovative, and implemented even though outcomes are uncertain; they are articulated rather than disjointed; and they are responsible and responsive to environmental needs at least as much as to considerations of organizational survival and aggrandizement. Bertram Gross puts the difference this way:

While the great value of Lindblom's approach has been to emphasize the sequential nature of decision-making and the huge limits on thoroughly rational analysis, he went too far in stressing the disjointed nature of the process He thereby ignored the necessity of focusing strategic decision making under certain circumstances, on major structural changes rather than a disjointed series of increments. The wisdom of Lindblom's analysis, however, lies in the fact that major structural change — even change of a revolutionary nature — cannot take place except through a series of small steps. These steps, however, must follow each other in accordance with some broad strategic considerations. They must be jointed, instead of disjointed. Hence, jointed incrementalism is one of the major principles of strategic decision-making. [41]

Distributive Equity and
Long-Range Social Planning

The simplified Webber list (pages 68, 70) emphasizes that careful attention to distributive equity is a requirement for long-range social planning. This is more than a normative and logical requirement; with growth in the technology of social indicators and related information-retrieval and feedback systems, there will be increasing capability to pay attention to "secondary" and "tertiary" consequences of actions, and there will be increasing efforts to anticipate them — which will encourage long-range social planning. Public pressure will ensure that organizations pay attention to such consequences. Clearly, the requirement that long-range social planning be closely attentive to distributive-equity issues would itself make necessary substantial participation by members of the environment. Corporations have not traditionally taken innocent cost-bearers and gratuitous gainers into account in their planning and programming. Government has been more self-conscious about the problem, and has depended on the processes of interagency negotiation and agency-executive-legislative negotiation to solve it. In recent years we have come to appreciate that this political and organizational process has very deep limitations. Thus, more explicit and systematic recognition of who gains the benefits, and who suffers the costs, will be a source of personal and organizational pain in the move toward long-range social planning — as well as a strong pressure for moving that way.

EVALUATION OF SOCIAL EXPERIMENTS
IN THE CONTEXT OF LONG-RANGE SOCIAL PLANNING

To assess the continuing relevance of the chosen goals, and the effectiveness of programs underway in the pursuit of these goals, evaluation must be a central and continuing part of future-responsive societal learning. Evaluation of the evaluation methods and purposes themselves would also be necessary in order to learn how, when, and what to evaluate. The process of designing social experiments so that they can be evaluated will be subtle and complex; only in the last few years has this begun to receive the quality of attention it deserves. Like the rest of long-range social planning technology, it is in a rudimentary state.

This reflects partly the state of behavioral science, and partly the result of so few opportunities in the past to develop and try out adequate evaluation procedures. Those responsible for most public service programs have resisted evaluating them, and in those rare cases in which evaluation has been requested, it has usually been done after the program was in operation. In such cases, evaluators are unable to get the information they need to compare conditions before with conditions after, or to properly control the variables under consideration. Often the organization requesting the evaluation has defined its project so narrowly that the evaluation is useless for the purpose of program redesign. Also, most evaluations have been made according to paradigms that simply were not sophisticated enough to handle the subject. As Donald Campbell has remarked, "With the most minor exceptions, it can be said for the United States that none of our ameliorative programs have had adequate evaluations."

This situation is starting to change; among other pressures, there are now legislative directives allocating a percentage of program funds for evaluation. But as of this writing, little has been done. Expenditure of the funds allocated for evaluation is not mandatory, so much has been avoided; and what has been done is inadequate. Also, evaluations are not integrated into organizational structures in a way that would assure that programs be designed so that they can be evaluated, and that evaluations will affect subsequent program activities.

Overall, even when evaluation is requested, the requester's attitude has been deeply ambivalent; there is always the fear that the evaluation may show that programs are not working. In that event, the agency or persons who promoted the program would be in trouble, and those committed to the program would have to shift their psychological investment. Members of organizations and their funding or administrative superiors have not approached the challenge of public service performance with an open, supportive, experimental attitude toward program outcomes. It is not surprising, then, that the development of effective evaluation methods has been thwarted, or that there are no built-in procedures to assure that evaluation findings will be used.

A factor contributing to new pressures for evaluation is the small beginning of deliberate social experiments such as those on the effects of a guaranteed minimum income, low-income rent subsidies, and educational vouchers. But these experiments are not yet imbedded in other long-range social planning processes that would give them the utility they need; they are more apt to deal with present problems, than with the product of future-responsive goals studies. Nor or they linked to government agencies and Congress in ways that would assure their impact across government operations. Nevertheless, both are steps in the right direction.

Two crucial, unsolved problems in designing evaluations appropriate to long-range social planning deserve mention here. First, what is the relationship of members of the environment, who are the "object" of the "experiment," to the "experimenters?" Obviously, there are grave ethical and ideological issues involved in the conventional arrangement, in which the subjects of the experiment do not know what behaviors are being evaluated (because that knowledge would alter their behavior). There are also deep methodological issues involved; one that is just beginning to get attention is the effect of this conventional arrangement on subjects' behavior, compared to the effect on their behavior when they are co-experimenters, or collaborators with the "experimenter." There are reasons to believe that the classic "scientific" experiment has produced a body of laboratory findings that essentially distort or trivialize our understanding of human behavior simply because of the stance the subject takes in the role of "subject." [42] How useful is it to know how people behave under the experimental conditions, when the legitimating norms will be different if the behavior is accepted as normal and conventional? (People who are part of an experiment in which, for example, they receive a monthly supplemental income when such income is not acknowledged as the right of every citizen, may well act differently than they would if such an income were legitimated as a right.)

More fundamentally, there is the question of whether the purpose of societal experiments — including the evaluation aspect — should be to gather data and test hypotheses, or whether it should be to provide a means by which "experimenters" and "subjects" alike learn new norms and behavior? To my mind, long-range social planning, as a procedure for societal learning, leans strongly toward the latter.

The fact that long-range social planning involves goals and public programs that would have their fulfillment well into the future poses a second basic problem in evaluation methodology, and hence for the conduct of future-responsive societal learning. How is the balance to be found between experiments that are comprehensive enough in time and scope to be meaningfully evaluated, and the social and economic costs that such comprehensive experiments might entail? Time duration is a particularly knotty problem. *When* is the utility of the program to be evaluated? The end point (if indeed there is one) is too late, if it should turn out that the program is counterproductive. Yet trying to make a definitive evaluation too early might subject the program to political and other pressures that could eliminate it for the wrong reasons, and, in the process, undermine attempts at changing over to long-range social planning. How then can we commit ourselves to long-term programs and goals, and at the same time evaluate and revise them continually, without destroying our very commitment? If there are answers, they will have to be discovered in the process of trying to meet the requirements for future-responsive societal learning; and they will be intimately related to ways of dealing with social-psychological resistance to changing toward long-range social planning.

Phases and Actors in Changeover Processes

Impressionistic as it must be, it will be useful to have an image — a "map" or "program" — of the kinds of phases and actors I have in mind when I refer to the process of "changing over" or "changing toward" long-range social planning. What follows derives from the circumstances and activities that seem to characterize organizations trying to move in the direction of long-range social planning, and from the formal literature on organizational change and related matters. However, it should be noted that, while a good bit has been theorized about the patterns of organizational change, and much has been written about what they should be, "there have been even fewer studies of the pattern of change than of its causes and consequences." [43]

The broad categories of influences bearing on the changeover processes are:

- The characteristics of the environment as it impinges on the organization.
- The state of long-range social-planning technology, as it develops in an organization and as it is available outside it.
- The ideas in good currency regarding the utility of long-range social planning and its technology.
- The circumstances that determine
- Who is pushing for long-range social planning in the light of aspects of 1, 2, or 3, and why; and
- The resources they can bring to bear in furtherance of their efforts inside and outside the organization.
- The circumstances that determine
- Who *opposes* moving toward long-range social planning in the light of aspects of 1, 2, or 3, and why; and
- The resources they can bring to bear in furtherance of their efforts inside and outside the organization.
- The personal, interpersonal, and organizational circumstances that determine what aspects of 1, 2, and 3 are screened out or emphasized through the selective attention to 4 and 5.

Those influences which are selectively attended to or ignored will change over time, in part as a result of accumulated experiences, including those associated with the changeover effort; and in part as a result of exogenous influences from new personnel, changes in organizational structure, and feedback forced on the organization by the environment.

This is the appropriate place to introduce the concept of "appreciation," as developed by Geoffery Vickers:

An appreciation involves making judgments of fact about the "state of the system," both internally and in its external relations. I will call these reality judgments. These include judgments about what the state will be or might be on various hypotheses as well as judgments of what it is and has been. They may thus be actual or hypothetical, past, present, or future. It also involves making judgments about the significance of these facts to the appreciator or to the body for whom the appreciation is made. These judgments I will call value judgments. Reality judgments and value judgments are inseparable constituents of appreciation; they correspond with those observations of fact and comparison with norm which form the first segment of any regulative cycle, except that the definition of the relevant norm or complex of norms, like the identification of the relevant facts is itself a product of the appreciation. The relation between judgments of fact and of value is close and mutual; for facts are relevant only in relation to some judgment of value, and judgments of value are operative only in relation to some configuration of fact.[4]

Elsewhere, Vickers emphasizes that although it is clear that we learn what to treat as information and what to value, we have very little understanding of how we learn these things.

Throughout this book I will assume the ubiquitous operation of the appreciative process; indeed, long-range social planning can be thought of as a self-conscious working out of the appreciative process at the organizational level. This process is operating when we call a human situation "natural," and draw attention to certain "facts" to validate that assessment. Thus, under most circumstances it sustains the definition of reality held by society at a particular time. When enough compelling anomalies accumulate, the appreciative process is central to the creation of a new definition of human reality that in turn becomes self-sustaining.

Among the most important appreciations in any group situation are those that have to do with what appreciations are permissible within the group: that is, there are limits to what one can question, or pay attention to, and still remain a team member. The constraints on what is "permissible" to perceive as relevant or factual may be different for groups within the organization, and groups in the environment. (For example, what is perceived by "establishment" law-and-order agencies as disruptive and threatening to social stability, may be seen by the dispossessed as new opportunities for access to membership in society.) Different persons and groups have, to varying degrees, different appreciative systems and different selective-attention characteristics — although within groups, the social forces to perceive in a consensual manner are very high indeed.[45]

With the appreciative process in mind, along with some of the circumstances that will affect its operation, let us look at the "phases" that might be abstracted from the ongoing processes of changing toward long-range social planning. The phases delineated here will help to emphasize that different needs and circumstances will be dominant as the changeover effort progresses over time.

- At some point, circumstances and the felt needs of those involved combine to produce a "selection" of motives and beliefs that result in the *intention* to initiate long-range social planning. (Quite a few organizations seem to have taken this step but have gotten no further.) If these persist and the proponents have the power to do so, other phases would be implemented:

- *Arrangements* would be made to initiate activities aimed at realizing the long-range planning intent. For example, committees are appointed, titles assigned, money allocated, enabling memoranda written. With people now enjoined to do things, this would lead to:

- *Conducting activities* for initiating long-range social planning; for example, future studies, goal-setting tasks, organizational-development programs. (Some organizations, including governmental organizations, have begun this stage.) Eventually this would lead to efforts aimed at:

- *Elaboration and integration of activities* for initiation of long-range social planning, into organizational norms and structures, and functions for trying to conduct long-range social planning as such. (A very few organizations, such as the YMCA and General Electric, seem to have just begun this stage.) As the organization and its environment learned how to do these things, the organization — and society — would be transformed into a:

- *Society operating according to the norms of future-responsive societal learning* (which, presumably, would include the requirements in the Webber list given early in this chapter).

In real organizations, things would not go this neatly. There will be much backing and filling, much personal pain and opportunity. Given the undesirability of rigidly controlling the people and processes involved (and our inability to do so), the phases certainly will not be clear-cut, or the sources of movement singular and one-directional. Environmental characteristics may be more or less propitious at different times. So, too, with the state of the art and philosophy of the technology for long-range social planning. It will be very important who or what groups in the organization or its environment become interested in or antagonistic to long-range social planning, or some facet of it; and these also will vary over time.

While conditions may converge felicitously to move the changeover process from phase to phase, a change in "input" may set back the effort, or may wash out the whole thing. At any point, the cost of redoing or moving ahead may appear too high, and the uncertainty or risk too great. The intent to move toward long-range social planning may die, or become encapsulated as ritual, or be converted into some form of planning other than long-range social planning. These counter-developments seem to characterize most of the experiences to date.

Since learning how to change toward long-range social planning will be long and difficult — even painful — it will require that certain needs be felt strongly enough to sustain the experience. Many of those working in organizational settings who have tried to initiate changeover efforts toward long-range social planning seem not to realize how difficult the task will be, and also seem to lack the motives or needs that would sustain such efforts. When faced with the complexity and difficulty of the task, the effort bogs down or dies. In view of this, it will be worthwhile to review impressionistically some typical circumstances that presently lead to the first phases of changing toward long-range social planning.

In what follows, Karl Marx's thesis that organizational change is forced or initiated from the outside, and Max Weber's thesis that change comes from within, are both operative. As often as not, in the societal situation we are concerned with, "inside" and "outside" will merge as members of organizations have an increasing portion of their role identity located outside the organization. (See Chapter 7.)

- A senior member of the organization becomes interested in long-range planning, or social planning, or a variant that uses some of the planning technology. He may simply be influenced by all the talk about planning in the management-oriented periodicals he reads, or by the high-level seminars he attends (much as were many executives who invested their company's capital in computers because it was the thing to do); or he may feel that the image of corporate or agency efforts to do long-range social planning will be good public relations. At any rate, emulating others (but often lacking strong motivation), he initiates some activities. Perhaps he contracts for future studies, or sets up a small long-range planning group, or invests in a management-information system (MIS) to give him the information he thinks he needs for planning, or to shake up his organizational sub-sections so they will start to plan. (Argyris has noted that MIS is often introduced through special task groups assigned to a small number of departments, so that the MIS effectively starts its test period in isolation from most of the company.) Or he has a favorite long-range problem and he puts some people to work on it. In other cases, the superior initiating the activity may be outside the agency where the activity will be undertaken. Usually the effort is uncoordinated and spotty.

  An organization faces a crisis, or a deep sense of malaise or frustration with itself. (The appreciation that there is "in fact" an organizational malaise that can be removed, is in part a result of the idea, increasingly in good currency, that organizational-development methods can help.) With the help of outside consultants, or using its own resources, the organization tries to understand what changes in organizational and environmental circumstances have produced the situation. Organizational consultants bring with them ideas that influence the organization to consider aspects of its relation to its environment that it has not thought about before. (According to Rogers and Shoemaker, "Some researchers . . . suggest that external sources are the most important catalysts of change for administrators of formal organizations." [46]) This leads to questions about how it should operate in the future, which introduces a self-conscious attention to the future as the context for making decisions. This in turn leads the organization to an intention to carry out the steps toward long-range social planning — usually without an understanding of what it will be getting into.

Under the influence of the professional fraternity's approval of long-range social planning, and with an eye to increasing their personal value to the organization, those (either inside or outside the organization) who are responsible for the organization's short-range planning, begin to apply their techniques to longer-range problems. They encourage their clients to expand their time frame, and they try to convince their superiors that the organization should and can expand its time frame. In the same way, those responsible for solving small planning problems try to move their organization toward working on more-comprehensive problems. Planning-oriented people in corporations and third-sector organizations (such as voluntary organizations, foundations, and colleges) try to move their superiors toward social planning in order to expand their "product-lines" and protect themselves from displacement by more-encompassing organizations, such as the federal agencies. Planning-oriented people in government agencies try to move their people toward social planning because, among other things, Congress and the Executive office keep adding activities and missions. Note that these moves toward long-range planning are not necessarily approved or known about by senior executives; sometimes they are the entrepreneurial or ideological moves of people with the skills, motives, organizational location, and legitimacy to push in these directions. Lack of senior-officer participation and support often leads to the demise, or at least the stalemating, of efforts to move toward long-range social planning.

At each phase of evolution of the changeover process, an internal sequence of "collective innovation-decision steps" seems necessary — though, depending on the conditions that precede arrival at a given stage of development, some of these steps may be bypassed. Rogers and Shoemaker offer a useful sequence in describing decision-making in communities; since the environment would play an integral role in the changeover toward future-responsive societal learning, reviewing it here will be useful. The sequence is:

- *stimulation* of interest in the need for the new idea (by stimulators);
- *initiation* of the new idea in the social system (by initiators);
- *legitimation* of the idea (by power-holders or legitimizers);
- *decision* to act (by members of the social system); and
- *action* or execution of the new idea.[47]

Rogers and Shoemaker stress that "these steps are not necessarily mutually exclusive, nor do they always occur in the exact chronological order."[48] Here is how they summarize the characteristics of the stimulator, initiator, and legitimizer operating in a community:

Stimulators of collective innovation decisions are more cosmopolite than other members of the social system. This characteristic provides them with fairly easy access to innovations, and the ability to perceive needs and problems of the social system. The initiators of collective innovation decisions are unlikely to be the same individuals in a social system as the legitimizers. Initiators are noted for their favorable attitudes toward change and for their knowledge of the system.

Legitimizers are the high status power-holders of the system who sanction the change. Therefore, the rate of adoption of a collective innovation is positively related to the degree to which the legitimizers are involved in the decision-making process.[49]

In organizations where efforts have been made to move toward long-range social planning, it seems to me that the stimulator and initiator are often the same person operating in a boundary-spanning role (see Chapter 12); occasionally the legitimizer, stimulator, and initiator are all the same person or group. But a lack of strong evidence of legitimation (beyond ritual pronouncements from the top) has usually thwarted the evolution of long-range social planning.

To apply their model of innovation decisions, Rogers and Shoemaker distinguish two means for diffusing innovations through the organization: a participative approach "in which there is a wide sharing of power, decisions about change being made in consultation with those affected by the change," [50] (which in our case would seem to mean just about everybody); and through "authority innovation-decisions," which involve five interrelated functions:

1. Knowledge about the need for change and innovation on the part of the decision unit;
2. Persuasion and evaluation of the innovation by the decision unit;
3. Decision as to acceptance or rejection of the innovation by the decision unit;
4. Communication of the decision to the adoption units in the organization; and
5. Action or implementation by the adoption units. [51]

It is important to note that in the long-range social planning situation, the kinds of groups and persons who would have to make such decisions at each stage, and then carry them out, may be among those resisting the introduction of the required changes, because they perceive long-range social planning as a threat to their authority.

Some summary comments about related developmental processes aptly suggest the complex and painful sequencing tasks that will be involved in changing toward long-range social planning. In what follows, E. Miller and A. Kenneth Rice are using as their example developmental problems in designing, building, and operating a new plant starting from scratch (on a "greenfield").

Our analysis suggests that, in most processes of institution- building, efforts to secure innovation will conflict with any attempt to secure commitment by involving the future members of the institution in design tasks. The only exception will be in the enterprise in which an individual or a small group, themselves the risk-taking entrepreneurs, can encompass the entire setting-up process. The setting-up task can then be contained within a simple system. If the task is large enough to require an internally differentiated organization, conflict will arise. Thus if the plant-design system does not include members of the future building system and the future operating system, first the builders and later the operators will be working to designs that they had no part in shaping. Predecessors' actions can then become alibis for current failures. Conversely, if the organization maximizes involvement in the design and building systems of members of the future operating system, innovation will be retarded.

The more general point is that conflict is inevitable in any setting-up process in which the task is to create a system with organized properties. Conflict and the attendant anxieties are likely to be stronger in the greenfield situation, where the heightened expectations at the beginning also exacerbate the ultimate feeling of let-down when — as must be so — the completed task does not live up to all the original expectations. The painful and destructive aspects of the creative process are perhaps easier to bear, however, if they can be anticipated and planned for.[52]

The reader should take what has been proposed here only as an image, not as a model of what would or should be the phases and kinds of actors involved in the changeover process. Let Rogers and Shoemaker echo earlier caveats about the comparatively modest state of our understanding of our society, or of the change processes operating in it:

Diffusion researchers have largely neglected the study of diffusion and adoption of innovations involving authority innovation-decisions; we know very little about the process by which authority decisions are made and organizational changes implemented.[53]

Long-Range Social Planning
Outside the United States

A frequent speculation suggests that the absence of extensive efforts to change toward long-range social planning in the United States is only superficially related to social-psychological phenomena, and is better understood in terms of the inextricable snarl of statutes, prerogatives, and traditions that characterize our hyperpluralistic society. Often attached to this speculation is the presumption that long-range social planning *is* underway in other parts of the world — at least in the socialist or communist nations, or in the Third World, where economic planning has been a continuing activity for many years.

Clearly, some countries, including Western European nations, are more deliberative about their development, at least over five-year time periods. How much more deliberative, how much more in the spirit of future-responsive societal learning as emphasized here, is not clear.[54] Gunnar Myrdal, for example, has argued that Third World planning has been economic planning, and that economic models have failed as social-planning technologies because they are simply wrong in their emphasis, and unresponsive to crucial social and psychological considerations. It might well be that differences in attitudes toward expertise, authority, and hierarchy; homogeneity of population; special historical experiences; different levels of aspiration and expected standards of social services, would provide better grounds for beginning long-range social planning elsewhere, if the attempt were made to do so. In this regard, Dror writes:

Developments have been different, for instance, in the Netherlands, where the constant pressures of critical hydraulic, social, political, and economic problems have required very good public policymaking merely for survival and have made much use of essential knowledge.[55]

On the other hand, Westin has speculated that

social psychological responses of the kind that inhibit efforts at long-range social planning are inevitable and natural consequences when human beings are set into the competitive and even combative relationships that the framers of the American Constitution saw as the way to inhibit the intensification of power in any one set of hands.[56]

Also, until the environment is perceived by local standards to be dangerously turbulent, other means of societal guidance may seem sufficient, and the rigors of long-range social planning an unnecessary burden. All such factors would affect the social-psychological setting since that is, by definition, the result of psychological processes interacting with social circumstance.

All things considered, *this is very much a book by an American, writing and reflecting on the situation in the United States.* Beyond this, questions of comparative national capabilities for moving toward long-range social planning, and the extent to which other nations are involved in the type of long-range social planning described here, are essentially unexplored.

1. Gross, B. "Friendly Facism: A Model for America." Social Policy, 1 (November-December 1970). *See also* Gross, B. "Planning in an Era of Social Revolution." Public Administration Review, 31(3) (1971), pp. 283-287. *See also* Morris, C. The Open Self. New York: Prentice-Hall, 1948, pp.166, 168.

2. Ozbekhan, H. "Toward a General Theory of Planning." *Perspectives of Planning.* ed. E. Jantsch. Paris: Organization for Economic Cooperation and Development, 1969, p.118.

3. Friedmann, J. "The Future of Comprehensive Urban Planning: A Critique." *Public Administration Review*, 31(3) (1971), p. 325. *See also* the rest of the May-June 1971 issue of *Public Administration Review*.

4. Jantsch, E. "From Forecasting and Planning to Policy Sciences." Paper for presentation at the AAAS annual meeting, Boston, December 26-31, 1969, p. 325. *See also* Jantsch, E. *Technological Planning and Social Futures*. London: Associated Business Programs Limited, 1972.

5. Friend, J. and W. Jessop. *Local Government and Strategic Choice*. London: Tavistock Publications; Sage Publications, 1969, p. 112.

6. Etzioni, A. *The Active Society*. New York: The Free Press, 1968, pp. 282-283.

7. Kahn, A. *Theory and Practice of Social Planning*. New York: Russell Sage Foundation, 1969. For a description of compatible policymaking and post-policymaking stages, *see* Dror, Y. *Public Policymaking Reexamined*. San Francisco: Chandler, 1968, pp. 15-16.

8. Kahn, op. cit., p. 62.

9. Dunn, E. Economic and Social Development: *A Process of Social Learning*. Baltimore: Johns Hopkins, 1971, pp. 133-134.

10. Webber, M. "Planning in an Environment of Change." *The Town Planning Review*, 39(3) (1968), p. 278.

11. Edited from a workgroup transcript and approved by Webber.

12. For detailed reviews and extensive biographies, *see* Ackoff, R. *The Concept of Corporate Planning*. New York: Wiley-Interscience, 1970. *See also* Steiner, G. *Top Management Planning*. Toronto: Collier-Macmillan, 1969.

13. *See Information Technology: Some Critical Implications for Decision Makers*. New York: The Conference Board, Inc., 1972. *See also Information Technology in a Democracy*, ed. A. Westin. Cambridge: Harvard University Press, 1971.

14. Michael, D. "The Individual: Enriched or Impoverished, Master or Servant?," *Information Technology*, op. cit., pp. 40-41.

15. For critiques of and proposals for a theory of social change *see* Bell, W. and J. Mau. *The Sociology of the Future*. New York: Russell Sage Foundation, 1971, Part I. *See also* Blumer, H. "Social Problems as Collective Behavior." *Social Problems*, 18 (1971), p. 299. *See also* Stogdill, R. *The Process of Model Building in the Behavioral Science*. Columbus, Ohio: Ohio State University Press, 1970. *See also Modern Systems Research for the Behavioral Scientist*, ed. W. Buckley. Chicago: Aldine, 1968. *See also Sociology and Modern Systems Theory*, ed. W. Buckley. Englewood Cliffs, N.J.: Prentice-Hall, 1967. *See also* Deutsch, K. *The Nerves of Government*. New York: The Free Press, 1966. *See also* McNamara, R. *Address to the Columbia University Conference on International Economic Development*. International Bank for Reconstruction and Development. Washington: 1970, p.10. *See also* Rokeach, M. *Beliefs, Attitudes, and Values*. San Francisco: Jossey-Bass, 1968, p. 166.

16. In personal conversation, 1971. Quoted by permission.

17. Ascribed to Professor J. Minus by Ratoosh, P. "Experimental Studies of Implementation," *Operational Research and the Social Sciences*, ed. J. Lawrence. London: Tavisitock, 1966.

18. David, H. "Assumptions About Man and Society and Historical Constructs in Futures Research." *Futures*, 2(3) (1970), p. 228.

19. Solo, R. "New Maths and Old Stabilities." *Saturday Review* (January 22, 1972), p. 47.

20. Bauer, R. et al. *Second Order Consequences: A Methdological Essay on the Impact of Technology*. Cambridge: M.I.T. Press, 1969. *See also* Maimon, Z. "Some Aspects of the Treatment of Costs and Benefits in Social Psychology." Discussion paper for the Center for Urban Studies, Wayne State University, May 1971.

21. Crecine, J. *Defense Budgeting: Organizational Adaptation to External Constraints*. Santa Monica: The Rand Corporation, 1970. *See also* Jones, E. *Systems Approaches to Multi-Variable Socioeconomic Problems: An Appraisal*. Program of Policy Studies in Science and Technology, Discussion Paper 103. Washington, D.C.: The George Washington University, 1963. *See also* McKean, R. and M. Anshen. "Problems, Limitations, and Risks." *Program Budgeting: Program Analysis and the Federal Budget*. ed. D. Novick. Santa Monica, Calif.: The Rand Corporation, 1965. *See also* Rivlin, A. *The Planning, Programming, and Budgeting System in the Department of Health, Education, and Welfare: Some Lessons from Experience*. Washington, D.C.: The Brookings Institution, 1969. *See also* Schick, A. "Can the States Improve Their Budgeting?" Brookings Research Report 120. Washington, D.C.: The Brookings Institution, 1971. *See also* Schultze, C. *The Politics and Economics of Public Spending*. Washington, D.C.: The Brookings Institution.

22. Rivlin, A. op. cit., pp. 57-58.

23. Hertz, D. "Has Management Science Reached a Dead End?" *Innovation* (now *Business Society Review*), (25) (1971), p. 14. *See also* Churchman, C. W. "Operations Research as a Profession." *Management Science*, 17(2) (1970). *See also* Dearden, J. "Myth of Real-Time Management Information." *Harvard Business Review*, 44(3) (1966). *See also* Hoos, I. "A Critical Review of Systems Analysis: The California Experience." NASA Report CR-61350. Berkeley: University of California, 1968 and Hoos, I. "A Realistic Look at the Systems Approach to Social Problems." *Datamation*, 15(2)(1969).

24. *Social Indicators*, ed. R. Bauer. Cambridge: M.I.T. Press, 1966, Ch. 2. *See also* Etzioni, A. and E. Lehman. "Some Dangers in 'Valid' Social Measurement." The Annals of the American Academy, 373 (September 1967). *See also Social Intelligence for America's Future: Explorations in Societal Problems*, eds. B. Gross and M. Spainger. Boston: Allyn and Bacon, 1969. *See also* Milsum, J. "The Technosphere, The Biosphere, The Sociosphere." *IEEE Spectrum*, 5(6)(1968).

25. In personal conversation. Quoted with kind permission.

26. Dunn, op. cit., pp. 254-255. *See also* Kahn, R. "The Justification of Violence: Social Problems and Social Solutions." *Journal of the Society for the Psychological Study of Social Issues*, 28 (1972), pp. 156, 161. *See also* Thomas, T. and D. McKinney. *Accountability in Education*. Research Memorandum, EPRC-6747-15. Menlo Park, Calif.: Stanford Research Institute, 1972.

27. Westin, A., "Information Technology and Public Decision-making." In *Harvard University Program on Technology and Society, 1964-1972, A Final Review*. Cambridge: Harvard University Press, 1972. p.60

28. Dial (1968) p.6. *See also* Urban and Regional Information Systems (1968). The evaluation reports in Part IV of the document, prepared by users of the sytems, make it quite clear that information useful for planning was not usually stored in the memory banks; see, for example, the reports of Alameda County, California (p.14); Alexandria, Virginia (pp. 24-25); Los Angeles (p.60); and Santa Clara County, California (p.88).

29. Salomen, J. "Science Policy and Its Myths." *Futures*, 1971 3(1), p.17.

30. For a corresponding emphasis on the complexity of environmental response, *see* Etzioni, op. cit.

31. Campbell, D. "Methods for the Experimenting Society." Paper delivered to the American Psychological Association meeting, Washington, D.C., September 1971, p. 14.

32. A superb anthology on this difficulty and related semantical problems is Lee, I. *The Language of Wisdom and Folly*. New York: Harper and Bros. (1949), especially Part VIII, "The Structural Patterns and Implications of a Language."

33. Etzioni, op. cit., Ch. 15.

34. Kahn, 1969, op. cit., p.23.

35. G. Steiner argues this persuasively; *see Top Management Planning*, Toronto: Collier-McMillan, 1969, pp. 94-99.

36. Simon, H. "Administrative Behavior," *International Encyclopedia of the Social Sciences*, vol. I. :New York: Crowell Collier and Macmillan, 1968.

37. Banfield, E. "Ends and Means in Planning," *Concepts and Issues in Administrative Behavior*, eds. S. Malick and E. VanNess. Englwood Cliffs, N.J.: Prentice-Hall, 1962.

38. Dror, Y. *Public Policymaking Reexamined*. San Francisco: Chandler, 1968, p. 48.

39. Schick A. "Systems Politics and Systems Budgeting." *Public Administration Review*, 24(1) (1969).

40. Lindblom, C. *The Intelligence of Democracy: Decision Making Through Mutual Adjustment*. New York: The Free Press, 1965. *See also* Wildavsky, A. *The Politics of the Budgetary Process*. Boston: Little, Brown, 1964.

41. Gross, op. cit., p. 85.

42. Rosenthal, R. *Experimenter Effects in Behavioral Research*. New York: Appleton Century Crofts, 1966.

43. Hage, J. and M. Aiken. *Social Change in Complex Organizations*. New York: Random House, 1970.

44. Vickers, G. *The Art of Judgment*. New York: Basic Books, 1965.

45. Hoopes, T. *The Limits of Intervention: An Inside Account of How the Johnson Policy of Escalation in Vietnam Was Reversed*. New York: David McKay, 1969.

46. Rogers, E. and F. Shoemaker. *Diffusion of Innovations*. New York: The Free Press, 1971, p. 307.

47. Ibid, p. 276.

48. Ibid, p. 275.

49. Ibid, p. 271.

50. Ibid, p. 316.

51. Ibid, pp. 315-316.

52. Miller, E. and A. K. Rice. *Systems of Organization*. London: Tavistock, 1967, p. 156.

53. Rogers and Shoemaker, op. cit., p. 315.

54. An excellent overall review of recent government and corporate planning efforts in Europe — with fascinating perspective on the United States included — is Shonfield (1965). *Also see* McNamara (1970b) and McNamara (1970, p.10).

55. Dror, op. cit., p. 249.

56. Westin, in personal correspondence.

⋆ Part Two ⋆

The Burden of Change:
Personal and Interpersonal Risks

Changing toward long-range social planning will require changes in the way people see themselves, relate to others, and find their meaning within the structure of those relationships and associated expectancies that we call organizations. In the chapters to follow, we will look at changes that will be required of people and of organizational structures: We will look at them from a social-psychological perspective, rather than from an economic, political, legal, or public-administration perspective. Of course these several perspectives overlap, because all perspectives unavoidably reflect the social-psychological properties of people and the structures within which they operate.

Observers examining the assets and limits of long-range social planning from these other vantage points usually assume or ascribe, however casually or uncritically, social-psychological properties to the human actors within their perspective. Each chapter that follows, then, deals with some requirement that would be placed upon a person performing within an organizational structure, in a changeover toward long-range social planning .

These requirements are such that, consciously or unconsciously, many people will feel threatened by them, and are likely to resist meeting them in a manner that would facilitate moves toward long-range social planning.

The sense that a situation is threatening is based on one's experience with the norms, and the arrangements for expressing them, that comprise our culture. (The contribution of those experiences may or may not be explicitly recognized: On the basis of past experiences, one may be able to calculate "objectively" the risks to self involved in a change — but that "calculation" may in fact be a response to unconscious or intuitive messages of impending threat.) If the people involved had been rewarded or punished for behaving in other ways, in keeping with different norms sustained by differently-constituted organizations, would the requirements for changing over toward long-range social planning still seem threatening? This very important question colors all the ensuing discussion; to some important but unknown degree, people will resist doing those things required by future-responsive societal learning — performing under high levels of uncertainty, acknowledging errors, trusting their colleagues, leaving socially-supportive groups, tolerating high levels of role ambiguity, and so on — if their experience has been such that, given their present situation, they would expect to suffer (or at least lose rewards) if they accepted these changes. So too, administrators will resist changing management procedures and reducing the barriers that protect the organization from its environment, if their experiences lead them to expect they would suffer because of what would happen if they complied.

Generally speaking, we can discern three kinds of resistance-to-change behavior:
- avoiding awareness of the need to change;
- rejecting the proposed behavior or value change; and
- arranging things so that no supporting structure of sanction and facilitation can develop to imbed the changed behavior and norms in the organizational processes.

We will note all of these resistances operating in response to pressures for change toward long-range social planning.

Generally, we expect an innovation to be "laid on" an existing organization. The typical experience associated with the introduction of innovation is that the essential structure and norms legitimizing the organization do not change — or are not changed deliberately. (Exceptions, where norms and structures have been altered by planned organizational change, are still comparatively rare — and in government, almost nonexistent.) Minor readjustments are made, to be sure, but if the requirements for operational and managerial change seem too large, most organizations will judge the innovation impracticable, and reject it. People tend to expect new technologies to affect their welfare by affecting them through conventional "rules of the game." Naturally, then, many people who would have to change with the introduction of long-range social planning into their organization would perceive the changes as threatening.

But what if long-range social planning and the change toward it were treated, not as the introduction of a technological innovation, but as a learning procedure and learning situation? And what if people *expected* their organizational and environmental norms and structures to be redesigned to reward that philosophy? Then they might not feel so threatened; perhaps some threats would disappear altogether. Of course, some people would fear learning and relearning; doubtless many do, because of their experiences as children and adolescents. At any rate, the reader should not lose sight of the likely relationship between resistance to long-range social planning, and what people expect of themselves and others, and of their organization, in the light of their previous experiences. I will try to emphasize this by suggesting from time to time possible ways of rearranging norms and structures so that the requirements need not be so threatening, and hence engendering of resistance. These alternatives derive from my position that long-range social planning can only be a learning procedure.

Since our appreciation here ("appreciation" in Vickers' sense, as explained in Chapter 2) is to be social-psychological, I will be emphasizing the ways in which a person's meaning for himself and others is defined, supported, and expressed through the structure of an organization, and through the norms that legitimize that structure. And I will emphasize how those structures and norms are reinforced by the people who find meaning by performing within them. While these pervasive reciprocal relationships are an expression of the human propensity to invent social reality (as discussed in Chapter 1), they are by no means all that comprise a human's sense of self, or all that holds together the structure of an organization. People have and find meaning outside their organizations — though often through other activities organized according to similar structures and norms. As Churchman and Emery have observed:

The properties of some groups might be defined in terms of a single organization, but an individual can be so defined only in terms of more than one organization. This is putting it mildly. If any individual could be described in terms of one organization we would have "organizational man," pure and simple. We do not think that he would be even humanoid. The individuals who carry the work of an organization are related as individuals and as groups to a multitude of other organizations. They cannot be defined as persons without reference to those varied interpenetrating relations.[1]

Organizational arrangements are reinforced by laws and by economic and political circumstances, among other things. In these times when the relationship between people and organizations is increasingly unsatisfying, it would be foolish to assert a one-to-one correspondence between the expressions of an organization, and the people it comprises. I hope this will disabuse the reader of any suspicion of simplistic assumptions on my part; nevertheless, I must add that people (perhaps especially those with government) find that much of the meaning in their lives is supplied by the norms and structures within which they work; and those norms and structures remain what they are because people, often unconsciously, wish them so.

Because the preferences of people and organizations, as they are conventionally expressed, constitute the social-psychological sources of resistance to changing over to long-range social planning, it is these preferences that I will emphasize. However, because it is clear that more people are now finding their sense of self insufficiently rewarded within their present organizational arrangements, I shall also consider ways people might change themselves and their organizations into something more meaningful.

In the following chapters, most of the changes necessary to move toward long-range social planning, as well as the suggestions for change in appreciative settings that are necessary for perceiving planning as a learning process rather than engineering, will lead the reader to wonder about the implication of these changes for the attainment, retention, and use of power. While "power" continues to be a rather ambiguous term, I mean by it what Roald Dahl described when he wrote, "A has power over B to the extent that he can get B to do something that B would not otherwise do." [2] (Raymond Bauer has pointed out that this would include such accomplishments as getting B to perceive his situation so that B realizes his self-interest lies elsewhere than he previously believed.) On first reading, much of what will be proposed may seem incompatible with what we now believe about the pervasiveness of aspirations to power, and the incentives to use and keep it. The reader may feel that most social-psychological sources of resistance to long-range social planning can be most easily explained as resistance to giving up power (or at least, that other sources are secondary to this one), and that, in giving up power or the quest for it, a person or organization would be foolish, irrational, or indifferent to survival.

I do not intend to explore the wellsprings of personal needs for power, other than to note that while some people have a *compulsive* need to seek power, many cultures — and many people within the culture of the United States — are not driven by that motive, or find ways to live so that it does not drive them.[3] While all organizations have to deal with personal needs for power, all organizations also have the instrumental need to accomplish the control described by Dahl. Often, though not necessarily, the two needs are expressed through the same individuals; and some of the suggestions I will make are aimed at disentangling the two, in favor of the instrumental. As Robert Kahn and Kenneth Boulding have noted:

*If a person seeks power only for instrumental purposes, we can
predict that his search will be bounded; he wishes to control other
people only insofar as that control will contribute to the attainment of
other goals. If, on the other hand, he finds the experience of
controlling others intrinsically rewarding, there may be few
limitations on the number of people over whom he will strive for
power, the magnitude of power to which he will aspire, or the kinds
of activity over which power will be sought. The wider and deeper
the search for power becomes, the more people and the more issues
in conflict will be encountered. Conflict is maximized when the drive
to power is neurotic, rather than pragmatic.*[4]

From time to time I will speculate on how the practice of long-range
social planning might reduce or change some needs for power. But
my general position is that the requirements for long-range social
planning do not remove the need for, or practice of, power: they
would, however, change its modes of expression and performance.
Kahn has suggested that the basis for influence might move away
from power based on legitimacy, or the ability to reward and
punish, toward power based on expertise. This statement makes
sense in light of the environmental context that makes long-range
social planning necessary. The pressures from the turbulent
environment, I believe, will be such as to outmode some forms of
power expressions, and introduce others.

For example, "embracing error" (Chapter 4) would remove
those means of getting and keeping power that went with lying,
hiding errors, or making others "take the rap." Power might go
instead to those most skilled in discovering the nature of the errors
for which they are responsible, or to those who expose the
incompetence of others who do a poor job of error detection, or who
try to hide their errors (perhaps even to the point of
misrepresenting the nature of the information their opponent could
have used to discover his own errors, if he had been responsible in
his role). Michel. Crozier's analysis of power in conventional
bureaucracies, and the role of uncertainty in the distribution of
power, seems supportive of this argument:

Power can neither be suppressed or ignored. It stems from the impossibility of eliminating uncertainty in the context of a bounded rationality which is ours.

In such a context, the power of A over B depends on A's ability to predict B's behavior and on the uncertainty of B and A's behavior. As long as the requirements of action create situations of uncertainty, the individuals who have to face them have power over those who are affected by the results of their choice.[5]

* * * * * * *

We can thus envisage two complementary sorts of discretion within an organization. The first one comes from the uncertainty of the task itself, and the second from the rules that have been devised to make it more rational and more predictable. As long as some uncertainty remains about carrying out the task, the most menial subordinate retains some slight discretion. And, in a way, as along as a human being is preferred to an automatic machine there will be some uncertainty. On the other hand, the rules that limit the discretion of the subordinate to a minimum can and will be used by the supervisor for preserving an area of discretion and the possibility of bargaining.[6]

Two more brief examples of how power might be applied in the context of changing toward future-responsive societal learning: One, instead of power depending on the preemption of knowledge, as it typically does now, it may devolve onto those persons and groups that can most effectively disseminate knowledge and get it used by their constituencies. (Ralph Nader's approach seems to be an example of this application.) Second, in some corporations, participative management procedures have increased the effectiveness of management; so, too, various forms of openness, trusting, and acknowledging uncertainty may provide new forms for the acquisition and use of power. My general point is expressed by Kahn and Boulding:

The argument for the essentiality of power to an organization is not an argument for authoritarianism. To say that an organization must be able to attain a certain level of power over the activities of its members is not to specify the bases and sources of that power. The basis may be punishment or identification with the organizational goal; the source may be a formal leader or the entire peer group.

*The list of such possibilities could be greatly extended; the crucial
point is that the amount of power which can be brought to bear
within an organization must be differentiated from the basis of that
power and the persons who wield it. It is essential that an
organization be able to exert power over the behavior of its members;
it is not essential that such power be concentrated in a few hands, or
enforced by threats or penalties.*[7]

Research tends to corroborate this position, as well as to reveal
many subtle and complex issues relating control (or power) to
organizational performance.[8] Hopefully, then, the foregoing
discussion will encourage the reader to imagine how power
motives could operate under future-responsive societal learning
changeover conditions, rather than to imagine people and
organizations abdicating power.

It is possible, of course, that the approach proposed here
would simply lead, in ways we cannot anticipate, to yet another
arrangement of incapability to deal with the societal problems. And
it is entirely possible — I think likely — that the old ways of
seeking, using, and holding power, when combined with and when
expressed through other sources of resistance, will make the
introduction of long-range social planning impossible. Likely, that
is, but not certain, because the changing relationships between
organizations and their environments are making the conventional
ways of doing things, including using power, less and less sufficient
unto the day, to say nothing of the future.

1. Churchman. C.W. and Emery. F. "On Various Approaches to the Studies of Organizations." in J. P. Lawrence (ed.). *Operational Research and the Social Sciences.* London: Tavistock. 1966. p. 82.

2. Dahl. R. "The Concept of Power." *Behavrioral Science.* 1957. (2). p. 202-203.

3. *See* Lasswell. H. *Power and Personality.* New York: W. W. Norton. 1948.

4. Kahn. R. and Boulding. K. (eds.) *Power and Conflict in Organizations.* New York: Basic Books. 1964. pp. 5. 6.

5. Crozier. M. *The Bureaucratic Phenomenon.* Chicago: University of Chicago Press. 1964. p. 158.

6. Id., p. 160. Crozier is subtle and insightful on bureaucratic processes. But his bureaucrats seem to be more obsessed by rules and rigidities than those in many federal bureaucracies. For a somewhat contrasting view of bureaucratic social psychology. *see* Blau. P. *The Dynamics of Bureaucracy: A Study of Interpersonal Relations in Two Government Agencies.* Chicago: University of Chicago Press. 1963. *Also see* Kohn. M. "Bureaucratic Man." *New Society,* October 28, 1971.

7. Kahn and Boulding. op. cit., p. 4.

8. *See e.g.* Tannenbaum. A. *Control in Organizations.* New York: McGraw-Hill. 1968.

3

The Requirement for
Living with Uncertainty

The very conditions that inform us that we live in a turbulent environment also tell us how little we understand about it. The perspective that leads us to want to institute long-range social planning to try to cope with this turbulence, emphasizes how presently inadequate are our techniques for quickly learning about our environment and doing something about it.

We want to eliminate poverty, crime, drug addiction and abuse; we want to improve education and strengthen family life, but we do not know how. Traditional measures are no longer good enough. Very different ones must be sought, invented, tried on a small scale, evaluated and brought closer to perfection. Many schemes will fail and the most profitable failures will be those that lead to the clarification of understanding of the problems. Many schemes will simply expose additional problems that social scientists will need to solve. Both design and evaluation are needed. . . .

The overwhelming complexity of the nation's social problems and their immediacy, however, should not blind us to our ignorance of ways to solve them.[1]

As our body of data increases, so too will controversies about how to interpret them, and whether they are really relevant. All this is especially true with regard to data used for designing and evaluating human-development programs.[2] Complicating all this will be the need to develop theory and data that take into account the growing self-consciousness of both plan designers and plan users about their own involvement in the unfolding of programs and their evaluation. This will be especially true when plan designers and plan users — and in some cases, plan evaluators — are overlapping groups. A state of mind of deep and continuing uncertainty characterizes those who choose to move toward future-responsive societal learning. Those who cannot live with high levels of uncertainty try to avoid it, along with the conditions associated with changing toward long-range social planning that will necessarily emphasize uncertainty. Todd La Porte notes in this regard:

Everyone and every organization confronts many kinds of uncertainties; for most of the time they are bearable. There is, however, some level of uncertainty which is not, at least if some relatively unaltered state of the personality or organizational structures is to be maintained. When that level or threshold of uncertainty is reached, then passed, feelings of discomfort increase. At some point they reach sufficient intensity that persons and dominant coalitions suffer fears for survival. Long before this point is reached searches begin to reduce the uncertainty of important relationships.

We must add that the reduction of uncertainty . . . is not necessarily a linear phenomenon. Neither persons not organizations necessarily attempt to extinguish uncertainty altogether. At low levels of uncertainty . . . important relationships are quite predictable and unchanging. This state of organizational boredom seems to prompt active attempts to increase the degree of stimulation, surprise, and uncertainty. Search for uncertainty is probably associated with the capacity for risk-taking and very stable situations. But stability does not characterize the state of most contemporary organizations. Rather, organizations everywhere are experiencing considerable destabilizing pressure and many surprising conditions. If uncertainty is sought there is no end of situations available to satisfy this search. It is quite the other way around — how do persons and organizations respond to relatively high levels of perceived contingency, inadequate cause-effect beliefs, hence uncertainty in a turbulent environment?[3]

Don Schon, building on the work of Frank Knight, makes an invaluable psychological distinction between the concept of risk and that of uncertainty.[4] Risk pertains when one believes that one knows what variables are involved in characterizing a situation; hence one can assign probabilities to outcomes that depend on those variables. Uncertainty pertains when one believes that one has either too much or too little information to feel confident about what variables define the situation. In this situation, no probability of outcome can be honestly assigned.

UNCERTAINTY AS A PSYCHOLOGICAL STATE

Throughout, I shall be referring to the *psychological* state of uncertainty. This should not be confused with the economic or decision-theory concepts of uncertainty. Aspects of behavior relevant for adequate logical responses to uncertainty, as defined in decision theory and economics, are quite different from the social psychological responses with which we will be concerned. We will be concerned with how people respond to the feelings, the anxiety, the fear, of knowing that they do not know. These feelings arise from the specter of losing control — at least of the situation, and perhaps of self — if the situation deteriorates, and from fear of being caught out in a mistake. Anxiety about losing control is probably grounded in the very nature of an organism that depends for survival on learning rather than on instinct.[5] However, it is much intensified in cultures, and especially in ours, that seem to use compulsive efforts to gain and keep control to cope with existential anxiety about "Who am I?"

The enormous emphasis we place on control is evidenced by our preoccupation with technology and material possession, that is, with control of the natural environment; by our often gratuitous or ritual emphasis on rationality; and by the huge investments of ideas and dollars that we make in "public relations" and advertising, which are aimed at controlling the directions of emotionality. The fear of being caught out in a mistake reflects the heavy emphasis our culture puts on the virtues and necessity of control of self and setting. of course, the results of this preoccupation with control has been highly rewarding in many ways for most members of the society, which makes the possibility of loss of control and being caught out in mistakes all the more fearful and anxiety-provoking. Without control and correct performance, the rewards could disappear.

Another way to understand this situation is to realize that anxiety produced by uncertainty results from the breakdown, or anticipated breakdown, of an established relationship between the individual and his human and natural environment. In this relationship the individual and society "collude" to establish order and form, a pattern, that differentiates and integrates the environment so that the individual can attend selectively to aspects of that "blooming, buzzing, confusion." A person's perceptions and sense of self have an order and form that correspond in critical aspects to the order and form in the outside world; the person's internal structure reflects the rewards and punishments experienced while learning to respond to and remake the external, societally given form and order. To some extent, of course, the relevant external environment that rewards the person has been uniquely invented by that person — that is, ordered and formed by him. But for most people, the internal structure is very largely sustained by the external one; the external environment provides most persons with most of their sense of their own order and form.[6]

Among other things, Western societies differentiate the human and natural environments into those things and events toward which one takes a "rational" stance, and those one is emotional about; and society also makes discriminations within these categories. (Of course, the societal definitions are not absolute and binding, as is increasingly evident in highly technologized societies among people moving away from conventional differentiations.) Once internalized, persons "know" those situations in which one must be rational and not emotional, where one can love but not hate, laugh but not cry. This "categorized self" then reinforces and defines the categorized outside, and so on in a self-sustaining interaction. Self then comes to be defined and sustained in important part by the external differentiations and integrations. (I would expect this to be especially so for persons whose careers depend on an "accurate" assessment of the "realities": persons in planning offices, decision-making roles, or in engineering, for example.)

Now, if there are changes in the outside world, there is likely to be a mismatch between the internal and external "reality" structures, and hence a loss of sustaining feedback. To the person, a shift in external structure means that the external world cannot be counted on to sustain the internal structure. To the extent the person depends on that external structure to keep self-organized, to keep the parts of the self separated and integrated, then there is anxiety about one's ability to keep the self in order. That is, there is felt uncertainty. There is a realization that one cannot keep the external environment under control in a way that in turn provides the input for keeping the self under control. There is fear that the separation of emotions and rationality will break down; that one won't know how to act, that one won't know what is rewarding or punishing. Under such threatening conditions the tendency is to overemphasize preferred order and form by becoming, for example, hyper-intellectual or hyper-emotional — whatever is in the direction of the previous match. In the extreme this becomes autistic behavior, reflexive behavior, essentially uninfluenced by what is going on outside the person. Another kind of response under conditions of uncertainty is to project onto the external environment the sense of dissolution that is occurring in the self; depending on how the environment is behaving, the feedback from it in response to the projected signals can further disrupt the sense of self — that is, the sense of ordered and formed beingness.

The formal literature dealing with psychological uncertainty is small — though it has always been a subject for novels, and occasionally it can be inferred in case-study accounts of decision-making in problematic situations. In this society it is difficult to get people to talk about their uncertainties, especially when their roles call for administrative skill and rational behavior — precisely the kind of roles where uncertainty becomes critically important for efforts to change long-range social planning under conditions of societal turbulence. The literature is also small because chronic and deep uncertainty has not been considered an important organizational matter; the ways of dealing with uncertainty were usually sufficient for the operating and personal needs of those who faced it. Those who succumbed to it were usually "phased out" as individuals and organizations. Usually we do not research "failures." Finally, there has been little incentive to study psychological uncertainty in the laboratory. It was not seen as a problem in a competitive society where belief in the virtues of survival of the fittest made the behavior unimportant, and therefore of low status as a research topic. Moreover, the kind of uncertainty we are going to deal with is deeply disturbing because it threatens the very self-image, the ego defenses, of the unfortunate sufferer. It is both unethical to stress experimental subjects in this way, and difficult to simulate a situation which would stress them to this degree.[7]

But this is not to say that uncertainty per se is a new problem for organizations, or for those who study organizational behavior:

Most of our beliefs about complex organizations follow from one or the other of two distinct strategies. The closed-system strategy seeks certainty by incorporating only those variables positively associated with goal achievement and subjecting them to a monolithic control network. The open-system strategy shifts attention from goal achievement to survival, and incorporates uncertainty by recognizing organizational interdependence with environment. A newer tradition enables us to conceive of the organization as an open system, indeterminate and
faced with uncertainty, but subject to criteria of rationality and hence needing certainty.

With this conception the central problem for complex organizations is one of coping with uncertainty. As a point of departure., we suggest that organizations cope with uncertainty by creating certain parts specifically to deal with it, specializing other parts in operating under conditions of uncertainty or near uncertainty. In this case, articulation of these specialized parts becomes significant.

We also suggest that technologies and environments are major sources of uncertainty for organizations, and that differences in those dimensions will result in differences in organizations.[8]

Thus, in a broad effort to extend research and theories about organizational behavior, James Thompson begins with major emphasis on the organizational task of coping with uncertainty, and with the assertion that uncertainty arises from the organization's internal technology and external environment. Thompson goes on to propose a number of ways that organizations reduce uncertainty. La Porte summarizes Thompson's proposals:

Internal strategies used in attempts to reduce uncertainty include the development of buffering units between the environment and the technical core, smoothing or leveling input and output transactions, and attempts to forecast or anticipate, then adapt to environmental change. When internal strategies are not sufficient to quell uncertainties and lower dependencies, organizations may pursue strategies which will decrease their dependence upon significant external elements . . .[9]

However, the important limitation in Thompson's description of organizational means for reducing uncertainty is that it does not deal with the consequences of being *unable* to reduce uncertainty to a psychologically-comfortable level and still deal with the issues characterizing our turbulent environment. By operating organizations, including conventional planning activities, so as to reduce the pain and impact of uncertainty by the conventional means delineated by Thompson, societal crises and dilemmas have accumulated to the point that they now require long-range social planning, which in turn requires that people and organizations learn to live constructively with uncertainty of the sort that can no longer be reduced to a comfortable level. As Argyris says,

Recently there has been a growing suspicion that the categories of organizational theory do not take into account new and emerging sources of uncertainty. . . . Traditional conceptions of organization have great difficulty in handling qualitative changes in organizational environment.

As interdependent relationships increase in number and rate of change, the capacity of common or uncommon sense conceptions to comprehend them declines. Management and policy processes, apparently useful in the past for control, falter as conditions to which they are applied no longer meet the assumptions of traditional measures. To the degree this is the case for contemporary organizations, the importance of increased environmental dependence and perceived uncertainty is likely to mount.[10]

On the basis of their observations of many situations, Don Schon and Todd La Porte argue that acknowledging high levels of uncertainty to self and to others is emotionally so painful, so anxiety-producing — particularly for those who see themselves as contributing to the rationality of their organization — that people will repress their awareness that they "know they do not know;" or they will avoid situations that confront them with uncertainty; or they will treat such situations as if they were not uncertain.[11] R. Nelson and others have noted:

Government policy making presently has . . . a tendency to delay for a long time the introduction of a new program because of uncertainties and then suddenly to jump in fully with a large commitment to a prescribed program, with no better knowledge base than before, when political pressures for doing something became strong. Once proposed or initiated, the program is then popularized among the public and in the Congress as a sure antidote, rather than as a promising probe of the environment.

This knowledge myth, which forces dedicated public servants to engage in charlatanism, seriously impedes the development of public policy. The channeling of large sums of money into programs predetermined on the basis of sketchy information narrows the range of alternatives that can be tried, and thus reduces the range of policy instruments that have to be tested. Further, it deters useful experimentation, since all programs are action programs. It places a high premium on actions likely to yield simple-minded quantitative indexes of immediate successes. . . . Conditions of great uncertainty call for imaginative and flexible probings, not vacillation between inaction and commitment.[12]

Contributing to this behavior is the expectation that members of the environment will demand certainty: and, not surprisingly, as members of the same culture as those in the organization, they often do expect it — or, at least, they fervently hope for it — from organization spokesmen.

Sources of Psychological Uncertainty

Throughout this book, we are contemplating how people and organizations face or avoid ambiguity, confusion, and ignorance about who they are and what they are doing, now and in the future. These questions arise in relation to the specific requirements for changing toward long-range social planning. But in most cases there is also a poignant and crucial source of resistance to meeting the other requirements — an exacerbated sense of uncertainty.

Uncertainty has been differentiated by J. Friend and William Jessop into three classes:

Class UE: uncertainties in knowledge of the external planning environment including all uncertainties relating to the structure of the world external to the decision-making system . . . and also all uncertainties relating to expected patterns of future change in this environment, and to its expected responses to any possible future interventions by the decision-making system.

Class UR: uncertainties as to future intentions in related fields of choice including all uncertainties relating to the choices which might in future be taken, within the decision-making system itself, in respect of other fields of discretion beyond the limited problem which is currently under consideration.

Class UV: uncertainties as to appropriate value judgments including all uncertainties relating to the relative degrees of importance the decision-makers ought to attach to any expected consequences of their choice which cannot be related to each other through an unambiguous common scale — either because the consequences are of a fundamentally different nature, or because they affect different sections of the community, or because they concern different periods of future time.[13]

Studying the planning for the rebuilding of Coventry, Friend and Jessop found that attempts to reduce uncertainty revolve around felt needs for more research, to reduce UE; more coordination, to reduce UR; and more policy guidance, to reduce UV. In a long-range planning situation, these three means for reducing uncertainty will be interdependent most of the time. Which one receives emphasis at a given time will depend on many considerations, including who — or what organizational subsystem

— is feeling what kinds of uncertainties most strongly, and who has the power and resources to do something about it. These problematic aspects will add their own contribution to the mix and press of uncertainties. Friend and Jessop report:

It gradually came to be apparent to us that many of the stresses which arose from time to time between the different parts of the decision-making system in Coventry could be attributed to a failure to bring about some reconciliation between such variations of perspective at a formative stage of the decision process. Extreme emphasis on the need for research (in our somewhat limited sense of resolving uncertainties in the external environment) could be seen to lead to an attenuation in time of the whole decision process, and often to an undue preoccupation with some of the more measurable variables; extreme emphasis on the need for coordination could often lead to the drawing together of more and more decisions under the umbrella of a single grand design or master plan, making it very difficult in the later stages for those concerned to review any alternative courses of action without calling the whole balance of the plan into question; and extreme emphasis on the need for policy guidance could lead to resentment in some quarters — particularly among the less senior officers — because of a feeling that too many issues were being taken out of the hands of experts and resolved at a political rather than an analytical level.[14]

All information brought into the organization that carries messages of turbulence will generate uncertainty. (Although of course, some feedback from the environment will sometimes reduce uncertainty; I am including feedback from the future, introduced via future studies, as well as from the present.) When values and feelings become strong considerations in decision-making and evaluation procedures, as they most certainly will, they too will generate uncertainty among the participants. We have so little experience with acknowledging our own feelings and those of others — especially when they conflict — that we don't know what to expect of them.

New managerial and administrative arrangements to facilitate the introduction of specific activities intended to meet the requirements for long-range social planning will also generate uncertainty, because we know that we know so little about the organizational and environmental consequences of implementing the new arrangements. Organizational restructuring, aimed at coping with turbulence and putting efforts at future-responsive societal learning into operation, will generate uncertainty, just as uncertainty is generated by the more modest and conventional attempts at restructuring being introduced today, in more-conventional organizations. What is more novel and of greater importance, uncertainty will be acute for those doing the restructuring as well as for those being restructured — not only because of uncertainty regarding the outcome, but because their own roles and status will be altered as well. Uncertainty recognized within an organization will need to be shared with members of the environment, so they can participate in the necessary societal learning rather than demanding or expecting certainty from the organizations upon which their welfare depends. Their responses to uncertainty in turn will further complicate the characteristics of the environment. Finally, all these sources of uncertainty will emphasize uncertainty about how to deal constructively with uncertainty, how to live with it rather than trying to avoid it or reduce it at too great a cost to societal learning — the very purpose of long-range social planning.

MEANS FOR AVOIDING UNCERTAINTY

The circumstances just summarized will be sources of uncertainty if they are faced squarely. But there are many ways to resist doing so. Some of those ways are described here in general terms; we shall later recognize how they contribute to resistance to other requirements that need to be met in order to change toward long-range social planning.

The most direct way to avoid uncertainty is to avoid situations rich in uncertainty. In our case this would mean avoiding information that demonstrates turbulence, and avoiding role and structural changes that leave both the initiator and the recipient of the changes uncertain about what to anticipate, and how to perform. As Peter Blau has observed, "The anxieties generated by the experience that one's knowledge is not always adequate for one's tasks can be calmed by making a ritual of conformity with those procedures with which one has become familiar." [15] (Another point, to be discussed in Chapter 4, is of profound importance: avoiding uncertainty also requires avoiding the recognition or acknowledgment of error.)

La Porte posits "ideological response" as another way used to cope with unwanted uncertainty:

Rather than withdrawing from the field, one engages with it on the basis of a cause-effect belief system which "explains" past uncertainties. Often such explanations are accompanied by programs of action to change the objective situation so it will coincide with the images of a "good" family, group, organizational structure or nation. [16]

As noted in Chapter 1, any explicit theory of what is "really" going on "out there" is subject to this tendency, whether or not it explicitly carries a particular political philosophy with it. Its social-psychological utility lies in telling one what to pay attention to and why, thereby removing from one's awareness much that would otherwise generate uncertainty — including evidence that one's perceptual and normative boundaries need resetting. This means of uncertainty-reduction will seduce many a would-be social engineer who defines his reality in terms of what his technology can deal with or what his theory emphasizes.

Apropos of this phenomenon, it is worth looking at the uncertainty-reducing virtues of an "idea in good currency." [17] Such ideas give aid and comfort because they are promulgated by professionals, and then amplified until they seem reasonable and valid in the reverberating circuit that connects professionals with their organizational clients. Such ideas have included disjointed incrementalism, the end of ideology, future shock, the impact of cybernation, urban renewal, Vietnamization, participant democracy, and the bag of strategic warfare tricks called escalation, deterrence, and massive retaliation. (Of course, I hope that the idea of long-range social planning as future-responsive societal learning, and the idea of error-embracing, also become ideas in good currency.) My point is not that these ideas are useless or misguided, but rather that they almost always become reified and influential far beyond their demonstrated utility. Due to their prestigious sources, the processes by which they become amplified, and their localized utility, they are grasped onto much more strongly than circumstances merit. Both promulgators and recipients evangelize the ideas with a fervor that, to those viewing the situation from other vantage points, smacks at least of proto-ideology.[18]

Schon demonstrates that a pervasive means for reducing uncertainty is to translate a situation of uncertainty into one of risk; that is, to act as if one knows what is *really* involved well enough to assign probabilities to outcomes. This gratuitous assignment of probabilities to situations that do not justify them is an endemic means of deluding oneself and others; often the need to reduce uncertainty is so great that the person justifies the assignment of probabilities by that most tenuous and attractive of rationalizations: "It's the best we can do," or "It's better than nothing." The information recipient, inside or outside the organization, having an equal or greater need to reduce uncertainty, colludes — unconsciously, cynically, or naively — first in accepting the rationalization, and then in forgetting that it underlies whatever arguments are put forth in support of the probabilities. In this regard, it is enlightening and terrifying to recall the spasm of ritualized rationality that shook national strategic planning directed to deterring nuclear attack or, failing that, to recovering from it. Endless books, reports, and study groups acted as if enough were understood about the motivations of people under stress and the dynamics of democratic society, to assign probabilities to the chances that the United States would recover, given various levels of nuclear attack and stockpiling of material resources. Other social-psychological processes that we will examine contributed to that state of mind, but the need to avoid acknowledging deep uncertainty about the future of democratic America was certainly a heavy contributor.[19]

One of the most serious consequences of this behavior is that the resulting emotional relief encourages all involved to believe they really do know what is important, what is going on. Consequently, not only do they ignore input that challenges that belief, but they entrap themselves in psycho-socio-political need to repudiate the fact of error when their risk-based models and programs fail in action. Important opportunities to learn from a perspective of uncertainty are thereby reduced or obliterated.

Still another means for attempting to reduce uncertainty is by various managerial devices aimed at "tightening-up" the organization. The ends sought in this way include increasing internal incisive action, controlling what goes in and out of the organization that could result in more turbulence, and reemphasizing the role and ability of management to reduce uncertainty by resorting to the traditional tightening-up ritual. In this regard, T. Burns and G. Stalker observe:

When individuals are frustrated in their attempts to get their own work successfully completed, when they are worried by the successful rivalry of others, when they feel insecure or under attack — these situations provoke an urge for the clarity, the no-nonsense atmosphere, of a mechanistic organization. It promises so many other dividends too. It is not only quicker to divide tasks into parcels, label them "responsibilities," and post them to subordinates or other parts of the structure; this kind of procedure has the connotations of visibly controlling others, and the appearance of knowing one's own mind, which are valued aspects of executive authority. Conversely, one has the security of unquestioned power through orders to subordinates, the security of knowing the limits of one's responsibility and of the demands and orders of superiors . . .

. . . Necessarily, when the environment or technical base of a concern is changing rapidly, the situation is alive with opportunities for advancement and transfer, alive also with actual or potential threats to the status, power, chances of success, or actual livelihood of some of the members of it. . . .

Under such threats there is bound to be latent or overt conflict between individuals or groups; and, as anthropologists have pointed out, hostility against persons in authority and aggressive action against rivals is often sanctioned by an appeal to traditional or other familiar values and modes of behavior.[20]

E. Miller and A. Kenneth Rice offer another perspective:

One observed all too often controls being imposed not to protect the task system from interference but to protect management against anxiety. Parameters are controlled not because they are relevant but because they are measurable. Their function is to create an illusion of certainty as a means of coping with intolerable uncertainty.[21]

Schon refers to some of these procedures as "propose-dispose" management schemes for channeling sources of uncertainty to them, either to be squelched or transformed into risk. Like the previous method, this one is comforting for all involved. It gives the feeling that those who know what to do are doing it. For a while it seems to work — until the manifestations of turbulence inside and outside surface again.

Corresponding to organizational tightening-up under conditions of uncertainty, may be personal tightening-up in disasters. (A disaster can be understood as a situation in which there is no supporting environment to give the feedback that once guided, energized, and informed one's sense of self and the world. It is a situation of acute uncertainty.) Studies of disaster behavior show that unless one's competence is such as to be functional in disaster (as expected of a doctor or clergyman), people and organizations tend to become rigid and perform in ways that are unresponsive to the environmental situation. Even some people with disaster-relevant competencies cease to adapt to the situation, and instead rigidly perform in ways that are counterproductive or irrelevant.

These essentially counterproductive means for reducing uncertainty will be amply evident as they are used to deal with efforts to introduce those changes toward long-range social planning that will increase uncertainty. It should be noted, however, that some people do and will see components of long-range social planning as uncertainty *reducers,* and will encourage their application for that reason. Management information systems and social indicators, among other technologies for long-range social planning, will from time to time really reduce uncertainty. At other times, they only appear to do so. Nevertheless, they will comfort those unable to live with turbulence and its concomitant high levels of uncertainty.

There is then a dialectic to be expected, and it will be noted throughout this book. While long-range social planning efforts will, far more often than not, increase psychological uncertainty, there will be times when knowledge and circumstance will converge propitiously with efforts to reduce objective uncertainty, times when things go as planned, when understanding increases faster than awareness of how little is understood, and when the exhilaration of collaborating in future-responsive societal learning gives new feelings of social potency. This variable reinforcement — familiar to golfers, slot-machine players, and even social engineers — will be a continuing stimulus to efforts to initiate long-range social planning, and an encouragement to others to join the effort.

Three types of responses to uncertainty are much more promising than those just reviewed, though at least two of them are subject to decline into the counter-productive forms described. The third type we know too little about, as yet, to know its strengths and weaknesses well.

The first type, which is really a class of organizational responses, is that which organizations typically use to deal rationally with uncertainty. (See La Porte's summary of Thompson's analysis, discussed earlier in this chapter.) Undoubtedly these will be used and modified to try and make long-range social planning feasible. But in their conventional forms they apply to a simpler world, in particular to one where uncertainty about value judgments played a far smaller part than it would when changing over to long-range social planning. In their present forms these means apply where first priority goes to organizational survival — to protection of (in Thompson's term) the "technological core" of the organization, rather than to environmental reconstruction for social growth, for self-actualization. In their conventional forms these responses set organizational well-being ahead of environmental well-being by constraining both organization and environment in ways inadequate for societal learning through long-range social planning. These uncertainty-coping means are probably too self-protective — "probably," because it is unclear where the balance should be between organizational survival and environmental development. In the past, belief in the beneficent operation of the hidden hand prevailed, and was translated into doctrines to the effect that what is good for a large organization is good for its environment. Contemporary experience asserts this isn't necessarily so, and it is now quite acceptable to propose everything from radical organizational self-renewal to self-destruct institutions.[22] Clearly, protection of "the technological core" will not do for long-range social planning, if that protection is at the expense of the uncertainty-acknowledging required for the growth of long-range social planning. Yet there must be "technological cores" if the environment is to have the much-needed organizational resources long-range social planning could help us learn how to get and use. Where and how the balance would be struck would be one of those things to be discovered through the learning context long-range social planning is intended to provide.

The second response is a special and increasingly-used version of the "Thompson-class" responses: greater use of professionals to discover, define, and to solve problems that otherwise would contribute to uncertainty. I do not intend "professional" in its original meaning of a person who, by virtue of skills, autonomy, and ethics, is responsible to the client in certain carefully-specified ways;[23] "professional" is used here in its vernacular meaning: as a specialist with credentials, who has special abilities for defining and solving problems relevant to and appropriate for his trained skill and his occupational allegiance. Here we will look at the ways in which professionals play an important part in uncertainty reduction.

The skills of professionals bring understanding and control where little existed before, through their perceptions of aspects of the organizations, which are different from those derived from historical perspectives and conventional organizational expertise. To this extent they provide a valid basis for uncertainty reduction. Indeed, it is in large part this capability that gives hope that the technology of long-range social planning can be used for societal learning purposes. Such skills are fundamental for discovering what aspects of the turbulent environment can be understood, transformed, and guided by scientific knowledge. The challenge, of course, is to prevent these important uncertainty-reducing capabilities from becoming either ritual or defensive — two counterproductive, uncertainty-reducing characteristics of professionals described next.

The professional's skills training, along with the definition of reality encouraged by the appreciative setting (in Vickers' sense) of their collegial community, into which they have been socialized through their skills-training experience, typically results in trained incapacity to recognize the enormity of the problems characterizing a turbulent environment. Their selective perceiving of the world leads them to see order and discriminability where others, not so professionally embedded, see complexity and problems linked to other problems, ad infinitum. This trained incapacity varies, of course, from person to person and from profession to profession. Also, developments in some schools that train public and private administrators and planners are enlarging the perspectives and tolerance for ambiguity among professionals-to-be. But as of now and for some years to come, the consensus of observers seems to be that many professionals — whether they be urban planners, systems analysts, or social workers — will strongly tend to hold professionally-reinforced definitions of reality that help them filter out much uncertainty. In particular, it seems that older professionals, self-recruited for and trained in the "management sciences" and the more analytic sectors of the behavioral sciences, are inclined to be more rigid about what constitutes reality, or more intolerant of or uninterested in ambiguous and uncertain definitions of it. For these professionals, the "other problems" are other professionals' problems. Most professionals seem to work well within a philosophy of disjointed incrementalism.

The emphasis on personal legitimacy associated with some professions also encourages strong identification with the special view of the world that characterizes the learned values, competences, and activities of the profession. Whatever challenges that world view necessarily challenges the criteria that bolster certainty about who one is. By perceiving the world in their professional way they reduce their own uncertainty to acceptable levels. This increases their willingness to involve themselves in situations that others try to avoid. But it also increases the chances of generating pseudo-problems and pseudo-solutions that, while they respond to the reality as perceived by the professional, do not respond to that as perceived by the environment.[24] What is more, the professional's special aura of legitimacy itself seems to reduce the uncertainty felt by his clients — which leads to another way the professional reduces uncertainty.

The attitudes and beliefs held by professionals about causes and effects, and what can be done about them, help reduce uncertainty for many of those who use their services. Their clients believe that professionals "know something," and that if someone knows something one has the power to control something, to bring about order where there was none before. Then too, the self-assurance that some professionals project, implying that they are bearers of a legitimized world view, gives some clients a feeling that things aren't so uncertain after all, that they really have the situation under control, or soon will.

A third constructive means for coping with uncertainty may be to openly acknowledge and share that state of mind. This is the most radical and most necessary approach if long-range social planning is to become a learning process. All of the means of coping with uncertainty, with the exception of the professional approach properly applied, encourage and sustain unconscious or deliberate hiding (usually from oneself, and almost always from others) of one's sense of uncertainty. Indeed, the rules of the game and the rewards that go with playing it usually require that participants act toward each other as though they are certain — or at least know the risks. The conventional definition of what constitutes effective human conduct, that says competent people know what they are doing, makes those who depend on the competence of others prefer, and often insist, that those they depend on do not face them with expressions of uncertainty. (As one federal executive put it: "Part of my job is to *look like* I know what I'm doing. Otherwise, morale would go to hell here. *Somebody's* got to look like they know where the end of the tunnel is in this madhouse!" But such subterfuge would be fundamentally self-defeating of any serious attempt to change toward long-range social planning. Because long-range social planning is valuable in an open society only if it is used as a means of learning how to guide that society, and because one of the things we need to learn is how to introduce and use it as a learning device, it is critical that those involved do not act as if they *already* had learned — as if they really knew what to do and how to do it. They cannot be models for others if they do not model the appropriate behavior in themselves, and in organizational expressions of themselves.

Philborn Ratoosh has pointed out to me that some people might be moved to tolerate an uncertainty-acknowledging style in leaders they want to depend on, if those leaders assert with certainty that the only way for them to be effective is to acknowledge their own uncertainty. The seeming paradoxical nature of this position is resolvable according to the generally-accepted position in symbolic logic that a statement about a statement is not bound by the constraints asserted in the original statement. Nevertheless, those not trained in the niceties of symbolic logic may not see it that way. More important is the question of whether a leader's own statements can change a popularly-held definition of what constitutes leadership. Perhaps if enough leaders took the same position, then their role redefinition will be accepted. But we know very little about the process by which redefined role characteristics come to be accepted.

ADVANTAGES OF ACKNOWLEDGING UNCERTAINTY

To learn requires recognizing what one wants to learn, and that means recognizing what one doesn't know. Otherwise, one cannot choose ways to learn or evaluate whether one has learned. Since long-range social planning requires both organizational resources and close, responsive linkages with the relevant environments, that recognition of ignorance must be shared among and contributed to by many persons; it cannot be secretive.

Sharing uncertainty can help ease the pain of carrying it alone, uncertain about who else feels uncertain, and even if uncertainty is appropriate to the situation. The emotional support that sharing could provide also would discourage the repression of uncertainty, by raising the level at which the anxiety becomes too great to bear constructively.

To be able to openly acknowledge uncertainty would make three critical contributions to the conduct of future-responsive societal learning. First, it would reduce the chances of undertaking planning in the mistaken belief, by the planning body or its environment, that one knows what one needs to know; hence it would increase chances for the tentative, exploratory mood necessary for societal learning. Rather than judge the effort as successful or unsuccessful in terms of predefinitions and precommitments — whether phrased in the rhetoric of certainty, of calculated risk, or of prudent investment — all would know that they were participating in a social experiment. All would share in the costs and benefits of the experiment, because it would be recognized that it is not really clear what should be done or how to do it, and that the only thing to do is to experiment in order to find out.

It is rather well recognized that under present conditions, poor people are increasingly opposed to being "experimented on." Aside from the fact that the situation we face requires experiments at all social and economic levels of the society (indeed of the world), the situation we are envisioning is fundamentally different from the present one in two ways: The environment would consist of people who would be involved in the design and evaluation of the experiment in which they take part; and by acknowledging uncertainty and embracing errors, those in organizations associated with the experiment would demonstrate that they were themselves part of the experiment, as well as being numbered among the experimenters. Whatever else offends those now "experimented on," they are certainly offended because the risks of failure or unanticipated consequences are not shared by the experimenters.

Second, acknowledging the limitations in the available facts and theory would encourage an atmosphere of trust and an attitude of permissiveness toward restructuring the problem at hand. This in turn would encourage creative approaches drawn from intuition, feeling, and hunch — sources usually ignored in order to "stay with the facts." By ignoring these sources, we are too often saddled with pedestrian and inadequate approaches.

Third, acknowledging uncertainty reduces the chances of people remaining committed to a single definition of reality. Typically, during the reign of an idea in good currency, failures in programs are taken to be a consequence of program choice or implementation, rather than a result of an inadequate model of reality.[25]

Prerequisites for Acknowledging Uncertainty

Open sharing of uncertainty is, I believe, a necessary condition to be met if efforts to change toward long-range social planning are to be effective; but it is in no sense a sufficient condition. Moreover, organizations — with the partial and very constrained exception of some research and development organizations —presently have no tested arrangements for such sharing. Indeed, under present operating conditions open acknowledgment of uncertainty within an organization is considered foolhardy at the very least; and sharing uncertainty between organization and environment would be decisively punished. The custodians of the image of organizational competence as now defined, and many of those in the environment who equate competence with certainty, would not stand for it.

Such an approach would require not only learning to trust, but also learning to transfer some of the potential "blame" for "failure" from others to self. This transfer will be refused, so long as the situation is defined as one in which failure results in someone (group) getting blamed — that is, someone running the risk of being punished and losing self-respect. This suggests that the norms and circumstances under which we reward and punish uncertainty must be altered — in homes and schools, and in that reflection and justification of home and school, the organization.

Acknowledging uncertainty and acting on it also requires skills in interpersonal behavior that most of us lack as members of task groups. To acknowledge that "I don't know" is to acknowledge that one's information or control is inadequate, or that one has been unable to make available to others the bases for control which one had been employed to provide. Under normal operating conditions this alone would be threatening enough; but there are additional threats to conventional definitions of competence as a decision maker or planner. If the formal data are acknowledged as insufficient for decision making, then hunch, intuition, and feelings would become irrepressible contributors to the planning process; and these are just what the "rational" approach in conventional organizations tries to eliminate.[26] Because we have succeeded in repressing, if not eliminating these factors, we have not learned how to use them; therefore we mostly fear them — in part because they seem uncontrollable, especially in ourselves.

To the extent that members of the environment are not constrained by role requirements that stress "rational considerations," environmental feedback will be rich in such extra-rational information. This, plus a cultural shift toward more expressive behavior, may facilitate the incorporation of "extra-rational" inputs into planning. This, in turn, may make it easier to cope with feelings and ideas that arise under uncertainty. Brainstorming, sensitivity training, and other proprietary schemes encourage expressing the extra-rational (although such expressiveness may be best sustained in organizations that are not burdened with a heavy sense of uncertainty).

Acknowledging that "I don't know" is dangerous enough, but acknowledging that "*we* don't know" would apparently, in our present scheme of things, leave little to keep our world together, little for us to count on. What is more, expressing the intuitions and feelings that would well up in a "we-don't-know" situation, runs counter to all canons of rational behavior set by and for professionals operating in formal organizations — particularly in government agencies. To support others in such expression would take much unlearning of interpersonal styles that have previously been highly rewarding — or have seemed to be. Learning to support feelings and hunches in others depends on learning to support such behavior in oneself. To do this requires a willingness to risk sharing these with others. This kind of learning does occur under

appropriate conditions, but it is painful and time-consuming —
and unless the learner's working context is supportive and
rewarding of these new skills, it atrophies. But
this unlearning and new learning are so upsetting, so fraught
with fantasized — and occasionally real — psychological dangers,
that people tolerate conventional behavior to the point of ignoring
gross organizational malfunctions, or rationalizing such
malfunctions as "natural" human negotiating behavior. If
uncertainty were routinely acknowledged, the content, process, and
procedures for programming, evaluation, goal-setting, changing
organizational design, and handling relationships with the
environment, would be quite different. Obviously, there will be
heavy burdens involved in learning what the new substantive,
interpersonal, and structural conditions should be. Reluctance to
assume these burdens will add to the resistance to changing over
to long-range social planning.

Haven't People Always Acted Under Uncertainty?

We shall continue to note the interplay of these reluctances, along
with the rewards of repressing uncertainty, in connection with
other changeover requirements. But at this point some response is
needed to the argument that "people have always acted under
conditions of uncertainty." My response is tentative: We need to
know systematically much more about how people act under
conditions of uncertainty, and how they contrive to protect
themselves from knowing that the situation is uncertain. But I
hope that what follows will help to differentiate the familiar
situations for which this argument probably holds, from the
conditions associated with trying to change toward long-range
social planning.

   The argument goes that people in responsible
administrative and executive roles have always acted under
conditions of uncertainty; whether or not they showed it, or
acknowledged it, they know it. The role of leadership, so the
argument goes, requires that this burden and its dissimulation be
accepted as part of the role.

My position is that it makes a profound difference whether one *shares* one's uncertainty, or whether one acts in ways that mislead people into believing that one really knows the risks involved. It affects what is expected, how arguments are conducted, what is concentrated on, and what feedback can be tolerated. It makes a difference in the trust that can be called upon, and it makes a difference in the image that the uncertainty-denier has of himself, and of the competences and response options he bestows on those he deceives. Geoffrey Vickers has speculated that one can stand a great deal more uncertainty when one can trust oneself and one's friends.[27] Indeed, as La Porte has noted, under such high-morale circumstances uncertainty might be sought as a challenge. But in the present and in the years ahead, those with whom we are concerned will be less certain of themselves and of their work associates or friends (Chapter 10), and this will make uncertainty about the environment less tolerable.

Additionally, trying to include in present actions the implications of future environments, seems to be psychologically a new situation, thereby changing the content of the uncertainty for the person who acknowledges this as his state of mind. In describing the implications of management information systems (MIS), which is a part of the technology required for long-range social planning, Argyris observes:

MIS requires managers with higher levels of intellectual and conceptual competence. They must be able to deal with the interrelationships among the facts. Typically, this is not a skill possessed by many executives. In the past, when data were incomplete a manger used intuition to fill in the many blanks with possibly valid data. Managers immersed themselves "in the facts" of their past experience. A sophisticated MIS is able to develop a much richer set of facts with past and present quickly summarized.[28]

In the past, a person's experience often told enough about the relevant variables so that, even if, in some objective sense, the decision-maker didn't know what was going on, his experiences afforded good basis for feeling that he really could deal with the situation. In the turbulent environment, past experiences, even those that were successful, will be less and less adequate for anticipating consequences. As Vickers has suggested, "there will be a greater mismatch between the degree of the world's predictability and controllability and the degree which [he] has come to expect."[29] In the past, information about the actual state of society was so lacking that leaders felt no real challenge to their definition of what "really" was going on. The very fact that one had been successful enough to get to a position of leadership "proved" that he knew what was going on. With moves toward long-range social planning and the concomitant use of data banks, social indicators, and simulation, competent administrators, planners, and executives must consider, to use J. W. Forrester's phrase, "counterintuitive" alternative interpretations of complexity, and will have to know that at a given time they have insufficient knowledge to choose between them. This will emphasize the uncertainty in the situation, at least as often as the technology provides them with a better basis for assigning risk. It will be much harder to avoid recognizing, or being told, that one "doesn't know."

In addition to these "in-house" indicators of uncertainty, there will be those from outside that will undermine the conventional means people have used to deal with uncertainty. The persistent challenge to legitimacy, the growth of competent advocacy groups and volunteer organizations representing different definitions and appreciations of reality, and the persistence of distrust toward government and corporations will mean that the practitioner of conventional means for coping with uncertainty will no longer have the rewards available that tell him his means of coping are working. In the future he will be not nearly so longer well protected from turbulence, or from evaluations of his responses to it.

1. Social Science Research Council (1968), quoted in Moynihan, D. "Counselor's Statement," *Toward Balanced Growth: Quantity with Quality.* Report of the National Goals Research Staff. Washington, D.C.: U.S. Government Printing Office, 1970.

2. Complicating this factor is the need to develop theory and data that take into account the growing consciousness of both plan designers and plan users about their own involvement in the unfolding of programs and program evaluations. This is especially true when plan designers and plan users — and in some cases, program evaluators — are overlapping groups.

3. La Porte, T. *Organizational Response to Complexity: Research and Development as Organized Inquiry and Action, Part I.* Working Paper 141. Berkeley: Center for Planning and Development Research, Institute of Urban and Regional Development, University of California, 1971, pp. 7,8. *See also* Cohen, A., E. Stotland, and D. Wolfe, "An Experimental Investigation of Need for Cognition," *Journal of Abnormal and Social Psychology,* (51), 1959; Berlyne, D. *Conflict Arousal and Curiosity.* New York: McGraw-Hill, 1960; and Schroder, H. et al. *Human Information Processing.* New York: Holt, Rinehart, and Winston, 1967, Ch. 3, pp. 34f.

4. *See* Schon, D. *Beyond the Stable State.* New York: Random House, 1971. *See also* Knight, F. *Risk, Uncertainty and Profit.* Chicago: University of Chicago Press, 1921.

5. *See* Kaplan, S. *Cognitive Maps in Perception and Thought.* Ann Arbor: University of Michigan, 1970.

6. The classic statement of this process of internalizing the external social environment, the "generalized other," is found in Mead, G. *Mind, Self, and Society.* Chicago: The University of Chicago Press, 1934. A related version is in Berger, P. and T. Luckmann. *The Social Construction of Reality.* Garden City: Anchor Books, 1966. *See also* Riesman, D., N. Glazer and R. Denney. *The Lonely Crowd.* New York: Doubleday Anchor Books, 1955.

7. *See* Driver, M. and Streufert, S. The General Incongruity Adaptation Level (GIAL) Hypothesis-II. Incongruity Motivation to Affect, Cognition, and Activation-Arousal Theory. Paper No. 148. Lafayette. Ind.: Institute for Research in the Behavioral, Economic, and Management Sciences, Purdue University. 1966. *Also see* Mumsinger, H. and Kessen W. "Uncertainty, Structure, and Preference." *Psychological Monographs: General and Applied,* 1964, p. 78.

8. Thompson, J. *Organizations in Action: Social Science Bases of Administrative Theory.* New York: McGraw-Hill, 1967.

9. LaPorte, op. cit., p. 20.

10. Argyris, C. *Applicability of Organizational Sociology.* New York: Cambridge University Press, 1972, pp. 3-4.

11. Schon, op. cit.; La Porte, op. cit.

12. Nelson, R. et al. *Technology, Economic Growth, and Public Policy.* Washington, D.C.: The Brookings Institution, pp. 173-174.

13. Friend, J. and W. Jessop. *Local Government and Strategic Choice.* London: Tavistock Publications; Sage Publications, 1969, pp. 88-89.

14. Ibid, p. 96.

15. Blau, P. *The Dynamics of Bureaucracy: A Study of Interpersonal Relations in Attitudes of American Men.* Chicago: University of Chicago Press, 1963, p. 91.

16. La Porte, op. cit., p. 8.

17. *See* Schon, op. cit., 1971, pp. 123, 128.

18. For a description of the ideological basis of disjointed incrementalism, *see* Schick, A. "Systems Politics and Systems Budgeting," *Public Administration Review,* 24(1) (1969). A scholarly polemic exposing the ideological basis of pluralism that undergirds interest-group liberalism is found in Lowi, T. *The End of Liberalism.* New York: W. W. Norton, 1969. For a symposium on "muddling through," cited in this book's Introduction, *see* Dror, Y. "Muddling Through — 'Science' or Inertia?" *Public Administration Review,* 24(3) (1964).

19. Based on personal observations as a staff social scientist with the Weapons Systems Evaluation Group, Joint Chiefs of Staff; as a member of the staff of the Gaither Committee; and as a sometime "expert" on civilian behavior under warfare conditions. *See* Michael, D. "Civilian Behavior Under Atomic Bombardment," *Bulletin of the Atomic Scientists* (11 May, 1955), and "Psychopathology of Nuclear War," *Bulletin of the Atomic Scientist* (18 May, 1962).

20. Burns, T. and G. Stalker. *The Management of Innovation*. London: Tavistock, 1961, p. 132.

21. Miller, E. and A.K. Rice. *Systems of Organization*. London: Tavistock, 1967, p. 263.

22. For example, *see* Gardner, J. "America in the Twenty-Third Century." *New York Times*, Editorial Page, July 27, 1968.

23. On the absence of necessary professional-client standards, *see* Gross, "The Need for New Managerial Values," (1970), Chapter 6.

24. Moynihan is illuminating on this; *see* Moynihan, D., "Eliteland." *Psychology Today*, 1970, 4(4).

25. *See* Caplan, N. "The Impact of Social Research on Policy Decisions." Invited address to the American Society for Public Opinion Research, May 19, 1971, Pasadena, California. Ann Arbor: Center for Research on Utilization of Scientific Knowledge, Institute for Social Research, University of Michigan.

26. *See* Dror, Y. *Public Policy Reexamined*. San Francisco: Chandler, 1968, pp. 149-153 and 157-159. Dror deplores the rejection of the "extra-rational" and insists it must be part of the policy-making process.

27. Vickers, G. in personal correspondence.

28. Argyris, C. "Resistance to Rational Management Systems." *Innovation*, 1970, (10), p. 34. (In 1972 *Innovation* merged with *Business and Society Review*.)

29. Vickers, G., op. cit.

4

The Requirement for Embracing Error

*We are in increasing danger of acting as if we knew
what we were doing, when we don't: and then not
being able to bear the consequences of having erred.*

R. BILLER[1]

AVOIDING AND REPUDIATING ERROR

Future-responsive societal learning requires acknowledging openly
the sources of uncertainty and risks inherent in fulfilling one
prerequisite for societal survival: preparing for the future through
present actions that take their direction from systematic
conjectures about the future. Changing toward long-range social
planning requires that, instead of avoiding and repudiating error,
we must seek it out and use the information derived from the
failure as the basis for learning through further societal
experimentation. Put more bluntly, future-responsive societal
learning makes it necessary for individuals and organizations to
embrace error. It is the only way to ensure a shared
consciousness of:

- the limitations of theories about the nature of social dynamics;
- the limitations on data for testing these theories; and
- the limited ability to control situations well enough to expect
  to be successful more often than not.

Under such conditions, embracing error is the only way to guarantee that members of the environment will be responsibly involved in specifying objectives, participating in experiments, and determining the characteristics of the evaluative feedback necessary for learning from the errors detected.

In our traditional attitude toward error, all incentives are directed toward rewarding organization members for denying the environment access to program planning or evaluation. Thus, if error occurs, the organization is able to avoid being punished by an environment that does not know about it nor is able to evaluate it, because it does not know what should have been accomplished. On the other hand, coopting members of the environment can be seen as a device for playing on *their* reluctance to embrace error. Those who join the organization's activities reap the rewards of affiliation and generally can be counted on to respond to organizational error the same way other members "naturally" do — by suppressing or repudiating it.

In our society, we presume that an error made by a member of an organization is the consequence of miscalculation, incompetence, bad luck, stupidity, or impotence in the face of social challenge. In one way or another, error seems to carry with it an aura of failure, of "unelectedness" in the Calvinist sense, and hence a taint of sinfulness. Failure is punished and success rewarded. We begin to learn this early in school, when we suffer the consequences of erring on tests or misjudging the teacher's ability to cope supportively with our error-acknowledging confusion or error-prone whimsy, imagination, and exuberance. John Holt has described this early conditioning:

He learns that to be wrong, uncertain, confused, is a crime. Right Answers are what the school wants, and he learns . . . countless strategies for prying these answers out of the teacher, for conning her into thinking he knows what he doesn't know. He learns to dodge, bluff, fake, cheat. . . . What the children really learn is . . . keep out of trouble, and get other people in . . . mean-spirited competition against other children . . . that every man is a natural enemy of every other man.[2]

This error-avoiding and error-denying behavior is reinforced by parental approval of good grades, which depend mostly on learning the "right answers." When the norms of school and home emphasize error-making and error-acknowledging as reprehensible, it is very difficult to revise them in adulthood.

So important is it to be right, that when a person or organization is allegedly in error, it is considered within the bounds of the ethic that sets the highest priority on organizational survival to assert that no error has occurred, or that if it did occur, it was unimportant. . . or that if it was important, it was someone else's fault. Succeeding by any of these gambits brings its own reward, at least to the extent that punishment is avoided. To the extent that the capabilities of an organization are judged by the competence of its leadership, a leader's error is usually not verified by actually punishing him or her for it — or, at least, the leader is not publicly or harshly punished at the time the error occurs. To do so would threaten the organization by undermining confidence in the much-depended-on role of leadership *per se*. Murray Edelman writes in this regard:

The assumption of responsibility becomes vital in a world that is impossible to understand or control, but the manner in which leaders are held "responsible" is highly revealing. It is expected of the top executive of every large organization that he will periodically proclaim his willingness, even eagerness, to take personal responsibility for the acts, and especially the mistakes, of his subordinates. Each time this stylized manifesto appears everyone involved experiences a warm glow of satisfaction and relief that responsibility has been assumed and can be pin-pointed. It once again conveys the message that the incumbent is the leader, that he knows he is able to cope, and that he should be followed.

In practice, however, it turns out that the message is the only one such ritualistic assumption of "responsibility" conveys. It emphatically does not mean that the chief executive will be penalized for the mistakes of subordinates or that the latter will not be penalized. On the contrary, it is ordinarily only the subordinates who suffer for mistakes. It is they who are fired, denied promotion or demoted, or hauled before a congressional committee to explain and be publicly castigated. So clear is the general understanding that the hierarchical chief benefits rather than suffers from the assumption of "responsibility" that his political opponents are outraged when, in a specific incident, he refuses to allow a subordinate to be identified and says he will shoulder responsibility himself. All concerned then understand that no one will in fact suffer at all and that the chief executive has scored heavily.[3]

Adversaries, whether they be political parties, investigatory commissions, crusading news reporters, or advocacy groups, try to place blame and exact punishment for error, but it is noteworthy how seldom the leadership really suffers when exposed and how blurred the issues become. This is true, in part, because very often the old concept of personal blame simply does not make sense in complex, interdependent organizations. Another factor is suggested in the quotation above. We don't want to believe that our leaders are error-prone. We don't want to undermine our institutions by seeing them as error-prone — at least, many of us don't.

In situations where societal learning is undeliberate, unconscious, and even seemingly unnecessary, given how well things are going, and given how little information and few effective advocates are available to make a legitimate case to the contrary, error-repudiation is "natural," inasmuch as it is amply rewarded. But when societal learning must become conscious and as rapid as possible, and when there will be increasing amounts of data purportedly clarifying the nature and source of error, it would seem that the "natural" response has to be to embrace error.

To better appreciate the difficulties in overcoming typical error-avoiding behavior, we return here to a further examination of the heavy emphasis our society places on control. In yesterday's world, characterized by scarcity and less interdependence, those personalities who could increase the likelihood of predictability were the same ones that could increase the likelihood of controlling access to survival resources, and vice versa. Those skills that led to control were found most frequently in those described as "compulsive" personalities; persons with a strong need to keep things well in hand.[4] This compulsive need to control, plus possession of the skills for maintaining and extending control, seem to characterize such professionals as inventors, engineers, managers, executives, elementary school teachers, and bureaucrats. Most organizations have evolved into structures that support and reward those who have the skill and the will to control the internal and external environment, and to arrange things so that the outcome is entirely predictable — that is, successful. Even in situations where less-compulsive performance is preferable, in order to deal constructively with less-predictable outcomes, there is still a strong tendency to maintain the structures and norms that encourage recruitment of and accommodation to compulsive styles of performance. Persons attach themselves to potential outcomes that are so hedged or so incremental that they are unlikely to be caught out in error; that is, they plan in ways they expect to end up in control of their own situation.

David Birch quotes an engineer in an aerospace firm doing advanced research and development: "One thing you find out around here very quickly is that you can't make a mistake. . . . So everyone sort of walks around delicately trying to get through the system without stepping in a hole." [5] This observation contradicts the prevailing belief that research and development organizations survive by taking innovative risks, which would mean that they would have to fail often and be able to absorb their errors constructively. Sometimes they do, but the internal culture is different from the one we are speaking about in ways that emphasize the social psychological difficulties public agencies have in embracing error. In "hardware" R and D failures, the project outcome usually cannot be faulted in regard to research technique or to theory applied at the time decisions were made, or to the data base subsequently used. Failure is usually attributed to nature being different from what human beings expected it to be, or to a *calculated risk* on research strategy. But if the calculated risk was taken on good, rational grounds, failure is seen as the result of nature having different properties, rather than a human being having displayed incompetence. It is accepted that there are limits to our knowledge about natural science. In the social area, however, any decision is seen as questionable, because theory, data, and research techniques are all challengeable. Thus, failure can be blamed on specific people rather than on a misunderstanding of social nature. In part, this is because people tend to believe they know the reality of social nature. They argue about it and challenge others' social theories, but the assumption is that "I am more right, and you are more wrong." Seldom do both acknowledge that they may both be wrong.

In the social situation, failure reflects on all aspects of the self-image. But failure in R and D need not reflect on technical competence, which is where the self-respect of the technician is located; therefore, a modest amount of error-embracing is sometimes feasible in R and D, whereas it is not in social planning. But only a modest amount, because in the long run technical competence becomes equated with overall ability to outguess nature. R and D organizations are designed to measure success on the average, rather than each time around. Such a standard of effectiveness is extremely difficult for public agencies to claim in the face of multiple and conflicting environmental demands, and in the absence of adequate evaluations.

Moreover, while this kind of error-embracing is provisionally acceptable at the technological level, it is almost invariably abjured by spokespersons who link the organization with the environment. Publicly, the organization still has to look like it really doesn't make mistakes; or that it has learned from the last ones, and next time everything will most assuredly work. Thus, an R and D organization is grudgingly allowed by its environment the opportunity to learn from its mistakes. But, in turn, it must give reassurances that it has indeed learned enough to eliminate error the next time. In the social policy and program areas, this assurance cannot be given. By failing to embrace error, the policy-maker avoids acknowledging that he may not learn enough from his mistakes to eliminate them next time. Aside from its political inexpediency, error-embracing seems to connote technical incompetence, and thereby personal inadequacy.[6]

This is not to say that all persons intensely committed to hard work or to a vision have a compulsive need to control or work in settings that encourage such behavior (though, if descriptions of their private and public lives are to be believed, many probably do). Nor are they uncreative and socially negligible; nor psychologically "strange" or dangerous by conventional standards. On the contrary, these persons often excel in intense commitment, hard work, skill, and will to control; in traditional terms, they are the epitome of a cultural ideal. At the same time, it is true that positions of control are likely to be more vigorously sought, more frequently filled, and more successfully operated by people with strong compulsive personalities. And these people, more than others, have an especially difficult time relinquishing control and accepting the fact that a situation in which they feel compelled to act is probably beyond their control and, as a consequence, likely to end in failure. While there are exceptions, arising from the mix of personalities and the press of events, it seems reasonable to propose that most people in positions of power and status, as well as those seeking power and status, have a deep need to avoid situations in which they are likely to "miss the mark." The prevailing "sensible" norm is epitomized by Charles Lindblom when he supports the political and logical reasonableness of disjointed incrementalism by warning that "nonincremental policy proposals are typically unpredictable in their consequences." [7] Such people represent a serious source of resistance to undertaking the changes required to move toward long-range social planning, because they are likely to be found at the organizational levels where initiating decisions are made, and because many professionals who think they want to promote planning find that, when long-range social planning is actually attempted, they still have the same strong need to control.

Leaders and members of organizations try to avoid acknowledging error, not only because it helps them sustain a view of themselves as people in control, but also because it elicits the support of members of the relevant environment, who, belonging to the same tradition, evaluate persons and organizations in the same way. For most people, neither leaders nor organizations are effective unless they commit few errors and act as if they do not intend to make any at all. Murray Edelman observes:

It can rarely be known what concrete future effects public laws and acts will bring. Economic interactions, psychological responses, the actions of foreign governments and of domestic groupings all contribute to uncertainty. Because men are anxious about impersonal, uncontrollable, or unknowable events, however, they

*constantly substitute personality for impersonality in interpreting
political events. They attribute wider maneuverability to leaders than
the latter enjoy. They want to believe that officials have the power
and knowledge to produce particular results.*[8]

Lewis Long of the National Institute of Mental Health has
suggested a related reason why members of organizations and
environments prefer their leaders to avoid embracing error. Error-
embracing revives painful feelings associated with childhood
experiences in which they suffered as the result of parental error.
One of the advantages of believing oneself to be an autonomous
adult is freedom from the threat of suffering further from misguided
parental behavior. Leaders who acknowledge error remind adults
that they are dependent upon those they choose to follow or work
for. Hence, they remind them that they can suffer again as they did
in childhood through the actions of these surrogate parents.

If long-range social planning is to be a societal learning
system, those in the environment must also learn how to condone
error-embracing. To do so, persons and groups in the environment
must give up the reassuring belief that there really are immutable
solutions to existing problems, a belief that is furthered by
excluding members of the environment from taking responsibility
for activities that constitute long-range social planning. If they
become part of an error-embracing, future-responsive societal
learning system, they can no longer sustain such expectations nor
routinely punish decision makers for error. Instead they become
part of the experiment, part of the error-embracing societal learning
structure. This kind of participation denies them the comforts of
ignorance and the satisfaction of blaming others for their exposure
to turbulence and uncertainty.

SOCIAL PSYCHOLOGICAL REWARDS
OF ERROR-EMBRACING

There can be certain social psychological advantages to embracing
error. For one thing, polarization over goals or choice of means can
be reduced, especially when it results from the assertion of
advocates that their position is right and would work if

implemented. An understanding that failure is possible, indeed likely, either way, eases the demand for commitment to the exclusion of all else, because it recognizes that all means and ends are likely to need changing as their weaknesses are discovered. Knowing in advance that there is no pressure to pronounce a goal or program successful, or to persist in it if it is unsuccessful, sometimes makes it easier to take a wait-and-see approach, knowing that a competing option could get its chance later, if the one being tried does not work.

It may sometimes be politically, economically, and operationally easier to attempt both approaches on an experimental basis, since neither approach has to be "sold" on the grounds that it will most certainly work. Acknowledging the likelihood of error before it occurs makes it easier to abandon the kind of rhetoric that anticipates no error, then requires further rhetoric to hide error, rather than learning from it. As a result, it is easier to set clear and meaningful goals. In fact, a norm of error-embracing makes it acceptable to revise goals and to evaluate programs. Certainly a chief contributor to our proclivity to substitute means for goals is a fear of failing to reach the goals, or of discovering that they are inappropriate.

Given the growing pressure to "tell it like it is," such a shift in perspective and style may not be impossible. Science, after all, rewards error-embracing, and major religious traditions emphasize that human control is fallible — a chimera — and that acknowledgment of error is not only praiseworthy but necessary for enlightenment. Shakespeare's "This above all: to thine ownself be true" is not questioned in principle. Moreover, among some of the more articulate young, and even here and there among older persons holding positions that traditionally were filled with the most aggressive of controllers, the cultural norm that emphasizes and rewards compulsive control seems to be weakening. But given the "naturalness" and the rewards of error-avoidance and error-denial, such a shift across a wide spectrum of environments is difficult — so difficult that only the increasing inability to hide errors may supply a sufficient incentive for placing a positive value on error-embracing.

Consider, too, that while acknowledging uncertainty requires error-embracing in order to cope and to learn, error-embracing requires acknowledging uncertainty. The loop is painful either way one goes around it. The incentive to avoid engagement with both conditions is multiplied and sustained by the unrelieved pain. But if people can bring themselves to embrace error, perhaps uncertainty and the turbulence that produces it will become less painful. Part of the pain results from anxiety and apprehension about the likelihood of committing error in a turbulent and uncertain world, and of being punished for it. If error-embracing is sanctioned, it should be easier to live with the presumed *consequences* of uncertainty, and to accept uncertainty as a personal and organizational condition of life.

Accountability Under Conditions of Error-Embracing

Although embracing error appears to be supported by the logic of learning and the experimental method in science, and although group process training provides evidence that it is not a psychological impossibility, there remains the question of accountability. The argument goes that if people are not threatened with punishment for making mistakes, errors will be made out of indifference, gratuitous distraction, or even maliciousness. In short, people won't work hard enough to avoid making errors.

I know of no completely convincing answer to this argument and its assumptions about what it takes to get humans to "do the right thing;" but appropriate accountability may, in fact, be possible. I offer these comments in the spirit of reducing resistance toward long-range social planning, because some of this resistance derives from a belief about what is "natural" for humans to do about committing and avoiding error.

In the first place, there is growing evidence that people need not be controlled like machines in order for them to generate accurate, efficient output. Sloth, negativity, and irresponsibility are not necessarily innate tendencies. The assault on hierarchical management systems and the demonstrable utility of shared goal setting between workers and supervisors and of participative-management systems give evidence that self- guidance and self-respect can produce responsibility, concentration, and positive involvement.[9] The threat of punishment implicit in the present meaning of "accountability" need not be an incentive for discouraging error.

A somewhat less-insulting image of humanity poses the question, "What incentive do you have to take risks, if you get rewarded whether or not you succeed?" Implicit in this "reasonable" formulation is the assumption that failure is quite likely to be the result of doing things differently from the way one is already doing them. But the argument for long-range social planning assumes that continuing to do the conventional thing is an invitation to disaster. Also implicit in the question is an assumption about human nature: "all things being equal, you will probably take the easy way out." Put that way, its falsity is obvious. It should also be noted that with efforts involving long-range social planning, the "success" of a program is likely to be evident only in some distant future; therefore, the rewards of success will be delayed. But along the way, there will be frequent opportunities to be a successful "teacher" or "learner," as error-embracing efforts reveal new knowledge, allow new understanding, and advance societal learning.

One of the many lessons to be learned by trying out different norms and procedures is how to reward error-acceptance and punish error-avoidance, so that appropriate accountability is maintained. We did not begin this era in full possession of such finely-honed standards; indeed, they are still in the process of evolution, as we learn the costs and benefits of punishment within our present social and organizational structures. We have learned to distinguish many kinds of errors of omission and commission, and to allocate punishments according to subtle or gross distinctions between them; an obvious example is the distinction made between degrees of homicide. Note, too, the present efforts to avoid gratuitous damage to children's self-esteem by removing the grade of "failure" from the lexicon of academic achievement; and the shift in allocation of "punishment" costs, from the worker to the employer, when the worker's error results in physical harm to himself that could have been avoided by a safety device. No-fault auto insurance, no-fault divorce, and legalized abortion all represent shifts in the definition of error or, more important, changes in the perceived utility of assigning accountability for errors. Consider, too, the implications of attempts to legislate compensation to manufacturers whose products cannot meet evolving FDA standards.

Henry David has pointed out that we do not expect ballplayers to bat 1000, though we reward most highly those who come closest. And we admire skilled athletes who try to break records, even if they fail; we admire them for their conscientious *attempt*. This sort of appreciation is a prerequisite for moving toward long-range social planning. This observation also emphasizes another prerequisite: access to and participation in the process by members of the environment. Fans do not expect players to bat 1000, because they are able to observe the workings of the game; moreover, most of them have had personal experience with trying to excel at some sport. There are no secrets about what is involved in failing or in succeeding. Because they understand the requirements for successful ball-playing and the problems of meeting them, fans content themselves with applauding skilled and systematic efforts that come off comparatively well. The same sort of dynamic could work to legitimize error-embracing in the area of societal development.[10]

A few areas in which a norm of error-embracing can be rewarded without encouraging gratuitous error can be imagined. First, there is a need to distinguish between those that result from deliberately undertaking programs for the purpose of long-range social planning, with the intent of learning from them for the social good, and those errors produced in more routine situations lacking such intent. An essential aspect of accountability is the requirement that a person or organization demonstrate that appropriate actions have been taken to seek out and openly report errors. Under this norm, what is punished is the *failure* to embrace error. Technical competence is partially measured by the ability to detect error, and the ability to use the information gained for learning more about where to head and how to get there. This competence is, in part, demonstrated by the capability to get the error-relevant information to the people who can most effectively do the learning and revising — whether they are in the organization or its environment. Such behavior must be rewarded because, by enriching the data base and reinforcing those conditions of trust needed to live creatively with turbulence and uncertainty, it helps make societal learning possible.

But how *much* error-embracing? If *everything* is exposed to everybody, doesn't it present a set of operational and interpersonal problems as intractable as error-denial? My response to this question has two parts; one involves principle, and the other, the practice associated with changeover efforts.

First, let's look at the principle. The interpersonal skills necessary for long-range social planning include the capacity for trusting others, for expressing feelings, nurturing interpersonal support, and so forth. These are skills that most of us very much need to improve not just on the job, but also in our personal lives. We have developed interpersonal styles that allow us to "make do" by keeping our defenses up, thickening our skins, and withdrawing from others. The plethora of books and training programs aimed at helping people become skilled in intimacy, group process, self-knowledge, and relationships with spouses, parents, children, supervisors, and supervisees is a symptom of the growing awareness that the traditional means of coping with one another are increasingly unrewarding. In a society that values open and supportive interpersonal relationships, error-embracing could well be valued as a way of learning more about ourselves and others, as well as about the society.[11] If error-embracing is valued, then the social psychological rewards from sharing the problem and learning from it will encourage error-embracing whenever appropriate. If long-range social planning is recognized as a prerequisite for self-conscious societal development, then error-embracing in some situations will seem to be a "natural" prerequisite for learning. In a turbulent environment, organizational structures will be altering, as will organizational-environmental arrangements. Under these circumstances, restricting error-embracing to some situations does not seem feasible, and I conjecture that, if established at all, that norm would diffuse throughout the social system.

Of course, we are not now such a society, and we are not going to become one during the period directly ahead, while we must be trying to change in that direction. What then "in practice?" In the time period just ahead, more people will be learning interpersonal skills. In addition to the widespread and growing appreciation of this need, the repertory of skills that can be learned, and the opportunities for learning them, are also growing. Of course, many people will not learn them; yet the evidence of error in public programs may become so irrepressible that it could become politically expedient to acknowledge the likelihood of error beforehand, and certainly at the time of the fact. What could be anticipated, then, is a situation in which some people and organizations, some of the time, will try error-embracing, and will be variously rewarded or punished for doing so. This, after all, is what we have done for a few decades with fiscal and monetary policy. It is what we do with international negotiations, shifting from open to secret activities and back again. There is no reason to argue for or suppose that an approach to societal learning as radical in its way as were, at their inception, Keynesian economics or Medicare, will be perfected or applied full-blown and consistently from the beginning. But even as these examples once represented radical responses to societal needs, and just as their practice inevitably shifted the definition of what is "natural" and right for society, so too may error-embracing come to play its "natural" part in long-range social planning.[12]

1. Biller, R. "Converting Knowledge Into Action: The Dilemma and Opportunity of the Post Industrial Society." *Tomorrow's Organizations: Challenges and Strategies*, eds. J. Jun and W. Storm. Glenview, Ill.: Scott, Foresman, 1973.

2. Holt, J. *The Underachieving School*. New York: Dell, 1970, p. 19.

3. Edelman, M. *The Symbolic Uses of Politics*. Chicago: University of Illinois Press, 1964, p. 79.

4. There are fundamental differences between a compulsive personality and an obsessive-compulsive neurosis. Generally speaking, the obsessive-compulsive neurotic is too preoccupied with internal struggles to be effective in controlling the environment, although his or her emotional needs and the desire for environmental control occasionally reinforce one another.

5. Birch, D. "The Model-Building Process and Its Interaction with Organizations: Two Exploratory Field Studies Involving Mathematical Decision Models." Thesis, Graduate School of Business Administration, Harvard University, 1966, p. 88.

6. I am indebted to Kai Lee, whose conversation with me regarding his research on R and D firms provided the substance for these paragraphs. I am, of course, solely responsible for what I have chosen to abstract from his observations, and for my interpretations.

7. Lindblom, C. *The Intelligence of Democracy: Decision Making Through Mutual Policy Making in American Government*. New York: The Free Press, 1965, p. 33.

8. Edelman, op. cit., p. 193.

9. Gooding, J. "It Pays to Wake Up the Blue-Collar Worker." *Fortune*, September 1970. *See also* Likert, R. *New Patterns of Management*. New York: McGraw-Hill, 1961.

10. David, H. "Assumptions About Man and Society and Historical Constructs in Futures Research." *Futures*, 2(3), 1970.

11. For related arguments, *see* the last paragraphs of Argyris, "The Incompleteness of Social-Psychological Theory: Examples from Small Group, Cognitive Consistency and Attribution Research." *American Psychologist*, 24(10), 1969.

12. With regard to the general thesis of this chapter, *see* Arendt, H. "Irreversibility and the Power to Forgive," *The Human Condition*. Chicago: The University of Chicago Press, 1958, pp. 218-219.

5

The Requirement for
Future-Responsive Goal Setting

There is a substantial literature, reflecting the state of mind of many planners and policymakers, which contends that goals for public policy cannot, need not, and should not be specified. The arguments go that 1) people can seldom reconcile value differences, but they can agree on means that serve their different goals; 2) people cannot rationally grasp enough of the issue at hand to set goals that are neither too broad to be guides to action nor too narrow to be other than program targets; and 3) even if their values are similar, people cannot resolve the goal conflicts inherent in the requirements for carrying out different tasks.[1] Thus the incrementalists conclude that "instead of simply adjusting means to ends, ends are, and should be, chosen that are appropriate to available or nearly-available means."[2]

THE MEANING AND PURPOSE OF GOAL SETTING

There is no denying the persuasiveness of these arguments under many conditions — especially in government. Yet there are truly limited, though vast, human and material resources to be applied to complex problems, and there are social purposes that must necessarily be realized in the future. There must be some basis, especially in government, for the selection of direction, commitment of effort, and allocation of resources, beyond the expedient, inertial motives that respond only to the present situation, which is itself an accumulation of past incremental actions. Nor, in a long-range perspective, is it sufficient to argue that ends should be chosen that are appropriate to available means, because future means can be made to differ from those available now, and because "availability" is a function of commitments made and actions taken earlier in pursuit of a long-range goal. Finally, in the light of the accumulating mass of societal problems, those who feel that planning is crucial for felicitous societal growth reject as a sufficient alternative to goal setting the processes that have dominated government actions:

Through various specific types of partisan mutual adjustment . . . what is ignored at one point in policy making becomes central at another point. . . . Similarly, errors that would attend overly ambitious attempts at comprehensive understanding are often avoided by the remedial and incremental character of problem solving. And those not avoided can be mopped up or attended to as they appear, because analysis and policy making are serial or successive.[3]

That there are both need for and great difficulty in setting meaningful future-oriented goals is evidenced by the comparatively feeble results from the growing number attempts to do so,[4] by cities, a Presidential commission, volunteer organizations, and agencies trying to meet PPBS goal specifications. For many reasons, these attempts end up as ritual statements, or just fade away. These experiences, combined with relevant theory, provide a basis for anticipating some social-psychological sources of resistance to goal-setting when its purposes would be to facilitate social planning for the future. The very reasons that make goal setting necessary provide sources of personal and organizational threats that will result in resistance to efforts to change toward long-range social planning.

Changing toward long-range social planning would require goal setting where values conflict, and where goals will need to be recognized as crucially important but possibly temporary, and evaluations will need to be designed accordingly. Moreover, it would be desirable for goals to be developed in other than crisis situations.

Goal setting as I mean it here is necessary in order for societal learning to occur. It is both a way of stating what is to be learned, and a necessary condition for discovering whether we are learning. It is not done to commit us to get from A to B, but to help us discover where we are and where we think we want to go, given our understanding of A and B — an understanding which is in part the result of committing ourselves to the task of goal setting. We cannot evaluate whether we are approaching a desired future condition without having specified how that condition is to be recognized. Nor can we evaluate the continuing relevance of chosen future conditions, unless there is a previous choice with which to compare our changing appreciation of what is important to avoid or attain in the future. A goal can refer to an end state, or to a desirable future condition that is not in itself an end state; or it can refer to establishing a norm. Geoffrey Vickers emphasizes that much of life is not aimed at end-point attainment, but rather at maintaining norms; and that the task of coping with the contradictory functions of balancing and optimizing organizational behavior by setting norms is more important and realistic than end-point goal setting for the purpose of getting from here to there.[5] I agree, especially for organizations dealing with a comparatively familiar band of internally- and externally-varying conditions responding to a comparatively short-future time frame. And I am sure that norm setting will be an important type of future-responsive goal setting, as I am using the term. But it also seems to me that in the public policy area, many of the goals to be set smack more of end-point targets and direction setting than of norm-setting.

The different types of goals could be represented by asking for ten million new houses by a given date, for housing of a stated quality for all within a given period, or for the application by a given date of a regulatory process for monitoring and revising housing standards. Goals are necessary because long-range planning activities extend over a long enough time to require reevaluation of means and ends as we move into the future, and because the future is likely to appear different enough from the present to allow and require choices among options that can only be attained in the future. Goal setting stimulates and provides the reference for scanning the future beyond and aside from the goal, thereby exposing costs as well as benefits that may be associated with the goal. It makes possible explicit understanding of the undesirable features that will accompany a preferred future. And it sensitizes and emphasizes the evaluation and goal-resetting processes that would become operative once goals were chosen.

Finally, long-range goals provide a kind of myth to which hopes and commitment can be attached.[6] Thereby, goals provide a symbolism for creating the future. They can become a statement of what we can be and an injunction to try; and, if societal learning is the mode, goals carry with them the obligation to evaluate and revise them over time. Fred Polak has much to say about the way images of the future provide a guide to the present. Goals, as used here, necessarily derive from images of the future, and encapsulate the meanings of that image. Of images of the future Polak says:

While mirroring man, they also hold up another mirror which shows him how he could and should be. To the extent that they can move man to look at the changing image reflected in this other mirror, they can help him grow into this new image. Positive images of the future create an active type of man, possessed of influence- optimism, indirect or direct, with regard to the future. Their dynamic power to compel the dramatic movement of cultural events through time lies in the human intermediary, in the man moved to action by his vision of the future. History does not unfold of itself, but evolves through man's evolving.[7]

RESISTANCE TO EFFECTIVE GOAL SETTING

When future-responsive goal setting is attempted in conventional organizational settings, it is upsetting — so much so that the activity usually dies aborning or ends as a ritual statement, too specific or too overblown to be useful for guiding and inspiring movement into the future, and disconnected from goal evaluation and goal revision processes. Misplaced expectations about the purposes and consequences of goal setting, which derive from social engineering assumptions and from the norms and behavior-defining competence in conventional organizations, result either in avoidance of goal setting altogether, or in so much anxiety and frustration that the activity is truncated and self-defeating.

Typically, when goal setting is attempted, it is done to avoid (or to gain a sense of avoiding) uncertainty. When participants succeed in stating and agreeing on goals, there is usually a tacit agreement: "This is what can be made to work out." Thus, implicit in the wish that goals be set is the hope that a consensus will be forthcoming on what constitutes reality, and which aspects of that reality merit attainment or avoidance. In this state of mind, if agreement on goals can really be reached, it implies a greater likelihood of order, and this anticipated reduction in uncertainty is comforting to contemplate. The hope that the act of goal setting will reveal an attainable future, and encourage tranquil participation in its attainment, comes through clearly in this comment by a staff member of a voluntary organization concerned with community action: "There's no reason why we can't get agreement on where we want to be in the future. Everybody really wants the same things out of life. And in this country, we've got the means to get those things if we get clear on them. All we've got to do is get together and stay together."

But effective goal setting for the longer term turns out, in fact, to confront those involved with new uncertainties. In the absence of a validated theory of social change, future conjectures are simply that — conjectures — no matter how artful, systematic, and rational the means of deriving them. While planners have more information than they once had, they have no reliable way of knowing whether they have the information they need for choosing among these conjectures in order to set goals.

Attempts to translate this uncertainty into a more comfortable form of risk requires an additional effort to better assess present conditions and the dynamics of change. But in the light of our inadequate understanding of social change (in spite of competing serious and pop sociology models purporting to describe it), examination of the present to get a better purchase on the future is far more likely to increase uncertainty than to reduce it. Thompson and Tuden have proposed a typology of decision making (which presumably includes decision making about goals) that emphasizes the uncertainty that infuses that act. The typology is built around beliefs about causation and preferences for possible outcomes:

- When there is agreement on both causation and preferences, the decision-making process is one of computation.
- When there is agreement about causation, but disagreement about preferred outcomes, the process is compromise.
- When there is disagreement about causation, but agreement about preferences, decisions are based on judgment.

But when there is disagreement about both causes and outcomes, decision making is by "inspiration." Inspiration would seem to be the most likely process for many future-oriented goal-setting decisions.[8]

If those involved in goal setting acknowledge to themselves and to their peers this fragmented and unvalidated theoretical and factual basis for setting goals with regard to the longer-range future, then restricting those goal choices to purely "rational" data and models becomes ridiculous or fraudulent. But if goal choices are not restricted to criteria based solely on data, theory, and so forth, then the door opens for preferences, values, ideologies, and the feelings that underlie them to become an explicit part of the goal-setting process.

The problems presented by this sort of goal setting are greater now than in the past. Even when values have differed among members of a goal-setting group in the past, the differences were far less than those expected in the future. A major condition that makes planning increasingly necessary is the absence of an agreed-upon value system with shared goals, priorities, and approved means for attaining them or for resolving conflicts over their priority. Sharply differing values will characterize the people filling the overlapping roles in which planning-relevant tasks are performed. This will be especially so because members of the environment must play an integral part in future-responsive societal learning.

In a brilliant and unique analysis of policy analysts and their work, Martin Rein has emphasized the ineluctable role of beliefs in such activities. He argues that, in the final analysis, the research for policy-making and program development, and the application or non-application of the research, as well as the choice of what is to be implemented, depends on professional and political creeds. But while the contributions of these creeds to the definition of problems, policies, and programs is evident, the contribution of beliefs is not attended to explicitly in the interpersonal setting in which planning-relevant activities are invented or decided upon. I am suggesting that one reason the central role of beliefs is not dealt with directly and constructively is because the idea of deliberately dealing with strong emotions is so threatening to those involved that planning-relevant activities, such as goal setting, are waffled so that the issues do not have to be faced and worked through. Moreover, attention to beliefs also undermines the authority of "science" by emphasizing the insufficiency of quantitative data. This undermining contributes its own modicum of emotions and compounds the threat.

Two social-psychological conditions intertwine here. The first is that serious attention to a more distant future will raise questions about social priority, moral stance, and the utilitarian justification for organizational survival. "Who am I?" and "What am I doing here as a person?" and "What is this organization doing here in the light of these possible futures?" have already become very uncomfortable questions for some members of organizations. Future conjectures examined for goal-setting guidance will often be mirrors reflecting ethical, personal, and operational obsolescence. Of course, other people with other values and other organizations will see instead new potential and purpose. But for those who don't like what they see, or are fearful of it, goal setting for guidance into alternative futures will be an emotion-laden activity and, as such, one to be avoided, particularly when another part of the group is perceived to like what it sees.

The second condition results from the oft-reinforced norm that personal feelings have no place in rational decision making. There is the *real-politik* injunction to "play it sensibly." Then there is the widely subscribed-to position that supports the efficacy of rationality *per se*, especially as enhanced by the techniques of management science. Both positions argue that feelings subvert efficiency and clarity in organizational goal setting. One important consequence of these viewpoints is that people seeking and attaining high-level policy positions tend to discount the contribution their feelings make to their choices. (While some will privately credit hunches or intuition, they will not acknowledge them publicly.)

By assuming the cloak of rationality and being rewarded for it with successively more powerful and central decision-making roles, those responsible for goal setting are often reinforced in a culturally-approved and occupationally-trained inability to deal constructively with their own feelings and those of people who are involved with them in such decisions. This trained incapacity to engage feelings constructively is not limited to those at the top. These individuals are the models for the approved behavior of junior aspirants, and what is more, they evaluate the performance of their subordinates. So the superiors' style of avoiding exposure to strong feelings heavily influences the norm. Thus, the strong tendency, as has been commented on and demonstrated often enough, is to repress feelings and avoid situations that might elicit them. (See Chapter 8.) Since during the changeover period, planners assume that there are strong value differences — perhaps among members of the organization, and certainly between the organization and the environment — and since these differences will be expected to be unresolvable by "rational" means of adjudication, goal setting will be avoided if possible, as too disruptive to be a part of a decision-making process. Thus, a major reason for resisting purposeful (as contrasted to ritualistic) long-range goal setting seems to be the fear of facing the intense feelings arising from value conflicts and ideological differences that accompany future-oriented planning.

In addition to the fear of facing open emotional conflict, those involved in changeover efforts would have to recognize that if they make goal commitments, actions to implement them should follow. Since these actions take place in a turbulent environment, feedback intended to assess goal achievement would often indicate that the actions are not succeeding, or that there is no way to know whether they are. There will be fear, then, that feedback that depends on goal specification will make it easier to be identified with erroneous decisions. Also, when goals are set well into the future, anticipations about the characteristics of that future are very likely to change over time; then goal-specifying tasks have to be undertaken anew, and the criteria for program evaluation altered. The reluctance to experience renewed exposure to intense feelings in renegotiating goals also encourages resistance to future-responsive goal setting.

These uncomfortable threats to status, values, and interpersonal relationships that accompany goal setting for long-range social planning will encourage members of organizations to use a number of readily available structural and interpersonal devices to resist serious goal setting.

Means Used to Resist Serious Goal Setting

The most familiar device is to set goals in such global or ambiguous terms that value differences are not engaged, and ostensibly goal-related activities are impossible to evaluate on their face. Nor need upsetting feedback from the present or the future be solicited. A second means is to encapsulate the goal-setting activity within a small group at the top who share mythologies and who then disseminate a goals statement for its ritual utility and public relations value. A third means is to set the future that is attended to close enough to the present so that future scenarios do not contain societal situations that require any shift from present goals or instrumentalities, accumulated out of past experience, according to which the organization believes it operates. Corporations that assess the future in terms of product-oriented markets, and government agencies that assess their relevant future as the duration of the present administration both have a realistic reason for short-term future perspectives and a good rationalization for avoiding the potential pain of longer-range, future-relevant goal setting.

A fourth device is to reject longer-range future studies on the grounds that "they are not specific predictions and anybody's guess is as good as anyone else's" — especially if "anyone else's" conjectures require no goal readjustment. Fifth, if goals are clearly stated , the subsequent uncertainty and need to revise the goals can be avoided by avoiding relevant feedback — that is, by structuring the organization so that it does not get or cannot use goal-checking information. A sixth device for avoiding goal setting is to base organizational and personal evaluations on comparisons of the present with the past, or with other ongoing analogous activities. A seventh means is to limit goal-setting to situations that can be treated as if the needed data and theory were in hand, so that the decision can be "rational," and feelings, values, and ideologies need not — indeed shall not — play a part; or, more correctly, shall not be acknowledged by the participants as playing a part. By excluding feelings and values, the situation is transformed into a ritual. Participants recognize that it does not face up to implicit conflicts; as a result, they lose interest and commitment and are indifferent to implementing the goals settled on. (However, some of the participants may accept the myth of knowledge sufficiency so that they are unaware of the essentially uncertain situation they are dealing with.) Eight, people avoid goal-setting by subscribing to the rationality and moral rightness of disjointed incrementalism, thereby also reducing their fear of making errors — in the short term. They also reap the rewards of reducing uncertainty by moving away from an unsatisfactory and clearly-defined situation in the present, rather than toward a chosen but problematic future.

ARE THERE WAYS TO REDUCE RESISTANCE TO SERIOUS GOAL-SETTING?

It appears, then, that social-psychological resistance to the kind of goal-setting required for moving toward long-range social planning will be formidable. Again, however, it is worth speculating about the possibilities of removing, or at least reducing, the social-psychological resistance by emphasizing the necessity of goal setting for societal learning. We have seen that, whatever else impedes serious goal setting, the following social-psychological contributions are important:

- inability to acknowledge great uncertainty;
- fear that one's errors will be more easily detected if goals are set; and
- fear of dealing with intense feelings in self and others over beliefs as to what constitutes the present and the future, and what priorities should pertain.

If we can stop thinking of goal setting as establishing a once-and-for-all commitment to a specific future, then we may be able to begin to learn if it can be done in ways that facilitate change toward a future-responsive society.

In earlier chapters we examined possible means of ameliorating the fear and anxiety attached to acknowledging uncertainty and embracing error. In later chapters we will examine other ways in which long-range social planning makes heavy demands on interpersonal competence in dealing with feelings, and we will look at possible means for enhancing these competencies. Perhaps these means, taken together, can facilitate our acceptance of goal-setting as a procedure for becoming clearer about what we need to do in order to move toward societal conditions that may be preferable to those of the present.

What about conflicts of interest and confrontations that leave no room for mutual exploration and learning? Some confrontations are simply beyond the capabilities of future-responsive planning. Many conflicts of interest may be lessened by jointly seeking longer-range goals, which by virtue of a shift in time-frame, put a different perspective on current confrontations. Emphasizing an experimental approach allows more than one goal or approach to be tried simultaneously, or if more than one is tried sequentially this may also encourage conflict resolution, for reasons discussed in our examination of error-embracing. In general, it is not clear what kinds of irreconcilable conflicts of interest will arise if organizations try to performing according to the characteristics of long-range social planning — which means that their environment is also involved. Probably new conflicts of interest will arise, just as happened when the poor became involved in decisions about urban resource allocation. Certainly the expression of feelings and beliefs will intensify as people work out their differences. But these expressions may also make it possible to resolve some conflicts that otherwise would have remained deep-rooted or subversive, precisely because goals were not faced squarely.

Daniel Moynihan has emphasized another difficulty confronting those who are serious about setting goals. His proposed means for easing the difficulty fits the position being developed here:

The difficulty with national goals is that they too quickly become standards by which to judge not the future but the present. In a sense, they institutionalize the creation of discontent. The setting of future goals, no matter how distant, drains legitimacy from present conditions. Once it is established and agreed upon that the future will have to be very different from the present, it becomes absurd to be content with the present. The past is annihilated. The most extraordinary progress counts for little if it has brought society only to a middling point in an uncompleted journey.

Yet the creation of discontent is in part the object of goal setting. Discontent is commonly a condition of creativity in an individual or a society: it is at all events an immensely useful spur to progress. The art of national goal setting, then, is to be realistic about what can be attained, and to use social data in such a way as to enable both the expert and lay publics to understand that progress toward any seriously difficult goal is going to take place by increments, and to measure that progress as it occurs (or fails to occur, which is often the case).[9]

Most certainly there are risks in dealing openly with these strong value issues and questions of priority. But the risks seem to me no greater than those attached to stumbling backward into the future — which surely is one of the results of not trying to set goals *in the spirit* of long-range social planning. I emphasize "in the spirit," because without a future-responsive, learning-oriented spirit, openness is disastrous, as numerous observers have pointed out in order to justify secrecy, ambiguity, and value avoidance in conventional planning situations.

1. Simon, H. "On the Concept of Organizational Goal." *Administrative Science Quarterly*, 9(1) (1964). *See also* Haberstroh, C. "Control as an Organizational Process," *Modern Systems Research for the Behavioral Scientist*. Chicago: Aldine, 1968.

2. Hirschman, A. and C. Lindblom. "Economic Development, Research, and Development, Policy Making: Some Converging Views." *Behavioral Science*, 7(2) (1962), p. 218.

3. Hirschman and Lindblom, Ibid, p. 216. For an elaboration of this argument, *see* Wildavsky, A. *The Politics of the Budgetary Process*. Boston: Little, Brown, 1964, especially the last chapter.

4. On the need for and difficulties besetting goal specification, *see* Colm, G. and Gulick, L. *Program Planning for National Goals*. Washington, D.C.: National Planning Association, 1968. On reactions to the National Goals Research Staff report, *see* Abelson, P. "The National Goals Research Staff Report." *Science*, 1970, p. 169, and "What Goals?" 1970.

5. Vickers, G. *The Art of Judgment*. New York: Basic Books, 1965.

6. Wieland, G. "The Determinants of Clarity in Organization Goals." *Human Relations*, 22(2), 1969. *See also* Arendt, H. "Unpredictability and the Power of Promise," *The Human Condition*. Chicago: University of Chicago Press, 1958, pp. 219-224.

7. Polak, F. *The Image of the Future*, vol. II, tr. E. Boulding. The Netherlands: A. W. Sijhoff, 1961, p. 117.

8. Thompson, J. and A. Tudlen. "Strategies, Structures, and Processes of Organizational Decision," *Comparative Studies in Administration*, eds. J. Thompson et al. Pittsburgh: University of Pittsburgh Press, 1959.

9. Moynihan, D. "Counselor's Statement," *Toward Balanced Growth: Quantity with Quality*. Report of the National Goals Research Staff. Washington, D.C.: U.S. Government Printing Office, 1970, p. 11.

6

The Social Psychological Burden
of Coping with the Future

Goal setting puts a particular emphasis on the future as the central focus for decision making. But all activities directed toward long-range social planning have an emphasis on the future, to a greater or lesser degree. So another common thread running through all these activities is the social psychological impact of coping with the future. We will explore some aspects of this coping in other chapters of the book, but will highlight a few important points in this chapter.

BELIEFS ABOUT THE FUTURE
AS A FUNCTION OF BELIEFS ABOUT THE PAST

When interviewed, those who were sanguine about the future invariably justified their expectations that conventional public and corporate governance could deal with the future by referring to past successes under conditions of crisis and change. In personal conversation, the historian and public administrator Henry David has suggested that people probably project their mood regarding the future from their personal interpretation of history.[1] P. Fraisse echoes this hypothesis when he writes:

The temporal horizon of each individual is the result of a true creation. We construct our past as well as our future. It is evident that adaptation is a characteristic of this activity. Man must somehow free himself from the state of change which carries him through life, by keeping the past available through memory and conquering the future in advance through anticipation. This control over time is essentially an individual achievement conditioned by everything which determines personality: age, environment, temperament, experience.[2]

Some implications of such a relationship between the future and the past merit further conjecture. The past, as experienced directly or absorbed vicariously, is a part of our self-image; it helps us explain to ourselves our successes, our failures, and how we arrived where we are. Moreover, our self-image is the fundamental reference by which we project ourselves into the future; it partially shapes our image of the rest of the world, an image that is also partially the product of our historically-derived image of ourselves.[3] One body of research, as reported by T. Cottle, strongly suggests that those who value achieving, and who have achieved, feel more potent with regard to their capacity to deal with the future than those who do not value achieving so highly:

If past-present connections are made through the sense of personal efficacy, control of activity or, more simply, autonomy, then present-future connections become the inferred extension of this autonomy. Inference gives life and meaning to the future. Prior achievement, therefore, breeds possibility and reinforces credible planning.[4]

In contrast, as Cottle observes in summarizing the research of others:

Anxiety, on the other hand, has been shown to deflect individuals away from the future and increase sentiments that success in personal action has a low probability of occurrence. . . . Thus, if anxiety causes an exaggeration of the future's dangers, achievement values reinforce an exaggerated sense of man's ability to control these dangers.

He warns, however, that

for the most part, definitions of past, present, and future remain unstudied. . . . Can one meaningfully discuss a future orientation, for example, if for some the future commences seconds from now, while for others an expanse literally of years appertains to what they themselves call the present?

How expectations about the future vary as a function of beliefs about the past is only beginning to be studied as a topic in behavioral science.[5] Such studies would further help us to understand reactions to attempts to change over to long-rang social planning.

Here, I must speculate in proposing a typology of relationships between past organizational experience and expectations about the future. First, the group sufficiently comforted by the organization's past competence to be able to look at futures: This group divides into those who expect the future to be like the past, and those who expect it to be different. The latter group can be divided into those who feel their organization will be able to operate more or less as it has before, just because it has been successful, and those who foresee a need for radical revision if the organization is to continue to be successful. This latter group seems to be very small, but if long-range social planning is to gain support, it will come from these people. We need to understand better the source of such ego strength, such a broad appreciative setting. Second, those who are sufficiently discomfited by the past performance of the organization to be apprehensive about the future: These people either will avoid attending to the future, or will attend to a future that is sufficiently like the present to keep their apprehension at a level that allows them to go on doing essentially what they have always done. Probably a few people who are discomfited by the past performance of the organization (although certainly not members of government agencies) can nevertheless look at radically different futures and recognize that their organization is obsolete or will die. But they do not publicly acknowledge this awareness, except occasionally as a prophetic incitement to radical self-renewal.

The degree to which identification with selected aspects of the organization's past affects the capacity to seriously consider really different futures would seem likely to be more highly correlated among successful than among unsuccessful senior personnel. For one thing, they are more likely to have a longer history with the government agency, and because of their success in rising toward the top, their self-images are more closely bound to the agency's history as they construe it. For another, a successful career has also usually required learning to hew to the agency line.

Overall, careerism probably is an important discourager of creativity, innovation, and risk taking because of the perceived or imagined dangers of stepping out of line. and insofar as it assures that the older officers within the system will hold the top positions of the agency, it assures continuity, stability, and conservatism in agency policy.[6]

Crudely put, most senior personnel will tend either to perceive that the future will be like the context in which they succeeded (else their sense of continuing to be successful would be threatened), or they will believe that the future will be different, but the means for organizational success will be the same. For such people the idea of changing over to long-range social planning from the mode in which they were successful would probably be repressed or ignored. In this light I would expect encouragement to move toward long-range social planning to come mostly from outside the organization, via consultants or newly-arrived members in the bureaucracy, from its political superstructure, or from legislative or executive directives. And this is the way the process seems to have operated.

Those senior members who can face the threat to their organization and themselves that the future seems to hold, and who can appreciate the need to move away from conventional operations and toward long-range social planning, become the innovative stimulus. so far, these people have been far more evident in private organizations than in government. To what degree being innovative and future-oriented though senior in the organization is a matter of personality, and to what degree it is a matter of organizational structure and history, are unknown, though both doubtless play a part.

FUTURE-THINKING AS A THREAT TO COMPETENCE

Trying to think seriously about the future poses another challenge to one's sense of competence: one must be able to absorb and incorporate new, complex and unfamiliar information. As I emphasized earlier, this information will be ambiguous, intricate, and incomplete, in contrast with the well-articulated construction about one's personal and organizational past that most people probably hold (at least if we accept the memoirs of successful people). A future different enough from the past to require a different way of dealing with it requires a shift in one's appreciative setting. Thinking oneself into the future requires the ability to think dialectically and cybernetically — that is, to think not only about trends but also about countertrends and about the trends that subsequently grow out of the contrasts between these two. My experience (and it is shared by others who try to help people think about institutional and social change) is that very few people are able to think this way.

Recognizing one's limits, especially if one has been successful in thinking in a linear and disjointed manner, is most disconcerting. As a result, in order to avoid recognizing their incompetence, people avoid exposing themselves to situations in which they need to think dialectically. That people attend seminars and lectures on the future is not incompatible with this conjecture. Listening to someone else do the thinking is not the same as trying to do it oneself. Nor is participating in a workshop on how to think about the future, which is likely to consist of the blind leading the blind. And too, many presentations about the future emphasize bits and pieces, so there is no need for the participants to think systematically about social trends.

All this competence-challenging input from the future must be dealt with in the midst of a situation already overloaded with information. Geoffrey Vickers describes the situation thusly:

Each schema derives its meaning both from the experiences which it subsumes and from its relation to other concepts similarly developed. Changes which would shake this conceptual system are resisted with vehemence proportionate to the extent of the threat;

and the extent of the threat varies . . . with the nature of the change involved. It is minimal when the change is by differentiation within an established concept; greater when it comes through the recognition of a wider category under which several established concepts can be subsumed; and greatest when it involves the dissolution of a concept and the distribution of its contexts among others.[7]

Information overload is not the only burden imposed by attending to a future that is not a projection of the past or present. This information, by its incompleteness, unfamiliarity, and inherently conjectural nature, increases the recipient's uncertainty about what it means, what to do about it, and, inevitably, what and who one is. While it is this very uncertainty that makes planning necessary, it also makes many people tend to avoid recognizing it, or to recognize it in ways that unrealistically attempt to impose some degree of certainty. As Richard Wohlstetter observes, "There is a good deal of evidence, some of it quantitative, that in conditions of great uncertainty people tend to predict that an event that they want to happen actually will happen."[8]

One could argue that such autism occurs only under conditions of great uncertainty. However, in the experience of a number of observers, persons usually attend to those forecasts in future studies that are compatible with what they want to happen or what they believe they can cope with because of past experience. Perhaps this is because the organization management that commissions such studies has already sensed an increasing uncertainty. Predictably then, the studies add more uncertainty to the situation than the management can deal with. A typical example emphasizes this important point. I was present at a long, detailed presentation, based on extensive data about the present and past, that was the basis for what was to be a long-range planning effort by one of the largest and most technologically sophisticated American firms. After a semi-public briefing, I commented privately to the chief of the project that if he were to consider some plausible alternatives intervening over the next years, his picture might turn out to be drastically different. Expressing both annoyance and astonishment at my misunderstanding of his situation, he pointed out that if his company took such possibilities seriously, it would be out of business (and so, I dare say, would he, if he pushed them too ardently).

Future studies can thus expose latent uncertainties. This exposure can, and occasionally does, encourage a reallocation of effort in light of those previously unrecognized contingencies. But more often, the exposure of latent uncertainties is resisted or ignored, simply because it adds too many variables to be acceptable. Often these uncertainties expose plausible future weaknesses in present arrangements, weaknesses that require more effort to correct than anyone wants to invest, especially if things are going well. People see the social costs and personal pain as too great, and reason that the future is subject to change anyhow. The common wisdom is, "I say, let my successor worry if these things happen. I've got problems enough putting out our stuff today. Besides, 'today' is what my boss is worried about — this year's dollars." Fear of exposing these latent uncertainties helps to generate resistance to paying serious attention to future studies.

Future Studies as a Source for Myths

Whether feedback from studies about the future contributes deliberately or unintentionally to the creation of new and compelling mythologies remains to be seen. I am not using myth in a deprecatory sense here. All coherent systems of belief are self-validating; they provide their members with direction and inspiration about what to pay attention to, and why it is important to do so.[9] Rollo May describes the role of myth in our lives:

The process of myth-forming is essential to mental health. Since myth is man's way of constructing interpretations of reality which carry the values he sees in a way of life, and since it is through myth that he gets his sense of identity, a society which disparages myth is bound to be one in which mental disorientation is relatively widespread.[10]

The social psychological pressures to create new myths are already strong. Contributing to these pressures is the tension between the need to appreciate alternative futures as a basis for long-range social planning, and the inability of future studies to give assurances about what the future will be. One way to resolve this tension is to become committed to a myth about what can be, and, inspired by that vision, to make a commitment to actions that increase the likelihood of its realization. This is what Dennis Gabor calls "inventing the future." [11] Fred Polak looks at this capacity in an historical perspective:

There is little doubt, to my mind, that the creative images of the future of Zoroaster, Isaiah, and Jesus, of Plato, Paul, Augustine, and Joachim, of Bacon, More, and Marx, etc., have through the centuries made the cultural history of the future. The Greek poets, thinkers, and dramatists, as well as those who rediscovered and revived them in the times of the Renaissance, ushered in a new time, just as the English and French philosophers of the Enlightenment foreshadowed and helped to bring about a revolutionary epoch, the German chiliastic-idealistic philosophers an evolutionary epoch, and Nietzsche and Spengler a reactionary epoch — all through their images of the future. . . .

The spirit of their own time spoke through these visionaries, it is true. But the goal-directed energy potential which they generated also determined to a significant extent which future out of a number of possibilities in a situation still open and fluid would become a part of the actual historical chain of events. They were not only prophets, but also agents who assisted in bringing about that which they predicted. Themselves under the influence of that which they envisioned, they transformed the non-existent into the existent, and shattered the reality of their own time with their imaginary images of the future. Thus the open future already operates in the present shaping itself in advance, through these image-makers and their images — and they, conversely, focus and enclose the future in advance, for good or for ill. [12]

While subscribing to a myth about the future would be, to some degree, unintentional, it need not be exclusively so. May explains:

We do not make myths or symbols; we rather experience them — mainly unconsciously as the source of the images of the charter of *the culture, such as the values, the goals, and the identity. By becoming conscious of the processes we can, however, mold our myths and symbols.*[13]

Historically, we have deliberately exposed ourselves to great myth-derived drama and literature in order to be inspired, informed, and, in some sense, changed in our appreciative setting. We might choose to do so with conjectures about the future, themselves an art form with their own dramatic trappings of complex and impressive rationalistic methodology. The problem is to encourage the inspiring, committing, and informing contributions of myth without losing our capability to reexamine it and revise it. I do not know how this can be done. Perhaps it cannot be done. Perhaps the important thing is to try, for the effort should change both our thoughts and our behavior. Or perhaps it is enough to subscribe to the myth that grows out of a concern with the future — the myth that a future in which future-responsive societal learning routinely takes place is both desirable and attainable.

1. David, H. "Assumptions About Man and Society and Historical Constructs in Futures Research." *Futures*, 2(3) (1970).
2. Fraisse, P. *The Psychology of Time.* New York: Harper and Row, 1963, p. 177.
3. These processes are extensively described in Mead, G. *Mind, Self, and Society.* Chicago: University of Chicago Press, 1934, and Berger, P. and Luckmann, T. *The Social Constuction of Reality.* Garden City, N.Y.: Anchor Books, 1966.
4. Cottle, T. "Temporal Correlates of the Achievement Value and Manifest Anxiety." *Journal of Consulting and Clinical Psychology,* 1969, 33(5), p. 549.
5. One of the few deliberate attempts in this direction is Bell, W. and Mau, J. *The Sociology of the Future,* New York: Russell Sage Foundation, 1971, especially Part One. *Also see* the seminal volumes Experimental Symposia on Cultural Futurology, 1970 and 1971.
6. Mosher, F. "The Public Service in the Temporary Society." *Public Administration Review,* 1971, 31(1), p. 58.
7. Vickers, G. *The Art of Judgment.* New York: Basic Books, 1965, p. 68.
8. Wohlstetter, R. *Pearl Harbor: Warning and Decision.* Stanford: Stanford University Press, 1962, p. 397. *See also* Webb, E. "Individual and Organizational Forces Influencing the Interpretation of Indicators." Research Paper P-488. Arlington, Va: Institute for Defense Analyses, Science and Technology Division, 1969, pp. 39-40.
9. Novak, M. *The Experience of Nothingness.* New York: Harper and Row, 1970. *See also* May, R. *Man's Search for Himself.* New York: Norton, 1953; and *Symbolism in Religion and Literature,* ed. R. May. New York: Braziller, 1959. *See also* Campbell, J. *The Hero with a Thousand Faces.* Princeton: Bollingen Series No. 17, 1968 and *The Flight of the Wild Gander: Explorations in the Mythological Dimension.* New York: Viking, 1969.
10. May, op. cit., p. 192.
11. Gabor, D. *Inventing the Future.* New York: Knopf, 1964.
12. Polak, F. *The Image of the Future,* vol II, tr. by E. Boulding. The Netherlands: A. W. Sijhoff, 1961, p. 124.
13. May, R. "Reality Beyond Rationalism," *Agony and Promise: Current Issues in Higher Education in 1969,* ed G. Kerry Smith. San Francisco: Jossey-Bass, 1969, p. 193.

7

How Long-Range Social Planning Intensifies Role Conflict and Role Ambiguity

As turbulence flows into an organization via feedback from the present and the conjectured future, it upsets the roles people assume in performing their organizational functions — roles that play an important part in helping them to define themselves. C. Lichtman and R. Hunt see roles as complementary expectations:

Social process [can be regarded] as an interaction of positions patterned in terms of these complementary expectations [about rights and duties] which are themselves called roles. Thus, role and its personalistic correlate, identity, represent the implications of social position incumbency and can be comprehensively described only with reference to other roles which bear a complementary relation to the focal role.

. . . since persons occupy multiple positions in life and are only partly involved in any single position they occupy, they have multiple identities that combine in various ways to affect their views and the enactments of their singular roles. And, whatever else may be involved, the modes of a man's participation in structured social intercourse will be reflected in his concept of himself and in the fabric of his personality.

. . . Roles are social phenomena — no doubt of that. However they are not only external "demands," they are dynamic interactive processes carried out by individuals who color their performances personal. By way of reciprocity, however, through their identity

implications roles become operationally integral to individual personality. Thus, roles more than link the individual and the social (or structural), they unite them.[1]

ROLE CONFLICT AND AMBIGUITY IN LONG-RANGE SOCIAL PLANNING

Relatively-stable organizational situations supply many psychological rewards. Most people find security in knowing who they are, which results from knowing what they are supposed to do, and vice versa. The sources of this satisfaction run very deep; simply put, they include being a predictable person in a predictable place, among other predictable people, and with comparatively predictable access to money and "work" friends. This comfortable situation is the antithesis of fighting to survive in an unpredictable, hence dangerous, world of scarce resources.

Of course, vigorous organizations, including government agencies, are not always tranquil, and life in them and the roles their members play are by no means totally stable. Some activities, such as those in the Secretary's office of a federal agency, are comparatively transient and often in turmoil, and roles may be full of conflict and ambiguity. Indeed, the role stresses and strains of such a working situation exemplify what lower levels in the bureaucracy might be like if faced with the requirements for changing over to long-range social planning. And that changeover would of course add greatly to the role-performance complexities in offices that now operate like those at the Secretary's level. We need to look, then, at the kinds of role conflict and role ambiguity that would additionally burden organization members who are changing toward future-responsive societal learning.

The personal strains thus produced among people with no stomach for the hustle and hassle of a "political" office (and often among those who do seek such activities) would absorb energies needed for substantive tasks, and could sap loyalties and commitment, stimulate painful self-searching and questions of identity, confuse communication, and lower trust. Therefore role conflict and ambiguity will exacerbate other threats to self and organization, such as those that arise from increased uncertainty, increased error, and increased organizational and environmental turbulence. Such consequences of excessive role conflict and ambiguity inhibit changing over to long-range social planning.

Role *conflict* exists when the role incumbent tries to carry out role-performance directives from persons he perceives as legitimate role-definers, but the directives require behavior he considers to be incompatible. (The "two-boss phenomenon" is an example.) Roe conflict also arises when carrying out one's own role conflicts with the role performance of others. Role *ambiguity*, as described by Kahn,

is conceived as the degree to which required information is available to a given organizational position. To the extent that such information is communicated clearly and consistently to a focal person [the role incumbent], it will tend to induce in him an experience of certainty with respect to his role requirements and his place in the organization. To the extent that such information is lacking, he will experience ambiguity. The relationship between the objective condition of ambiguity and the intensity of the ambiguity experience for a certain person will be modified by various properties of personality.[2]

Role conflict and role ambiguity together produce serious personal stress, and their reflection in performance has serious organizational consequences:

[Role conflicts] generally have the following effects on the emotional experience of the focal person: intensified internal conflicts, increased tension associated with various aspects of the job, reduced satisfaction with the job and its various components, and decreased confidence in superiors and in the organization as a whole.

The strain experienced by those in conflict situations leads to various coping responses — social and psychological withdrawal (reduction in communication and attributed influence) among them.[3]

* * * * * * *

The ambiguity experience is predictably associated with tensions and anxiety . . . and with a reduction in the extent to which the demands and requirements of the role are successfully met by the role occupant.[4]

*   *   *   *   *   *   *

. . . the presence of conflict in one's role tends to undermine his relations with his role senders, to produce weaker bonds of trust, respect, and attraction. It is quite clear that role conflicts are costly for the person in emotional and interpersonal terms. They may also be costly to the organization, which depends on effective coordination and collaboration within and among its parts.[5]

Studies conducted at the Institute for Social Research have demonstrated that management and administrative job stress, in part the product of role conflict and ambiguity, and intensified by responsibility for other people (who themselves are struggling with role conflict and ambiguity), "are primarily responsible for many of the chronic diseases that have been hitting American males hard in middle age, notably the big one, heart disease."[6] Hardest hit are those hard-driving "compulsive" organizers and controllers commented on earlier.

In all, the stresses and consequences would seem most serious for those kinds of people who would be involved in initiating and carrying out the changeover toward long-range social planning. Kahn continues:

Of the various forms in which role conflict is encountered, two emerge as characteristic of the high-conflict, innovative roles: interpersonal conflict and intra-role conflict. Each of these takes a special guise in such cases. The interpersonal conflicts of the innovator are fought out around his proposals for innovation, a kind of continuing battle of new guard versus old. The intra-role conflicts of the innovator stem from his engagement and commitment to the creative, nonroutine aspects of his job and his corresponding disinterest and disdain for the routine or uncreative demands placed upon him; as a result he experiences a conflict between these two categories of role requirements, both legitimate and unavoidable, but only one truly ego-satisfying.[7]

. . . role conflict is greatest where the prevailing expectations in role set emphasize low rules orientation, low closeness of supervision, and low universalism — that is, in groups which deviate from the general organizational norms in the direction of permissiveness, autonomy, and a willingness to deal with people in individualized, personal terms. Moreover, the tension scores of focal persons are significantly higher in role sets which deprecate orientation to rules and closeness of supervision.[8]

In view of these unpleasant consequences, we can expect people to try to avoid the stress of role conflict and ambiguity by resisting the changes that produce, or are expected to produce them — in our case, those associated with the changeover to future-responsive societal learning. Moreover, the resistance will not come solely from those who are being compelled to change. Those who inaugurate the changeover may also find themselves caught up in unexpected role stress, which may well undermine their enthusiasm. In fact, *all* organizational roles are subject to alteration. How to reconstitute them and how to relate them to each other in less conflicting, less ambiguous ways will be a major learning task for organizations trying to move toward long-range social planning.

In this chapter we will not look at specific role changes. Instead, we will examine some special contributions to role conflict and ambiguity — contributions made by the turbulent environment on the one hand, and the requirements of long-range social planning on the other. We will look at conflicts and ambiguities engendered by arguments about what constitutes role legitimacy, role competency, and role responsibility under such circumstances. In what follows, I will conjecture about situations that arise from the conflicting and ambiguous messages that role incumbents receive from relevant role-information "senders" (who may also be incumbents). These ambiguities and conflicts will have an impact on the receivers, who perceive or anticipate them at the performance level, where interaction takes place with others, who will also be experiencing ambiguity and conflict in carrying out their ambiguous roles. Both the anticipation and experience of role conflict and ambiguity will be stressful. In the absence of much experience with changing toward long range social planning, it is more useful to consider the logical and social psychological aspects of the problem than to try to anticipate specific operational features. In chapters to follow, the reader will recognize many of the general principles discussed here in the more specific operational situations, in which role conflict and ambiguity (often grouped together as "role stress") will be rife. A major purpose of this chapter is to aid in that recognition.

ROLE STRESS FROM CHALLENGES TO LEGITIMACY

There is a widening challenge to the legitimacy of any established organization's purposes, priorities, and procedures that seems to be a concomitant of our contentious, complex, and intensely communicative society. Who has the right to do what (including planning and making demands) is increasingly open to question. While some challenges to legitimacy derive from generational differences, many more are not generation-bound at all.[9]

Because people assume a wide range of overlapping and conflicting roles, questions of legitimacy will challenge them in their roles both inside and outside of the organizations. Some people will face new problems in justifying their organizational roles to those outside, while some will have a problem justifying their organizational role to themselves when they see themselves from the vantage point of their other roles. This does not mean that people are unable to reconcile roles, or that all will recognize themselves to be in conflict situations. But it probably does mean that the broader the educating experiences of the role incumbent, the greater likelihood there will be of being in conflict or hard-pressed to legitimize oneself to oneself.[10] Some of the very kinds of people who will seek to facilitate changing toward long-range social planning will be those who are complex enough in character and intellectual attainment to experience self-doubt and self-searching regarding their own efforts to cope with difficult and interdependent ethical, operational, and personal problems. Others seeking to implement long-range social planning may not be so burdened. Those whose personality or skills tend to make them indifferent to questions of legitimacy may ignore or resent such challenges. (Those who find their rewards in designing and applying highly quantitative, logical, and technological approaches to social problems seem more prone to this reaction; but not all of them fall into this category, nor do all of them have a monopoly on indifference or obtuseness.) And some, who by training or temperament are susceptible to challenges to their legitimacy, may find the additional uncertainty about self and situation too much to bear, and cease to pay attention to those who would impose the new definitions.

An inability to see one's own legitimacy as open to question distorts the use of feedback from the environment. A self-image that is so self-protective that it cannot seriously attend to questions about legitimacy is too defensive to deal with ambiguous situations in the trusting, feeling-laden, and supportive manner necessary to understand and live constructively with questions of legitimacy. Rather than becoming learners about legitimacy issues, they are likely to blame others for raising such issues, as they continue to pursue more rigid planning styles. Out of these legitimacy challenges will arise some extremely difficult and divisive interpersonal issues, which complicate role definitions within and among organizations. We have already seen this in the anguished and embittered divisions in some universities that are the result of faculty members taking sides with various student demands. Similarly, student groups are often divided over what constitutes legitimate means of representation.

Martin Rein has reviewed some of the dilemmas of legitimacy associated with planning — more specifically, with the legitimization of roles:

(There are) three strategies that reformers and planners rely on to legitimate their actions. Each appeals to a different aspect of the democratic process: the need f or consensus among elite institutional interests; the reverence for science and fact; and the validation of pluralism, diversity, and conflict on which democracy depends for its vitality. The dilemma seems to be that reform that works with the establishment, searching for a consensus, tends to lose its soul and its purpose. It abandons its real feeling and commitment for the poor as it sacrifices innovation and reform for survival and growth. Yet, any program that is based solely on a fight for the rights of the poor and that fails to work with established institutions not only is likely to create conflict, but also may fail to generate any constructive accommodation that can lead to real reform. Organizing the poor on a neighborhood basis cannot achieve very much fundamental change. Vision is limited to issues around which local initiative can be mobilized; most typically there is failure to give attention to broad social and economic policy. Research can interfere with both functions, for it can be used, in Gouldner's graphic term, as a "Hamletic strategy" or delay and procrastination,

*responsive to political realities, while avoiding action that will
provide authentic services for the poor. Research can compete with
reform for resources, and it may pursue competing aims. The
documentation of social injustice, which seeks action by
confrontation, may embarrass the bureaucracies and make
cooperation with the reformers more difficult. But without research,
without some kind of objective analysis of the consequences of
action, social policy moves from fashion to fashion without ever
learning anything. It is, after all, useless to continue to create
innovations and to spread new ideas if one never checks to see
whether the new ideas and innovations are mere fads or whether
they do indeed produce any kind of demonstrable change.*

*How then can these dilemmas be resolved? The answer, I believe, is
that they cannot, for the contradictions are inherent in the nature of
American social life.*

*. . . The search for a welfare monism that rejects pluralism and
conflict only fosters utopian illusions. When all three strategies are
pursued simultaneously in the same organization, internal conflict
develops over time.*

*. . . Fragmentation of function does not, however, resolve the
dilemma; it serves only to exacerbate the problem of
interorganizational relationships as lack of coordination becomes a
perpetual crisis.*[11]

Another kind of dilemma will arise for members of an
organization who are loyal to it because it is trying to move toward
long-range social planning, but who voice questions about
legitimacy of the sort Rein delineates. They may weaken motivation
in others to persist in the effort, or they may find themselves
rejected or muzzled for offering unwanted "internal" feedback:

*It must be realized that loyalty-promoting institutions and devices
are not only uninterested in stimulating voice at the expense of exit:
indeed they are often meant to repress voice alongside exit. While
feedback through exit or voice is in the long-run interest of
organization managers, their short-run interest is to entrench
themselves and to enhance their freedom to act as they wish,
unmolested as far as possible by either desertions or complaints of
members. Hence management can be relied on to think of a variety
of institutional devices aiming at anything but the combination of exit
and voice which may be ideal from the point of view of society.*[12]

To leave the organization removes the possibility of influence from inside (though perhaps one may become even more influential outside). Yet to remain quiet and let the legitimacy dilemmas remain unappreciated undermines the very purpose that makes the effort worthwhile in the first place. If there is a way to cope effectively with these dilemmas it is apparently in some other normative context than the conventional one. Perhaps it is a context that emphasizes future-responsive societal learning. Certainly, it will take a lot of societal learning to find out.

Thus, at the very time long-range social planning could have a chance to create new, legitimate organizations and activities, its promoters will have to cope with the heavy psychological burden of challenges to their legitimacy from themselves and from others in their organizations and environments. Their sense of competence probably decreases with a sense of increased uncertainty. Their sense of satisfaction with their competence also decreases with challenges to their legitimacy. And with challenges to legitimacy comes uncertainty about identity and role.

Questions of legitimacy, plus other sources of uncertainty that result from opening the organization to feedback as required by future responsive societal learning, also increase role ambiguity. Role incumbents become defensive and rigid in order to avoid feelings of increased uncertainty. And as rigidity increases, so too does resistance to assuming the learning mode required to learn new roles. If those espousing long-range social planning cannot feel legitimate, and cannot believe they are seen as legitimate, they will simply not be able to build the motivation needed to undertake the required role re-learning. And since legitimacy carries with it definitions of accountability, questions of legitimacy will also raise questions about who and what is accountable. This, too, increases role ambiguity, uncertainty, and the likelihood of counterproductive consequences associated with an anxious state of mind. The interdependent personal costs and benefits of role ambiguity and role conflict are usefully described in the following observation about their effects on personnel in a corporation undergoing major changes:

*Moreover, and equally important, the insecurity attached to
ill-defined functions and responsibilities and status, by increasing
the emotional charge of anxiety attached to the holding of a position,
increased also the feeling of commitment and dependency on others.
By this means the detachment and depletion of concern usual when
people are at, or closely approaching, the top of their occupational
ladder, the tendency to develop stable commitments, to become a
nine-to-fiver, was counteracted. All this happened at the cost of
personal satisfactions and adjustment — the difference in the
personal tension of people in the top management positions and
those of the same age who had reached a settled position was fairly
marked. Such a cost seems, in the present state of knowledge about
the effective operation of working organizations, to be an inescapable
element of successful adaptation to growth and change.*[13]

ROLE STRESS CONCERNING COMPETENT AND RESPONSIBLE PERFORMANCE

At least some of the issues discussed below about what constitutes
competent and responsible role performance, are perennial
arguments, unsolved or variously solved in conventional
organizations. They are reiterated here because they are intensified
under conditions of trying to introduce long-range social planning.
This is due partially to the state of the environment, and partially
to difficulties in shifting from an appreciation of planning as social
engineering to an appreciation of planning as a means for societal
learning. These circumstances make roles even more conflict-laden
and ambiguous than normal, thus generating more internal and
external upset. This upset increases the threat to the sense of
competence felt by those required to change, as well as by those
seeking to induce change.

First, the various definitions of what constitutes competence
and responsibility will come from philosophical differences,
ambiguous research findings, and contending normative theories
rampant among professionally-connected role definers, as these are
reflected in journal articles, graduate school curricula, training
seminars, job specifications, conference speeches, and so on.[14]

A second source of definitions of role competence will be the
special interests in an organization's environment: protest groups,

consumer groups, advocacy planning groups, and other volunteer agencies.

A third source of conflicting and ambiguous role definitions will be some of the role players themselves, who may acquire conflicting definitions of competency and responsibility as they cross the boundaries between their work place and the environment "outside." Many professionals who will be drawn to long-range social planning identify themselves with an overlapping, intertwining network, in which role distinctions are increasingly blurred between work and ethnicity, work and gender, work and religion, and work and community. Persons develop a sense of their personhood by combining their perception of other people's definitions of who they are, with their own definition of who they are. Therefore, these "extra-organizational" role definitions are often in conflict for priority and emphasis with those operating in the more narrowly and conventionally defined work situation.

Finally, conflicts and ambiguities about responsibility and competence in role performance will arise from contending definitions provided by the political structure. This is a crucial source of stress for public agencies and other organizations that are dependent on government funding. There are certain to be contradictory messages from political leaders, constituencies, and professional colleagues about the utility or disutility of risk-taking, error-embracing, and uncertainty-acknowledging in a political setting, which itself is in the process of change. Issues of legitimacy, competence, and responsibility will converge around the balance between what needs to be done on the basis of professional beliefs and knowledge, and what needs to be done on the basis of *political* beliefs and knowledge.

While it is widely acknowledged that planning cannot be divorced from politics, that appreciation does not now provide he roles, norms, or structures for felicitously combining planning and politics. These questions of role competency and responsibility in a political setting have been informatively explored by others.[15] Our task here is to recognize that under the conditions we are examining, this source of role stress will be especially upsetting and will probably be avoided, insofar as possible, by conventional obscurantist tactics. To overcome the tendency to resort to such tactics will require that those who fill the politician's role, whether in the legislature or appointed by the incumbent administration to run a government agency, must themselves be participants in learning how to change over to future-responsive societal learning, and must be strong proponents for doing so. Since the relationship between planning and politics is by no means invariably dominated by the politicians — they are dependent on agency expertise for guidance and ideas — the possibility of bringing politicians into the learning mode need not depend on their unilaterally deciding to do so.[16]

Robert Burco, a planning consultant, has studied and personally experimented with the differences between the characteristics of the competent and responsible "expert" in planning-related activities, and what seem to him to be the requirements for experts who want to try to facilitate movement toward long-range social planning. His summary of these characteristics emphasizes the variety of role stresses that will be involved. As with all such categorizations, the impression of polarized extremes is conveyed too strongly; in reality, neither the old nor the new expert is so completely differentiated. Nevertheless the general direction of emphasis seems appropriate.[17] (See chart on page 203.)

Three more substantive issues can be discerned in which role stress over the appropriate demonstration of competence and responsibility will intensify:

1. The balance the role incumbent must set between using the technical skills of rational planning, and using the intuitive skills that transcend or give perspective to the directions forwarded by techniques and technologists;

2. The degree of attention the role incumbent should pay to the ethical aspects of planning activities, above and beyond the

Characteristics of Two Types of Experts

Old Expert	**New Expert**
Solution Oriented (defines a problem in terms of a solution) bounded emphasis on primary effects simplifying assumption accepting	*Problem* Oriented (explores a situation to find the problem) unbounded secondary and tertiary effects complexifying assumption challenging
Question *Answering* Expertise professional error denying	Question *Asking* Expertise extra-professional error embracing
System *Closing* elitist technocratic comforting conflict masking product oriented	System *Opening* democratic public threatening conflict exposing process oriented
Organization *Captive* protected "hired gun" institutional client-oriented	Boundary *Spanning* exposed free floating personal issue-opportunistic
Politically *Explicit* late in political process choice related well-defined expectations	Politically *Ambiguous* early in political process issue formulating uncertain expectations

Robert Burco

ethical positions supported by the ignorant, the naive, or the practitioners of the conventional wisdom in the organization and its environment; and

3. The extent to which the role incumbent should be able to facilitate group task competency in management processes and interpersonal relationships.

Consider the first item above. The very nature, variety, and complexity of formal planning technology, and the high professional identification of the planner-proponent with that technology — an identification established through intensive training in its use, and legitimized by his value commitment to rationality — will strongly tend to make many technologists vigorous advocates, but with a comparatively narrow view of what constitutes a social problem or a social answer. His own advocacy that he perform his technical role, and that others perform their roles so as not to produce role conflict or generate role ambiguity, will be supported by a general organizational bias toward ever greater rationality. This thrust toward greater rationality will be reflected in role-definition messages sent to policymakers by others besides the technologists involved in planning. At the same time, other experts, including that most important and rare expert, the generalist, will be drawing vociferous attention to the limits of the technologies, telling executives, planners, and administrators that competent and responsible role performance requires that they not depend too much on the technology, that they should define role competency in broader or different terms. And various groups in the environment will deprecate those technologies as too rationalized to be responsive to human needs and aspirations, too confining of the definition of a social problem or its solution. The blends of technique and intuition that role senders will define as acceptable for specifying various decision-making and planning roles will be in continuing ferment, and those filling the relevant roles will find themselves confused and in conflict.[18]

The level of ethical understanding to be deemed appropriate for the roles we are examining will be a perplexing and abrasive question. The issue revolves not only around questions of legitimacy, but arises from an appreciation of the

growing power humans have to intervene in their societal
processes, even though we are essentially ignorant about how
to anticipate the consequences of our actions. It also arises from
a growing awareness that decisions regarding the long-range future
must be made with full awareness of our ignorance. To be sure,
socio-historical conceptual systems like Marxism and religion make
anticipated futures the basis for present actions,
and for the ethics that justifies them. But in the United States
we believed that the future would take care of us, that destiny
was on our side.[19] Now that image of the future is changing;
future conjectures present us with alternative images of the
future, and require that we choose between them. We will no longer
be able to act as if we were ignorant of our options, or
as if we expect the future to work itself out to our benefit. Thus,
explicit valuing and choosing between values will have to become
self-conscious acts surrounded by ethical controversy, and
fraught with complexity and emotionality.

The pressures to plan, along with the exhilarating and
devastating experiences of trying to learn to plan, will begin to
change our sense of human priorities and tradeoffs; and this will
change the ethical bases for choosing one approach or problem
rather than another.

The very idea of an experimenting society is rich in ethical
dilemmas, at least within the present cultural setting; and as
attempts are made to change toward future-responsive societal
learning, those dilemmas have to be faced and learned from.[20]
Which persons or groups are to get which resources or what ends?
Under what circumstances do unborn generations have rights to
survival and amenities that override our own "rights" to alter
ourselves and our natural environment? Differing definitions,
arising from self and from professional, environmental, and
managerial role senders, will assert that decisions should be based
on one or another ethic — as we see in the controversies over
legalized abortion and marijuana. There will be definitions of role
competence that stress pragmatic skill over ethics (or require the
capacity to blur ethical distinctions), definitions that stress action
rather than reflection, and so on. Workable ethical systems,

infused with the power and insight of wise people, have slowly evolved through trial and error; but those involved in changing over to long-range social planning will face the burden of deliberately trying to discover viable ethical principles. For people who have been protected from that obligation by working within large organizations, this will be a heavy burden indeed. For some, the obligation to be especially enlightened about ethical theory and practice is certain to bring them into conflict with others who assiduously try to avoid the introduction of that kind of complication in the performance of their roles.[21]

Accepting a role definition that highly regards the abilities and obligations to encourage and to use interpersonal skills (Chapter 8), and sustaining the opportunity costs and personal stress involved in using them, will be more of a problem for those at the top, but it is will also be a problem at the middle levels of government organizations. Middle-level managers and administrators will increasingly be exposed to definitions of role competence that emphasize these skills. Some are learning, and more will learn these skills as part of their professional training, and in exposure to other professionals in the applied behavioral and management sciences. But for years to come, many effective managers will reject these techniques, and will fear exposing themselves to the experiences through which they can be learned.

To the extent that senior people in an organization are older people, secure in a self-image that has evolved in conventional organizational-environment settings, they will have more trouble changing their role definitions to include interpersonal competencies. Their own role-definition messages tell them that they are where they are because they "get things done" by intellectual superiority, or charismatic domination, or finesse at interpersonal manipulation, or by ruthlessness. A large part of the self-image of their role has to do with their "poker playing" skills and their belief in and ability to capitalize on the organizational norms that made success dependent on such role-performance definitions. Seldom, if ever, have they been rewarded for sharing power, being open, trusting or engendering trust, or being honest. But interpersonal skills necessary for supporting a learning norm require these competencies; and successful development of group task skills requires allocation of substantial opportunity costs, extending over several years, to learning those skills and restructuring the organization to use them.

Role Effectiveness

Most important, it takes explicit commitment from the top to provide the supportive atmosphere needed if the training is to be more than ritual, or is not to fade out altogether. What little evidence there is makes it clear that the same kind of commitment is necessary for any serious effort at planning to make any headway: the participation of top personnel in the training or planning efforts. Otherwise, the unavoidable message is that those below need it, but those at the top do not. This defeats the very intent of the training, because it is always clear to those below that those at the top need the training at least as much as they do. If the top avoids such involvement, then the whole effort becomes defined as ritual, and no one will take the political risks or the time, or make the psychological effort involved, to gain the greater group-task competences that can be provided by such training. If the training is mad obligatory by top management, as it sometimes has been, the purpose is also foiled, because coercion is not compatible with learning the conditions for openness and trust that the training is supposed to provide.

Thus the role definitions that many people at the top accept as applying to them, and which they and their peers apply to each other, will conflict with role definitions advocated by growing numbers of people that top administrators and executives also pay attention to: professionals, clients, some other top executives, highly competent junior executives, consumer spokesmen, and writers for the prestigious media. These will more frequently insist that top people are truly skilled and competent only if they develop interpersonal skills. But the role conflict will become even more poignant and pressing. In all large organizations, and certainly in government, conventional executive role performance requires repressing feelings of uncertainty, to say nothing of not sharing those feelings with others; it requires repressing acknowledgment of error; and it requires discouraging the expression of strong feelings about values. Thus role style will conflict with the psychological need executives will feel to share their distress over environmental and organizational conditions that appear, in their way, to threaten the viability of conventional top management roles.

1. Lichtman , C. and R. Hunt. "Personality and Organization Theory: A Review of Some Conceptual Literature." *Psychological Bulletin*, 76 (1971), p. 151.

2. Kahn, R. et al. Organizational Stress: Studies in Role Conflict and Ambiguity. New York: Wiley, 1964, pp. 25-26.

3. Ibid, pp. 70-71.

4. Ibid, pp. 25-26.

5. Ibid, p. 71.

6. McQuade, W. "What Stress Can Do to You." *Fortune*, 85(1) (1972), p. 102. *See also* French, J. and R. Caplan. "Psychosocial Factors in Coronary Heart Disease." *Industrial Medicine*, 39(9) (1970).

7. Kahn, op. cit., p. 127.

8. Ibid, p. 161.

9. *See* Slater, P. *The Pursuit of Loneliness*. Boston: Beacon Press, 1970. *See also* Bell, D. "The Cultural Contradictions of Capitalism." *The Public Interest*, (21) (Fall 1970).

10. On education for these experiences, *see* Erber, E. (ed.), *Urban Planning in Transition*, Part III. New York: Grossman, 1970.

11. Rein, M. "Social Planning: The Search for Legitimacy." *Journal of the American Institute of Planners*, 35 (1969), p. 242.

12. Hirschmann, A. *Exit, Voice, and Loyalty: Responses to Decline in Firms, Organizations, and States*. Cambridge: Harvard University Press, 1970, pp. 92-93. *See also* Flacks, R. "Protest or Conform: Some Social Psychological Perspectives on Legitimacy." Journal of Applied Behavioral Science, 5(2) (1969).

13. Burns, T. and G. Stalker. *The Management of Innovation*. London: Tavistock, 1961, p. 135.

14. A most perceptive exercise in delineating different definitions of role competence is found in Archibald, K. "Three Views of the Expert's Role in Policymaking: Systems Analysis, Incrementalism, and the Clinical Approach." *Policy Sciences*, 1 (1970). *See also* Gans, H. "The Need for Planners Trained in Policy Formation." *Urban Planning in Transition*, ed. E. Erber. New York: Grossman, 1970, pp. 239-245.

15. For a look at the past, *see* Marris, P. and Rein, M. *Dilemmas of Social Reform*. New York: Atherton, 1967. For conjectures about the future, *see* Marini, F. (ed.) *Toward a New Public Administration*. Scranton, Pa.: Chandler, 1971.

16. *See* Peabody, R. and F. Rourke, "Public Bureaucracies," *Handbook of Organizations*, ed. J. March. Chicago: Rand McNally, 1965. *See also* Wildavsky, A. *The Politics of the Budgetary Process*. Boston: Little, Brown, 1964.

17. Burns, R. "The Assessment of Technology as a Problem in the Distribution of Technical Expertise." Private paper, December 1971.

18. *See* Moynihan, D. "Counselor's Statement," *Toward Balanced Growth: Quantity with Quality*. Report of the National Goals Research Staff. Washington, D.C.: U.S. Government Printing Office, 1970. *See also* Archibald, op. cit.

19. *See* Heibroner, R. *The Future as History*. New York: Grove Press, 1959.

20. *See* Rivlin, A. *Systematic Thinking for Social Action*. Washington, D.C.: The Brookings Institution, 1971, pp. 108-119.

21. Boulding, K. "Ethics of Rational Decision." *Management Science*, 12(6) (1966). *See also* Tead, O. "The Ethical Challenge of Modern Administration," *Ethics and Bigness*, eds. H. Cleveland and H. Laswell. New York: Harper and Row, 1962.

8

The Necessity for Greater Interpersonal Competence

Acknowledging uncertainty, embracing error, and changing roles are not only individual acts calling for intrapersonal strength and skill. In the context of changing over to long-range social planning, they are *interpersonal* transactions. They depend on reciprocal competencies.

Feedback from a problem-filled present and a future full of questions carries a potential threat to preferred programs and the deeply held beliefs they incorporate. This ever-present potential for goal and program changes threatens the survival of socially supportive groupings that are attached to potentially disposable tasks. Resistance to the conditions that produce these threats can be lowered only if people have others with whom they can share their fear and anxiety, and find the imagination and support to risk experimenting in order to learn anew. But sharing to promote creativity and learning under such conditions of stress and conflict depends on trust and emotional support, which in turn depend on interpersonal openness. Openness requires the occasion and the ability to express strong emotion: feelings of commitment, fear, enthusiasm, and anxiety; feelings of rejection, anger, hostility, and affection; and feelings about ideas, actions, and persons.

Changing toward long-range social planning will depend on the ability of people and organizations to sustain far more trust, openness, emotional support, and expression of strong feelings. Unless people increase their interpersonal competence in these areas, and unless there are changes in organizational structures that support and encourage such competence, the resistance to meeting the requirements for long-range social planning will be invincible.

EVIDENCE OF INTERPERSONAL INCOMPETENCE

In order to appreciate why lack of interpersonal competence will result in resistance to changing toward long-range social planning, let us look at some research findings. Despite ritual protest or honest disagreement from people unaccustomed to interpersonal effectiveness, the evidence points one way: to endemic interpersonal incompetence and organizational structures that sustain it when it comes to giving and accepting trust, openness, support, and feelings. As Warren Bennis has noted:

Americans, in general, pay fulsome lip service to all forms of cooperation, teamwork, togetherness, etc. The problem is that there is no social translation of this ethic. Indeed, many observers of the American cultural scene point to the discrepancy between individualism, as expressed in Jeffersonian democracy, and cooperation, as expressed in the original confederation of states. The resultant dilution of both ethics is what David Reisman calls "antagonistic cooperation": we feign harmony and act autonomy.

This is no easy conflict to resolve. There is a necessary dialectic between the individual and the group, identity and community. . . . The problem of [horizontal] collaboration presses. As professional workers join large-scale organizations in increasing numbers, as tasks become more complex and interdependent, as diverse specialists come together for relatively short periods of time to solve problems, as responsibilities become too complex for one man`s comprehension, new social inventions of collaboration are imperative. . . .

The problems of vertical collaboration stem from qualitatively different stresses than the horizontal type. Predominantly, a superior controls the means to the need satisfaction of his subordinates. From this basic structural fact springs all the difficulties which separate bosses from employees, fathers from sons. Experience and research demonstrate conclusively that subordinates tend to withdraw and/or suppress views that are at variance with those of the boss, invent political solutions rather than engage in joint problem solving, allow their superiors to make mistakes, even when they, the subordinates, know better. For their part, superiors desire an atmosphere of trust in order to encourage authentic communication, but they rarely understand how to create and maintain — or even trust — this atmosphere. . . . research demonstrates that upward communication depends on three factors: (1) trust between superior and subordinate, (2) the perceived power of the superior from the point of view of the subordinate, and (3) the ambition of the subordinate. To the extent that the superior and the subordinate do not trust each other, to the extent that the subordinate sees the superior as having higher power, and to the extent that the subordinate is highly ambitious, upward communication is restricted. In short, power without trust is the main condition of poor communication between ranks.[1]

In a summary of several of his own field studies, Chris Argyris supports and extends Bennis' observations. From his field studies Argyris infers:

Individuals did not, nor did group norms, support their owning up to their feelings, being open to their own and others' feelings. There was almost no experimenting with ideas and feelings and also no trust existing in the groups. Rarely did individuals help others to own up to, be open with, and experiment with ideas and feelings. People rarely said what they believed about the important issues if they perceived them to be potentially threatening to any member. They preferred to be "diplomatic," "careful," "not to make waves." Under these conditions, valid information about unimportant issues (task or interpersonal) was easy to obtain. It was very difficult to obtain valid information regarding important issues (task or interpersonal). It was very difficult to problem solve effectively about these important issues since people tended to cover up important information. Also, individuals rarely received valid information about threatening issues.

The game of telling people what they "should" hear and the consequent lack of valid information understandably led individuals to be blind about their impact upon others.[2]

Argyris concludes that these behavior characteristics are sustained by typical beliefs about organizational efficacy, held by people who behave that way:

These data suggest that individuals tend to hold three basic values about effective interpersonal relations. They are:

1. In any given interpersonal relationship or group, the important behavior is that behavior that is related to the accomplishment of the purpose or task of the relationship or of the group.

2. Human effectiveness increases as people are rational and intellective. Human effectiveness decreases as people focus on interpersonal feelings and/or behave emotionally.

3. The most effective way to tap human energy and gain human commitment is through leadership that controls, rewards, and penalizes, and coordinates human behavior.[3]

Echoing Bennis, Argyris further observes:

We may tentatively infer, therefore, that the "typical" interpersonal universe tends to be populated with individuals, groups, and organizations that tend to create an interpersonal world in which the conditions facilitating effective interpersonal relationships tend to be infrequent. Effective interpersonal relationships tend to be conceived in terms similar to the superior-subordinate relationship. At any given moment, A, if he is effective, is carefully and covertly diagnosing B (since openness is not sanctioned) and is acting on his unilaterally determined attributions about B. The individuals also tend to be blind to the negative impact of their relatively low degree of openness, expression of feelings, risk taking, and the low potency of the norms of individuality and trust. Indeed, they tend to see these concomitants as "natural."[4]

The literature is replete with research substantiating such devastating evidence about the way people typically behave toward one another, and the beliefs about appropriate interpersonal behavior.[5] Nevertheless, it is demonstrably within the realm of normal human behavior for people in groups to be more trusting, open, supportive, and self-knowledgeable, and to expose themselves to strong feelings and strong interpersonal conflicts. Argyris reports on some of his research findings:

T groups began with the typical [interpersonally incompetent] pattern and after several sessions, if successful, developed the atypical pattern . . . in which feelings are expressed and risks are taken; in which helping others to own, to be open, and to experiment occurs; and in which the norms of conformity and antagonism become less

potent whiles the norms of individuality and trust become more
potent [i.e., Pattern B behavior].

. . . The phrase "if successful" is emphasized because not all T
groups become effective; indeed by our scoring methods a minority
develop into Pattern B. Task-oriented groups have also been changed
to produce B interaction patterns. The development of Pattern B
therefore is not limited to T groups.[6]

Such findings are not limited to Argyris' work or to
T-group techniques. Other approaches used by other
practitioners and researchers have also been effective.[7] Too few
definitive tests of these procedures have yet been made, and there
has been very little application undertaken within government.
The facilitating organizational structures to reinforce and effectively
use the training are for the most part undeveloped, and under
conventional arrangements the rewards have discouraged frequent
experiment of this type, which is necessarily risky and
uncomfortable.

People need other kinds of interpersonal skills training than
they conventionally receive in this society, but organizational
structures must be changed to use and sustain that training.
Argyris' observations emphasize that interpersonal incompetence is
sustained by the structures within which men express or repress
themselves:

New developments for rational decision-making often produce
intense resentment in men who ordinarily view themselves as
realistic, flexible, definitely rational. Managers and executives who
place a premium on rationality, and work hard to subdue
emotionality, become resistant and combative in the back-alley ways
of bureaucratic politics when such new technologies are introduced.

These reactions sound paradoxical. Yet they stem from ingrained,
almost unconscious processes in American organizational life. Waves
of fear, insecurity, and tenacious resistance arise unbidden from the
bowels of the organization. Strange but true.

It`s also understandable in human terms. It does not happen
because men are stupid. It happens because of their long and
successful education in organizational survival, where they learn

deceit, manipulation, rivalry, and mistrust — qualities endemic to our present organizational structures.[8]

Bennis elaborates:

Information and understanding are necessary but not sufficient components for inducing change. More is required if the change is to affect important human responses. For human changes are bound up in self- image and its maintenance and the complicated context of the social life and groupings which help to define and give meaning to the individual's existence. If intended change is perceived to threaten (or enhance) the self-image, then we can expect differential effects. If an intended change is perceived as threatening the social life space of the individual, then safeguards must be undertaken which ensure new forms of gratification and evaluation.

In short, I am saying that human changes affect not only the individual but also the social fabric and norms from which he gains his evaluation and definition of self. It means, quite probably, that thinking solely about the individual's understanding of the change and its consequences is not enough.[9]

Organizational studies by T. Burns and G. Stalker lead them to the following comments, which emphasize the links between interpersonal incompetence and organizational structure — and in passing, emphasize also the special stress these contribute when an organization is trying to change itself to respond to a changing environment:

The translation of organizational difficulties surrounding the person into charges which can be made against others, or a technical problem of relationships into an emotional one, is a characteristic human process familiar enough when it is worked out in terms of national or international politics or inter-class or inter-racial conflicts. This is not to say, of course, that the reverse is true, that all emotional difficulties are resolvable into technical problems. Nor does it permit the emotional charges engendered by the process to be written off as irrelevant or superficial. People are often unfair to subordinates and others, ignorant where they assume knowledge, prone to see dangers or hostility in situations where none threatens, or clumsy and insensitive, or selfish, or lazy, and the people with whom they deal will dislike them for it. Yet what we have described was a general process repeated in a number of different firms, with very different casts performing very similar sets of parts. The recurrent appearance of a number of similar difficulties which were construed by informants in terms of the personal characters of other people suggested very strongly that the cause lay in what was observably common — the situation and the organizational vicissitudes of the concern. The origins of the trouble, also, dated from the introduction of the development group into the concerns, when, we must assume, there was a general willingness on the part of top management and the newcomers, to make the new venture succeed, and at least a chance of gaining the support of other members of the concern for an effort aimed at improving its chances of survival.[10]

It is important to reemphasize the effect of organizational structure on interpersonal behavior, lest the perspective be lopsided. It must also be emphasized that while there is evidence that people can become interpersonally competent, there is no theory for deliberately designing organizational structures so that, when combined with the operating requirements for using the organization's technology, members can optimally use their improved interpersonal skills. There are organizations that have invented arrangements that have led to improvements in their performance. Out of these experiments and others, informed by the requirements for changing over to long-range social planning, should have come some tolerable theories for designing better systems. With these should come better chances for the acceptance of the requirements for changing toward long-range social planning.

Before examining the implications for organizational structure, it is useful to look briefly at specific examples of situations that necessitate much greater interpersonal competence if the requirements for changing toward long-range social planning are to be met.

EXPRESSING AND COPING WITH FEELINGS

Almost all aspects of the requirements for long-range social planning are bound to elicit strong feelings; this is especially true of goal-setting, evaluation, and program changes. If there is no opportunity to express feelings in connection with the circumstances that elicit them, they will be displaced into other activities, thereby complicating and obstructing them."[11] Strongly felt differences over goals or means, which are transformed instead into "logical" or "political" attitudes, or which are simply ignored and left vaguely unsettled, inevitably seem to arise, wrapped in circumstantial camouflage, to corrode and destroy subsequent programs. Societal learning will not occur under such conditions, because neither positive nor negative feelings are explicitly and constructively included as part of the information needed for choosing alternatives and priorities. If feelings are excluded, the activity becomes a charade, a ritual, a game, or a means to other ends. Whatever the choices made or actions taken, people will impute intentions that cannot be validated, and the occasions for distrust will multiply.

This is and will be especially so in the public arena, where sub-cultural differences of age, color, education, lifestyle, and income will contribute to different values, different feelings about those values, and different styles of expressing those feelings. The insistence by nonprofessional lay persons that their feelings get into the activities in which they participate with professionals, exasperates and threatens the professionals. The professionals' transparently unsupportive or misdirected responses generate hostility and distrust among the lay people. Usually neither group is trained in the skills needed to use feelings constructively. Without such training, either the *expression* or the *repression* of feelings, as part of the dialogue and issue, tends to increase rather than reduce turbulence and complexity. Consider the complications that occur when people impose on "establishment" types arguments containing feelings, without also working on the problem raised by the inability of these more conventional persons to deal effectively with emotionally-laden messages. However, training *can* help.[12]

When professionals — particularly bureaucrats, administrators, managers, and technical consultants — meet among themselves, the problem arises differently. Inside the organization, feelings simply are not verbally expressed; or if they are, it is assumed that the person is acting, not "really" feeling.

There is no easy way to tell if it is "an act," because the participants are too unskilled at working in group situations involving feelings, too unwilling to trust themselves or others with real feelings, and too anxiety-ridden to probe more deeply in a situation where the probers would not know what they were getting into. "It just isn't done, and it's not the way to get things done."

When feelings are consciously or unconsciously excluded, self-respect withers — along with commitment, willingness, and eagerness to risk the self in learning how to plan in a turbulent society. When strong feelings go unexpressed or remain unengaged because they are successfully (though perhaps inadvertently) ignored by those who should respond to them, they turn back upon their source and enfeeble it. In our culture, emotional depression, which destroys vitality and creativity, seems to be the usual consequence of not expressing or acting on what one feels strongly. Those feelings of depression arise from the self-disparagement, the self-hate we feel for not respecting our own feelings, which are at very core of our sense of self.[13] In many people this feeling of self-disrespect is projected outward into feelings of hostility toward the person and circumstances that ignored those feelings. Whatever way, creativity and learning are frustrated, and distrust and interpersonal ambiguity increased — so that changing toward long-range social planning is further resisted or avoided altogether.

Feelings associated with conflict cannot be eliminated by repressing, obscuring, or ignoring them. But they can be managed productively by making them part of the activity in which they arise. Otherwise they generate further feelings of distrust, self-hate, hostility, or cynicism, and they encourage short-sighted manipulativeness. As Bennis notes:

Basically, conflict arises from two structural sources: (1) vertical, between ranks; (2) horizontal or between various groups and departments. Bureaucratic strategy for resolving vertical conflicts depends solely on a vague "law of hierarchy," and an unvague implication: when in doubt, the boss decides. The bureaucratic strategy for horizontal disputes depends on the equally vague "law of coordination," with an assist from the "rule of hierarchy" when the former fails. In other words, the boss arbitrates and then rules.

There is a third, more informal, rule that is typically practiced as a last resort. The boss calls the disputants together and invokes the "rule of loyalty" for the general good. The "rule of loyalty" is a curious one, for more often than not its effects are undesirable and tensions are aggravated, rather than relieved. One of the basic, but often unrecognized, paradoxes of organizational life is that its chief device of integration tends to induce excessive in-group cohesiveness at the price of intergroup cooperation.[14]

When conflicts in feelings are openly acknowledged, they become part of the information-defining options, expectations, and operating styles of the task. Often they can stimulate new ideas that reconcile the conflict. In any event, open recognition of feelings increases trust, and reduces ambiguity and confusion in enormously complex and uncertain situations.

I am not arguing that feelings must be the only basis for engaging in the activities comprising long-range social planning. Far from it. I am arguing that if feelings cannot be openly expressed and effectively included among the factors that go into those activities, then two things will happen: the activities will be far weaker and ineffective than they need be; and acknowledging uncertainty, embracing error, setting goals, evaluating programs, and other such requirements for social planning, will be impossible.

Offering Support

Interpersonal skills are also necessary to supply the emotional support people need to risk the role changes that long-range social planning requires, and to live meaningfully in the midst of the conflict and ambiguity that such role changes trigger. Changing one's roles in the direction required for long-range social planning means more or less risking the reconstruction of one's self-image, which often is frightening to undertake. For example, the crucial and protean function of spanning boundaries (see Chapter 12) is sure to be an ambiguous and conflict-laden role. Adopting it is certain to generate strong feelings in both the boundary spanners and their constituencies. These people depend heavily on the spanners for information, but fear the autonomy and power they wield through real or fancied understanding of what is really going on across the contending and collaborating groups. Filling that role calls for especially good interpersonal skills, both from boundary spanners and those they span. It demands support from others — support that can be trusted to be honest and perceptive in its evaluation of what is happening to the persons who are changing their roles amidst conflict and ambiguity. Honesty and perception require both self-understanding and the understanding of others, as well as the skill to combine these into supportive and relevant interpersonal transactions.

Help is another form of support that people in this society manage very poorly. *Giving* help without patronizing or depreciating the recipient is difficult for us to do. *Receiving* help without resisting or feeling submissive is equally difficult. People giving help are anxious about being rejected, and people accepting help are anxious about being dominated. This form of interpersonal incompetence is regularly displayed in almost any group setting when members try to "be helpful" by introducing an idea or suggestion for advancing the task at hand. Unless the group has learned how to give and accept help, or unless its members have worked together long enough to have learned how much they can trust each other, a new idea will be "shot down" by being ignored, attacked, or transformed into something else without checking with the originator as to what was really meant. On the other side, the person proffering the idea will do so diffidently, aggressively, or loquaciously, depending on his or her learned style for trying to anticipate the reaction. Indeed, many persons will not risk offering help or responding to it, in order to avoid the experiences that go along with the process. More effective giving and receiving of help can be learned by using the techniques for overcoming the various forms of interpersonal incompetence described here.[15]

In the society envisioned here, we will have to depend on highly imaginative ideas that have little, if any, support in "hard" data and reliable theory. Necessarily, these ideas will have to derive from feelings, intuition, and "hunch," more than from logic. A willingness and desire to help by sharing and by urging "way out" ideas — especially those based on intuition, hunch, and feelings, unprotected by a shield of logic — will depend on the proposer's estimate of how far he can trust his audience to respond supportively. Putting one's intuitions on the table almost anywhere (and certainly in a government agency) takes courage, trust, commitment, and high hope. Therefore intuitions are usually presented in disguised form, as the result of logical analysis, or as implications for policy decisions. By appearing to be more solid and less "hunchy" than they really are they lose some of the power they might have to stimulate the intuition of others. To offer an intuition or a hunch "raw," so to speak, would be an invitation to subtle or openly derisive undermining by colleagues who are threatened or offended by the "illogical" source of the ideas, and the emotionally expressive style of presenting them. Indeed, under present conditions a person operating in a conventional setting would not even be likely to conceive of a new idea, especially a "wild" one. We will have to learn how to support and encourage those intuitive ideas in formal organizational contexts even though, at the same time, these contexts will be necessarily and increasingly pervaded and legitimized by the techniques and values of professionals who define themselves by their skills in explicit, data-based, logical thought.[16]

SELF-UNDERSTANDING

Self-understanding is a prerequisite for learning how to change over to long-range social society. The critical function of self-understanding as a prerequisite for undertaking other personal and interpersonal learning activities aimed at changeover is emphasized by C. Sofer. His numerous field studies of efforts at organizational change, and his own involvement in them, have led Sofer to propose that, in general,

One of the key events that discourage a group attempting to change is the discovery that significant changes can rarely be made merely by persuading other people to act differently. Sooner or later one must alter that last sacred object, oneself. Whatever has been said before, or acknowledged at the intellectual level, the impact of this depresses and retards the group.[17]

But that self-understanding can only be learned in relationships with other people; more precisely, it can only be verified and refined by practicing it in transactions with others. Interpersonal skills are needed to improve self-understanding, and self-understanding is needed to improve interpersonal skills. This is not a chicken-or-egg dilemma. Rather, it is a dialectical process that requires people to develop both skills through cycles of self-consciously working alone and together. This opportunity requires growing levels of interpersonal trust, and the openness of relationships that verifies that trust. As Argyris has observed:

The greater A's defensiveness, the less the probability that he will create conditions where he can receive helpful (descriptive nonevaluative) feedback [about his behavior]. However, the greater the defensiveness of B, the greater the probability that he will give distorted feedback to A. Thus, A is in a human bind. He will not learn unless he is willing and capable of learning, and unless B is willing and capable of helping him learn. He will not tend to be willing and capable unless A helps create the conditions in which B will not be highly defensive. The opposite is also the case. A cannot decrease B's sense of self-acceptance without hurting his own. If A hurts B, B will respond defensively, and the feedback A will receive will either be designed to hurt him or it will be distorted, which may have a negative effect on it.[18]

Greater self-understanding is imperative if we are to increase our ability to recognize and live with uncertainty, complexity, and error. Inherent value contradictions and ethical dilemmas that we hide from ourselves by avoiding uncertainty, denying error, and repressing conflict over values, goals, and organizational arrangements, become all too evident when we try to meet the requirements for long-range social planning. Struggling inside ourselves with value conflicts, and shifting our appreciative setting and behavior toward ourselves and the world are difficult, anxiety-producing experiences. Without interpersonal support, most of us will lack the will and strength to risk going along with changeover efforts; we will resist relearning on the "outside" because we would sense that it would cost us too much on the "inside."

SUBGROUP AFFILIATION

In situations where turbulent environments are mostly shut out and where knowledge is sufficient to maintain a stable relationship between the organization and its environment, that stability is reflected in the general stability of task groups within the organization. These task groups invariably evolve into *sentient groups* — groups that provide their members with the social rewards of membership. So great are the rewards, that any reorganization of task groups to meet changed goals usually proves to be personally disruptive, and people, tasks, and the organization as a whole suffer accordingly. In long-range social planning, regrouping becomes the norm rather than the exception, and those who participate in changeover efforts will have to learn how to depend less on permanent sentient groups and more on transient groups to provide the needed social support (see Chapter 10). Warren Bennis and Philip Slater emphasize this aspect of subgroup affiliation as follows:

> As routine tasks become automated, those requiring human participation will increasingly relate to the boundaries of current experience — to invention, ambiguity, unusual synthesis, catastrophic changes, and so on. This means that the skills required will include larger quantities of creativity, imagination, social perception, and personal insight, and will hence draw upon all layers of the personality with maximum involvement and commitment. Such involvement will tend to drive other social affiliations out — temporary systems will inherently be what Lewis Coser calls "greedy organizations" — but only temporarily so. Instead of partial commitment to a relatively large number of groups over a relatively long period of time, we will see relatively total commitment to a single group over a short time period — the organizational equivalent of "serial monogamy" (in which a person may have several spouses but only one at a time) replacing a kind of organizational polygamy.[19]

This too will call for interpersonal skills in quickly establishing trust, openness, and support for feelings and ideas in new or transient group affiliations. A very few research and development firms, which Miller and Rice consider the prototype of this kind of relationship) are already investing in trying to develop such skills.

Trust

In Chapter 14 we shall look at the sources of resistance that may arise over changes in the management of an organization's information resources that would be required to facilitate moving toward long-range social planning. This resistance has to do with who is to have access to what data and the programs for using them. This is already a chronic problem, especially with urban data banks. Data give power, and those who have data do not trust those who do not, to use data in ways that protect the interests and aspirations of those who do. Those who do not have the data distrust the interests and aspirations of those who do, and distrust the motives the data-possessors have toward them. The result, so far, is just what might be predicted in hierarchical, closed, environment-avoiding, error-avoiding systems, which discourage trust and openness. The trusting relationships needed to overcome these and related counterproductive conditions cannot be imposed by fiat, and they cannot be created simply by imposing "experiments" in data sharing. Such experiments are being made, but the fundamental distrust apparently continues. The openness and trust required for changing toward long-range social planning will have to come about as a general consequence of improved interpersonal skills, along with organizational restructuring that would reinforce new norms based on more trust.

Collaboration — not only for data sharing, but at all stages of long-range social planning — requires what R. Walton calls a "problem-solving decision process." [20] Reviewing an array of research and theory, Walton arrives at a number of propositions suggesting that collaboration that produces flexibility, experimentation, interaction, supportiveness, and positive affect, also further enhances trust; while bargaining produces the opposite situation. [21] As a result, he concludes that:

Under conditions of hostility and low trust, persons will adopt competitive behavior strategies in the decision process. For example, one adopts decision patterns which involve furnishing another with less information and less accurate information when one dislikes or distrusts the other. . . . Negative attitudes lead to perceptual distortions, which in turn lead to competitive decision-making. . . . Strong negative affect often leads one unit to interfere with the other unit's activities, just to frustrate the latter's goal achievement.[22]

Distrust is an endemic operative in government processes, as was knowingly delineated by Aaron Wildavsky in his description of the various styles by which agencies go politicking for their budgets.[23] There is good evidence that distrust grew in the United States between 1964 and 1969, especially towards politics, peacekeeping, and communications.[24] And whatever other factors lead to confrontation politics, persistent mutual distrust is certainly one of them. Whether distrust must always be part of confrontation is unclear. Do different appreciations of a situation invariably engender distrust, or might they be the basis for joint learning through societal experimenting? There seems to be no good reason why conflict must breed distrust, if the conflict is dealt with openly for the purpose of resolving it and learning from it. To what extent can organizational experiments aimed at increasing internal trust be sustained, if distrust is brought into the organization via those members of the environment involved in the process of long-range social planning? Indeed, to what extent can trust be extended within the organization, as more of its members bring into the organizational setting the values and roles rooted in their environmental allegiances? These are questions that can only be answered by deliberate efforts at learning to do long-range social planning. The problem is that societal learning depends on improving the level of trust. Fortunately, it is possible to gain improvements in the ability to trust; it remains to be seen whether the improvements would be sufficient to permit and encourage moving toward long-range social planning.

The methods of organizational development alluded to earlier have already demonstrated their usefulness for improving interpersonal competence in a number of corporations and third-sector organizations. If the thesis of this book is correct, the rewards of conventional, interpersonally-incompetent behavior will decrease, while the pressures to try changing toward long-range social planning will increase. Therefore I expect increased incentives to design person-structure-technology systems that reward interpersonal competence, and more incentives for organizations, especially government agencies, to try them out.

1. Bennis, W. *Changing Organizations*. New York: McGraw-Hill, 1966, pp. 199-202.

2. Argyris, C. "The Incompleteness of Social-Psychological Theory: Examples from Small Group, Cognitive Consistency, and Attribution Research." *American Psychologist*, 1969, 24(10), pp. 895-896.

3. Ibid, p. 899.

4. Ibid, p. 900.

5. *See*, for example, any of the works of Argyris, Bennis, Schein, or Rice, or any issue of the *Journal of Applied Behavioral Science*.

6. Argyris, op. cit., p. 878.

7. Recent issues of the *Journal of Applied Behavioral Science* are illustrative. *See also* Rice, A.K. *Learning for Leadership*. London: Tavistock, 1965.

8. Argyris, C., "Resistance to Rational Management Systems." *Innovation*, 1970 (10), p. 29.

9. Bennis, op. cit., pp. 175-176.

10. Burns, T. and Stalker, G. *The Management of Innovation*. London: Tavistock, 1961, p. 143.

11. A.K. Rice's research at the Tavistock Institute, London, emphasized this phenomenon. For an earlier formulation of the process, *see* Rice, op. cit.

12. An extraordinary and so far apparently successful attempt to facilitate task skills among various representatives of the environment and the guiding organization, by exposing all participants to group process skill training has been the Hartford Development Project, under the guidance of the American City Corporation, Columbia, Maryland, 1972. M. Hoppenfeld tells me that the training vastly facilitated working on touchy issues openly and effectively, and as a result generated great commitment to the tasks.

13. *See* the classic Horney, K. *The Neurotic Personality of Our Time*. New York: Norton, 1937.

14. Bennis, op. cit., p. 199.

15. One of the most striking and effective learning devices available in this area is a "game" called "The Helping Hand Strikes Again." Invented by Prof. F. Goodman, School of Education, University of Michigan, it has been used to teach schoolchildren and social workers, among others, how badly people give and receive help, and how to do it well.

16. For an elegant description of the relationship between logical and nonlogical thinking in connection with decision-making, see Barnard, C. Appendix ("Mind in Everyday Affairs"), *The Functions of an Executive.* Cambridge: Harvard University Press, 1938, pp. 301-322. *See also* Gore, W. *Administrative Decision-Making: A Heuristic Model.* New York: Wiley, 1966.

17. Sofer, C. *The Organization From Within.* Chicago: Quadrangle Books, 1962, p. 156. *See also* Jung, C. *Two Essays on Analytical Psychology.* Cleveland: World Publishing Co., 1956, pp. 204, 237-238, 276.

18. Argyris, C. *Interpersonal Competence and Organizational Effectiveness.* Homewood, Ill.: The Dorsey Press, 1962, p. 20.

19. Bennis, W. and P. Slater. *The Temporary Society.* New York: Harper and Row, 1968, pp. 92-93.

20. Walton, R. "Theory of Conflict in Lateral Organizational Relationships," *Operational Research and the Social Sciences,* ed. J. Lawrence. London: Tavistock, 1966, p. 414.

21. *See,* for example, Friedlander, F. "The Primacy of Trust as a Facilitator of Further Group Accomplishment." *Journal of Applied Behavioral Science,* 1970, 6(4), and Deutsch, M. "An Experimental Study of the Effects of Cooperation and Competition Upon Group Processes." *Human Relations,* 1949, 2, and Deutsch, M. "The Effect of Motivational Orientation Upon Trust and Suspicion." *Human Relations,* 1960, 13.

22. Walton, op. cit., pp. 423-24.

23. Wildavsky, A. *The Politics of the Budgetary Process.* Boston: Little Brown, 1964. (Chapter III is a fascinating recounting of the various devices by which those in the budgeting process trust each other to misrepresent facts, interests, and needs according to agreed-upon procedures, trusting to "process politics" to come out with the best solution on the average.) *See also* Schick, A. "Systems Politics and Systems Budgeting." *Public Administration Review,* 24(1) (1969).

24. *See* Rotter, J. "Generalized Expectancies for Interpersonal Trust." *American Psychologist,* 26(5) (1971).

⋆ Part Three ⋆

The Burdens of Change:
Structural and Organizational

9

Organizational Restructuring
and the Social Environment

Part of the environment may be represented by organizations that act as boundary spanners between clients and targeted government organizations. Another part may be the diffuse collections of people who are the deliberate or inadvertent beneficiaries – or victims of governmental activities. These people may from time to time organize into specific interest groups or into competing groups with the same interests.[1] Here, we will limit our attention to conjectures about the structural requirements for linking servicing organizations and publics, and the implications of these requirements for overcoming social psychological resistances to long-range social planning. My primary emphasis will be on how these organizations are affected, though I will note, too, some complications for the environment. The magnitude of the linking requirement and the need for it are summarized in terms compatible with my approach by D. and A. Wilson:

We live in a culture that focuses on decisions and decision makers. Our status ladder's top rung is for the executive; our highest rewards are for those who make our choices. In emphasizing the opting, we too frequently ignore the options. We relegate to a subsidiary role the generating of the alternatives among which the choice must lie and the testing of whether the candidate options adequately exhaust the possibilities open to us or do justice to our creative powers. In emphasizing the optors, we also too frequently ignore the criteria by which the choices are made. We tend to leave unexamined the unprogrammed pressures that intrude into the decision making process. The spotlighting of the most dramatic part of the action — the decision itself serves to render less visible the rest of the action; the decision maker, the decisions already existing in the decision making process, and in the yardsticks or pressures by which the choice is made.

In order to bring into perspective these overlooked but vital components of choice governing our movement into the future, we must bring before our citizenry the germinal ideas, the research programs, the unfolding trends, the prospective opportunities, the incipient threats, possibilities, probabilities, forecasts — all of the ingredients that go together to generate our options. We must view these ingredients and their implications not when the newspapers tell us that they have arrived as options on the decision makers' desks, but as long beforehand as is possible in order that they may be understood, discussed, assessed, and given appropriate support or opposition according to our preferences. Participation in the generation and assessment of options is the citizen's responsibility in a democracy. Citizen participation cannot be secured only through expression of choice after options are printed on a ballot. By then, the future has to a large degree already been shaped. In an age of rapid change a way must be found for the citizen to participate in the generation and selection of the options.[2]

· Certain social trends and circumstances are especially important as the context for relations between the environment and servicing organizations. As an increasing number of educated people become more and more aware of the tension between social costs and benefits in any given program or policy, the demands of special-interest and consumer-oriented groups will proliferate. These demands will be intensified by the availability of increased amounts of social indicator data on who is getting, or not getting, what. This information explosion will be augmented by laws that facilitate citizens' rights in criticizing and pressuring government agencies and private corporations. Challenges regarding their commitment, legitimacy, and competency are partly the legacy of an endemic distrust of government and large organizations of all sorts. Efforts to avoid changing norms and structures (especially in government) and the continuing exposure of incompetence and duplicity will sustain that distrust. The growth in the number of professionals eager to assume advocacy roles means that the public will be able to draw upon a pool of skilled professionals who know what information and services to demand on behalf of their clients and what to do with the information when they get it.[3]

The public interests represented by these advocates and by organizations, especially voluntary organizations with their component of skilled professionals, will increasingly demand access to public-agency planning activities and information about these agencies' intentions, ongoing programs, and evaluative feedback. They will often be in a position to supply their own data and propose their own plans, such as advocacy planning for the poor and a wide spectrum of public-service watchdog groups.

Some groups will make short-run demands, while others will demand long-range organizational responses (though they may not be recognized as such). Meeting demands for immediate action may actually require long-range social planning, while some allegedly "long-range issues" may not be long range at all. Certain demands by the poor for immediate relief and demands by the affluent for preservation of the natural environment are contrasting examples. Part of the structuring task will be to arrange organizational-environmental relationships that encourage shifts in time perspectives appropriate to goals, means, and knowledge.

Organizations can respond to these demands by refusing to acknowledge them, by pretending to acknowledge them, or by collaborating with the demanders to cope with the situation. On the face of it, it doesn't appear that organizations can pursue the first course indefinitely and still survive. As to the second course, no government agency is able to sufficiently secure its internal workings and its data base to protect itself from exposure, as congressional efforts to increase public access to information, and the chronic dribble of exposés and leaked reports amply demonstrates. Organizations will be unable to prevent leaks so long as there is an increase in the number of professionals inside the organization who do not rigidly separate their bureaucratic loyalties from their roles as members of the environment. Indeed, in a crunch, their loyalty will be more likely to go to the "consumer" than to the agency.

The third option, then, seems to be the one that organizations will have to learn to live with if they are not to suffer the pains of being exposed or displaced by more effective agencies. If they do try to respond, their effectiveness will depend on their ability to increase their boundary-spanning resources; to disseminate data, ideas, and plans, internally and externally; and to make the internal shifts in organization needed to respond to changes in present and anticipated clientele, service mixes, and evaluation approaches. This shift will not come easily for most planning staffs, which are already burdened with the overload that is the result of insufficient financial or statutory support, and of outmoded styles of planning. (The director of city planning in one large city expressed the mood of a number of his colleagues: "There are too many people around to meddle in too many city issues to get anything really in place.") Whatever other organizational functions these capabilities facilitate, they are crucial to meeting the requirements for changing over to future-responsive societal learning.

An example will illustrate the structural and psychosocial transformations involved. In response to advocate planning pressures to do thus-and-so, an agency, an administration, or a political party trying out a future-responsive societal learning approach states publicly: "We don't know the answers, and you can't prove that you do either. The task for both of us is to acknowledge our uncertainties and then design together experiments to resolve them." In this way, confrontation and loss of face are avoided and societal learning advanced. Under such circumstances, organizations trying to move toward long-range social planning may gain power, compared to organizations that refuse to change, because their relevant environments see them as choosing flexibility, open to alternatives and helpful in proposing alternatives.

Reducing public distrust and inventing effective means for members of the environment to participate in societal learning is very difficult, especially when the learning does not promise instant gratification. Effecting environmental changes seems even more difficult than overcoming organizational resistance, but if it cannot be done — and it becomes impossible to say whether society can evolve quickly in this direction — it seems to me that the whole enterprise of future-responsive societal learning becomes unfeasible. Organizations have not made this their mission because it has not been a purpose of society to adopt or implement such a goal. If some organizations were to adopt a stance of uncertainty-acknowledging, error-embracing other organizations in the environment would probably find it easier and more worthwhile to wait out the evolution of programs, while still supporting and being involved in a serious evaluation of those programs and their goals. Also, if an organization were trying to change toward long-range social planning, those of its members who also had strong roles in the environment could urge a supportive stance and help shift environmental appreciation to the need for future-responsive societal learning. Obviously, the whole of society cannot change over at once, but it is possible that certain members of it could change enough to find it rewarding to continue to do so, and hence find themselves in a positive feedback mode that accelerates the acceptance of future-responsive societal learning.[4] (See the Epilogue.)

Another component of the environment that requires restructuring if long-range social planning is to be attempted is that one comprised of other organizations, other government agencies, voluntary organizations, legislatures, and nongovernmental providers of funds. In examining this component, it should be emphasized that useful theory (to say nothing of research) on interorganizational processes is woefully inadequate. The conceptual problems are as basic as how to think about an organizational "boundary," especially in complex, interactive situations like those found in government organizations. As R. Tripathi notes:

> Most organization theorists concede that the environment of an organization is an important determinant of its behavior and functioning. Yet, it is true that environment has entered into the equation of organizational functioning only tangentially, often as a constant or a "given," but not as a variable.[5]

Statutory distinctions look good on the books, but they do not help, especially under changing conditions of the sort we are assuming. What is more, directives from legislatures to government agencies are sometimes deliberately, but usually inadvertently, contradictory or ambiguous, further obscuring and complicating a systematic understanding of the way organizational structures and norms, combined with the mix of bureaucratic and free-swinging interaction among their members, interact at the interorganizational level.[6]

Let us consider two other important observations. All organizations in the public sector will be faced with internal and external pressures for and against long-range social planning, but these do not come at the same time nor to the same degree. Nor will efforts to try to move toward long-range social planning, which may, in turn, influence the direction of further efforts, happen in the same sequence in all organizations. Second, all organizations face uncertainty about what other organizations are doing, and they are unclear about the degree to which they can collaborate or compete in anticipated future situations. This uncertainty will be the residue of traditional relationships between agencies, modified and complicated by shifts in norms and structures produced by attempts to introduce long-range social planning. Even without intending to do long-range social planning, their source of uncertainty will increase because they will find themselves having to apply the systems philosophy (in part because they are increasingly dependent on skilled persons who think in these terms). As a result, organizational mandates and the boundaries of their relevant environments, functions, and programs will become less clear.

Both collaboration and competition can be expected, and either can be constructive or destructive to changeover efforts. To the extent that working with environmental groups means opening up data and program information, one of the chief means of competition — privileged access to information — is eliminated or at least reduced. To the extent that specific environmental demands affect more than one organization, organizations will find it worthwhile to learn to collaborate.

There is an interesting dilemma to be noted here. Each organization needs more information about its environment, either to serve it effectively or to try to control it in the interests of organizational survival. More information becomes available if agencies pool information. But pooling reduces organizational autonomy, as the organization becomes increasingly dependent on more and more information, and begins to trade it with other agencies, corporations, and third-sector organizations.

As turbulence increases, along with uncertainty and the risk of error, organization members will become more inclined to share with other organizations the social psychological burdens of coping. Together, they may learn to embrace error and try to anticipate it through long-range social planning. As they collaborate, uncertainty about the intentions of other organizations will be reduced, and that rewarding state of affairs could in turn strengthen the incentives to move toward long-range social planning.

For government, increased collaboration will require rewriting of legislation and the reallocation of the prerogatives of congressional oversight, but the loss in control this represents for some representatives, who jealously protect their turf, could turn out to be in their interest by redistributing the burden of coping with error and uncertainty, in a world where it is increasingly difficult to hide either one. As older legislators are replaced by fresh faces, it is possible that the shift in perspective will open up the possibility of statutory and procedural innovation.

For many reasons, including the social psychological ones, this shift, this redistribution of power, this redefinition of what constitutes power, will not come about quickly or easily. Therefore, we must expect the conventional attractions of competition and efforts at organizational aggrandizement to persist. To a point, this is helpful to changeover efforts. If members of an organization see long-range social planning as a means for advancing their own interests, it gives them the impetus to change in that direction. Much planning that is to be done within organizations is not contingent on more cooperation from other organizations than is usually available. To be sure, in the absence of collaboration, uncertainty about the intentions of other organizations increases, but when long-range social planning is directed toward societal learning, one of the things learned is the cost of competition versus the cost of collaboration. Also, precisely because long-range social planning is a means for societal learning, competition between agencies or programs within agencies for the purposes of "proving" that one approach to a problem is more effective than another (or that both approaches together are more effective than either separately) can be a desirable aspect of the process, *if* learning remains the first priority.[7]

The structural requirements for interorganizational long-range social planning, along with their social psychological concomitants, seem similar to the requirements for effective relationship between organizations and the nonorganizational parts of their environments: much more boundary-spanning capability, shifts in organizational differentiation and integration, shifts in "products," and changes in management processes. The next few chapters will examine some of these specific requirements.

1. For a discussion of these matters and a substantial bibliography, see Etzioni, A. *The Active Society*. New York: The Free Press, 1968.

2. Wilson, D. and A. Wilson. "Toward the Institutionalization of Change." Institute for the Future, Working Paper 11. Middletown, Conn., 1967, p. 23.

3. *See* Arnstein, S. "A Ladder of Citizen Participation." *Journal of the American Institute of Planners* (July 1969). On the general question of participation of the environment in determining the future, see Cahn, E. and J. Cahn. "Citizen Participation," *Citizen Participation in Urban Development*, ed. H. Spiegel. Washington, D.C.: NTL Institute for Applied Behavioral Science, 1960; Clark, K. "Problems of Power and Social Change: Toward a Relevant Social Pathology." *Journal of Social Issues*, 21(3) (1965); Clark, T. "The Concept of Power: Some Overemphasized and Underrecognized Dimensions–An Examination with Special Reference to the Social Community." *Social Science Quarterly* (December 1967); Coser, L. *Functions of Social Conflict*. New York: The Free Press, 1956; Coser, L. *Continuities in the Study of Social Conflict*. New York: The Free Press, 1967; Edelston, H. and F. Kolodner. "Are the Poor Capable of Planning for Themselves?" Washington, D.C.: NTL Institute for Applied Behavioral Science, 1968; Gamson, W. *Power and Discontent*. Homewood, Ill.: Dorsey Press, 1968; and Pickering, G. "Voluntarism and the American Way." Center for a Voluntary Society, Occasional Paper 7. Washington, D.C., 1970.

4. On changes needed in structure and in the performance of the environment in order to allow more effective policymaking, see Dror, Y. *Public Policymaking Reexamined*. San Francisco: Chandler, 1968, Chapters 19 and 21. *See also* Friend, J. and W. Jessop. *Local Government and Strategic Choice*. London: Tavistock Publications; Sage Publications, 1969; Smelser, N. *Theory of Collective Behavior*. New York: The Free Press, 1972.

5. Tripathi, R. "A Review of Conceptualizations of Organizational Environment and Studies of Environment-Organization Relationships," (Manuscript prepared for University of Michigan's Organizational Psychology Program, December 1971).

6. *See* Lowi, T. *The End of Liberalism*. New York: W. W. Norton, 1969. Some admirable tussles with interorganizational processes are exemplified by Evan, W. "The Organization-Set: Toward a Theory of Interorganizational Relations," *Approaches to Organizational Design*, ed. J. Thompson. Pittsburgh: University of Pittsburgh Press, 1966; Halperin, M. *Why Bureaucrats Play Games*. Washington, D.C.: The Brookings Institution, 1971; Levine, S., P. White, and B. Paul. "Community Interorganizational Problems in Providing Medical Care and Social Services." *American Journal of Public Health*, 53(8) (1963); Levine, S. and P. White. "Exchange as a Conceptual Framework for the Study of Interorganizational Relationships." *Administrative Science Quarterly*, 5(4) (1961); Litwak, E. and L. Hylton. "Interorganizational Analysis: A Hypothesis on Coordinating Agencies." *Administrative Science Quarterly*, 6(4) (1962; and Long, N. "The Local Community as an Ecology of Games." *American Journal of Sociology*, 64(3) (1958). On the insufficiency of theory or practice for dealing with interorganizational arrangements at the federal level, see Mansfield, H. "Federal Executive Reorganization: Thirty Years of Experience." *Public Administration Review*, 29(4) (1969) and Warren, R. *Interorganizational Field as a Focus of Investigation*. Waltham, Mass.: Brandeis University, 1968.

7. We have regularly used synthetic competition procedures in the weapon systems area. An ailing aerospace firm would be declared the "winner" of a developmental or prototype contract in order to keep it alive. In the auto industry, for years the putative evils of monopoly or oligopoly were avoided by a not-so-tacit government/ industry agreement not to wipe out American Motors. The same kind of philosophy might be made to operate among government agencies for the purpose of stimulating future-responsive societal learning.

10

The Requirement for Changes in Sentient Groups

There is a body of experience and research going back to the works of Mayo, Roethlisberger, and Dickson that distinguishes between the worker as a task-oriented person in a task-oriented group and the worker as a person oriented to a group of people within a psychologically defined work space.[1] The latter has been succinctly described by Miller and Rice as "the group to which individuals are prepared to commit themselves and on which they depend for emotional support."[2]

THE FUNCTIONS OF SENTIENT GROUPS

All stable task groups develop a sentient, or emotional, component. It is often suppressed or repressed in the performance of the task, but nevertheless it influences group members in many ways: how they go about their tasks; how they reward each other for performing task-oriented or sentient-oriented roles, how they introduce new members to the norms and performance styles of the group, and how they handle conflicts that arise between sentient-related and task-related demands.[3] In the situation we are contemplating, organization members will deeply need the emotional support and commitment that sentient groups provide. In the face of the turbulence and uncertainty that accompany changeover to long-range social planning, anxiety must be allayed and a sense of personal "location" provided. The strain of role ambiguity and role conflict also needs easing. Those initiating such changeover efforts and those who are asked to make the changes must turn to others for support as they try to cope with the challenges that impinge from both inside and outside the organization. Under these insecure conditions, people will use their sentient groups to gain the psychological strength they need to resist change, accept it, or try to institute it themselves. For some people these sentient groups exist within the organization; for others, they are found outside the work place. Or, lacking such affiliations, individuals may turn in upon themselves, in an attempt to isolate themselves from turbulence and uncertainty, and the anxiety they produce. The former response is far more typical, but the latter is not infrequent among leaders in high places. One way or the other, the functions served by the sentient group will be especially important in determining reactions to efforts to change toward long-range social planning under the organizational circumstances with which we are concerned.

Effective task performance depends heavily on the relationship between the person's task group and the person's sentient group.[4] As Miller and Rice remark:

Forms of organization in which task and sentient groups coincide may have relatively high short-term effectiveness; in the longer term, such groups can inhibit change and hence can lead eventually to deterioration of performance, and in consequence to social and psychological deprivation rather than to satisfaction.[5]

Within this observation lie some critical dilemmas, both real and false. As defined herein, both long-range social planning and the process of reorienting organizations toward a compatible philosophical and operational mode are themselves learning activities — more specifically, research and development activities. All these arrangements and activities are thereby subject to change. Sentient groups that discourage change are inimicable to learning and to implementing what is learned. And strong sentient groups, melded with task groups, reduce the credibility and usefulness of boundary-spanning activities. (See Chapter 14.)

One of the chief social psychological purposes that sentient groups serve is to provide people with a feeling of security, imbeddedness and continuity.

Sentient groups are also the locus of a person's sense of commitment. Thus, anything that threatens to break up a person's sentient group is resisted; one's very sense of self is threatened because the group helps define and sustain that sense of self. Conventional management also sees the melding of task group and sentient group as in its interest. Note, however, that not all members of a group that has a mix of task and sentient functions are equally "in," either in their own eyes or those of other members of the group. The degree to which a member is "acceptable" affects his or her response to innovations that the group as a whole seeks to reject or accept. When task and sentient group are identical, then loyalty to the task is heightened and things get done with less external coercion and managerial intervention than would be required otherwise. Although the following quotation refers to Rensis Likert's studies in industry, the same circumstances pertain in office situations.[6]

Analysis confirmed the impression that one of the ways the high-producing managers are achieving better communication and more accurate perceptions is by building greater peer-group loyalty. The results also show that the greater the peer-group loyalty, the greater is the agreement between the foremen and the men as to what constitutes a reasonable figure or standard.[7]

When the task group and sentient group are separate entities, it appears that introducing task change is easier, but generating organizational loyalty is harder. This will be especially true in government agencies, where employees see their work as having a special potential for advancing their commitment to sentient groups outside the organization. Some professionals in government and corporations feel it is immoral for one's "inside" values to clash with one's "outside" sentient-group affiliations. If the work situation is frustrating or unproductive in terms of task accomplishment, or if other jobs look more attractive from the perspective of fulfilling sentient group commitments, or if the effort to change in the direction of future-responsive societal learning seems too threatening, these individuals may be more inclined to "exit." [8] Leaving may disrupt ongoing activities, especially if these persons are managers who could take with them information the organization wants to keep secure. In the absence of sentient group affiliations located within the organization, the conflict-resolving utility of appeals to loyalty noted earlier are seriously reduced. Management that needs to feel in control finds such a situation extremely threatening. Thus, management also will resist breaking up sentient groupings for the purpose of changing toward long-range social planning if it fears the loss of loyalty or feels unable or unwilling to undertake a different management style to compensate for losses in sentient group control. This is especially true if the sentient groups to be disbanded are those with which managers themselves identify.

On the other hand, sentient groups seem necessary as the buffers and sustainers for those who take on the task of innovating in the direction of long-range social planning. In theorizing about the implications of successful efforts to introduce new weaving technology into a textile manufacturing organization, Miller and Rice observe that, as a rule,

what is important is the relative balance of sentience of groups committed to the status quo and groups committed to change. Efforts by other workers to replicate elsewhere the experimental changes in weaving cited above often foundered through a failure to create initially a strong sentient group committed to experimentation. It was only such a group that could provide the necessary protective boundary within which innovation could be encouraged to take place. In the case of the loom-sheds already referred to, however, once the new autonomous groups had established themselves, they acquired their own valency and froze into a new status quo, and the group committed to experimentation disappeared. . . To maintain adaptiveness, the greatest sentience must remain vested in a group committed to change.[9]

In some situations sentient groups can provide the emotional support to risk change, especially when it is generated within the group. Blau observes:

The social support of the group also makes it easier for officials to adopt new practices, since it lessens their need to find emotional security in familiar routines. Social cohesion, therefore, paves the way for the development of new adjustments. In addition, it furnishes the group with instruments for instituting them.[10]

Three relevant examples of the application of this property of sentient groups were noted during interviews for this book. In Los Angeles, [then] Chief City Planner Calvin Hamilton was making large changes in the composition and functions of the planning staff. He deliberately introduced schemes that built sentient group support for undertaking new means of establishing and maintaining programmatic activities. Among other things, he used organizational development techniques to teach the interpersonal competencies needed for creating work groups that could both risk and develop organizational changes.

Within the Bureau of Research of the Office of Education, David Bushnell developed a highly innovative curriculum for seventeen school districts around the country. A number of activities were introduced deliberately to bring the involved superintendents together to share their experiences in ways that effectively made them into a strong sentient group. Part of Bushnell's reason for emphasizing sentient-group building was to increase the likelihood that these superintendents would find enough strength to continue to risk innovations in the event federal funding dried up — which is what happened.

Thompson Ramo Wooldridge (TRW) has frequent occasions to establish temporary task groups around aerospace engineering development. These groups work together intensively and careful not to develop sentient group attachments that isolate them from other groups involved in the same project. Effective interaction is critical. Therefore, before these teams begin work, they spend time under the guidance of an in-house organizational development staff, becoming sensitized to each other's work styles and social support needs. They also learn which sentient-group tendencies are likely to interfere with their working relations with other team involved in the particular work they face. (For example, two such teams were a rocket engine test team working in the field and an analysis and development team, miles away, at the computers without proper preparation it was likely that each team would misinterpret well meant actions by the other as stupid or willfully indifferent.)[11] They also learned techniques for dealing with such tendencies, and these were used — usually with the help of the organizational development staff — when signs of such misinterpretations were noted in the intense working situation that follow.

A major component of many organizational development techniques is improving interpersonal competence so that sentient groups can realistically and openly support their membership in the risks of changing.[12] It may well be that a major source of a sentient group's resistance to innovation from outside the group is its inability to move beyond conventional interpersonal support to the support required to understand and face up to what each needs to give and receive in order to share the hopes and fears that go along with the process.

In sum, it appears that many sentient groups are likely to resist efforts to change toward long-range social planning, but that sentient groups skilled in interpersonal competencies, groups that participate in planning changeover efforts, and groups specifically designed for introducing long-range social planning are likely to facilitate change attempts. Thus, changeover requires the dissolution of sentient groups built around routines and values that resist long-range social planning, and simultaneously the establishment of other groups that favor the proposed changes, plus the establishment of temporary sentient groups to support those most directly involved in designing and implementing the innovation. An important planning goal will be to learn how to institute intense but changeable group identifications.[13] Clearly the task of restructuring sentient groups will be time-consuming, difficult, and complex. It will be a learning process in itself.

Sentient-Group Characteristics

Professionals

We can gain a greater appreciation of how sentient group responses will aid or hinder changeover efforts by looking more closely at sentient-group characteristics of professionals. Some of these people may be innovators of long-range social planning and some may be resisters. It is important to have in mind some of their psychosocial attributes, as they are reflected in sentient group needs. Their resistance to or support of efforts to change toward future-responsive societal learning will be a function of how they regard their sentient groups, since organizational restructuring will alter or eliminate those groups.

When professionals find their tasks frustrating or their roles ambiguous, or when they need more assurance about their social usefulness than the organization provides, some find their sentient groups outside the agency, perhaps exclusively so. An important sentient group for professionals has been their professional association. Miller and Rice observe:

The sentient groups to which professional men and women commit themselves and from which they draw their support are the professional associations and their related learned societies. Membership is a qualification to practice. And the sanction to practice those professions that are concerned with the lives, liberties, and property of their clients has, in our society, the force of law. Society, in effect, not only defines the boundaries of the task system and of the sentient system, and separates them, but also, through the sentient system, controls professional conduct in the task system.[14]

The big professional associations are also victims of the turbulent society. They are racked with internal dissension over purpose and means: splintering or threats to splinter are the order of the day. Consequently, members sometimes feel that the traditional legitimized basis for controlling their professional conduct has been threatened, although they still cling to a collegial association for a sense of commitment and emotional support.

One result is the growth of splinter associations that provide their members with strong sentient group rewards, certainly stronger ones than the parent organizations can provide in turbulent times. The need for a sense of commitment and emotional support in an uncertain world encourages the proliferation of doctrinaire distinctions in ways akin to the intense subgroup differentiation that characterized sixteenth-century Protestantism.[15] This splintering happens because of increasing specialization; those practicing new specialties need the status and support that a professional organization provides. Related to this process is the splintering that occurs in professional associations when members disagree about the association's position on social issues — the same issues that give impetus to long-range social planning. That is to say, new professional skills *plus* a particular viewpoint about their appropriate application to societal problems become the basis for new professional organizations. This fragmentation of sentient groups increases the problem of sustaining the organizational loyalty of professionals to their agencies or corporations. At the same time, it may increase professional support for efforts to change toward long-range social planning.

Top Decision Makers

What about the relationship between sentient groups and task groups at the top-management levels of an organization? More specifically, how do the sentient groups of executives affect their response toward long-range social planning? We have little systematic knowledge of these matters, though much has been reported, more or less anecdotally, in novels and case studies. These are the people who see themselves as "successes." Their self-image tells them they *know* what they are doing and how to do it. At the same time, these are the people who must deal with the inpouring of the turbulent environment across their organizational boundaries, bearing with it a threat to their self-image. And these are the people who must provide the necessary stimulus and continuity of support for efforts to change toward long-range social planning. It is important, therefore, to speculate upon how well their sentient groups can sustain their personal image of success, meet their emotional needs, and ground the location of their commitment, thus advancing efforts to change toward long-range social planning.

In times of crisis, the sentient groups and task groups of top decision makers coalesce. To a degree, this coalescence seems to be the case for everyday deliberations also, but under normal conditions the executive or manager in charge is able to maintain an effective operating distinction between sentient and task group demands. However, in crisis or under stress, the distinction tends to blur and usually (but not invariably) the interpersonal processes operative in sentient groups become dominant, even though the task at hand is still the ostensible objective. The turbulent environment outside the organization and the efforts to change or resist change inside the organization, with all that implies about uncertainty and error, mean that the situation will be stressful. It is important to keep in mind some special characteristics of high-level deliberative groups when sentience and task purpose fuse.

Under conditions of high stress, these sentient groups often resist change in perspective and performance by resorting to what Irving Janis, who has studied a number of such events in government, calls "groupthink."

Above all, there are numerous indications pointing to the development of group norms that bolster morale at the expense of critical thinking. One of the most common norms appears to be that of remaining loyal to the group by sticking with the policies to which the group has already committed itself, even when those policies are obviously working out badly and have unintended consequences that disturb the conscience of each member. This is one of the key characteristics of groupthink.[16]

Janis describes the "main principle of groupthink" as follows:

The more amiability and esprit de corps there is among the members of a policy-making in-group, the greater the danger that independent critical thinking will be replaced by groupthink, which is likely to result in irrational and dehumanizing actions directed against outgroups. . .[17]

. . .While I have limited my study to decision-making bodies in Government, groupthink symptoms appear in business, industry, and any other field where small, cohesive groups make the decisions.[18]

Miller and Rice, drawing on their field research experience with corporations and other nongovernmental organizations, have a similar message with further insights:

We have seen that any transaction across enterprise boundaries, an essential process for any living system, involves the drawing, temporarily at least, of new boundaries. And the drawing of new boundaries contains the possibility that the new boundaries will prove stronger than the old. Any transaction across enterprise boundaries has in it, therefore, the elements of incipient disaster, in which not only are essential tasks undone, but sentient systems are destroyed as well.

We can learn something more from the examination of disaster. The destruction of boundaries is so stressful that somebody has to go, or has to be believed to go, to pieces — somebody or some group has to carry the role of panic leader. In more normal situations, religious sects, immigrants, racial groups, delinquents, or other socially condemned minorities can threaten, or be perceived to threaten, the integrity of group boundaries. The preservation and protection of adequate sentient boundaries often depend, therefore, on finding or inventing other groups on whom can be projected the feelings and behavior that, if retained within the sentient group, would destroy its sentience.[19]

These independent findings suggest that when faced with crises and stress from the turbulent environment, executive group members are likely to use the sentient group qualities of their work situation to "push away" the uncertainty and threat of making errors that a learning posture in fact requires. The resistance from an executive's sentient group may be formidable if the members respond in a groupthink manner to the crises that are precipitated by the environmental feedback an organization needs to learn how to change.

Resistance to change by sentient groups performs a valuable stabilizing function by smoothing over disruptive input to organizations. This function may be appropriate in organizations doing routine operations or facing routine stresses, but is likely to be counterproductive in a planning situation, with its attributes of novelty and heavy stress. This is especially so because the aura of expertise and inaccessibility that surrounds senior groups protects them from accusations of incompetence, even though they are very likely to be operating by groupthink norms when under stress. What is more, those who depend on senior groups for their status or resources usually do not want to believe that their superiors are so psychologically vulnerable; it is more reassuring to blame events or other groups. Were they able to resist this tendency, however, the alternative groups could serve as valuable resources for facilitating social planning.

It is worth noting that sentient groups are by no means necessarily comprised of open, trusting, deeply supportive members. Interpersonal incompetence seems as great in such groups as elsewhere. In fact, groups of executives or administrators may be particularly wary of testing the depth of mutual understanding, commitment, and willingness to risk on behalf of others. When task groups and sentient groups overlap, a number of devices, ostensibly directed toward task accomplishment, are often used to avoid testing the availability of mutual support. Often a group will operate without questioning certain assumptions about its "client." "Getting on with the job" or "meeting the deadline" (which often is not as immovable as it seems) are a few of the other excuses administrators use to avoid exploring the values, goals, priorities, and feelings that are usually inherent in any task. In these ways they avoid exposing differences that might well go beyond their group's ability to support its members. Indeed, the dynamics of group-think can be understood as a partially unconscious collusion by members of the group to avoid testing each other's camaraderie and emotional support by ignoring the fact that a situation may be a "moment of truth."

Those senior executives and managers who innovate in the direction of long-range social planning can be divided into two groups: those who are naive about the personal changes required of them and their group, and those who are knowledgeable about this requirement. Consider the first category. By their very appreciation of the need to attempt a changeover, these executives are likely to be a member of overlapping task groups and sentient groups that are exposed to the turbulent environment. Hence, they are better able to deal innovatively with crisis and stress, or at least to resist certain groupthink tendencies. As these executives and their sentient groups attempt to innovate toward long-range social planning, their exposure to organizational resistance and to information from boundary spanners inside and outside the organization will help them realize the profound structural and interpersonal changes that are necessary. They will have to reassess previously arrived-at definitions of competence and usefulness to the group and to the organization and allow for the inevitable shifts in appreciation, self-image, and status. Without special preparation, most groups cannot face this kind of reassessment. This is especially so for well-mannered people who have worked together for the rewards of mutual esteem. Whether, during this period, the innovator/executive's sentient group finds that it has the will to face these interpersonal readjustments, or whether it reverts to more familiar avoidance responses, depends on the confluence of many factors, including those discussed here. The point to be made is that while an executive's sentient group is capable of providing the emotional support he needs in order to sustain the risk and discomfort of moving toward long-range social planning, it is problematic whether the group can actually fulfill this critical function.

The knowledgeable executive or manager will already have begun the interpersonal competence training and the structural reorganization that must precede effective movements toward long-range social planning. Irving Janis points to a number of structural means for reducing the tendency to groupthink and notes that they have worked successfully.[20] While very little has been done to link these personal and structural changes with regard to sentient group affiliations, there are a few organizations, mostly nongovernmental, that have moved rather well in this direction. In these settings the executive's sentient group becomes less hierarchical and status-bound, and as a result, is able to absorb more information from the organization and the environment. This type of group is better prepared to handle the emotional aspects of long-range planning, without the counterproductive consequences we have examined elsewhere.

In spite of these pioneering efforts, groupthink persists, and the structural and interpersonal changes that Janis, Likert, Miller, Rice, and others have recommended for improving organizational responsiveness continue, for the most part, to go unimplemented. There are still executives around who are ignorant of organizational development technology. More often, the recommended procedures remain unimplemented because the changes demanded of the innovating officer and the overlapping sentient groups and task groups are too threatening to the self-images of competence built up in earlier days. Those with seniority within an organization feel a special need to maintain their self-image in the face of societal turbulence. This need will be especially strong in government agencies, where trying to move toward long-range social planning will create greater uncertainty than in nongovernmental settings. Under these conditions, sentient group support will remain a much more important indication of personal success and accomplishment than evidence from the environment. Unambiguous evidence in the environment will be hard to find, and many others will contend for it.

In this regard, it is important to note that under ambiguous conditions or when rewarding feedback from the environment is a long time coming — both characteristics of the long-range social planning situation — people tend to seek more immediate sentient-group feedback as evidence of competence or acceptability. But this solution has a cost: no one makes enough of an effort to make sure that the planning will have a real impact on the organization. The planning-oriented people get their assurance of competence and value from other planning-oriented people — their local and extended sentient groups — not from the people who should be using their efforts. Thus planners, frustrated because their efforts do not result in action, compensate by exchanging expressions of support with other frustrated planners and would-be plan users, instead of leaving the organization or seeking other means to make a difference within it. To be sure, this behavior is by no means limited to the planning fraternity, but it is especially important from our perspective.

Mid-Level Administrators and Managers

The influence of sentient-group membership on mid-level managers seems similar to that felt by professionals and senior personnel. As managers and administrators gain experience, they, too, look to their associations or splinters thereof for sentient support. Some, however, find their sentient groups among their immediate staff and among associates attached to the office's programs or administrative activities.

Some mid-level people will have received training in organizational development skills, and they will not so upset by the loosening of control that follows when stable and loyal sentient groups dissolve. Indeed, in the interest of organizational learning, they may encourage such dissolution. Others, lacking such training or values, will become anxious and resist changes that threaten to dissolve their stable and reliable sentient groups. Those responsible for the performance and morale of these employees will carry a heavier burden in coping constructively with their fears. If those responsible are managers who themselves fear or want to avoid the loss of control over subordinates that a conventional sentient group provides, they will be especially resentful of efforts to move toward long-range social planning and especially intent on sabotaging them. Organizations such as those described earlier that move toward less structured organizational settings lose personnel at all levels who cannot deal with the greater ambiguity and changes in their sentient group's openness. If sentient groups change over time, as moving toward long-range social planning requires, managers will have to learn how to deal with this source of internal turbulence.

A General Electric study highlights a number of matters dwelt on in this chapter. The study was carried out to anticipate the corporation situation, but it would seem to apply to government as well:

Compounding the problems caused by an organization in a virtually constant state of flux will be the greater mobility of managerial, professional, and technical personnel. In a fluid organization setting, and in an economy of tight labor markets, it will become progressively easier for an individual to consider his prime commitment to be to his profession and / or his self development, not to a single organization. Predictably, therefore, a key problem will be that of motivating individual commitment to organizational goals: predictably, too, however successful an organization may be in this regard, it will also (in a sense) fail, for the turnover of this type of personnel is almost certain to increase, even under the best of circumstances.[21]

Either the General Electric authors overlooked the need which "managerial, professional, and technical personnel" will have for sentient associations or they assume that professional commitment will fill that need. For those who are unsatisfied by that option, the attractions of mobility will be in conflict with those of more lasting interpersonal associations. Others will move in the direction that Bennis and Slater have suggested: toward intense, short-lived, sequential associations. The point is not that everyone will need the same kind of sentient arrangement. Quite the contrary. The point is that changing toward long-range social planning will make it necessary to change the sentient group arrangements. In the process, many people will be required to change the ways in which they find interpersonal support and commitment. They may resist or welcome structural changes, but either way, they will discover that moving toward future-responsive societal learning is a long and difficult journey.

1. Mayo, E. *The Human Problems of an Industrial Civilization*. New York: Macmillan, 1933; Roethlisberger, F. *Management and Morale*. Cambridge: Harvard University Press, 1941; and Dickson, 1946.

2. Miller, E. and A. K. Rice. *Systems of Organization*. London: Tavistock, 1967, p. 253.

3. Bion, W. *Experiences in Groups*. New York: Basic Books, 1959 and Rice, A. K. *Learning for Leadership*. London: Tavistock, 1965.

4. Warwick, D. "Socialization and Personality," *The Management of Urban Crisis*, eds. S. Seashore and R. McNeill. New York: The Free Press, 1971, Chapter 13, pp. 386-393.

5. Miller and Rice, op. cit., p. 253.

6. On the prevalence and utility of "normative compliance" in professional situations see Etzioni, "Shortcuts to Social Change," *The Public Interest*, a(12) (Summer 1968).

7. Likert, R. *New Patterns of Management*. New York: McGraw-Hill, 1961, p. 55.

8. Hirschman, A. *Exit, Voice, and Loyalty: Responses to Decline in Firms, Organizations, and States*. Cambridge: Harvard University Press, 1970.

9. Miller and Rice, op. cit., p. 260.

10. Blau, op. cit., p. 259.

11. Katz, D. and B. Georgopoulos. "Organizations in a Changing World." *Journal of Applied Behavioral Science*, 7(3) (1971). Also see Mead, M. and P. Byers. *The Small Conference*. The Hague: Mouton, 1968. The photographs and text in the latter reference are invaluable for elucidating the interplay between task and sentient group needs and the kinds of competencies necessary to meet both.

12. Bennis, W. and P. Slater. *The Temporary Society*. New York: Harper and Row, 1968. This book is imaginative and perceptive as regards the personality requirements for temporary affiliations. These conjectures are well based in social, anthropological, and psychological research. See also Hyman, H. "Reference Groups," *International Encyclopedia of the Social Sciences*, Vol. XIII. New York: Crowell Collier and Macmillan, 1968.

13. Bennis and Slater (1968) are most imaginative and perceptive on the personality requirements for temporary affiliations. These conjectures are well based in social, anthropological, and psychological research. There is also a large body of research and theory on "reference groups" that is complementary to the subject of this chapter. For a review and bibliography in this area *see* Hyman (1968).

14. Miller and Rice, op. cit., p. 254.

15. Shapley, D. "Professional Societies: Identity Crisis Threatens on Bread and Butter Issues." *Science*, 176 (May 19, 1972). *See also* Dumont, M. *The Absurd Healer: Perspectives of a Community Psychiatrist*. New York: Science House, 1968. The latter explores the changing professional criteria for performance and relevance in the mental health area.

16. Janis, I. "Groupthink Among Policy Makers. *Sanctions for Evil*, eds. N. Sanford and C. Comstock. San Francisco: Jossey-Bass, 1971, p. 43.

17. Ibid., p. 44.

18. Ibid., p. 76.

19. Miller and Rice, op. cit., p. 268.

20. Janis, op. cit. See also Wilensky, H. "Organizational Intelligence: Knowledge and Policy in Government and Industry. New York: Basic Books, 1967 and Webb, E. Individual and Organizational Forces Influencing the Interpretation of Indicators." Institute for Defense Analyses, Science and Technology Division, Research Paper P-488 (Arlington, Va. 1969).

21. "Our Future Business Environment." General Electric Co., Future Study (1968)), p. 44.

11

The Requirement for Frequent Organizational Restructuring

Changing toward long-range social planning requires a capability for frequent organizational restructuring. As defined by Paul Lawrence and James Lorsch, differentiation refers to "the difference in cognitive and emotional orientation among managers in different functional departments, including differences in time orientation and interpersonal orientation." [1] Integration refers to "the quality of the state of collaboration that exists among departments that are required to achieve unity of effort by the demands of the environment." [2] In other words, to achieve the requisite variety, subcomponent managers of an organization should have the cognitive and emotional orientations, and collaborative arrangements that permit the activities for which they are responsible to match the demands from the environment.

WHY A RESTRUCTURING CAPABILITY IS NECESSARY

The empirical evidence and the conceptual model provided in the study cited above are supported by cybernetic theory as expounded in W.R. Ashby's fundamental "law of requisite variety." [3] This law states, in effect, that the repertory of responses an entity can make to its changing environment is determined by the degree to which its complexity mirrors the complexity of the environment. Ideally, an organization is differentiated and integrated to the same degree as those aspects of the environment to which it is supposed to respond.

Because long-range social planning enlarges both input from the environment and the variety of participants engaged in planning efforts, it demands an effective matching of the organization to its environment through internal differentiation and integration of activities. As members of the organization are more exposed to the environment, they would begin to perceive it as differentiated and integrated into a variety of patterns corresponding to the appreciative settings in the organization and among members and groups in the environment that influence the organization. Herbert Simon notes in this regard:

Anyone familiar with organizational life can multiply examples . . . where different problems will come to attention in different parts of the organization, or where different solutions will be generated for a problem, depending on where it arises in the organization. The important point to be noted here is that we do not have to postulate conflict in personal goals or motivations in order to explain such conflicts or discrepancies. The discrepancies arise out of the cognitive inability of the decision makers to deal with the entire problem as a set of simultaneous relations, each to be treated symmetrically with the others.[1]

The task here is not to propose the best way to differentiate and integrate an organization, but rather to show that these appreciative settings will be changing when doing future-responsive societal learning. The organization will have to redifferentiate and reintegrate itself accordingly, accepting this as the normal state of affairs.

There will be strong resistance to performing the task at hand; hence, resistance to changing toward future-responsive societal learning. Achieving the appropriate redifferentiation and reintegration means doing more than the typical organizational "shake-up." It means changing the communication patterns, authority relationships, and systems of specialization — not only as they occur within the organization but as they interact with the environment. And it will mean changing appreciative settings as regards task ends and means, and as regards relationships with the environment. There are consequences, then, for members' sense of self and their relationship with others. Since the outcome of the changes will be problematic, many will resist giving up the certainty of the existing arrangement. Role conflict and role ambiguity will be accentuated, questions about individual usefulness will arise, and sentient groups will be broken up. Uncertainty will increase, not only because more information is flowing in from the environment, but because the redifferentiation and reintegration process itself introduces new operational and interpersonal uncertainties. To the extent that people must revise their appreciative settings, personal anxiety and uncertainty will increase as well. Moreover, the chances for error multiply. Although these consequences, or even the anticipation of them, may generate strong resistance, it is absolutely essential that an organization acquire the capability to continuously redesign its structure and norms in order to achieve future-responsive societal learning.

Whatever the prevailing appreciative setting, the environment will be differentiated and integrated in terms of the products (things, services, ideas, imagery, events) its various members need and want, and also in terms of the consequences resulting from what they do with these products. As we are beginning to understand, consumption has consequences that extend far beyond the needs of the consumer, and it is to this larger domain that long-range planning must respond. Of course, no perceived pattern of differentiation or integration can structure the environment completely; a turbulent environment always has undifferentiated and unintegrated properties, which under some conditions may quite overwhelm those aspects of the environment that at other times seem structured and regulatable if not precisely predictable. (How and with what frequency this turbulence is able to overwhelm the structured and regulatable, are key questions.)

To try to change toward long-range social planning, organizations will have to be structured differently and more elaborately than conventional organizations. In particular, they will need capabilities for:
• scanning the present and future environment;

- interpreting information so obtained; and
- applying it to the evaluation, transformation, and design of programs, policies, and organizational structure.

All agencies claim to perform these tasks, but if they do so at all, they do not direct the kind of attention to them that moving toward long-range social planning requires. That is to say, they do not differentiate tasks so as to make them match the environment's differentiability that, in turn, generates feedback indicating whether needs and wants have been met or unmet. Even more glaringly absent are those integrative means within organizations that could insure that useful information is being gathered and applied.

CONDITIONS THAT STIMULATE RESTRUCTURING

Good social-indicator data will heighten the pressure for redifferentiation and reintegration by isolating those categories of the environment that need more refined and targeted services. Later on, these data can serve an evaluative function. However, the environment may also redifferentiate itself, for whatever reason. Specifically, it may redifferentiate itself in response to the categories suggested by the social indicator data, as these are interpreted either by the relevant agency or by advocate interpreters in the environment. The agency must then redifferentiate and reintegrate itself accordingly, or else deal with the operational, ethical, and role stresses that result.

How often and to what extent an organization will need to restructure will depend on the circumstances, though it seems reasonable to speculate that it will be more rather than less frequently when the rewards of this planning mode become obvious.

In addition to the influence of social-indicator data, two other stimuli to restructuring merit mention. One is the theoretical reformulations about the nature of society and the services it requires. In an extraordinarily perceptive and stimulating paper, Nathan Caplan and Steven Nelson argue that social psychology researchers and theorists tend to blame the person rather than the system for deficiencies and inadequacies. They make a case for understanding that behavior is also a product of the system, and that "solutions" to social problems are as likely to require systemic change as personal transformation.

If Caplan and Nelson are correct, then as more "blame-the-system" or "blame-the-person" theories develop, there will be conceptual revisions about the sources and consequences of social problems such as crime, drug abuse, pollution, and the disintegration of the family unit. As these ideas gain good currency they lead, in a long-range social planning mode, to organizational restructuring of programs, functions, and procedures in ways that are appropriate to the newly-invented image of reality.

Another strong stimulus to restructuring will come from information forced into the organization from its environment. Urban riots, loss of motivation in young blue-collar workers, professional and public service unionization, and environmental disasters are examples of environmental stimuli that lead to restructuring.

Restructuring, as with other requirements imposed by long-range social planning, is not a completely new experience for organizations. In government, restructuring of sorts (though chiefly cosmetic) happens with every change of administration. Corporations also restructure periodically. There is evidence that as they become larger and more complex, they become more horizontal in structure and use committees more than the hierarchical line of command for decision making.[5] The resistance generated by such restructuring efforts can provide insight into what to expect from efforts to change toward long-range social planning.

SOURCES OF RESISTANCE TO RESTRUCTURING

Conventional restructuring is different in degree and kind from the differentiation and integration needed for long-range social planning. Some of the resistance to conventional restructuring can be understood as resulting from the expectation that the norms of the organization will remain the same, even if the table of organization is different — that restructuring is an exceptional state of affairs, rather than a normal one. People neither expect restructuring to be normal, nor do they design it that way.

There are, however, some partial success stories. In some research and development organizations, restructuring is understood to be a continuing process, to the degree that project teams expect to be broken up as projects are completed. Even though they have been self-recruited, those involved experience certain social-psychological costs as well as benefits.⁶ We need to know much more about this kind of arrangement and its implications for people and organizations in the public sector.

In successful restructuring, accomplished through the techniques of planned change, resistance is heightened by inadequate attention to the prevailing social-psychological circumstances. Therefore, if the restructuring is to occur more easily and with fewer adverse consequences, some of the procedures designed for continuing redifferentiation and reintegration should emphasize attention to these circumstances.

Restructuring of functions and activities results in the reallocation or dissolution of authority, which is formally prescribed by regulations, and informally achieved through demonstrated task-competence and interpersonal qualities within sentient groups. The satisfactions that accompany one's command of predictable patterns of influence — the satisfactions of power — may be jeopardized. Others may see an opportunity to attain power for themselves. Again, as with sentient groups, restructuring impacts those who have the authority to initiate such changes, as well as their subordinates. In some situations, superiors must make substantial alterations in their own span and expression of authority. As Lawrence and Lorsch observe:

The locus of influence to resolve conflict is at a level where the required knowledge about the environment is available. The more unpredictable and uncertain the parts of the environment, the lower in the organizational hierarchy this tends to be. Similarly, the relative influence of the various functional departments varies, depending on which of them is vitally involved in the dominant issues posed by the environment. These are the ways in which the determinants of effective conflict resolution are contingent on variations in the environment.⁷

Shifting the definition and location of relevant information threatens the powers-that-be, and will be resisted. In a large government agency or corporation, components are organizations in themselves. As Norton Long points out:

> . . . *every organization with any drive towards autonomy is concerned with achieving control over the information it needs for decisional independence. Control over the communication of information requisite to key decisions is to an important degree control over the decisions themselves. This fact often plunges the most seemingly harmless fact-gathering enterprise into the storms of politics.*[8]

In conventional bureaucracies the tendency is to resolve conflicts hierarchically; but if the intent is to change toward future-responsive societal learning, that form of conflict resolution is inadequate. It is equally inadequate as a means for establishing the conditions and criteria for redifferentiation and reintegration.

Attempting to reintegrate the differentiated components generates a host of social psychological problems and sources of resistance. First, there is the difficult task of looking at the environment and the organization with fresh eyes in order to create a design "template." Second, there is the task of designing operational processes for establishing, maintaining, and evolving integrated components. Those who have the power to establish and maintain relations between components have the power to adjudicate conflicts and alter relationships; thus, new integrative arrangements will mean new allocations and distributions of authority. Those threatened by the loss of their power and sense of usefulness will resist the changes.[9]

In Chapter 12 we will examine a potentially potent integrative mechanism called boundary spanning, and the resistance it is likely to elicit. But the fact is that we know very little about designing effective integrative mechanisms, much less systems of integrated components that are alterable in response to changes in the environment. As James Thompson suggests, "Although reorganization [or the pretense thereof] is a frequent phenomenon in complex organizations in modern societies, our social-scientific understanding of it is meager, and largely derived as a by-product." [10] Miller and Rice elaborate on this point:

Specialization of technology and product in sub-enterprises or separate enterprises can no doubt increase the efficiency of the parts, but until new forms of organization are invented, with activity system, task group, and sentient group adequately differentiated and their interrelations controlled, it is not certain that greater efficiency of the parts will necessarily add up to greater efficiency of the whole. [11]

Since there is neither a shared body of experience about procedures for establishing integration in complex, changing organizations, nor a theory of integration derived from research, there exists no established repertory of skills sufficient to tie together the multiple aspects of personnel, structure, and planning technology. [12]

Especially talented persons have helped some organizations redesign themselves using a combination of art, skill, and knowledge of behavioral science. [13] But designing an organization so that it has the capability for *continual redesign* results in an organization vastly different — in design, membership, and norms — from a redesigned organization *per se*. Changing over to long-range social planning clearly requires the former.

In sum, frequent redifferentiation and reintegration has unsettling social-psychological effects, producing its own internal turbulence and threat to a sense of status, belonging, autonomy, and certainty. The very fact of frequent revisions will increase occasions for conflict and decrease the legitimacy of formal authority, placing a much heavier demand on the organization's ability to manage conflict by nonauthoritarian means — means that also facilitate the kind of learning needed to restructure in conformity with the requirements of future-responsive societal learning.

Lawrence and Lorsch propose that:

the possibility of more systematically planning and implementing conflict resolution procedures hinges on establishing a baseline in terms of the required and actual patterns of differentiation in an organization. This baseline establishes the frame of reference for tackling the conflict resolution problem in an orderly fashion. This clarifies what the conflict is all about, what creates the differences of judgment, and what knowledge is relevant to its resolution. From this vantage point we can see why conflict must be accepted as a continuing result of living in a complex civilization. Resolution is not then put up as some final Utopian answer, but simply as a sensible solution to today's issue — with awareness that basic and legitimate differences will generate new conflicts to be resolved tomorrow. From this baseline managers can move more directly toward designing procedures and devices that are adequate for processing the flow of conflicted issues that will surely arise.[14]

Note, however, that this approach assumes agreement on what the "required" patterns of differentiation should be. In our situation, organizations must discover these patterns themselves, by assessing the impact of services that have been rendered according to a particular model of environmental differentiation and integration. Thus, as usual, the only way long-range social planning requirements for organizational differentiation and integration can be met is if those involved see it as a learning procedure. In this case, as with goal-setting, they would agree to experiment by trying to match the organization's internal structure with a model of the environment's structure. Means for arriving at such temporary agreements to experiment and revise must be among the things to be discovered via long-range social planning. Certainly, it involves an appreciation of other matters described here, and it takes a willingness to shift to a norm of societal learning.[15]

1. Lawrence, P., and Lorsch, J. *Organization and Environment: Managing Differentiation and Integration.* Cambridge: Harvard University Press, 1967, p. 10.

2. Ibid, p. 11.

3. Ashby, W.R. *An Introduction to Cybernetics.* London: Chapman and Hall, 1956.

4. Simon, H. "On the Concept of Organizational Goal." *Administrative Science Quarterly,* 9(1) (1964), p. 17.

5. Tripathi, R. "A Review of Conceptualizations of Organizational Environment and Studies of Environment-Organization Relationships." Manuscript prepared for the University of Michigan's Organizational Psychology Program, December 1971.

6. Glatt, E. and M. Shelley. *The Research Society.* New York: Gordon and Breach, 1969.

7. Lawrence and Lorsch, op. cit., pp. 157-158.

8. Long, N. The Administrative Organization as a Political System." *Concepts and Issues in Administrative Behavior,* eds. S. Mallick and E. Van Ness. Englewood Cliffs, N.J.: Prentice-Hall, 1962, pp. 145-146.

9. In the U.S. government, the task of redifferentiation and reintegration is as difficult on the interorganizational level as it is within a single unit. The combination of psychological and statutory resistance to restructuring is so great that the only effective recourse seems to be to establish new, independent agencies. The task of integration with other agencies is left to the uncertain, slow, and usually erosive processes of committees and congressional pressures, even though injunctions to coordinate with other agencies are written into the enabling legislation. Observers and legislators alike agree that legislators, at least at the federal level, don't want autonomous integration among agencies, but prefer to oversee that task themselves. Effective autonomous integration necessarily requires redifferentiation of legislative committee fiefdom boundaries and, as a consequence, the reallocation of congressional authority, status, and other prerogatives. In effect, there are no established, reliable integrative procedures presently available that can be counted on to provide an interagency equivalent of an effective intra-organizational integration (which in itself is rare enough). One response to this situation, which reflects other changing perceptions of professionalism, legitimacy, and management philosophy, has been the aforementioned development across agencies of an informal, *sub rosa* integrative mechanism consisting mostly of bureaucrats exchanging information for the purpose of problem-solving rather than agency survival.

10. Thompson, J. *Organizations in Action: Social Science Bases of Administrative Theory.* New York: McGraw-Hill, 1967, p. 79.

11. Miller, E. and A. K. Rice. *Systems of Organization.* London: Tavistock, 1967, p. 266.

12. For instance, researcher James Lorsch has emphasized to me that his research compares organizations as they are. He has not yet studied the ways in which they come to be differentiated and integrated nor why they stop at the point they do. Also excellent criticisms and reservations about the potential of organizational development theory and practice to specify structure design requirements are in the literature. [Argyris, C. "Resistance to Rational Management Systems." *Innovation,* (10) (1972). *See also* Bennis, W. *Organization Development: Its Nature, Origins, and Prospects.* Reading, Mass: Addison-Wesley, 1969. *See also* Bowers, D. "Perspectives in Organizational Development." CRUSK-ISR Working Paper. Ann Arbor: Center for Research on

Utilization of Scientific Knowledge, Institute for Social Research, University of Michigan, 1971.] Also available are many studies that provide a sense of the difficult conceptual problems involved in fusing personal, structural, and technological change.[Georgopoulos, B. "An Open-System Theory Model for Organizational Research," *Organizational Behavior Models*, eds. A. Negandhi and J. Schwitter, Kent, Ohio: Kent State University, 1970. *See also* Leavitt, H. "Applied Organizational Change in Industry: Structural Technological, and Humanistic Approaches," *Handbook of Organizations*, ed. J. March. Chicago: Rand McNally, 1965, pp. 1144-1170. *See also* Hunt, R. "Technology and Organization," *Academy of Management Journal* (September 1970). Two descriptions of research needed in this area are found in Bennis, W. *Changing Organizations*. New York: McGraw-Hill, 1966, pp. 181-211; and Mohr, L. "Determinants of Innovation in Organizations." *The American Political Science Review*, 62(1) (1969).]

13. Bennis, W., K. Benne, and R. Chin. *The Planning of Change*. New York: Holt, Rinehart and Winston, 1962 and 1969 (revised). *See also* Blake, R. and J. Mouton. *Corporate Excellence Through Grid Organizational Development*. Houston, Tex.: Gulf, 1968. *See also* Beckhard, R. *Organization Development: Strategies and Models*. Reading, Mass.: Addison-Wesley, 1969. *See also* Bennis, op. cit. *See also* Schein, E. *Process Consultation: Its Role in Organization Development*. Reading, Mass.: Addison-Wesley, 1969. *See also* Walton, R. *Interpersonal Peacemaking: Confrontation and Third-Party Consultation*. Reading, Mass.: Addison-Wesley, 1969. *See also* Zimbardo, P. and E. Eabesen. *Influencing Attitudes and Changing Behavior, A Basic Introduction to Relevant Methodology, Theory, and Applications*. Reading, Mass.: Addison-Wesley, 1969. For examples of integrative mechanisms that have worked, but under much stabler conditions, *see* Likert, R. *New Patterns of Management*. New York: McGraw-Hill, 1961.

14. Lawrence and Lorsch, op. cit., p. 224.

15. Lawrence and Lorsch conjecture on some aspects of how this learning can be facilitated: *The viable organization of the future will need to establish and integrate the work of organization units that can cope with even more varied subenvironments. The differentiation of these units will be more extreme. Concurrently, the problems of integration will be more complex. Great ingenuity will be needed to evolve new kinds of integrative methods. The viable organizations will be the ones that master the science and art of organization design to achieve both high differentiation and high integration . . . To conceive new organizational forms and to develop the managerial behavior needed in these viable organizations, managements will rely increasingly on formally designated organizational development departments. These departments, staffed by trained specialists in the behavioral and administrative sciences, will be involved in planning new organizational forms for the effective utilization of human resources and in training managers to operate effectively in these settings.... As the demands for both differentiation and integration become more acute, top management will also find it necessary to devote more and more of its explicit attention to the achievement of these organizational states.* Ibid, pp. 238-239.

12

The Requirement for
More Boundary Spanning

Boundary Spanning as Integral
to Long-Range Social Planning

On the one hand, conventional organizations do what they can to
reduce the need for boundary spanning, and its internal
turbulence-generating consequences, by trying to control their
environments. On the other hand, the very societal conditions that
create the need for long-range social planning, indicate that there is
little potential for controlling the environment.

Throughout this chapter we will be looking at boundary
spanning as an activity that occurs across the boundaries of
components *within* an organization, and across the boundary
between the organization and its relevant environment. In large
organizations the same sources of resistance seem to arise whether
the threats and opportunities come from another subsystem or
from a consumer group, Congress, a city council, or another
agency. I will not usually distinguish between an organization and
its subsystems in discussing their boundary-spanning relations.

Because more information technology will be used by
organizations and their environments, there will an increase in
information that clarifies the distribution of the consequences of an
organization's activities; of the interaction of activities between
organizations; and of the interaction of those activities with

turbulent properties of the environment that are independent of the organization's activities. This increase in information will pressure organizations to pay more attention to who is being burdened with social costs or blessed with social benefits. This in turn will increase the need for them to use boundary spanners to connect themselves with other organizations, in order to enhance the rewards and reduce the costs to the environment. Anticipating environmental demands will encourage attention to the future, and once an organization begins to try to anticipate relevant futures and evaluate programs in terms of future impacts, its internal and external linkage needs will change and grow.

With social indicators and computer-facilitated disaggregation of clientele, there will be pressures to differentiate the environment into many more special clienteles and situations. Differentiation of clienteles means dealing with more demands, including more coalitions and volatile groups, which will require more highly-skilled boundary spanners. It has already been demonstrated that heavy organizational costs must be sustained in order to provide more discriminating services (though in less sophisticated form) through client-differentiating feedback supplied by boundary spanners in citizen-participation and advocacy-planning situations.

In their classic study of the dilemmas of eliminating poverty through community action, Peter Marris and Martin Rein emphasize that "concerted social policy [must] rest on a consensus, and the creation of a consensus involves, like any compromise, conflict, intrigue, and ambiguous accommodation." [1]
The question for us is whether the conflict, intrigue, and ambiguous accommodation need be so great that concerted social policy must always founder, and future-responsive societal learning will be impossible. Some of the difficulties encountered could be ascribed to the absence of *effective* boundary spanning. Fear of being co-opted by the spanner, spanner fear of being co-opted, distrust, misunderstanding, subversion of the spanner, disagreement on representativeness — all are evidence of the inability of those involved to cope with the threats and ambivalence

that boundary spanning contains, and will contain until we learn how to use it appropriately.[2]

As a result, an organization clearly will need more boundary spanning in order to relate itself usefully to its environment; and it will have to cope with the internal consequences of new boundary-spanning activities, resulting from the importation of turbulence and uncertainty and from the requirement of coping with the input by internal reorganization. As we have seen, changes in the environment will require restructuring of the organization if it is to provide adequate functional responses; and if the organization is to allocate its resources effectively and evaluate its programs in terms of overall organization goals, this redifferentiation must be integrated internally. All this will require increased efforts at internal and external boundary spanning to the relevant and changing sub-environments. Inside and outside the organization, those who feel that more boundary spanning is needed will have to seek the competencies and structures to support this crucial activity.

The social-psychological situation will further complicate coping with information feedback in general. Organizations and their members will have to cope not only with the information produced by boundary spanning, but with the fact that this information is carried, and frequently generated, by human beings performing that function. Thus personal and interpersonal matters will be ensnarled in this form of feedback more than in dealing, say, with social-indicator data.

The boundary-spanner function will be protean: scanning, stimulating data-generating activity, monitoring, evaluating data relevance, transmitting information, and facilitating interpersonal intercourse. The spanner is in one way or another a carrier of information between systems of activity, and as a carrier he is a system for both feedback and generation of information. Being human, he will be fallible in what he observes and reports; and activities he initiates for the purpose of generating information may not turn out as he intended. He is thus especially vulnerable to error, and because of ambivalence toward him, his messages will often be ignored, repressed, rejected, or distorted. Inevitably,

the boundary spanner's function will be ambiguous, conflict-laden, ambivalently performed and responded to, and
thus precarious. Boundary spanners will often be distrusted and resented by all the spanned parties; yet they will also be depended on by those pushing for or pushed toward long-range social planning. Without the boundary spanner's commitment and skill, long-range social planning will be impossible to initiate, much less to institutionalize. This ambivalence and confusion will create additional resistance to changing over to long-range social planning, but it will also facilitate inadvertent moves in that direction.

TYPES OF BOUNDARY SPANNERS

Before looking in more detail at the social-psychological sources of resistance to boundary spanning, two kinds of boundary spanning merit mention.

First, recall that there are five *cognitive-affective* boundary-spanning tasks[3] that are associated with each stage of changeover:
- stimulating interest in the possibility of long-range social planning, or of some facet of it;
- initiation;
- legitimation;
- action decisions; and
- implementation or routinization.

These activities will be responsive to each "stage" of the changeover process itself. Second, there will be the *structural* boundary-spanning tasks that stretch across organizational subsystems, functions, or offices to the environment.

In our situation, there would be boundary spanning at many levels, to serve and stimulate many activities; Boundary spanners would often be advocates, trying to influence their peers and superiors, and providing them with information with which to influence others.

R. Havelock's encyclopedic review of innovation methods[1] has led him to propose several categories of "knowledge-linking roles," which are valuable to have in mind. (See chart on p. 276.)

A boundary spanner effective at stimulating interest in moving to a particular stage of long-range social planning may not be the same person who can legitimize that interest. The style, substance, and circumstances of boundary spanning will vary, and different persons and groups may be more or less appropriate for particular tasks. However, in cases where persons have been assigned the task of developing a long-range planning capability, or have invented the task out of their own inclinations, the multifarious spanning tasks have been done by one or a very few people in each organization. Consequently, there have been heavy personal and organizational costs.

The boundary spanner committed to changeover to long-range social planning will have to try to arrange his activities so that he can make interpersonal and informational contacts to sustain him personally, while not threatening those they seek to link; and to allow him to gain and use the information and ideas needed to move others to support long-rang social planning. This means he must seek out and bring together people and information concerned with

- the future;
- what they are doing about that future and about each other, including their arguments and agreements;
- what other organizations are doing regarding long-range social planning; and the nature of the relationship of their organization to its environment, and vice versa.

In the turbulent environment, all of these linkage efforts will require the boundary spanner to relate to the outside with understanding and skill, as carefully as he relates to the inside of his organization, or he will quickly be seen by his external links as exploitative, imperialistic, manipulative, and untrustworthy.

Varieties of Knowledge-Linking Roles

Role Type	Function
Conveyor	To transfer knowledge from producers (scientists, scholars, developers, researchers, manufacturers) to users (receivers, clients, consumers).
Consultant	To assist users in identification of problems and resources, to assist in linkage to appropriate resources; to assist in adaptation to use: facilitator, objective observer, process analyst.
Trainer	To transfer by instilling in the user an understanding of an entire area of knowledge or practice.
Leader	To effect linkage through power or influence in one's own group, to transfer by example or direction.
Innovator	To transfer by initiating diffusion in the user system.
Defender	To sensitize user to pitfalls of innovations, to mobilize public opinion, public selectivity, and public demand for adequate applications of scientific knowledge.
Knowledge-builders as linkers	To transfer through gatekeeping for the knowledge storehouse and through defining the goals of knowledge utilization. To transfer through maintenance of a dual orientation: scientific soundness and usefulness.
Practitioner as linker	To transfer to clients and consumers through practices and services that incorporate the latest scientific knowledge.
User as linker	To link by taking initiative on one's own behalf to seek out scientific knowledge and derive useful learnings therefrom.

Robert Burco

RESISTANCE TO BOUNDARY SPANNING

In general, the boundary spanner will facilitate feedback from the environment, and between subgroups in the organization. Boundary spanners will seem threatening to other members of the organization, and to members of the environment, because they carry sensitive information to others. They perforate boundaries of subsystems within the organization, threatening their autonomy, their secrets, their security, and their unexamined *raisons d'être*. Moreover, they encourage the joint use of planning technology, which in itself threatens conventional subsystem autonomy.

At the same time, boundary spanners directly experience environmental turbulence, then report and interpret this experience to those who hear about it only indirectly. Because it is crucial, this information-diffusion process is almost certain to be a source of disturbance. By their very presence, boundary spanners encourage the environment to produce information it might not otherwise recognize it possesses, and which it can benefit by producing. Thus, they may enlarge the range of demands on their organization, but also the sources of support.

There will be strong inclinations to resist such "invasions," even if it means abjuring information available from the spanner's "invasion" of the subsystem at the other end of the link. The most direct resistance will be to activities introduced by boundary spanners in order to facilitate one or another aspect of changing toward long-range social planning.

Resistance to the boundary spanner can be accomplished by so constraining the person that he is recognized, and recognizes himself, as playing a ritualistic role, in which he is not to be trusted or taken seriously. Organizations regularly ritualize boundary-spanning activities in order to appear "in touch," while exposing themselves to a minimum of uncertainty, error recognition, and pain of reorganization. Advertising is often the agent for this ritualized boundary spanning (consider expressions of "shared" concern for the environment, and puffery about new arrangements to ensure a direct response to customers' complaints). Ritual is sometimes the intent of Presidential Commissions, White House Conferences, and special advisory panels. Assigning boundary spanners to the morass of organizational committees is a standard method for undermining their effectiveness — though sometimes this backfires.

Tavistock Institute research on group processes has illuminated another means for resisting disturbing input: people are frequently chosen for boundary-spanning roles (though the motives behind the choice are often unconscious), as a means of getting them "away" from core activities of the subsystem which, other members feel, are upset by the presence of the spanners-to-be.[5] Also, members of the sentient group associated with a task may feel the group will be strengthened if they eject those who are not totally committed. Finally, it usually appears to such groups that there may be some benefit in linking themselves to the environment, and thereby gaining more information about it. Often, however, this is a rationalization, since those members of organizations who would find long-range social planning uncomfortable, would prefer to minimize the amount of nonroutine information they must deal with. Those who believe in the need for social planning, and seek to implement it in a situation where that belief is not widely shared (which would characterize most bureaucratic activities) would create just such a disturbance. There would be a strong tendency, then, to move them away from the core of the activity by linking them to the outside. But removing this source of internal turbulence is gained at the cost of heightening uncertainty and anxiety.

On the one hand, the boundary spanner may come to identify more with the organization or persons spanned *to*, than with the organization spanned *from*. If this happens, he could subvert or desert the original organization, or at least discard its norms and purposes. (This of course is well known to organizations like the Department of State, which regularly rotates Foreign Service officers and brings them home for reindoctrination.) During the effort to change over to long-range social planning, there will indeed be occasions for the spanner to be seduced away from his organization. Kahn suggests that for boundary spanners associated with future-responsive societal learning, removing them from that role from time to time would serve two purposes: to permit the spanner to indoctrinate other organizational personnel with outside perspectives, and to relieve the spanner of the role strain attached to the boundary-spanning function.

To date, the frustration and the sense of marginality associated with the boundary-spanning roles related to long-range social planning have been so punishing that people in these roles usually find their cognitive and affective support — and therefore their allegiances — outside of the organizations they are trying to change.[6] This situation will persist even if changeover attempts are made; outside his organization, the boundary spanner is more likely to find more supportive people who are involved in the technologies related to introduction of long-range social planning, such as seminars and research studies. For some boundary spanners, these activities will be both cognitively and affectively attractive. Operating free of embroilment in the enormously difficult and frustrating tasks of organizational change, these groups will be intellectually wide-ranging and imaginative; the people involved will often offer each other more emotional support and shared commitment than boundary spanners find in their "home" organization. Moreover, these people will not be ambivalent toward the spanners, nor will they subject them to the institutional and personal pressures that will exist within their own organization as they try to change it toward long range social planning. Other agencies may also appear seductive, if only because the "grass is greener" syndrome is especially prevalent when frustration and a sense of tenuous organizational loyalty are chronic, as they are likely to be for many boundary spanners.

On the other hand, some boundary spanners will have enough task-group and sentient-group support within their own organizations to find the challenge of facilitating changeover efforts deeply rewarding. This is especially likely to be so for boundary spanners who are skilled in organizational-development techniques. They will be better able to anticipate and understand what is or is not happening, and better able to interpret the slings and arrows they suffer not as personal attacks, but as expressions of the situation.

For the less-fortunate boundary spanner, the threat of defection will create uncertainty, and hence anxiety, in those who commissioned them, whether they were commissioned to enhance linkages with the environment outside their boundaries, or as a means of reducing internal turbulence. But by rejecting the spanners, the powers-that-be must also worry about persisting organizational turbulence, and its ability to erode allegiance. Moreover, they must also consider the threat to organizational survival that may result from information revealed by the ex-boundary spanners — information that could expose organizational weaknesses (and, not incidentally, the weaknesses of those who made possible the occasion for defection in the first place). As Anthony Downs observes:

All top-level officials (and many others) are frequently in danger of being embarrassed by revelations of their illegal acts, failures, lack of control over their subordinates, and sheer incompetence. . . .

Even the most brilliant and impeccably ethical leader of any large organization will eventually develop some skeletons in the closet because of the nature of large organizations. This is particularly likely if his organization's functions involve great uncertainty, rapidly changing environments, large expenditures, and heavy pressures from external agents.

. . . No leader of any large organization can avoid undertaking acts he does not want made public. Therefore, the desire for personal loyalty among subordinates is a universal phenomenon among such leaders.[7]

This threat is very real in a turbulent society, where roles outside the organization will often interact with roles performed inside the organization.

Individuals with a long-range social planning perspective often have competencies growing out of that perspective that are increasingly in demand. At the same time, their perspectives and their corresponding feelings of urgency about getting on with long-range social planning make them more indifferent to parochial values about organizational prerogatives and public relations images. It will be a growing threat to error-denying, uncertainty-resistant organizations and environments, because in the very nature of their activities, many who seek the boundary-spanning role see themselves as expendable. They come from environments, and carry self-images, that value problem solution over organizational stability — even over organizational survival; and there seem to be more such people produced in our changing, multi-valued environment.

Finally, the boundary spanners' special opportunities to discover more rewarding affiliations will stir in others the embers of discontent and frustration that always warm the yearnings of persons struggling to be meaningful in upsetting, uncertain situations. Coping with perhaps unsought, but nevertheless self-generated, pressures to look farther afield, as boundary spanners do, will add to their personal burdens. These stirrings, transformed through the ubiquitous psychological process of projection, can lead them to question the organizational loyalty of their boundary spanning colleagues. An unconscious desire of the entrenched to avoid these uncomfortable states of mind will provide yet another incentive to restrain boundary spanners, and, in the process, to resist efforts to change toward long-range social planning.

Ambivalence toward the boundary-spanning function when applied to planning activities is evidenced by the reluctance of top executives to commit sufficient resources to developing this function, even when they assign it. The rationale offered is that they want to see what will develop before they invest too heavily; but investing meagerly practically guarantees that those who are given the boundary-spanning roles will have too few resources to do an adequate job. Usually the assignment fails because the spanners are worn down by frustration and antagonism, or because they are reassigned by higher authorities who have decided that their activities bring too little payoff, or too much disruption to the organization.

Within this situation lies another source of ambivalence toward boundary spanners intent on furthering the change toward long range social planning. It resides in executives and managers; from those at the top, on down through those responsible for the various subsystems that must be linked to meet the requirements for long-range social planning. Boundary spanners, especially those performing as long-range planners, come to understand the ramifications of the interactions between the subsystems better than the subsystem administrators do. The spanners see the picture broadly, "from above," whereas the subsystem administrators are rewarded for seeing their activities narrowly, from the vantage point of what most benefits their subsystem. The executives at the top rarely see the detailed interactions of their own organization; their perspective and reward come from looking outward at the relationship of their organization to its environment. These executives really have little control over or understanding of the interactions between their subsystems. Information coming up to them is deliberately filtered and distorted to protect the senders, and interaction between subsystems is supposed to be managed by their subordinates.

The role of boundary spanners, however, frees them from the reward structure that constrains the actions and perspectives of middle-level managers. Thus, they are able to obtain information, and to derive implications from it, that they can apply to an understanding of the organization that is different from that available to top-level or middle-level management. Boundary spanners learn things and put them together in ways that are potentially threatening to the autonomy and authority of executives and middle-level administrators, threatening their feeling of competence and control. This is not to say that boundary spanners are more competent or should be in more control than the administrator or executive. While the spanners' perspective is likely to be broader, it will be different from theirs, partially because, not being in a management role, spanners do not completely understand that perspective — just as those inside the organization have trouble getting the spanners' "feel" for the turbulence outside. These mutual inadequacies of understanding and response to each other's needs can only he reduced if time, resources, and self-conscious efforts are committed to acknowledging them and working on them.[8]

The uncertainty and anxiety attached to the establishment of boundary-spanning activities, whether to gain environmental contact or to reduce the impact of an internal disturbance, is succinctly summarized by Miller and Rice:

> In general, the setting up of any intergroup relationships involves the drawing, temporarily at least, of new boundaries. And the drawing of new boundaries contains the possibility that the new boundaries will prove stronger than the old — that the new boundaries will enjoy a great sentience than the old.
>
> Potentially, therefore, the setting up of any intergroup transactions has destructive characteristics since the relationships involved may destroy, or at least weaken, familiar boundaries. But any open system, in order to live, has to engage in intergroup transactions. The members of any group are thus inevitably in a dilemma: on the one hand, safety lies in the preservation of its own boundary at all costs and the avoidance of transactions across it; on the other hand, survival depends upon the conduct of transactions with the environment and the risk of destruction.
>
> . . . Clearly, the more numerous the members who 'represent' an enterprise to its environment, the greater the chance of inconsistency; and hence, as we have postulated, of reducing investment in the enterprise boundary.[9]

Burdens and Incentives Experienced by Boundary Spanners

In Chapter 7 we examined the psychological burdens produced by ambiguous or conflicting roles. Here, I note only that boundary spanners will unavoidably be subject to heavy role stress.

Another burden will often be added to those already described. A decision to influence an organization, or parts of it, to change toward future responsive social learning involves adding another work load on already overloaded persons. At whatever level or source the initiative comes from in the organization, people who think in terms of long-range social planning must already have been formally or informally in touch with many trends and activities beyond those that occupy them in their jobs. Otherwise, they would hardly appreciate the need for future-responsive societal learning, much less be motivated to initiate it — especially given the rewards that go with conventional organizational perspectives. Such persons are almost certainly already overloaded by organizational and extra-organizational activities. But initiating long-range social planning requires spanning beyond conventional organizational boundaries and activities to garner the conceptual and operational ideas and resources. And this boundary spanning means further overloading, with concomitant exhaustion and emotional discomfort.

Most boundary spanners will perform that function by virtue of some specialized competence that they or their superiors believe legitimizes the linking function. As a result, for years to come the boundary spanner can be expected to provide his own contribution to the resistance to changing over to long-range social planning. This resistance will derive from the trained incapacities associated with the boundary spanner's special competencies: The professional socializing experiences of many who fill these roles will have produced personal styles of behavior as perception that militates against their easy acceptance by others not similarly socialized. More specifically, since many aspects of long-range social planning technology will depend on mathematical-logical styles of thinking, persons with these skills are likely to find themselves by choice or assignment bridging the proposed planning activity and the conventional organizational activity they hope to influence. But by training, and sometimes by temperament, persons who use these cognitive styles are often obtuse to the point of being, or appearing to be, downright arrogant about the priority and rightness of their expertise.[10]

In contrast, there is the boundary spanner who is "all heart," who has analogous trained incapacity to recognize the need for rational learning relationships between the organization and the environment. For these spanners, that which ought to get planning attention may seem to be ineffable, transcending all efforts to embed it in a systematic societal learning system, or it may seem to be a matter that can only be dealt with by those in the environment who have lived the situation."

Therefore, there will be the task of structuring the organization and its organizational interfaces in such a way that the cognitive and interpersonal inadequacies of the boundary spanners can be dealt with openly and constructively in order that boundary spanners can learn to enlarge their interpersonal skills and substantive knowledge. This again emphasizes the reciprocal aspects of building a trusting, open, uncertainty-acknowledging, error-embracing organization by improving the interpersonal competencies of its members, and changing the norms and structures that sustain them.

In view of the conflict-laden, ambiguous, and potentially frustrating role that inheres in boundary spanning, why does anyone choose to perform it? There seem to be several rewards. For one intent on pushing for changes toward long-range social planning, the role could be particularly potent. The incumbent has the opportunity to define new realities and opportunities among groups that need to collaborate if these changes are to be tried out. His access to information beyond that known within the boundaries of any subsystem, and his comparative freedom to interpret and embellish the implications of that information, afford him special opportunities and resources to be influential. As boundary spanner with the aim of moving toward long-range social planning, his monitoring activities could afford him and his sponsors special opportunities to channel and regulate developments in that direction. Whether these goals are fulfilled is another question. So far they haven't been, and most of those with whom I am familiar have sooner or later given up the role — or have been forced out of it. But for those aspirants yet to come, these can be potent enticements — especially if they are naive about the matters discussed here.

Motives like these are also bolstered by other psychologically-rewarding aspects of the role: a sense of omniscience and the expectation (sometimes the realization) of influence.

The boundary spanner knows more than the groups he spans because he has access to more sources of information, and because he has the incentives and resources to make more interpretations. The additional facts and interpretations are what makes him valuable (as well as what makes him threatening). The feeling of knowing more, and being more valuable because one knows more, is heady stuff indeed. It has kept more than one boundary spanner going in the face of hostility, rebuff, and only occasional influence.

For some, there is the satisfaction of feeling powerful by virtue of their omniscience Not only may they influence, but they can defect — with all the potential for upset that implies. Sometimes they do both; but even when they don't, the belief that they can influence by defecting sometimes compensates for the frustrations and rebuffs.

Related to the satisfaction of feeling powerful is the satisfaction of operating clandestinely. Boundary spanners know that efforts to introduce planning activities are bound to be resisted, at least by superiors who have attained their status by commitment to bureaucratic routines, or who are political appointees for whom the requirements for long-range social planning would jeopardize their ambitions or operating styles. Hence, some spanners feel a special satisfaction in the opportunity to transform conventional roles into boundary-spanning activities, to establish alliances outside the formal lines of authority, to beat the system while operating within it.

And finally there is the feeling of mobility that such spanning tasks inspire, as well as the experience of wider horizons and exposure to more people and situations and alternative career opportunities. This, too, helps compensate for inadequate or unreliable in-house recognition.

Of course, in addition to those who seek the role, there will be persons and groups who are assigned to boundary-spanning activities, whether they like it or not, because in the eyes of their superiors their present roles or organizational titles seem right for the job. But they may not be at all right for the job, and they may not want it either, although some may come to like it for the feelings of power and omniscience it provides. However, for others, including some members of in-house planning staffs, the psychological burdens may well be intolerable. Many persons who, from their location in the table of organization, would seem to be "naturals" to further the cause of long-range social planning, in fact will sabotage such efforts because they are unable to operate effectively under conditions of high role ambiguity, role conflict, and vacillating, ambivalent support. This will be true for many who recruited themselves for and trained in the more rigid conventional skills and professional standards of city planning, land-use planning, operations research, computerized data processing and simulation, and other such areas of quantitative expertise. Some administrators, recognizing this fact of life, have made humane use of it. When reorganizing their planning activities to make them more flexible and open to the environment, those people who are unable to deal with "turbulence at the interface" have been deliberately shifted to jobs that emphasize routine.

A number of those compensations associated with boundary spanning have to do with real or fantasized behavior by the role incumbents, of precisely the kind that generate hostility and anxiety among their clients. Those who fill the role may find in it compensations that are truly threatening to those dependent on them.

Thus, those who need the services of boundary spanners may have valid reasons for their fears. These fears would be less valid if the boundary-spanning role were valued enough by the organization to provide direct rewards instead of fantasized omniscience and power. But as long as users are ambivalent, the role is unlikely to be positively valued with any consistency. The dilemma is unreal, however; making boundary spanning more acceptable organizationally and more rewarding personally requires the personal, interpersonal, and structural changes mentioned throughout these chapters. What seems clear is that boundary spanning cannot be incorporated as an essential part of long-range social planning merely by imposing or overlaying that activity on conventional organizational norms and structures.

1. Marris, P. and M. Rein. *Dilemmas of Social Reform.* New York: Atherton, 1967, p. 137.

2. *See* Moynihan, D. *Maximum Feasible Misunderstanding.* New York: The Free Press, 1969. *See also* Arnstein, S. "Maximum Feasible Manipulation." Third Conference on Crises, Conflict, and Creativity, National Academy of Public Administration, July 1970.

3. *See* Chapter 2, "Phases and Actors in Changeover Processes," pp. 95-104.

4. Havelock, R. et al. "Specialized Knowledge Linking Models," *Planning for Innovation.* Ann Arbor: Institute for Social Research, Center for Research on Utilization of Scientific Knowledge, 1971, Ch.7, pp. 4-5.

5. In conversation with A.K. Rice. *See also* Rice, A.K. *Learning for Leadership.* London: Tavistock, 1965.

6. Based on numerous interviews. See also Duhl, L. "Creation of Forecasting and Planning Mechanisms." American Academy of Arts and Sciences, Commission on the Year 2000. Unpublished paper, Vol III of the Commission's Working Papers.

7. Downs, A. *Inside Bureaucracy.* Boston: Little, Brown, 1966, pp. 71-72.

8. An observation by R. Bauer.

9. Miller, E. and Rice, A.K. *Systems of Organization.* London: Tavistock, 1967, pp. 23-24.

10. It is generally acknowledged that the Pentagon experts assigned to indoctrinate civilian agencies in PPBS, in the wake of President Johnson's Executive Order that civilian agencies use PPBS, did a first-rate job of alienating almost everyone by their "arrogant, insufferable, know-it-all" attitude toward the civilian innocents. This impression seems so widely shared that there is no reason to doubt that arrogance was evident.

11. *See* Cottrell, L. and E. Sheldon. "Problems of Collaboration Between Social Scientists and the Practicing Professions." The Annals of the American Academy of Political and Social Science, 346 (March 1963). *See also* Moynihan, D. "Eliteland," Psychology Today, 4(4) (1970).

13

How Conventional Organizations Resist the Requirement for Information Sharing

The intimate and reciprocal relationship between the person and the organizational structure is sharply exemplified in the resistance to requests to share information garnered and used by sub-units in the pursuit of their mission.

THE PRESENT STATUS OF INFORMATION SHARING

There are many types of information that persons and organizations resist sharing. The forms and circumstances of resistance can be expected to vary to some degree, depending on the kind of information involved, but I will not attempt such a detailed description here; that is more appropriate for later systematic studies. Nevertheless, it is worth noting some of the types of information that are people will resist sharing. This will help explain why information sharing is so crucial to efforts to change toward societal learning through long-range social planning.

Information sharing includes the exchange of data, data sources, and data collecting methods; program instructions for processing, combining, disaggregating, and summarizing the data; interpretations of the data and the theories or assumptions upon which interpretations are made; and decisions about who has access to any of the above, including who is obligated to use what data, programs, or interpretive concepts as a basis for organizational action.

Today a person's or sub-unit's power in an organization rests on the capability to preempt information. There are several advantages in preempting information, though no one advantage is exclusively determined by information control, nor is it usually the only determinant of power, influence, and invulnerability. But it can be a formidable asset, one that is well worth protecting under present norms. By controlling access to information, persons can protect themselves somewhat from challenges to their authority, because others lack the information they would need or could use to dislodge them. To some extent, they can protect themselves from accusations of inefficiency or unimaginativeness, because they have control of the information others need to prove their case. They can protect their appreciative setting about what constitutes the relevant reality in their environment by the kind of information they collect. This self-serving image of reality gives them a measure of value in their own eyes. They can define their situation very much as they choose, because they have information about it that others lack. And they can bargain with information for power and status and for other information they need to improve their control capability and status.

Resistance to sharing information also benefits those who ought to use the information if they could get it. By not having more information to expand the considerations they should apply to their interpretations and decisions, uncertainty is not increased and the risk of error from decisions made in an unfamiliar larger context is lessened. A person or his unit remains responsible only for what can be done in the face of constraints on the information available to them. In other words, the rule "live and let live" often supports information preemption.

Yet moving toward long-range social planning depends fundamentally on overcoming resistance to relinquishing the advantages gained from information preemption. Every aspect of the planning process will involve the sharing of information found in the discrete units of an organization. Moreover, this sharing must extend to constituencies in the environment, and to other organizations involved in overlapping service areas. Unless the data base and the assumptions for interpreting and applying it are shared with the environment, societal learning will be impossible. Also, the very legitimacy, utility, and viability of service organizations will depend, in part, on their ability to respond positively to demands for information from constituency representatives skilled in data interpretation and utilization. (There is, of course, endemic resistance in federal agencies to sharing information with the public.)

Experience clearly supports the theoretically-based conjecture that conventional organizational structures and norms encourage strong resistance to this requirement for changing toward long-range social planning.

Those familiar with ongoing efforts to use information-sharing systems such as urban data banks and management information systems conjecture that resistance will continue. According to Anthony Downs:

Within city governments, those who actually control automated data systems gain in power at the expense of those who do not. Most city officials are acutely aware of this potential power shift. Each operating department naturally wants to retain as much power as possible over its own behavior and its traditional sphere of activity. Its members are especially anxious to prevent "outsiders" from having detailed knowledge about every aspect of the department's operations. Hence nearly every department with operations susceptible to computerized management will at least initially fight for its own computer and data system controlled by its own members.[1]

STRUCTURAL SOURCES OF INFORMATION PREEMPTION

Overcoming these resistances to information sharing will depend upon changing the structural arrangements that reinforce and reward personal and interpersonal behavior and self-images that resisting change. We need to look, then, at what seem to be the structural sources that encourage resistance to information sharing. Wilensky serves our purposes well when he explains them as the result of hierarchy, specialization, and centralization. With regard to hierarchy, he writes:

Information is a resource that symbolizes status, enhances authority, and shapes careers. In reporting at every level, hierarchy is conducive to concealment and misrepresentation. Subordinates are asked to transmit information that can be used to evaluate their performance. Their motive for "making it look good," for "playing it safe," is obvious. A study of 52 middle managers . . . found a correlation . . . between upward work-life mobility and holding back "problem" information from the boss; the men on their way up were prone to restrict information about such issues as lack of authority to meet responsibilities, fights with other units, unforeseen costs, rapid changes in production, scheduling or work flow, fruitless progress reports, constant interruptions, insufficient time or budget to train subordinates, insufficient equipment or supplies, and so on. Restriction of such problem information is motivated by the desire not only to please but also to preserve comfortable routines of work: if the subordinate alerts the boss to pending trouble, the former is apt to find himself on a committee to solve the problem. . . . Hierarchy blocks communication; blockages lead to indoctrination; indoctrination narrows the range of communication.[2]

Argyris reinforces this view:

At the upper levels, subordinates tend to "think positive" (remain within the tolerance limits arbitrarily set at the top); they react primarily to crises; they tend to create win-lose competitions between groups for resources and esteem; they hide information; and they create "just-in-case-the-president asks" files.[3]

Specialization is an important source of resistance. As Wilensky notes:

As a source of information blockage and distortion, specialization may be more powerful than hierarchy. . . . Each service, each division, indeed every sub-unit, becomes a guardian of its own mission, standards, and skills; lines of organization become lines of loyalty and secrecy. . . . Top men . . . are reluctant to let their subordinates "take on" rivals by asking for information for fear that their unit will betray weakness, invite counter-inquiries, or incur debt. While information can also be used to persuade potential allies and to facilitate accommodation with rivals . . . it is more commonly hoarded for selective use in less collaborative struggles for power and position.[4]

A second source of resistance from specialized sub-units will be their reluctance to risk present operating styles and rewards in order to use untested information-sharing technology. As specialists, their "objective" estimates of the high economic, political, and operational costs of shifting to an information-sharing system based on the latest information technology has a valid rational component. However, their estimates are also likely to be a rationalization for continuing to do things the familiar way — a way that is less uncertain, hence less prone to error, and less likely to require personally-upsetting restructuring. Negative estimates will confront advocates of long-range social planning with a particularly sticky kind of argument to overcome, especially since many executives and managers
prefer the rationalization offered by their conservative experts, to facing the consequences of information sharing. In this regard, Argyris writes:

There is a deeper reason for executive resistance. It's rarely discussed because executives themselves are rarely aware of it. This basic, unspoken reason usually surfaces after lengthy discussion about the probable long-range effects of MIS.

At this point managers slowly begin to realize that fundamental changes will be required in their personal styles of managerial thought and behavior. That's when the danger signals start. Those other stated objections — lack of knowledge and the primitive state of the art — are important, but only temporary. Eventually they will be overcome by research and dissemination of knowledge. But concern and fear about what MIS will do to managers — what it will reveal about the way they've been operating all this time — is what creates the basic resistance.[5]

Wilensky's third structural contributor to resistance to information sharing is centralization:

Related to the information pathologies of hierarchy and specialization is the dilemma of centralization: if intelligence is

*lodged at the top, too few officials and experts with too little accurate
and relevant information are too far out of touch and too over-loaded
to function effectively; On the other hand, if intelligence is scattered
throughout many subordinate units, too many officials and experts
with too much specialized information may engage in dysfunctional
competition, may delay decisions while they warily consult each
other, and may distort information as they pass it up. More simply,
plans are manageable only if we delegate; plans are coordinated in
relation to organizational goals only if we centralize.*

*. . . In the minds of political, military, and industrial elites the
advantages of centralized intelligence have apparently tended to
outweigh these dangers. Most executives have been less concerned
about preserving the independence and objectivity of their experts
than about controlling them. For their part, the experts, seeing a
chance for greater influence, have not been loathe to secure guidance
from the top.*[6]

Argyris writes:

*As the informal modes become explicit, information comes
increasingly under the control of top management. The top level
starts to see things it never saw before. Middle managers feel
increasingly hemmed in. In psychological language, they will
experience a great restriction of their space of free movement,
resulting in feelings of lack of choice, pressure, psychological failure.
These feelings in turn can lead to increasing feelings of helplessness
and decreasing feelings of responsibility. Result: a tendency to
withdraw or to become dependent upon those who created or
approved the restriction of space of free movement.*

*Sound familiar? MIS can do to middle and near-top management
exactly what the job specialization itself does to lower-level
employees.*[7]

There are ways to reduce these oppressive adverse effects,
as demonstrated by the evolution of divisionalized large
corporations. To also achieve this in government would require a
radical redesign of bureaucratic structures and the relationship
between executive and congressional control of the agencies. This
would also be true at the state and local levels. More basically, it is
unclear that the philosophy inherent in corporate decentralization
is appropriate for defending or pursuing the public interest. The

reconciliation of conflicts within and among agencies, and of the purposes of Congress and the Executive Office, does seem to require some kind of top management that knows more and more, even as it requires the same down the line — which brings us back to Wilensky's dilemma, just quoted.

As I have repeatedly emphasized, attempts at changing toward long-range social planning will have to be *learned* from if the effort is to advance, or at least have a chance of persisting, in the face of the many failures and sources of resistance we have examined. But learning will itself require an information-sharing system to facilitate just that purpose. An additional organization function would have to be integrated: an information-sharing system for applying the learning to further efforts at long-range social planning. A general observation by Wilensky emphasizes the additional organizational-redesign task implicit in the requirement for a learning-system, information-sharing structure:

Other things being equal, the larger the size, the greater is the public impact, the more intense is the problem of internal control, and the more resources are available for the intelligence function. The more specialization, the more interdependent are the specialized parts, the greater the cost of failure of any one part, and, therefore, the more resources devoted by each to keep track of the others, and the more staff at the center to coordinate the whole. Moreover, greater specialization increases the difficulty of recruitment and training, and the amount of effort needed to secure information about morale and performance. Finally, the more heterogeneous the membership or constituents of an organization, the more ambiguous, diffuse, diversified, and numerous its purposes or products; this more complex structure of goals means more variables to consider and a more urgent problem of coordination.[8]

If organizations try to meet these requirements by the conventional means of hierarchy, specialization, and centralization, organizational learning for changing to long-range social planning will not be possible: information will not be sufficiently shared.

Some Unresolved Dilemmas

If there is a way out of the auto-regenerative set of resistances to sharing information, it certainly requires a willingness to acknowledge uncertainty and embrace error. Information sharing could be disastrous for the donor if the recipient uses it to further those organizational and personal needs that are rewarded by the same norms that make it worthwhile to resist information sharing. Discreet sabotage, deceit, and duplicity are usually rewarded by the conventional structures if they serve organizational survival or, sometimes, sub-unit aggrandizement. There is no reason to believe that such well-learned performance styles will be given up easily by people who have found them rewarding, and thus expect the same behavior from others.

On the other hand, there will be the environment of clamorous constituencies and advocates insisting on access to information. Once some information, and the premises regarding its applicability, are partially shared with the environment, it becomes difficult to know what can be guarded, and whether it is still worth being jealously guarded — especially if other persons and other agencies are advancing themselves by sharing with their environments.

However, there is an important dilemma here, one that would need to be worked through. One advantage in controlling access to data is that it reduces outside pressures. There is less distraction and interference because there is less basis for queries, questions, challenges, and arguments. All systems, including biological systems, control the information they allow to influence them, partly by controlling the amount of information they share with the environment.

Even as congressional demands for information do at times claim most of the creative and top administrative resources of an agency under fire, unlimited access to information could immobilize the agency, leaving it too little time, energy, and ideas to do more than provide information. Societies, especially their repositories of power and information, have vacillated between being relatively

inaccessible and relatively accessible to information, though inaccessibility has been the more
frequent response.

Nevertheless, if we wish to move toward future-responsive societal learning, it can only be done by increasing access to information. What the rules of the game should be, if we want to provide access to information but also protect the information-sharing organization so that it can accomplish its other functions, is one of the many procedures yet to be learned, through attempts to move toward long-range social planning. But while pressures from the environment will tend to force data sharing within an organization, they do not of themselves provide the direction for effective and humane changes in the structure, supportive norms, and interpersonal behavior that have traditionally sought to gain advantages from information preemption. Directions for these changes are to be found, I believe, among considerations of the kind we have attended to in other chapters.

Additional directions for structural change appropriate for information sharing for future-responsive societal learning can be discovered by examining the most encompassing information-seeking and information-using requirement for changing toward long-range social planning — namely, the pervasive solicitation and application of feedback from the present and future environment.

Before turning to this broader subject in the next chapter, I must acknowledge one aspect of information sharing that is already so much a part of the dialogue that I shall not expand on it here: the problem of individual privacy and freedom, and the extent to which these rights are threatened or protected by the preemption or sharing of information, on the one hand, and by the organizations that do the preempting or sharing, on the other. The issue is complex and holds deep dilemmas. How to live with or resolve these dilemmas depends in part on what conjectures about future personal values and societal needs are emphasized as a basis for present action. Much has been written on these issues;[9] they remain unsolved, and the balance between the private and public interest remains obscure and contentious.

1. Downs, A. "A Realistic Look at the Final Payoffs From Urban Data Systems." *Public Administration Review*,(27(3) (1967), p. 208.

2. Wilensky, H. Organizational Intelligence: Knowledge and Policy in Government and Industry. New York: Basic Books, 1967, p. 43

3. Argyris, C. "Resistance to Rational Management Systems." *Innovation*, 1970 (10), p. 30.

4. Wilensky, op. cit., p. 48.

5. Argyris, op. cit., p. 30.

6. Wilensky, op. cit., p. 58.

7. Argyris, op. cit., p. 32

8. Wilensky, op. cit., pp. 38-39.

9. Harrison, A. "The Problem of Privacy in the computer Age: An Annotated Bibliography." Memorandum RM-5495-PR/RC. Santa Monica: The Rand Corporation, 1967. *See also*, Michael, D. "Speculations on the Relation of the Computer to Individual Freedom and the Right to Privacy." *The George Washington Law Review*, 33(1) (1967). *See also* Miller, A. *The Dossier Society*. Ann Arbor: University of Michigan Press, 1971. *See also* Westin, A. *Privacy and Freedom*. New York: Atheneum, 1967.

14

The Importance of Feedback
and the Resistance to It

Information feedback is the *sine qua non* of cybernetic systems.
It is through feedback that a system evaluates where it is in
terms of where it intends to go. It is the means by which error is
detected, and thereby it provides the basis for learning how to get
from here to there, through changes in performance that result in
successive reductions in error. Of central importance for long-range
social planning, feedback also provides the information needed for
learning what now constitutes "here," and for deciding whether to
continue to try to get "there" in the future. That is, it provides the
basis for evaluating whether the appreciation of
"here" and "there" needs to be revised. In the nature of the situation
with which we are dealing, the very process of learning through
feedback provides the means for making changes in definitions of
"here" and "there," along with the means for linking them through
time via programmatic actions, and the means for evaluating those
actions.[1]

WHAT CHARACTERIZES APPROPRIATE FEEDBACK?

Ideally, the feedback process consists of:
*   Putting into the environment "output" signals — that is,
    symbols, materials, or events intended to produce specific
    results.

- Detecting in the environment signals, presumably related to the results, that can be used to assess the effectiveness of the output signals.[2]
- Detecting other environmental signals that can provide a context for analyzing the meaning of the gap between intended and actual results.
- Detecting other signals that can provide a context for revising goals and objectives and hence for revising programs intended to produce specific results.
- Gathering the signals in forms that can be interpreted.
- Bringing the signals into the initiating organization (or other organizations assigned the task of feedback analysis).
- Evaluating the meaning of the feedback in light of objectives and goals, and the programs intended to meet them.
- Disseminating the evaluation in such ways that it is in fact *acted on* by the organization so as to change or otherwise influence the output signals.

In spite of the centrality of feedback for system adaptation, most human organizations use a very poor quality of feedback under most conditions — indeed, it is often so misleading that it is worse than no feedback at all. There are many reasons why this is so in organizations that are responsible to complex environments. As discussed in Chapter 2, there are serious technological and conceptual inadequacies in most schemes. There is always the question of whether turbulence, in Emery and Trist's sense, is so great as to block out all evidence of the relationship between organizational output and environmental impact. There are ambiguities in goals and objectives that make it difficult, if not impossible, to specify what feedback to retrieve. There are also contradictions and ambiguities inherent in the statutes and other directives that determine the scope of government mandates. (This situation is beginning to change, however, with the growing understanding that society is a system, not a collection of recipients for categorically-funded programs.) There are time constraints and money limitations and all those other characteristics of the organization's operating context that permit no more than, in Herbert Simon's phrase, "bounded rationality."

HOW FEEDBACK INTERACTS WITH ORGANIZATIONAL STRUCTURES

But other factors weave through and exacerbate these circumstances by sustaining the personal, interpersonal, and structural arrangements that make familiar constraints more persistent and obstructive than they need to be. These are social-psychological factors that revolve around the needs of the organization's members to be protected from turbulence, uncertainty, error, and sentient-group instability. People resist doing what needs to be done to retrieve and use better feedback, to the degree that it removes the social-psychological advantages that organizations provide by avoiding feedback.

Even if the social-psychological sources of resistance to better feedback were removed, other sources of feedback enfeeblement would still be there, and would need to be overcome. And all these sources operate as they do, to some degree, because the social-psychological rewards — or as Henry David puts it, the benefits of calculated ignorance — discourage overcoming them. Doubtless the comforts of not knowing, because the feedback is either absent or unrevealing, have contributed to a disinclination to work hard at evaluation technology, and to risk trying it in the real world. Similarly, the comforts of ignorance have made it easier to live with the disadvantages of sub-unit autonomy and competition. So, too, with the disinclination to expose internal conflicts, either to resolve them or to make them catalysts for overall organizational accomplishment vis-à-vis the environment. Even if attempts are made to change the feedback process in ways that are appropriate for long-range social planning, they will not succeed if the benefits of calculated ignorance as a source of resistance is not considered as carefully as other factors obstructing effective feedback.

The structural arrangements that exist between the organization and its environment, and the structural arrangements within the organization for dealing with feedback, contribute to resistance to the use of feedback. As R. Rosenthal and Robert Weiss have observed:

An organization is a system of structured relations. But an organization also acts, and such actions imply intellectual, rational, decision-making processes. Both organization structure and the nature of the intellectual phase of organizational life (decision making) limit the modern organization's ability to absorb feedback information, especially data regarding second-order social consequences. Learning how to perceive or detect these consequences is difficult; it is even more difficult to make these perceptions effective within the organization.[3]

As is true in all these matters, the interdependence of persons and structures makes precise distinctions misleading and awkward. This is especially pronounced in the interplay between two factors: organizational doctrine and mission definition, which determine what aspects of the environment will be emphasized; and organizational structure (specialization, authority relations, and communication patterns), which determines how doctrine and definition will be processed in transactions with the environment.

Doctrine and mission tell the members what to pay attention to. But the components of organizational structure (expertise, boundary spanning, environment scanning, terminals for seeking and retrieving information, etc.) determine what will be collected and introduced into the organization. The choice of whom decision makers will listen to depends on their definition of mission and their definition of what they can do with what they read or hear. What they feel they can do is partly determined by how they perceive the way in which the organization's authority system deals with information from their level, and partly by how they themselves view the information. I need not belabor this fairly obvious generalization.[4] But it will be useful presently to typify several important arrangements that organizations use to avoid feedback from the environment. This will help us appreciate the formidable task of dealing with resistance to feedback, and hence with resistance to attempts to introduce feedback-dependent aspects of long-range social planning.

An organization's structural components, interacting with personal and interpersonal factors, will significantly affect whether or not feedback, once obtained, will be shared or encapsulated. Other factors, such as the structure of sub-unit differentiation and integration, contribute to the willingness or reluctance of members to process information so that it will be available within the time constraints that may ultimately determine its utility. I will not attempt to show how various internal arrangements and responsibilities may affect the processing of feedback. Here I will conjecture only about how organizational structures facilitate resistance to feedback — how they help people resist using the information itself, and also resist redesigning structures that might facilitate that use.[5]

Ideally, feedback should help reduce uncertainty by clarifying the extent to which an intended result is presently on track, and the ways in which it is not; and by discriminating among options by feeding into the present carefully worked-out conjectures about the future. Sometimes this happens, and when it does, those espousing a planning perspective gain support. But far more often feedback about the present and the future produces irritation, exhaustion, and anxiety, because it increases uncertainty or renders worthless that which was held to be certain. If it is richly reflective of the environment, it imposes more information on users than they can manage — information rich in cognitive, valuative, and emotional content. If users wish to reject some of it as "irrelevant," "awkward," or "outside their responsibility," then means for sorting it out must be invented, and this calls for new screening procedures and new arrangements of subgroups in the organization. The creation and implementation of these procedures will carry heavy opportunity costs in already overburdened organizations.[6]

It is generally recommended that more groups in the environment feed back more information to organizations, both as a means for informing and influencing organizations, and for stimulating members of the environment to participate in planning. J. Friend and William Jessop write about the necessity for responding to the law of requisite variety:

The law of requisite variety suggests that a system of strategic control will only succeed to the extent to which it can develop a similar level of complexity to the system it sets out to influence; it can never, however, be expected to achieve this if it is forced to rely entirely on the scanning abilities of one individual or even a single small group of individuals who occupy a central position in relation to the agencies concerned. It is here, if anywhere, that potential may exist for drawing on the diversity of perspectives which may be provided by a larger body of representatives, particularly where these are directly elected on a ward or constituency basis, and therefore have a direct motivation to keep in touch with events and pressures within defined sectors of the total community system. If the strategic control group can find effective ways of drawing on the existing scanning functions of all elected representatives, it may thereby considerably enhance its own internal capacity to identify areas of relevant connection between agencies.'

But as the number of advocates increases, and more authorities and experts take sides; and as we see increases in the amount and variety of feedback that is asserted to be relevant for decision making, policy formulation, evaluation, and the rest, it will become increasingly difficult to know what to pay attention to. What might be interpreted as signals, with enough time and resources to sort and compare them, will instead become mere noise. The overwhelming tendency, when faced with such information overload, is to withdraw into familiar perspectives and styles of performing. In that case, we would be pretty much where we are now, with selected feedback used to reinforce positions rather than to facilitate societal learning. Moreover, the feedback will seldom be definitive, and this grossly complicates the question of what to do with it and who is responsible for the doing. For a long time to come, such information will demonstrate to the professionals involved in long-range social planning and to their organizational and interorganizational constituencies, the limits to our understanding of what is going on "out there;" and how puny is our ability to do anything effective about it.

One of the things to be learned through long-range planning efforts is how to live constructively with noisy, "non-definitive" information. A major task will involve learning what constitutes a signal that can be meaningfully transmitted into the environment; that is, a signal that the environment will be able to recode and retransmit in forms that allow the organization to evaluate its activities. Many signals into the environment will turn out to not "recode" in these ways. Only as a result of the development of powerful theory relating specific kinds of social change to the properties of signals, will improvements in signal generation and evaluation occur; and theory development will depend on successive analyses and alterations in what are hopefully referred to as "social indicator" data.

Social indicator designers are not only the ones faced with problems. Adjustment of signals into the environment and *from* the environment means that the programs that produce them, and the functions that facilitate them, will also subject to change, as is the personal, intellectual, and emotional commitment to a particular program. So too, with the sentient-group supports that invariably develop among people associated with a given program. It means that feedback will expose the failures, as well as the successes, of programs and projects.

This, in turn, will confront program proponents with the task of acknowledging error — indeed, of seeking it out, of embracing it in the interests of learning how to create better programs. Feedback can raise questions about the sufficiency of original goals and planning for achieving them. This raises the harrowing question of who is accountable for acquiring information about the errors, and who can be trusted with it. And it poses the difficult task of dealing with personal and interpersonal conflict over goals, values, and feelings. In short, feedback will present all recipients with the likelihood of deep intellectual and emotional discomfort — provided they expose themselves to the information in the first place.

The personal and interpersonal burdens of adjusting preconceptions to more information, and the strains of coping with uncertainty and its repercussions in the organization, have been explored in earlier chapters; our concern here is with possible structural consequences. For example, those responsible for initiating administrative-managerial responses to feedback face the task of reorganizing program activities in response to the feedback implications. This requires dealing with others' errors as well as one's own, with shifting mandates and roles, and with removing people from programs to which they are committed and with which they have an intimate identification. These realignments will place heavy social psychological burdens on initiators and receivers. Typically, private and public bureaucracies are chronically overloaded with struggles arising out of competition and conflict between internal empires and external demands. The idea of having to adjudicate these struggles, in addition to those arising out of planning-oriented feedback, will simply be too much for most people most of the time. They will tend to respond with avoidance behavior, unless the circumstances force or reward them to do otherwise.

STRUCTURAL MEANS TO AVOID FEEDBACK

It should come as no surprise, then, that people have structured organizations (and organizations have structured people) in such a way as to avoid unfamiliar feedback. Roughly put, organizations arrange to receive a minimum of turbulence-generating feedback, and to use as little as possible of what they do receive.

One avoidance process involves structuring the organization so that sub-units are rewarded for using indicators of organizational *input* to the environment, as though they represented what was going on in the environment in response to them. Use of this device has been endemic in organizations that do not use profit and related measures as their feedback signal of environmental response. Historically, this approach represented widespread naïveté about the relationship between "input" and "output" in cybernetic systems. It also reflected the absence of technology needed for data processing and analysis. But naïveté was sustained by a reluctance to face the consequences of abandoning it. However, this means of avoiding feedback is beginning to be undermined by a growing recognition of the need for cost-benefit type analyses as a basis for public welfare program selection. Cost-benefit studies set the stage for defining the feedback needed to check the anticipated relationship between the symbols, material, or events put into the social system and the results produced by them.

Meantime, the perennial argument continues to be made that *some* measure is better than no measure, and that input indicators are the best that can be done in the absence of validated theory that relates input to output. Thus, recognition of ignorance is avoided and "some measure" becomes a reinforcer for the extant organizational structure and bestows its rewards on the members. "No measure," however, has the virtue of signifying ignorance, and therefore the need to invent and seek valid feedback.

Feedback that is disrupting because it is unfamiliar is also avoided by structuring the feedback-retrieval process so that it selects from the environment only those signals that are compatible with the structure and norms of the organization. As Wilensky notes:

The tendency of bureaucratic language to create in private the same images presented to the public never should be underrated. In domestic policy surely such bogeys as "the balanced budget" have worked similar mischief . . . Francis Bacon's warning that man converts his words into idols that darken his understanding is as pertinent today as it was three centuries ago.[8]

In the past, the environment was placid enough that learning about highly complex and changing social issues could be minimal, or at least slow.[9] Survival of the organization depended upon comparatively predictable intra-organizational and interorganizational bargaining among fund sources, stable constituencies, and formal internal structures — in contrast to the presently changing environment. Hence structures and norms were designed to respond to congressional feedback (or feedback from whatever sources the organization depended on), rather than to new environmental feedback.[10] In corporations, the familiar signals to which they are structured to respond usually have to do with profit or related measures such as corporate growth, market share, and public image.

As discussed in the chapter on corporate long-range social planning (see Appendix), corporations typically have not sought feedback on the extra-market consequences of the production, distribution, or consumption of their products, most notably the external costs to both nonconsumers and consumers. As a result, the new, consumerism and a concern for the natural environment have created new sources of feedback that have been disrupting to corporations and for the most part resisted, notwithstanding their advertising to the contrary. Corporate organizational structures have rewarded inattention to these matters, and therefore they are mostly populated by persons who see themselves as competent partly because they successfully fill roles that reward such inattention. Governmental agencies and their personnel have similarly restricted feedback to that which is comfortable because it is compatible with "recognizing" special constituencies and with specifying the conditions for communicating with the organizations through specific organizational sub-units or boundary spanners.[11] Peter Blau comments on feedback in government agencies:

An organizational need was not met by operating officials unless it or the fact that their tasks had become routine disturbed them sufficiently to interest them in making the required innovation. By the same token, external dysfunctions cannot be expected to disappear unless they are transformed into organizational needs, which means that their occurrence is so deleterious for administrators or for all officials that they are compelled to make adjustments. This raises the problem of developing democratic techniques that enable the public or its representatives to hold officials specifically accountable for the various consequences of bureaucratic operations, thus converting external dysfunctions into internal needs of the organization that disturb its personnel. The difficulty of finding solutions to this problem is matched only by the urgency of doing so.[12]

Put in another relevant perspective, only some environmental sources of support or criticism are deemed legitimate. And "legitimate" generally means those values, behavior, and environmental auspices that are compatible with the program and information-processing structure, and thus are understandable and approved by the servicing agency. As a result, much of what an agency ought to be receiving as feedback is screened out as unreliable, misguided, irrelevant, or politically infeasible.[13] At the same time, some feedback is overly responded to because it fits personal and organizational biases. H. Wilensky refers to this practice as follows:

This is not to say that symbols in support of established policy and comfortable prejudice inevitably serve as a substitute for policy deliberations. It is to say that facts, arguments, and propaganda directed at friends and enemies alike, in and out of an organization, can be self-convincing. Executives and politicians often become persuaded that the world of crisis journalism they create and respond to is the real world; many a decisionmaker is in this way diverted from things which really happen or which are not happening but should be. Many a leader becomes captive of the rhetoric he customarily presents or of the media image he projects. Students of modern society have given too little attention to this reverse action of propaganda — the effect on the people who themselves make the news. If supplying the symbols that guide executive action is "window dressing," it is the kind of display that tells us what is in the store.[14]

Since legitimacy criteria also function to justify the structure of organizational activities, they are a powerful means for reducing uncertainty about what knowledge will be needed for decision making, interorganizational relations; and choosing appropriate values. But this increase in certainty encourages a routinized perspective which in turn can be transformed into structural arrangements that reinforce the prevailing definitions and screen feedback in ways that leave the organization as little disturbed as possible. But resistance to feedback utilization will be increasingly vulnerable as uncertainty about organizational legitimacy increases among members of the organization, and as parts of the environment continue to challenge organizational legitimacy. Whether this vulnerability can be used to facilitate movement toward long-range social planning depends on the simultaneous occurrence of other circumstances to be discussed in the Epilogue.

Another way a prevailing definition of legitimacy is used as a feedback-reducing device is to structure the organization so that it only attends to feedback from those parts of the environment that produce feedback compatible with the organization's output signals. Those in the environment who do not respond to these signals do not increase organizational turbulence: By the criteria of legitimacy subscribed to, they have excluded themselves from organizational responsibility by not responding to the signals offered to them. In this situation the members of the organization convince themselves and others that "we've tried," but that the environment was indifferent, or antagonistic, or unappreciative of their efforts. The fault, then, is in the environment, not in the organization's input to that environment. The fact that the environment doesn't make a corresponding "effort" to respond removes the organization from any further obligations toward it. Such an approach permits legitimacy distinctions between the "worthy" and the "unworthy" poor, between the "self-helping" and the "lazy" ethnics, between "appreciative" and "unappreciative" recipients, and it results in the familiar process of "creaming off" the environment.[15] It also allows the organization to ignore or be ignorant of feedback it ought to be using as input to its conjectures about the future, which in turn should be affecting its goal and program choices.

In the extreme, organizations try to avoid undesired feedback by threatening to deny services or take punitive action. Examples of such tactics are midnight checkups by social welfare agencies; General Motors' effort to "get something on" Ralph Nader; firing an internal source of threatening feedback, be it a corporate engineer, a Defense Department critic, or a Food and Drug Administration chemist; cutting off resources, such as funds or legitimating auspices supplied by research-supporting agencies; or retracting tax-free status, as the Internal Revenue Service did to the Sierra Club; or sweeping up antiwar protesters without recourse to due process.

Serious and systematic attention to feedback from the future, via future studies, is avoided by using these same devices. Future studies can be written off as illegitimate because they do not meet conventional standards of verifiability (though often they are overly legitimized by their champions, simply because they do meet other conventional professional standards). They remain unnoticed or unused because the organization is not structured to take in feedback from this quarter; there is no niche for it. They are ignored because organizational structure rewards management and personnel for the production of input that responds to existing opportunities. This, it is presumed, will take care of the future. This presumption is often the expression of the same kind of avoidance technique that fails to question the certainty behind other input measures accepted as reliable indicators of impact on the environment.

Yet vicarious exposure to the future is a necessary part of an organization's feedback if it seeks to change toward long-range social planning. Otherwise there is no way to evaluate the feedback from the present in terms of anticipated impact in the future. Two devices serve to resist future-oriented feedback, with its freight of uncertainty and problems. One means is to attend only to future-oriented feedback that is compatible with present activities and expectations. The other is to avoid gathering any information that presages future developments which would be upsetting for the organization; that is, to avoid carrying out steps 3 and 4 in the feedback sequence (described at the beginning of this chapter). By concentrating on what is expected and familiar, the organization can overlook signals that might be precursors to discomforting or even irresponsible disconnects between present actions and future outcomes. In this way the organization also avoids the requirement to seek and use other, more contextual conjectures about the future, which, if combined with precursor information from the present environment, probably would be even more upsetting. If we think of future studies as a form of feedback that is resisted as such, it is easier to understand why such studies are frequently commissioned but seldom used if they are incompatible with present operations and perspectives.

Sometimes feedback that has the potential for increasing uncertainty does find its way into an organization. Usually it is forced into it from outside sources or is introduced by its own boundary spanners or boundary spanners to it, such as consultants. Occasionally it is inadvertently produced, as when new senior personnel bring in a different appreciation of environmental reality. Sometimes it is produced by deliberate efforts undertaken within the organization, such as internally generated program evaluations, or a decision to invite the environment to become part of the organization (for example, adding members of the environment to the organization's advisory boards). Sometimes it is generated through future studies, which may be commissioned deliberately to shake up the organization, or may do so inadvertently.

Whatever the means by which the turbulence-generating feedback is produced, and however it gets into the organization, its impact is most often attenuated, diffused, obscured, and otherwise reduced, usually to the point of impotence. As Rosenthal and Weiss observe:

The structure of interpersonal relationships that permits the organization to coordinate the actions of its members often blocks, or at least severely limits, communication of information between the feedback system and the rest of the organization.[16]

The means for limiting communication have been well described and documented.[17] Essentially, they consist of three processes:

1. Progressively screening out turbulence-generating feedback as it moves up through the system (see Chapter 13).

2. Distributing the task of discovering and coping with the implications of the feedback between contending and competing subgroups, which lack the intention, mandate, substantive skills, or interpersonal skills to cope with the threat to values, goals, and images of competence, or to cope with the requirement for error acknowledgment and creative reprogramming and restructuring.

3. Transforming the feedback into concepts and categories that allow the decision maker to treat it as if it called for only the application of familiar approaches and commitments. This reduces anxiety about one's competence and the competence of others. It also reduces anxiety about purpose. In this way information overload is kept within tolerable bounds.

Rosenthal and Weiss observe:

Over time an organization fabricates an idealized self-image, which becomes a sort of mythological basis for the organizational ideology that explains "What the hell we are doing." The elements of fantasy in the view of the organization involve, usually, some distortion of reality and, therefore, prejudice the evaluation of incoming information . . . In some degree organizational myths are essential for continuity of purpose. If the myth of "What the hell we are doing" is overly responsive to signals from the environment, it cannot serve as an organizational balance wheel. Yet at some point there is an optimum balance between the benefits of continuity of purpose and the costs of biased information.

. . . It seems probable that no organization actively seeks feedback information that contradicts such necessary organizational beliefs unless, of course, it is provoked to do so by some kind of crisis.[18]

REDUCING RESISTANCE TO FEEDBACK

There are, then, many rewards derived from the structural arrangements that protect an organization's members from the disruption encouraged by feedback, with its threats of overwhelming uncertainty, exposure of error, and questions of legitimacy and purpose. Two changeover questions are posed by this situation: How can the organization overcome the resistance that protects it and its members? and How can this be done so that the organization doesn't over-respond or under-respond to feedback from the present and the future? Indeed, this second question contains another: What would characterize an effective balance in a changing and problematic world between over-response and under-response to feedback?

Whatever else is involved in dealing with these questions, certainly two capabilities are critical. The first is a capability to reduce fears and anxieties about competence, purpose, and status, which are elicited by the threat that feedback will provide more information to more people about the environmental consequences of certain activities. Reducing such fears depends on discovering how to replace the present structure and norms with ones that can sustain and reward a learning context. If that happens, the very information that is feared may be actively sought out because of the opportunity for improvement it provides. Such a shift might reduce the tendency of organizations to over-respond or under-respond to unexpected feedback. Certainly some portion of either response is simply an effort to "cover up," sometimes expressed as panic, other times as withdrawal. However, this shift to a learning norm still leaves unresolved other knotty issues about allocation of effort and resources for decision making. Hopefully, once the social-psychological rewards of resisting extensive use of feedback are reduced, restraints on imaginative approaches to weakening other constraints can be loosened as well.

The second capability has to do with the ability of the environment to force greater openness and responsiveness to feedback. Everything we have examined makes it clear that a very large part of the incentive to change has to come from the environment and from those organizational members who, in role identification or function, link themselves to that environment. To be such a counterforce to internal resistance, members of the environment must learn what feedback to supply; and this is not always the feedback they *want* to supply. Nonetheless, members of the environment, organized into information-generating entities, will have to become more sophisticated about what constitutes useful and valid information about their needs and wants, and how to obtain and provide such information in forms that organizations can effectively understand and use. And they must become more sophisticated about the structure and processes of the organizations into which they force-feed information.

In what follows I am referring to the nongovernmental, noncorporate components of the environment — that is, voluntary organizations and ad hoc groups. Elsewhere, I have described the role of these organizations as reality redefiners and as resources for generating future-responsive policy and program-influencing information. They generally want to force feedback for changing those corporate and government organizations whose actions affect various aspects of the general welfare. But in order to meet the requirements for doing so, voluntary organizations will have to overcome the same sources of internal resistance to undertaking future responsive societal learning.

If voluntary organizations can make such changes (and a few are working very hard to do so), then they may be able to force salient information into old structures to give leverage to those proponents of long-range social planning who are also trying to make their organizations more feedback-responsive. There are universities and even high schools that have learned to respond to a greater range of feedback than they used to. In some situations they have even learned a little about how to continue to respond to changes in feedback — though it has taken traumatizing crises to move them that far. Of course, responsiveness to feedback is not the only requirement for long-range social planning; but when its ramifications are recognized, it seems to be nearer than any other requirement to being sufficient unto itself.

1. Bauer, R. "Societal Feedback." *The Annals of the American Academy of Political and Social Science*, 373 (September 1967) and Webber, M. "The Roles of Intelligence Systems in Urban-Systems Planning." *Journal of the American Institute of Planners*, 31(4) (1965).

2. There is a generally unremarked-on subtlety in the feedback process that becomes critical in the societal situation because the matching process is so poor: "the output message must be in such a form that when it acts on the [environment] the [environment] will be able to generate a message which is usable by the feedback system for controlling the output source. [Components of systems] exist as systems because they can generate signals to which they can respond: when they cannot do this they cease to be [parts of] systems. (Michael, 1954, p. 4).

3. Rosenthal, R., and Weiss, R. "Problems of Organizational Feedback Processes." In R. Bauer (ed.), *Social Indicators*. Cambridge: M.I.T. Press, 1966, pp. 316-317.

4. For a description of many interrelationships of this kind, *see* Downs, A. *Inside Bureaucracy*. Boston: Little, Brown, 1966.

5. For suggestions about what to do structurally to reduce avoidance or distortion of feedback, *see* Wilensky, H. *Organizational Intelligence: Knowledge and Policy in Government and Industry*. New York: Basic Books, 1967 and Webb, E. "Individual and Organizational Forces Influencing the Interpretation of Indicators." Institute for Defense Analyses, Science and Technology Division, Research Paper P-488. Arlington, Va.: 1969. But the problem of making the transition to those structures has not been dealt with in psychosocial terms, nor is there an adequate empirical base of comparative studies demonstrating which process works better.

6. Meier, R. "Information Input Overload." *Libri*, 13 (1963); Downs, A. *Inside Bureaucracy*. Boston: Little, Brown, 1966, Chapter 15; and Miller, J. "Information Input, Overload, and Psychopathology." *American Journal of Psychiatry*, 116 (1960).

7. Friend, J. and W. Jessop. *Local Government and Strategic Choice*. London: Tavistock Publications; Sage Publications, 1969, p. 132.

8. Wilensky, H. *Organizational Intelligence: Knowledge and Policy in Government and Industry*. New York: Basic Books, 1967, p. 22.

9. For an illuminating insight into the historical circumstances of a tranquil domestic environment that encouraged the promulgation of "process politics," otherwise recognizable as "disjointed incrementalism," *see* Schick, A. "Systems Politics and Systems Budgeting." *Public Administration Review*, (1969), 24(1).

10. The classic delineation of organizational structures and norms for getting and using feedback useful to the federal budgetary process is Wildavsky, A. *The Politics of the Budgetary Process*. Boston: Little, Brown, 1964. *See also* Seidman, H. *Politics, Position, and Power: The Dynamics of Federal Organization*. New York: Oxford University Press, 1970.

11. "When a business or government agency is under the administration of scientific management, it's clients may feel that they are not getting the service they are entitled to. But service to the client — at least as the client perceives it — is not what keeps scientific management in business. Under modern Taylorism, management's performance is judged not by the clients' perceived welfare, but by their *demonstrable* welfare. And since the managers themselves design the criteria that demonstrate welfare, demonstrable welfare can be counted on to increase." Thompson, V. "How Scientific Management Thwarts Innovation." *Trans-action*, 1968, 5(7).

12. Blau, P. *The Dynamics of Bureaucracy: A Study of Interpersonal Relations in Two Government Agencies*. Chicago: University of Chicago Press, 1963, pp. 263-264.

13. "One way organizations adapt to the unreliability of information is by devising procedures for making decisions that can ignore possibly relevant information: they develop 'special coding categories.' " Cyert, R., and March, J., *A Behavioral Theory of the Firm*. Englewood Cliffs, N.J.: Prentice-Hall, 1963, p. 110. Related observations, though not interpreted in terms of legitimacy, are made under the rubric "coding scheme barrier" to communication in Frohman, M., and Havelock, R. "The Organizational Context of Dissemination and Utilization." *Planning for Innovation*. Ann Arbor: Institute for Social Research, Center on Utilization of Scientific Knowledge, 1971, p. 7. They also cite several studies demonstrating this phenomenon.

14. Wilensky, op. cit., pp. 23-24. The most illuminating and devastating analysis and description of this situation is found in D. Boorstin's *The Image: A Guide to Pseudo-Events in America*. New York: Harper and Row, 1964. *Also see* Downs, op. cit.,

15. *See* Caplan, N., and S. Nelson. "On Being Useful: The Nature and Uses of Psychological Research on Social Problems." *American Psychologist*, 1973, 28(3). For an incisive summary of the history of American social-work attitudes toward the poor, concerning what it is "proper" to do to improve the lot of the "worthy," *see* Lubove, R. "Social Work and the Life of the Poor." *The Nation*. May, 1966, 202.

16. Rosenthal and Weiss, op. cit., p. 317.

17. *See* Wildavsky, op. cit.; Wilensky, op. cit.; Webb, op. cit.; Downs, op. cit.; and Rosenthal and Weiss, op. cit.

18. Rosenthal and Weiss, op. cit., pp. 321-322.

⋆ Epilogue ⋆

Outlook for Change:
Potential and Threat

For the purposes of this Epilogue, it will be useful to summarize
the path this book has followed. I begin, then, by repeating some
words that were used in Chapter 1 to indicate where we would
be going.

A BRIEF REVIEW

Changing toward long-range social planning would require that
people working in organizations, and in the social and natural
environments linked to them, find it rewarding to:
- Live with and acknowledge great uncertainty.
- Embrace error.
- Seek and accept the ethical responsibility and the conflict-laden
  interpersonal circumstances that attend goal setting.
- Evaluate the present in the light of anticipated futures, and
  commit themselves to actions in the present intended to meet
  long-range anticipations.
- Live with role stress and forego the satisfactions of stable on-
  the-job social-group relationships.
- Be open to changes in commitment and direction suggested by
  changes in the conjectured pictures of the future and by
  evaluation of ongoing activities.
     To be able to learn these things will require basic changes in
the way people view themselves and others, and in the

organizational norms and structures that facilitate and reward some behaviors, and punish others. It will also require changes in the way members of the environment view themselves and the organizations that serve them.

I have argued that people, organizations, and environments can succeed in changing to meet these requirements only if long-range social planning is accepted as a learning process, rather than as social-engineering technology; and that the social-psychological context for trying to change toward long-range social planning will be fundamentally influenced by the requirement that such planning be treated as a future-responsive learning procedure. Several reasons for this bear emphasizing by way of introducing the question of feasibility.

First, the social technologies for facilitating this learning process are underdeveloped, because the social-science theories, and the data needed to refine and test them, are inadequate for understanding and delineating complex, changing social systems. It is not clear how much systematic and useful information about societal dynamics can be developed, and we face a long period of learning, of research and development, in order to create theory and technology applicable to long-range social planning.

Second, we will have to learn *how* to change toward long-range social planning. We will have to learn how to introduce the requirements for long-range social planning in ways that will not result in their rejection, or distort them into ritual or into rigid, dehumanizing social-engineering exercises. We will have to learn what organizations and their members need to do to function effectively as part of a future-responsive societal learning arrangement, and we will need to learn how organizations and their members can change over to functioning in those ways. The development of individuals must be articulated with the development of organizational structures that are able to redesign themselves continuously, and both individuals and organizational structures must be able to incorporate the evolving technologies of long-range social planning. A long period lies ahead for learning what organizational techniques to apply, and how to apply them, to introduce long-range social planning into organizations.

Third, we shall have to learn *as a society* how to change to future-responsive societal learning. A particularly difficult research and development activity will have to do with learning how to incorporate members of the environment into the process of long-range social planning. Incorporation is mandatory because members of the environment share norms and expectancies that reinforce the norms, structures, and personal self-images that will produce resistance to long-range social planning. Shifting the norms and expectations of the environment so that they permit or encourage organizations to experiment with learning how to meet the requirements for long-range social planning will require the environment to participate in the learning, to be part of the learning system. Moreover, at all stages of long-range social planning there will be a need for ideas, arguments, perceptions, and information from those in the environment who will be affected by activities guided by long-range social planning. But we do not know how to incorporate "input" from the environment in the long-range social planning process: what constitutes competence, relevance, and effective procedure has yet to be discovered.

Finally, we shall have to learn what things in a turbulent world *can* be guided and regulated, and which of them it is necessary or desirable to regulate. There are no ready-made, tested "solutions," or even adequate coping procedures, for any of the major societal tasks; and even when a wide-ranging "solution" can be proposed, candid examination reveals that the means for implementing the proposal are not available. These need to be invented, developed through the process of future-responsive societal learning. We shall have to learn what it is that we can try to manage through long-range social planning, as well as how to manage what we can.

I have tried to show that resistance to changing toward long-range social planning reflects images of human nature, and expression of those images, that are incompatible with the requirements for long-range social planning. These images, and the expression of them, have resulted in the organization of human behavior in ways that set organizational survival above the anticipatory responses to the future that are appropriate to environmental development; that seek to attain and maintain power through aggressive and possessive actions; encourage "*petit Eichmanism*," or a narrow view of our responsibilities; and sidestep serious, future-responsive goal setting. We reward forms of organizational life that at best discourage societal learning, and at worst, make it impossible. Instead, people are rewarded for behaving in ways that are producing an ungovernable and unsatisfying society, made all the more unsatisfying because efforts to counteract this situation move in the very directions that exacerbate it: more novelty, distraction, image-making, security-seeking, more "nowness," more separatist "individuality" and splintering autonomy.

HOW I DEFINE "FEASIBLE"

In this light, it would seem that innovators who would attempt to move organizations toward long-range social planning would have to be naive — or reconciled, through deep conviction, to struggle with long odds against success. I intend this study to thin the ranks of the naive. As for "technological fixes," after-the-fact laws, "marketing" of public goods and services, consumer advocacy, and other such means, they seem inadequate in themselves for meeting the larger requirement that society learn how to self-consciously guide itself into a chosen future. But they can help, by slowing down the flow of consequences from incompetent and inadequate guidance systems, thus allowing much-needed time for learning how to institute future-responsive societal learning. And they can help generate an awareness of the need to move in a more deliberate, comprehensive, and more future-responsive directions. I suspect that they are doing these things, and I propose that, in spite of counterforces, moving toward future-responsive societal learning just may be feasible.

By "feasible," I mean that circumstances seem to be developing that could help establish enough of a learning-by-planning mood to moderate the growth and adverse consequences of societal entropy; and if this occurs long enough, and in enough places, we might have time to learn to be some other kind of society: one that lives by the requirements of future-responsive societal learning, in order to develop humanely. What such a society might be like would depend on the kind of learning experiences that are undergone in "getting there." Emergent, unpredictable consequences, inherent in any learning experience, will here be made all the more unpredictable by the ubiquitous interjection of social events that lie outside systematic incorporation into theory.

As Edgar Dunn argues, mankind has always evolved by building on, and learning from, an accumulating social reality. A relevant example here is the U.S. Constitution; about its genesis, Rexford Tugwell observes:

We tend to think today that agreement in 1787 about the Constitution was much more unanimous than it actually was. The 1787 convention was a tumultuous one. The framers, in the interest of compromise, actually left a great many things undone; a lot of things were left to future development simply because they could not agree.

Alan Westin comments (in personal correspondence):

The nature of 18th-century constitution-making (an exercise in the rationalism and higher law concepts of the Enlightenment of that time) was indeed to be remarkably brief. . . . [The Framers] did deliberately write in majestically vague concepts, and they did fully expect the various agencies of the Republic they were creating to give definition and meaning to the grants and denials of power they had labored over. And, they certainly did leave unspecified or only partially developed these points of basic constitutional power on which sectionalism, economic interests, and other divisions did not allow a cohesive majority to be gathered.

Feasibility means to me that enough experiments could be undertaken, enough stages in the long-range social planning process tried out, to demonstrate possibilities and utilities sufficient to generate a momentum that would encourage others to try to change toward long-range social planning, and to become environments that would support these experiments. We have begun to be more self-conscious about the need for social experiment; feasibility would mean that some organizations and their environments were willing and able to experiment with a different image of man, and different organizational norms and structures to support that image, in order to try to learn how to change toward long-range social planning.

Feasibility, then, would depend on a willingness to entertain an appropriate alternate image of man, his purposes, and the means for accomplishing them; and upon the availability of circumstances that provide occasions to try out and learn from that different way of being and doing. In what follows, I shall try to show that within ideas and experiences now beginning to receive serious attention, there may be the makings of an appropriate alternate image. Then I shall try to show that we can expect occasions and developments in society that, aided and abetted by this alternate image, might provide opportunities to learn about how to change toward future-responsive societal learning.

THE HUMAN-POTENTIAL IMAGE OF HUMAN NATURE

The image of human nature I shall consider is surrounded by a penumbra of sycophants, proselytes, wishful thinkers, and millenarianists — from whom I disassociate myself. The new image is unclear at this time, partaking of a variety of sources and promulgated with sometimes contradictory and diverging emphases. It is still aborning in this changing world: the fine points and specifics, and the arguments about them, are unimportant for our purposes. If, in the long view of history, this image turns out to be viable, what is being thought about it now will probably appear, to future generations, as murky and fragmented as ideas about human nature during the late Middle Ages and the Age of Enlightenment now look to us.

While the phrase "human-potential image of human nature" sounds as though it carries a specific definition, it does not. The "image" is at this time a collectivity of partly congruent, generally divergent images, and should be understood as no more than that.

The human-potential image and philosophy derive from religious, philosophical, aesthetic, and psychological viewpoints that have persisted for so many centuries that Huxley labeled it the Perennial Philosophy. As Willis Harmon points out:

The Perennial Philosophy is not new to Western culture. It is present in the Rosicrucian and Freemasonry traditions. Its symbolism in the Great Seal of the United States, on the back of the one-dollar bill, is testimony to the role it played in the formation of this country. It also appears in the Transcendentalism of Emerson, the Creative Evolution of Bergson, and the extensive writings of William James.

In recent years new contributions to its formulation have come from humanistic psychology, especially from Erich Fromm, Carl Jung, J. D. Laing, Abraham Maslow, Rollo May, G. Murphy, and Carl Rogers; from the theological-political-philosophical writings of such as Martin Buber, Harvey Cox, Teilhard de Chardin, Henri Marcuse, and A. Watts; from some of the theoretical writings of behavioral scientists studying group processes and organizational development, such as Chris Argyris, Warren Bennis, and Donald McGregor; from recent work with biofeedback systems that have demonstrated that humans have the ability to intervene in their "autonomic processes," thereby helping to legitimize Eastern psychology and philosophy; and from the use of chemical agents to "expand consciousness."

And what is very important, many executives, administrators, and professionals, exposed to learning occasions based on these theories and perspectives, have discovered that there is much more to themselves and to others than they had realized. Young people often find it satisfying to express themselves publicly on these matters, and some young people (by no means the majority) have been most vocal in espousing and expressing facets of this image of man and human nature. But the hard research and thought have come mostly from older members of society, and my experience and that of others suggests that there is a scattered but growing commitment to the tenets of the human-potential philosophy among professionals, and among high-level corporate and government administrators.

These few people, as champions and as boundary spanners, may be in positions to encourage the organizational development — the improvement of interpersonal and intrapersonal skills — needed to meet the social-psychological requirements for a changeover to long-range social planning, and the restructuring of organizations to reward those improved skills. Of course, there are far more people in positions of power, or seeking it, who do not share this emerging perspective; but with the influx of young professionals and administrators already exposed to these ideas in business schools and schools of planning, in departments of psychology, encounter groups, meditation sessions, and the like, their numbers will increase over the next few years. (Add to this the fact that young people are moving more rapidly into administrative roles.)

The image has appeal elsewhere, too: indeed, many of the ideas and experiments come from outside the United States. However, we have no idea, really, of how many people, of what kind, and where placed, it takes to "make a difference" when it comes to shifting societal perspectives.

For the purposes of this chapter the human-potential philosophy could be put roughly as follows: Human beings are part of nature, not separate from it. Persons are linked to other persons and to the rest of nature in ways that transcend the conscious, rational mind, and thereby have access to a far wider range of being and becoming than the everyday definitions of man, and the structures of our society, acknowledge or reward. These linkages and resources, if acknowledged and cultivated, encourage a drive toward compassionate and loving self-actualization, even toward transcendence, and away from exploitation of self and others, away from compulsive needs to control and manipulate; away from the canons of logic and science as the only expressions of reason; away from valuing scientific rationality over feelings and intuition; away from excessive need for possession of material things; and away from preoccupation with greater material growth and comparative social status. For individuals and organizations, the direction points toward more openness; a much wider range of cognitive and affective experience and intercourse; and shared development through responsible social evolution.

Some believe that the weaknesses in the conventional view of humans, demonstrated by the declining state of the society, together with the attractiveness of the human-potential view of human nature as a myth around which to reconstruct social reality, provide the thrust for, in Thomas Kuhn's words, a "paradigm shift." There are indeed fascinating analogies between the conditions in society today that appear to be encouraging a redefinition of social reality, and the conditions that lead to a fundamental change in the definition of physical reality. But to my mind, preconditions for the equivalent of a scientific paradigm shift do not really exist in the changing and ambiguous world of everyday society. For one thing, scientific paradigms are far more definitive than social paradigms; this makes the demonstration of anomalies much more impressive, and the need to deal with them more compelling. As Kuhn notes:

Without the special apparatus that is constructed mainly for anticipated functions, the results that lead ultimately to novelty could not occur. And even when the apparatus exists, novelty ordinarily emerges only for the man who, knowing with precision what he should expect, is able to recognize that something has gone wrong. Anomaly appears only against the background provided by the paradigm. The more precise and far-reaching that paradigm is, the more sensitive an indicator it provides of anomaly and hence of an occasion for paradigm change.

What is valuable in the paradigm-shift metaphor is the strong suggestion that a major shift may be underway in — to use Geoffrey Vickers' term, which I prefer — the *dominant mode of appreciation*; and that this will produce new questions about what humans can be. As a result, what are now political, economic, and social "impossibilities," might become feasible.

The contemporary version of the human-potential philosophy now developing, as I understand it, is in many ways compatible with, and supportive of, the social-psychological requirements for moving toward long-range social planning. To be interdependent and part of nature suggests a communality, a symbiosis, that could make it less necessary to fear some loss of personal control, if others were to share a supportive sense of mutual responsibility and mutual implication. Being *in* nature emphasizes that each of us is unavoidably linked to and dependent on nature (which includes other people), and that the rest of nature is dependent on each of us. Given this mutual dependence, humans must be as responsible as they can be about their part in creating the future. But since humans are only a *part* of nature, what happens in the future is only partially a result of present actions. On the one hand, humans cannot expect the future to go as they would wish unless they try to guide it. On the other hand, they cannot expect the future to go the way they wish just *because* they try to guide it. Hence it is our responsibility to try to create a responsive future, but we cannot expect to succeed as we could if we were really in control — that is, if we were *outside* nature. This appreciation could make change and instability seem a more "natural" human condition, because humans would not see themselves as insulated from nature, as we do when we act as though we were outside of nature: conquering, or overcoming, or breaking through it.

With this outlook, error-denying could seem foolish, and embracing error could be a natural mode of adjustment — of learning — rather than a threat symbolizing loss of control, and therefore punishable. The anxiety attached to uncertainty could decrease if there were a sure feeling of being imbedded in the universe. This could reduce the stress caused by role ambiguities and conflicts; or stress could remain high, but without the anxiety now associated with losing control or with being caught in error. The reduction in defensiveness brought about by acknowledging uncertainty and embracing error could result in increased mutual openness, understanding, and supportiveness. This in turn could encourage seeking, rather than avoiding, feedback. A more relaxed tentativeness could replace hard-driving, compulsive forwardness.

In some versions of the human-potential image, however, there is a position that is antagonistic to the requirements for future-responsive societal learning: this is the "do-your-own-thing" mystique — bound to the moment, insular in perspective, and committed, at the group level, to unconstrained group autonomy and action now. This is not to say that there is no historical justification for demanding local autonomy and immediate action; but acting on that historical justification in these ways is incompatible with the requirements for moving toward future-responsive societal learning.

Acknowledging themselves as part of nature, humans would emphasize the systemic, the ecologic, the emergent condition of man. At the same time, with emphasis on the naturalness of compassionate and loving self-actualization, one's sense of self and relatedness would be strengthened, so that neither excessive dependence on others, nor excessive preoccupation with independence from others, would be necessary. Both of these behaviors are typical today; they are evidence of a sense of being an incomplete or empty self. A strengthened sense of self and relatedness could lead to less emphasis on autonomy *per se*, more emphasis on collaboration — and therefore more boundary-spanning. Hence there could be less fear of loss of a particular sentient relationship, and more willingness to try new organizational structures.

Emphasis on the complementary utility of emotions and logic for validating experience, and for evaluating alternatives, could encourage less defensiveness, and more experimentation with approaches that appeal simultaneously to both aspects of human creativeness and commitment. This could also make the arguments more open to one or another scheme for goal setting, program choice, and evaluation; and it could stimulate more occasions for trust, and, in that atmosphere, for more social experimenting. Organizational behavior that was not directed by careful attention to alternative futures would be seen as irresponsible — as being incompatible with being part of nature, which includes in its present forms the seeds of the future.

And so on. My point is hardly to prove that such changes would in fact occur, but rather to suggest that if social reality were constructed out of this definition of the nature of man, then on the face of it there would be ample justification for, and legitimization of, a future-responsive societal learning style of being and doing, as the natural way for humans and their institutions to perform.

Nor am I proposing that such a changed image would result in the removal of conflict or the elimination of power in human affairs; certainly not over the years ahead when this new image would be contending with — and at best, only occasionally substituted for — the prevailing image of the nature of humans. Occasions for conflict and for the use of power would change, and the ways in which conflict and power were expressed would change too. My feeling regarding the influence this new image will have on conflict and power is well expressed in a statement by Robert Kahn pertaining to research on role stress:

The issue . . . is not the elimination of conflict and ambiguity from organizational life; it is the containment of these conditions at levels and in forms which are at least humane, tolerable, and low in cost, and which at best might be positive in contribution to individual and organization. The present research implies four ways in which this goal might be approached: by introducing direct structural changes into organizations, by introducing new criteria of selection and placement, by increasing the tolerance and coping abilities of individuals, and by strengthening the interpersonal bonds among organizational members.

That observation was written before the human-potential image attained the attention it claims today; clearly, though, role-stress research, as part of the psychology of organizational behavior and change, has contributed to the present status of the new image.

Certain examples of approval of the human-potential image of human nature deserve our attention because they come from unexpected sources where, if approval were to spread, the feasibility of trying to change toward long-range social planning could be substantially enhanced. Of course, public expressions of interest are not evidence of active engagement, any more than the public imagery about long-range social planning corresponds to what is actually happening. However, just as that imagery is influencing people to see planning in a positive light, making it an idea in good currency, with increased possibilities for invention and innovation, so too with attention to the new image of man. Moreover, it is my strong impression that, inspired by the image, individuals in the most unlikely places are in fact exploring unfamiliar ways to satisfy desires that Philip Slater argues are deeply and uniquely frustrated in American middle-class culture:

1. The desire for community — the wish to live in trust and fraternal cooperation with one's fellows in a total and visible collective entity.
2. The desire for engagement — the wish to come directly to grips with social and interpersonal problems and to confront on equal terms an environment which is not composed of ego-extensions.
3. The desire for dependence — the wish to share responsibility for the control of one's impulses and the direction of one's life.

Consider, for example, the characteristics that top executives of two major American corporations expect future managers to display — characteristics that, they emphasize, will require changes in corporate structure and norms in order to attract such managers. One executive lists the desired characteristics this way:

High level of education; minimum loyalty to company; concern with maximum authority as individuals; desire for social concern by businesses; rejection of authoritarianism; interest in the whole environment; decreasing sense of tradition; individualistic dress and grooming; open, direct communication; acceptance of "feelings" as essential data.

The other, an executive vice-president in one of America's largest firms, sympathetically describes these characteristics as:

Openness; non-materialism; identity related to age category; I-Thou; trust; love; use of small groups; identity with alienated groups; personalization (anti-technology); moralistic concern with humanism and self-knowledge.

George C. Lodge, Professor of Business Administration at Harvard Business School, has this to say:

The new ideas are all around us: harmony between man and nature, individual fulfillment as part of an organic social process, a right to survival and income, a sharp distinction between consumer desires and community needs, the role of the state as vision-setter and planner.

. . . The old idea of individualism is largely a useless antique. For the majority of Americans a sense of fulfillment and happiness will derive from their place and participation in a purposeful, organic social process; their talents and capabilities should be used to the fullest, and they should have maximum involvement in the decisions by which the process is conducted and directed.

. . . The costs of neglect are real. It is all too likely that worker malaise and discontent will bring increased pressure for wage increases which companies may well grant, hoping money will buy satisfaction, and thus productivity, when in fact it won't.

. . . Paternalism won't work because there is no father and there are no children. There is only a collection of human beings with different capabilities who are needed to perform different functions. And how they are organized is something upon which they must generally agree. Perhaps the workers should select the manager, in some cases.

. . . Whatever the techniques, this transition will place a serious burden on existing management. In many instances, managers may in fact be deciding whether or not to relinquish their own jobs and authority in the name of a more efficient and useful collective.

In the last few years *Science* magazine has begun to publish articles concerned with states of being and images of reality, that would have been out of bounds for such a publication just a few years earlier: such titles as "a Cartography of the Ecstatic and Meditative States," by an experimental psychiatrist and pharmacologist; "Sensuous-Intellectual Complementarity in Science," written by a chemist; "States of Consciousness and State Specific Sciences," by an experimental psychologist. The *Wall Street Journal*, which we may reasonably assume chooses non-financial articles that it believes will appeal to its particular readers, has featured a page-one article that ran two full columns, describing research indicating that plants can sense human feelings toward them, as well as the biological state of other animals. Whether or not the respective editors and referees share the views of the authors, it is significant that they now believe such views are proper subject matter for *Science* and the *Wall Street Journal*, and that enough readers of those publications will find them interesting and appropriate.

Whether or not positive views about the human-potential image are widely held, it appears that those who see themselves as idea-disseminators and opinion influencers believe that they are widely held. And, very likely, that is one means by which prophecies become self-fulfilling.

Other, more-familiar issues that are fully compatible with the perspectives emphasized in the human-potential image, would depend on future-responsive societal learning for their resolution. These include concerns about the natural environment and an "ecological ethic" (to use Lynton Caldwell's term); commitment to radical change in the status of the dispossessed, the marginal, and minorities; strong control of technology for social welfare; and the reassessment of science as the crowning expression of man's competencies, and of the ethical consequences of it. Much of what is discussed, proposed, and implemented with regard to these issues tacitly accepts the prevailing definition of human beings, though quite a few critics either subscribe to versions of the human-potential image, or deplore the prevailing one. at any rate, whatever the assumptions about man's being, preoccupation with these powerful social issues certainly will not discourage perceiving new and additional human potential, and other social realities that might be less likely to engender resistance to attempts to change toward long-range social planning.

The human-potential image seems to be a fact, and its spread seems likely. As noted by Robert Kantor:

The recognition of the divine in man is widely diffused through the literature of religion and of mysticism. What is not so generally visible, is that an identical recognition is now spreading through the journals of psychology. In fact, there is a convergence of religion, psychology, and education. They share a growing unity of concern beyond the proper forming of a social self in each human. Their concern now is with the cultivation of the subjective self that also lives in every man.

The extent to which this image could facilitate efforts to change toward future-responsive societal learning is only speculation, but on the face of it, it also seems likely. The next question is: Are there societal circumstances that are likely to expand the plausibility of the human-potential image, and provide occasions for the credibility of the philosophy to be demonstrated?

Before discussing specific situations that may enhance feasibility, let us acknowledge the ubiquitous role of inadvertence — the occasional influence in the direction of long-range social planning that might be exerted by persons, technologies, or roles introduced into organizations for different purposes altogether, or for the ritual or image of long-range social planning. Persons may at any time find themselves involved in long-range social planning as a result of the circumstances we shall look at now.

ORGANIZATIONAL DEVELOPMENT AS FACILITATING FUTURE-RESPONSIVE SOCIETAL LEARNING

I have referred throughout to growing recognition of this approach in corporations, third-sector organizations, and (in principle, if not nearly so much in practice) in government. Among the elites of established organizations there is growing appreciation of the utility and validity of the findings of behavioral science to the effect that fulfillment of higher human needs and aspirations is increasingly necessary for effective organizational performance. More and more executives are aware of the arguments — and sometimes the evidence — that openness, trust, and all the rest "pay off." Warren Bennis sees those espousing organizational development as reflecting the following philosophy:

(1) A new concept of man, based on increased knowledge of his complex and shifting needs, which replaces the oversimplified, innocent push-button or inert idea of man.
(2) A new concept of power based on collaboration and reason, which replaces a model of power based on coercion and fear.
(3) A new concept of organizational values, based on an humanistic existential orientation, which replaces the depersonalized, mechanistic value system. I do not mean that these transformations of man, power, organizational values are fully accepted, or even understood, to say nothing of implemented in day-to-day organizational affairs. These changes may be light-years away from

actual adoption. I do mean that they have gained wide intellectual acceptance in enlightened management quarters, that they have caused a terrific amount of rethinking and search behavior on the part of many organizational planners, and that they have been used as a basis for policy formulation by certain large organizations, mainly industrial leviathans, but also by many other non-industrial institutions.

There is no reason to believe the direction of this trend will reverse; when practiced, it usually proves rewarding, and it recruits executives, managers, and professionals who are searching for a more rewarding human condition. Since it seems to improve performance, it also appeals to the conventional view of humans and the conventional goals of organizations, particularly corporations. But as more business school graduates who have been exposed to the processes and philosophy move into positions of authority and influence, emphasis on compatibility with the human-potential image should increase. Increased use in other sectors should help legitimize its application in government, especially when younger generations of bureaucrats, political appointees, professionals, and consultants move into authority and influence, and as legislators partake of similar experiences and ideas before assuming their elected positions.

Another favorable consequence of the growing emphasis on organizational development merits recognition. It must be evident that the social-psychological requirements for changing toward long-range social planning would also be functional for organizations or their components that will not themselves be involved in activities needing long-range social planning; examples might be some distribution and service-dispensing components of large organizations. Such organizations are increasingly investing in organizational development. It would seem that the greater the number of people and organizations that find it rewarding to behave in some of the ways needed to move toward long-range social planning, the more likely that there will evolve networks of organizations and people sympathetic to such planning, and willing to risk collaboration in ways that would at least be less resistant to long-range social planning efforts. The more that organizations find they can work together, the less uncertainty they will have to bear about other organizations are going to do, about sabotage and double-dealing. Under such circumstances, the atmosphere surrounding tactics and strategy for preserving and extending organizational autonomy is likely to change. Non-government organizations have often found that more can be accomplished with less effort by enlarging participation in management and policy decisions — if organizational development has preceded such enlargements. So, too, organizations may find more satisfaction, including a kind of exhilarating autonomy of competence and direction, through collaboration based on the sort of behavior and structures argued for here, than they now find in the typical defensive, closed, and narrowly protective organizational behavior. Some sources of turbulence might be reduced as a result, and the satisfaction this provides could encourage more behavior and structures sympathetic to efforts to change toward long-range social planning.

SOCIAL CRISES AND DISASTERS AS FACILITATORS OF FUTURE-RESPONSIVE SOCIETAL LEARNING

One consequence of our inability to regulate our society, at least as it is presently operated, will be frequent crises and disasters. Some will be sudden, like an urban insurrection or a lethal inversion layer; others will be cumulative, like Vietnam, mercury poisoning, or power shortages. Such crises and disasters have important potential to encourage moves toward long-range social planning.

First, crises and disasters will demonstrate that leaders and administrators are unable to carry out successfully the solutions they claim to have to social problems. As disasters and crises accumulate, it will become clearer to more people that those who run the government really don't understand the problems: that they are unable to operate their own organizations productively and creatively, and that they are unable to guide coherently and felicitously the natural and social environments for which the accept or claim responsibility. In spite of all the technological and managerial resources they have or claim to have, it will be evident that they are unable to make things work the way they promise they can — or claim they have. It will become unavoidably evident that in an increasingly complex world, conventionally-behaving leaders and executives are simply incompetent or inadequate.

Second, some people seeking to lead may try to do so by acknowledging to their environments that they are uncertain about what to do because they are uncertain about what is happening in the present, to say nothing about the future; hoping thereby to demonstrate honesty, courage, wisdom, and humility. They may also choose to embrace error rather than deny it, pointing out that all leaders are in fact inadequate on the basis of their records, but haven't the courage or honesty to admit it. Having embraced error and acknowledged uncertainty, they may invite their followers to share in *learning* a way through.

This approach would terrify and revolt people who, in their own uncertainty and fear of error, need the kind of leader who believes and acts as if he knows. As M. Hall observes:

Anxieties are provoked when one hears about the danger of external attack, or the imminent collapse of the economic system, or the disintegration of his sound, virtuous country. These factors mobilize a sense of anxiety and a sense of the need for action. They also make one perceive his own limitations. Now suppose this anxiety-ridden, helpless citizen can attach himself to an effective leader, can identify with him. He lessens his own anxiety and no longer feels helpless.

But among persons subscribing to or susceptible to the human-potential image there is, along with a respect for candor, an appreciation that complex situations can be experienced in many ways, leading to quite different versions of "telling it like it is." Some loss of control doesn't upset them. They accept error more easily as part of the human condition, as something to be learned from. And they believe that control is best exercised through participatory processes that share power and purpose. This group increasingly includes senior people in all kinds of organizations, who have had responsibility in the midst of complexity, and who have had the opportunity to test their beliefs against the need to get things done with finite resources and time. Such people could encourage leaders to move toward long-range social planning, and help sustain efforts to do so.

Third, it is during the aftermath of a disaster that organizations are most subject to drastic restructuring and redirecting. The environment that sustained their norms and operating style is changed, and either does not provide the expected feedback, or produces unexpected feedback. Indeed, a disaster can be thought of as the withdrawal of sustaining feedback. Lacking these regulating and constraining inputs, the organization is vulnerable to a metamorphosis.

Usually an organization "reorganizes" itself into essentially what it was, and so does its environment. But things need not work that way: The disaster of the Great Depression resulted in a permanent shift in the norms and structure of the federal government in the direction of developing and supplying public welfare services. The disaster of World War II contributed to the creation of the European Trade Community. The disasters of the urban uprisings in the United States in the 1960s and 1970s intensified attention to racist norms and structures. And the disasters of student uprisings have led in some places to changes in the structure and norms of university governance.

Without significant preplanning, recovery into a transformed structure and norm system that could encourage social-psychological processes able to meet the requirements for changing toward long-range social planning is almost certain to fail. Among other things, this preplanning would need to include training for interpersonal competence; without such skills, it would be virtually impossible to use the disaster as a lever to move toward long-range social planning. Many people, pushed by their experience with the disaster or crisis, will feel an intensified need to keep things under control. At the same time, the fluid post-disaster context will seem both an opportunity in which to capture control, and a threat that control is slipping away. Both perceptions will intensify pre-disaster behavior patterns acting in the service of pre-disaster norms.

However, organizations that believe themselves right and healthy are unlikely to do such pre-planning, or to provide funds for it, because that would imply an inability to avoid disaster; and acknowledging such impotence, either publicly or privately, is more than most leaders can manage. Therefore, in the event of a disaster we will have to depend on the skills available in organizations that have previously undertaken organizational development for reasons other than disaster planning. However, it might also be that if they possessed those skills — including, crucially, self-understanding — leaders could face acknowledging the inability to avert disaster. (I know some who acknowledge this today.) With that strength they might be able to initiate some contingency planning that would facilitate moves toward long-range social planning when disasters occur.

Another characteristic of the social psychology of crisis and disaster must be acknowledged. In the crisis stage preceding disaster, unless they have been trained to avoid doing so, members of organizations tend to retreat into forms of behavior that have been well learned because they were successful in the past. They are very likely to cut themselves off from information they should have to cope with the reality of the looming disaster; instead, they selectively attend to information that is compatible with their previously-learned successful behavior, including hierarchical command procedures. These procedures are followed because they have a history of success that leads back to childhood. Such behavior increases distrust in the environment and heightens a sense of beleagueredness. It would make post-disaster experiments with future-responsive societal learning highly unlikely.

SOCIAL INDICATORS, SOCIAL EXPERIMENTS, AND DISTRIBUTIVE EQUITY AS FACILITATORS OF FUTURE-RESPONSIVE SOCIETAL LEARNING

Those seeking more efficient government, more agency productivity and accountability, more "bang for the buck" in social investments, and those seeking more humane and rewarding government in the public interest, share a growing appreciation of the potential utility of data collected to evaluate the social state of the nation. To this we may add the thrust of consumerism, volunteerism, concern with the natural environment, and the pressures for decentralization into quasi-autonomous neighborhood and lay-organized activities, of such social services as public health, education, and welfare for the poor. These circumstances, which are facilitated by and encourage the growth of the human-potential image, would seem to hold opportunities for future-responsive societal learning.

These different interests and groupings will disagree strongly and often about whether the right data are being collected to estimate particular social conditions, and they will disagree strongly about whether the correct interpretations are being made from a given set of data. Intense arguments will be inevitable, at least as long as models of what constitute social processes and their causal interrelations are underdeveloped and unevaluated. In the absence of error-embracing and acknowledgment of uncertainty, and in the absence of guiding future perspectives, these arguments will most likely bog down in familiar disarray, and decisions will probably be made in familiar but increasingly-unacceptable ways. Instead of this outcome, these differences could be used as the basis for competing and collaborative societal experiments at the very local level, as well as on a regional and national scale. To go beyond *ad hoc* experiments would require moving toward meeting the requirements for future-responsive societal learning. If this were seen as the desirable direction in which to go, the human-potential image, as a model of appropriate norms and behavior, would make it easier to work with the uncertainties and conflicts inherent in changing toward future-responsive societal learning.

At the same time, social-indicator data will force more organizations, especially government, to face up more directly and comprehensively than ever before, to questions of distributive equity. Government agencies and many private organizations face futures in which increasing data and advocacy skills will force them to make preoccupation with the public interest paramount. Inevitably, then, they will have to try to anticipate the costs and benefits to the social and natural environment, of conditions that could increase or decrease equity for one or another group, and they will have to seek or at least cope with feedback for their actions. In other words, they will have to move toward long-range social planning. A willingness by management to indulge, if not support, the new image of humankind — especially if it becomes an idea of some currency — would make it easier to survive the crunch of environmental pressures on one side and internal resistance to long-range social planning on the other. Those inside and out who do subscribe to the new image would be strengthened in their efforts to undertake actions aimed at facilitating moves toward long-range social planning. If these efforts began to be rewarding, indulgence could change to commitment.

PLANNING AS A FACILITATOR OF FUTURE-RESPONSIVE SOCIETAL LEARNING

It is hard to imagine the idea of long-range social planning weakening, if society holds together long enough to be outraged and terrified by its disarray. Measured by the number of publications, popular concern with the future would seem apparent. (However, without research we do not know how much is serious interest, how much Sunday-supplement curiosity, how much various attempts to relieve or rationalize generalized anxiety, and how much is simply promotion.) More academics and more students are taking an interest in policy research and future studies. Organizations in and out of government are making new efforts to set goals, and are thinking about reexamining organizational structures and evaluating activities. Advocacy planning and counter-planning are almost institutionalized. Consulting firms are increasing in all these areas. Many people in and out of government are being caught up in the idea that there is a need for long-range social planning. And positions of authority and responsibility will increasingly be filled by younger persons who, by their advanced stage of personal development, believe in these changes and intend to act to facilitate them. It seems to me, then, that an elaborated idea about planning may develop good currency: that if we are to plan, we must change ourselves in the direction of believing in and acting out the human-potential image of social reality.

Bertram Gross, having reviewed the evolution of planning and conjectured about societal trends, concludes with a statement that well expresses what I expect will be an appealing idea in good currency regarding long-range social planning:

Genuine human rationality is essentially a process of learning and . . . any learning process involves not only the acquisition of knowledge and skills but also the development of new values and interests. In this case, if we are to escape the icy grip of technocratic planning, we must develop a humanist style of learning through planning and a theory of planning as widespread social learning. This is what we must learn if we are to escape the new superhighways to post-industrial serfdom and begin to release the vast potentials for humanist reconstruction.

FEASIBLE, BUT HOW HOPEFUL?

Even taken together, these potentially-supportive circumstances are pathetically thin reeds to lean on, or to weave into a hope that long-range social planning as a means of societal learning could become pervasive in, say, the next two decades. As of now, the human-potential view of man is attractive primarily to the intellectually or economically affluent. Most people apparently "don't know what they're missing" from the perspective of their conventional viewpoint; for them, survival, security, belonging, and esteem are much more attractive goals than self-actualization. Peter and B. Berger have argued that if those espousing variants of the new image cannot find congenial circumstances within conventional norms and structures, they will be quite adequately replaced, in accordance with the familiar process of circulation of the elites, by people who have no doubts about the sufficiency of the conventional norms for being and doing. The Bergers conclude:

There is no reason to think that "the system" will be unable to make the necessary accommodations. Should Yale become hopelessly "greened," Wall Street will get used to recruits from Fordham or Wichita State. Italians or Southern Baptists will have no trouble running the Rand Corporation.

This suggests that for many years it will probably be much easier for the many in power who hold to the traditional definition of the nature of humans, to ignore the requirements for future-responsive societal learning, and to try where they can, to plan in the spirit of social engineering — what Gross calls "technocratic planning." Social engineering may well be attempted where coercion, manipulation, and control seem right and reasonable to those holding to the traditional image of human beings, where it could seem feasible and correct to social-engineer the control of delinquency, crime, drug abuse, or job training.

A social engineering approach could be undertaken within conventional organization structures and norms, avoiding contact with the environment, substituting technological ritual and pseudo data for acknowledging uncertainty or embracing error, and so on. Organizational resistance would be minimal because planning these activities would be treated as if no changes in men or organizations were required — just more exotic engineering techniques applied to planning for, rather than with, the environment. One can hope that out of the inevitable failures that would result — failures due as much to their inhumanity as to the inadequacy of a social-engineering approach — would come appreciation of the need to move away from the conventional image of the nature of humans and the norms of organizational and interpersonal behavior that reflect it. But the denouement is more likely lead to the rejection of any kind of planning, in favor of authoritarian leadership.

Bennis, who was among the most optimistic about the impact of organizational development, as caused by and causing a shift in values that would encourage self-actualization, has described in a most instructive and error-embracing article some fundamental organizational dilemmas he now sees us faced with:

the threat to legitimacy of authority, the tensions between populist and elitist functions and interdependence and complicity in the environment, the need for fresh metaphors, the discontinuities between microsystems and macrosystems, and the baffling competition between forces that support and those that suppress the adoption of democratic ideology . . .

Some of these dilemmas are deepened by the progress of the new image of man, making its way amidst the expressions of the older one. And we can each add our visions of countertrends and conditions in the society that would be almost certain to overwhelm the circumstances I have suggested as supportive of changes toward long-range social planning. To my mind, the most threatening is the likelihood that social crises and disasters will be dealt with in ways that will destroy the opportunities, the new definition of social reality, and the proponents needed to create the conditions for future-responsive societal learning. The authors of a highly authoritative 1972 study on attitudes toward violence indicate one such potential source of destruction. M. Blumenthal, R. Kahn, F. Andrews, and K. Head wrote in *Justifying Violence: Attitudes of American Men* (Institute for Social Research, University of Michigan).

The fact that almost 50 percent of American men felt that shooting was a good way of handling campus disturbances "almost always" or at least "sometimes" is particularly disturbing. . . . That 20 percent of American men considered it appropriate for police to kill in these circumstances indicates the ease with which many people accept violence to maintain order even when force so used is entirely out of proportion to the precipitating incidents. The data imply that willingness to reach for a gun is easily evoked . . .

The fact is that we really don't understand the processes of change in this society, which is so complex that it has no historical precedent. That is why we must turn to future-responsive societal learning. We don't know what it takes to make a difference, to produce a change, in the definition of social reality that would be akin to Kuhn's paradigm shift. We don't know how to measure or perceive clearly the dialectics of trend and counter-trend, value and counter-value, image and counter-image.

For example, it is easy to assert that although the Perennial Philosophy is perennial, it has never been realized, except by a few; and that what is really going on is a perennial welling-up of that part of human nature that finds comfort in fantasies of being more than we can be. It is easy to demonstrate that, in large groups at least, humans have never behaved according to the human-potential image, no matter how much they might have aspired to. It is easy to conclude that they won't and can't this time around, either; indeed, the bulk of this book would support that position.

But it is also arguable that there has never been a convergence of circumstances like those we now face, where more and more people of all ages know how enormous are our powers, how rudimentary our abilities to control them, and how precarious and finite the natural and social environments in which we must act out this struggle with ourselves. It can be argued that by knowing these things, and by recognizing the existential circumstances that reveal them, we are creating a social setting different from any that existed in the past. Moreover, growing numbers of people know that they know, and know that growing numbers of other people *also* know, that our societal condition is historically unique. This may provide a real potential for beginning to redefine our natures, and for beginning to create social arrangements that validate and sustain that definition.

It took the circumstance of agriculture to make civilization possible, with its concomitant changes in the definition of man. It took the circumstances of technology to produce the density and complexity of interactions that characterize our society — including our increasingly shared dissatisfactions with the more prevalent definitions of human nature and our increasing shared aspirations for something akin to the Perennial Philosophy.

As a basis for learning to become a future-responsive learning society, by learning how to do long-range social planning, this is not much to go on. But if the thesis of this book sounds reasonable, we had better make the most of it.

⋆ Appendix ⋆

Long-Range Social Planning
in Corporations

*[Ed. Note: This Appendix originally appeared
as Chapter 4 in the 1973 edition]*

*AUTHOR'S NOTE: At the time I was writing this chapter, Pierre Wack and
his colleagues at Royal Dutch/Shell in London were inventing and refining
the design of scenarios to influence the mental maps of executives and
planners in that corporation. One consequence of this early work was that
Shell became prepared for the possibility of an oil price rise, which came to
pass in 1973, the same year this book was published. The scenario success
and Royal Dutch/Shell's prestige subsequently legitimated scenario-based
planning and stimulated other corporations to engage in and very gradually
to recognize the learning process inherent in it. Because all this took place
after this book was published, there is no mention here of what was to be
the future role of scenarios in planning and learning.*

Although it is generally acknowledged that in coming years
corporations will be increasingly, if ambiguously, involved in the public
interest, our concern in this book is with organizations that are legally or
morally obliged to respond to the public interest, namely government and
some third-sector organizations However, the widespread imagery about
ongoing long-range planning in corporations makes it desirable to review
the corporate situation. Certainly some readers are already familiar with

the limits of corporate long-range planning, and its insufficiency for long-range *social* planning. Other readers, however, do not know what in fact seems to be going on—or not going on—but do have strong impressions from the media and from speeches by corporate executives that a great deal is happening. This chapter is for those in the latter group who may believe that the problems we examine in this book have already been solved in corporations.

What follows is derived from the technical literature on what corporate planning should be; from the media that report what is happening in the corporate planning world; and from interviews with highly competent "insiders" and consultants to corporations.[1] What follows is based on more than a cursory look at the condition of corporations but on far less than a systematic examination. My purpose here is not to resolve the questions and conjectures raised by this exploration, but to propose that they are worthy of further study. As Shonfield has written:

The significant facts about the behavior of private enterprise are less readily established than about governments. This is partly because of the sheer volume of disparate elements, each pursuing its own separate interest, which make up the private sector; at best, one is dealing with statistical aggregates. The other factor which makes the study of the public sector easier is that even at its most secretive its actions in the conduct of economic policy are, in a democracy, subject to scrutiny, whereas private enterprise has often managed to escape it. . . . Economic analysis, during most of the time that it has been practiced as an academic discipline, has been much less concerned with what businessmen actually do than with what they would do on certain assumptions, including the major assumption that they are strictly rational men.

. . . there is a lack of systematic data on which to base precise and comprehensive generalizations in this field. Many of the changes which have occurred are in any case so recent that it would be surprising if much more were available at this stage than suggestive indications of underlying trends. The development of business planning is an obvious case in point. There is no way of measuring its significance. [2]

With due appreciation, then, that there may be more to the story, it appears that much that is claimed for and done in the name of corporate planning is related in practice and spirit only dimly to what is proposed in this book. Since my only research purpose for examining corporate planning efforts was to see if it might illuminate the problems and possibilities public organizations would face when attempting to change over to long-range social planning, there seemed no point in probing further. However, while the goals and conditions that set the conventional context for corporate planning are basically different from those we are concerned with, the developing social situation is leading a few corporations to try to move toward a mode of long-range social planning that is more akin in process, and perhaps even in spirit, to what I propose. As of this writing, to my knowledge only a very few corporations (most notably General Electric) have even described planning intentions that are in the direction proposed here. Whether these intentions can be implemented, whether the psychological resistances can be overcome and the organization restructured and values and norms shifted, and whether the corporation could still operate as a profit-making entity, all remains to be learned. Many corporations will someday face the issues and psychological processes described in this book but none has actually gone far enough in its long-range social planning development efforts to face them yet.

In what follows, I will first very briefly review the conventional setting for corporate planning, and then suggest some developing conditions that will put corporations in a context more akin to that of public agencies, with corresponding unfamiliar requirements which will complicate the introduction of long-range planning.

The Conventional Corporate Situation Today

Executives associated with corporations where one might expect long-range social planning like to think of themselves as advanced and responsible planners. The aspirations held by higher-level corporate management personnel about what they and their organizations should become are changing. These people are influenced by images of the potency and potential of planning, systems approaches, computer simulations, and so on, and by the imagery that says that these are the things that advanced organizations are using and doing. (This influence by imagery, promulgated in the corporation-servicing media and by the organizations catering to corporate executives, seems similar to the earlier imagery that seduced many organizations to invest in computers without really knowing what to do with them.) Thus they tend to see whatever planning effort they have as in the vanguard and as influential throughout the organization — whether the planning activity is two people looking ahead twenty years at the state of society or twenty people doing sophisticated but comparatively narrow, market- or capital-investment planning. However, most senior personnel have little understanding of the processes of innovation and change in their own organization, being concerned primarily with money flow, market share, and so on. D. Ewing described the situation in realistic terms:

Managers at the division level are likely to have spent much of their working lives in their present or other divisions. Their "real world" is the people they see and work with every day, the products they manufacture, the physical facilities of the division, and the projects that are underway in the division. Customers and customer complaints are real: the products produced for them are tangible and are probably well understood. How well the product works and how efficiently it is produced are probably the result of innumerable personal challenges, successes, and failures. . . .

At the corporate level, in contrast, it is all too easy to feel that the real world consists of "the corporation" and those quantified abstractions which show how the corporation is doing with respect to the outside world — profit and loss statements, balance sheets, the market price of the stock, and so on. "What does it mean in earnings per share?" is often the all-important question with regard to division proposals or problems. The real world at the corporate level becomes the external and quantitative measure of corporate performance and health; divisions can all too easily be regarded as suppliers of financial statements which merely fit into the vast corporate totals. [3]

Thus, senior personnel tend to be naive when assessing the alleged impact of planning on actual organizational behavior at lower levels.[4] However sincere, their responses to questions about the operational impact of planning cannot be accepted as valid.

Examination of the social psychological aspects of present and past corporate efforts to change toward long-range planning is complicated by other factors. Much of what has been represented as advanced long-range social planning has been mere public relations.
As J. Martino observed:

It is unfortunately true that for the past five years or so, long-range planning and technological forecasting have been 'in' with corporations. Articles in the Wall Street Journal, the Harvard Business Review, and Fortune have spoken glowingly of the virtues of technological forecasting as a component of corporate long-range planning. Hence, many corporations set up long-range planning groups more for the purpose of impressing the stockbrokers, or the public, or the executives of competing corporations, than for the purpose of making and implementing long-range plans. These groups were little more than window-dressing. Is it surprising, then, that when the crunch came many of them were disbanded? They were, after all, serving no useful purpose other than the advertising value gained from them, and when business is bad there are more effective ways to spend advertising money. [5]

In the absence of studies in depth it is difficult to know whether one is dealing with naivete or cynicism.

It is important to realize that many corporations actually doing some kind of long-range planning that includes a social component, have the military as their chief client. This means that critical aspects of their planning are classified. Of even more significance for this study, the planning that has been done *so far* has been done in a situation where the organization-environment relationship and the goals of planning are profoundly different from those that characterize open systems confronted with changing, conflict-filled environments and social needs and wants.

Many corporations, and probably all the large ones, do plan. But except for a handful, they do so in ways different from those proposed here for different goals, usually for different reasons, and until very recently, in a different environmental context. Long-range planning in corporations seems for the most part to be far less practiced and perfected than its imagery implies. Corporate foresightedness usually extends from six months to two years, with five years usually being the extreme. [6] A recent survey by W. Hall of seventeen major banks, public utilities, and manufacturers concludes:

Most of the planning models which are being used are not significantly influencing the actual strategy formulation process within the firm. [7]

In the words of one analyst: "We run our planning model regularly, sending the output to a committee composed of our executive officers. Frankly we don't know what they do with the results — but we suspect nothing." A senior executive in another firm who receives projections from a corporate financial model provides another perspective when he comments: "All of the senior managers in our firm believe that these corporate models should be providing valuable information, but we just don't know what use to make of it. [8]

Conventionally, the corporation's consumer environment was passive compared to today: it simply sold its products to those who wanted to buy, and sometimes it created markets in its interest. Government regulations have usually been in the interest of, sometimes at the request of, the corporation. Of course, corporations have battled mightily among themselves, but the purpose of the battle has always been the same — organizational survival and growth, never the public interest, and that also simplified the corporation's environment. Intrinsically, the chief organizationally-shared goal was profit, or was profit-related, like the size of the market share. Thus goal choosing was chiefly instrumental: how to make a profit. Correspondingly, the most salient feedback data from the environment were indicators of profit and loss, or share of the market, or some such profit-related measure. To be sure, there were other kinds of feedback from the corporation's sub-environments (such as suppliers and distributors), but these sub-environments were comparatively easy to differentiate externally and matched internally through functionally specified activities (such as purchasing and marketing). The interpersonal and organizational relationships between the corporation and its sub-environments were understandable and essentially predictable. People played by the same rules: especially, they shared the value of negotiating a reasonable profit for all concerned—most of the time.

The profit goal in typical corporate situations has meant that, given the rapid obsolescence of so many products, the time frame for planning has had to be short. For some products like steel mills, aircraft, or computers, the time frame has been longer (as much as a decade), but the goal-setting task (will it contribute to profit) remained comparatively simple, and the procedure for getting from here to there appeared clear. The tangible product requirements defined the steps along the path.

Product development took place under conditions of proprietary secrecy, as well as it could be maintained. During the research and development stages the environment was ignorant of what was going on, or what little environmental feedback there was, in addition to product purchases, began only after the product was marketed. Sometimes what was developed was influenced by market research, but consumer involvement was always at the wish and under the control of management. Deliberate creation of consumer markets was an option open only to the largest corporations, and has been a unilateral procedure chosen and implemented at the discretion of the corporation, and in its interests.

Typically, the corporate product had been a tangible physical product. The characteristics of the product itself imposed a structure and direction on the planning of its development and dissemination. Commenting on the conditions that affect the usefulness of that basic tool and conceptual style of long-range social planning, C. DiBona has observed:

Some areas may be neater or inherently more tractable than others. The more the subjects of investigation are preplanned, the more they depend on the characteristics of large pieces of equipment with few operating modes and the more they are determined by early large events, then the more likely they are to be analytically tractable. These areas are less likely to be influenced by unpredictable behavior and states of training or to be dependent upon a myriad of small encounters. [9]

Physical things have to fit together; some things have to fit before other things; things have to have specific properties in time and space. The articulatedness inherent in properties of the product itself provides a scaffolding, a reference system, upon which to construct the instrumental goals, the time frame, the feedback requirements, and the means for assuring implementation of the feedback messages. Indeed, all the requirements for long-range planning can be met, and sometimes have been met in practice, once the product specifications to be developed have been stated: they can be met because the properties of the product impose their requirements on the people seeking to realize those properties. The internal corporate environment is stabilized by the operations-structuring and information-specifying constraints of the hardware.

This same situation has been determinate in government programs that are considered products of successful planning. The question, "If we can put a man on the moon, why can't we apply the same management and technological know-how to remaking our cities?" is in large part answered by the fact that Apollo was in effect directed by the properties of materials and the artifacts into which they were arranged, while city problems are directed by people and social processes: management and technological know-how cannot interlock nearly so well in this situation.[10]

The research and development corporation or the organization with an important research and development subsystem have more complex planning tasks, and generally longer time perspectives. But since the research and development is almost invariably on physical products, the uncertainties that plague the social planning area are substantially absent. Nevertheless, as Don Schon has demonstrated, organizations are generally unable to deal with the uncertainty introduced by radically new research and development produced in their own organizations. They succumb to psychological processes of the sort to be discussed later.[11]

In essence, then, when conventional corporate planning was undertaken it was with a rather clear sense of knowing where the corporation wanted to get, and knowing how or what was likely to get it there. And the product could be tested in private, thus allowing careful assessment. (In contrast, social technologies cannot be tested "inside" the organization. This enormously complicates evaluation and it changes, sometimes unpredictably, the relationship of organization and environment.)

This kind of corporate planning is much more like scheduling than long-range social planning. Indeed, moving ahead in the absence of that scheduling-like clarity has been deemed a poor risk, and when attempted at all it has been done in ways that hid the riskiness, or rather the uncertainty, from the environment — including that most relevant environment, the stockholder. Product development and marketing choices were only constrained by the expectations of profit-loss risks and by legal restrictions, though good public relations were deemed an important concomitant of the profit-loss context. And legal restrictions often could be subverted, indefinitely ignored, diffused, or changed by the big corporations.

But even though the problems, perspectives, and organizational arrangements for corporate planning have been different in spirit and simpler than they were for long-range social planning, corporations seem to have been burdened with some of the same social psychological problems that I shall conjecture will be involved in changing over to long-range social planning in the public arena. D. Mockler, observed these problems as corporations struggled to computerize their operations during the late 1960s:

In sum, much is known about planning, but not enough corporate managers understand how to put it into practice and use sophisticated mathematical and computer tools. As a result, they are not equipped to direct the money spent on planning into the most effective channels. At the same time, executives frequently are unwilling to change existing organization structures and to give planners the tools they need to get the job done. As a result, the planner often works in a vacuum, acting as a sounding board for corporate management's futuristic thinking but isolated from the operating realities of the organization. Bolder and better directed experiments with planning techniques, organization, and administration are thus needed if this important function is to live up to expectations for it. We will, I believe, see many such experiments in the 1970's. [12]

D. Ewing argues that, as much as anything else, the very high failure rate in corporate planning is due to indifference to the human factor in doing and implementing planning:

Planning has gone wrong because it has been defined too often in terms of economic analysis, production capacity projections, distribution schedules, acquisition formulas, forecasts of demand, and other bloodless criteria — in these terms almost to the exclusion of the "people" aspects. As a result, there has been a tendency for the art and knowledge of planning to proceed in one direction while the art of management and leadership has proceeded in another. [13]

The Developing Corporate Situation

The evolving corporate situation today is becoming much more like that of government agencies. The environment is active: both consumers and non-consumers, beneficiaries and victims of the corporation's products, are insisting that the corporation has responsibilities beyond making products available for purchase. The multifarious intricacies of natural-environment protection already confront them. Social indicator data will be used often by activist and advocate interests in the environment to confront and complicate the pursuit of corporate interests. Corporations will have to face the complex problem of who is to carry the burdens and reap the benefits of what have been "externalities": the secondary consequences of corporate activities will be demonstrable. This in turn means corporations will have to think and choose in terms of additional goals that may come to compete in priority with profit, and they will have to think farther ahead in societal terms.

In addition to dealing with an active external environment, corporations will have to face an increasingly active internal environment if they wish to recruit workers and executives from the most thoughtful and competent of the younger generations.[14] Carrying their more complex self-images, job satisfaction requirements, and multiple roles into the work situation, these younger employees will disturb the organization's conventional perspectives about the proper conduct of the corporation. This means that corporations will be less able to plan in secrecy: there are almost certain to be more internal leaks — as in government agencies now — and there will be increasingly legitimated demands by external groups for representation in major corporate decisions that may affect their welfare through secondary long- and short-term repercussions. The pressures for consumer representatives on corporate boards, and the effects of laws and regulations for consumer protection, will mean that corporations will be comparatively less able to go their own way. They will have to see their future and evaluate their present state in terms that attend to much wider considerations of corporate self-interest than those that affect their market and profits.

Corporations are now discovering, when they find they lack product-servicing personnel because of demographic and job skill changes in the society, as corporations seeking to market services rather than goods have discovered, a totally different task is involved when the goal becomes the development of people and institutions instead of the development of things. In this case they start by not knowing how to get from here to there. Increasingly, corporate goals and the means for reaching them will cease to be matters of risk calculation around tacitly agreed-upon goals. Instead they will become more matters for argument, rich in uncertainty, error production, and psychological discomfort. G. Steiner writes about the evolving corporate situation:

As P. Drucker points out, "the most common source of mistakes in management decisions is the emphasis on finding the right answer rather than the right question." A primary job of management is to find the right problem and to define it. This, however, has not always been an easy thing to do. Very frequently, as Gross points out, to ask the question, "What is the problem?" of members of an organization will, if not summarily brushed aside, lead to acute internal discomfort. The reason is that it usually is a very difficult question to answer. Most organization problems, and all really important ones, turn out to be clusters of many interrelated problems. [15]

By comparison, when conventional corporate planning has been done it has referred to and guided activities essentially unconstrained by or unresponsive to the very conditions that make long-range social planning necessary. In this newly developing situation, the extent to which corporations will have to plan in and for circumstances similar to those facing public agencies will depend on the extent to which the environment requires them to do so, through public pressures or laws and regulations, and on the extent to which corporations choose to become involved in activities that require them to do so. This situation is only beginning to unfold; hence the capability of corporations to deal with the social psychological factors in order to change toward long-range social planning, in furtherance of corporate purpose, is only beginning to be a real question. E. Stabler echoes this view:

As for corporations themselves, there are still many that haven't succumbed to the notion that they're obliged to do anything but turn a profit. Others profess a social conscience but don't really mean it; they just recognize a public-relations fad when they see it. But behind the ballyhoo of anti-littering campaigns, self-congratulatory advertisements, and hot air from all sides, some major corporations are taking steps that they contend represent sincere efforts to gear social dimensions into their day-to-day operations. So far, the vast majority of these actions are in the realm of dealing with minorities. [16]

It remains to be seen if these social dimensions will play a part in long-range *social* planning in corporations. Given the difficulties most corporations have faced in doing any planning beyond the next fiscal year or the next product change, there is every reason to expect that they will have to struggle with the same psychological difficulties described here.

Corporate responses to the pressures to move toward long-range social planning take the form of buying future studies (particularly participating in Delphi-type forecasting exercises); sending their top executives to training seminars on long-range social planning and on the future; establishing in-house planning staffs (or more usually, planning persons); setting two- to five-year operational and developmental targets; and holding retreats and executive training programs aimed at improving interpersonal skills and team capabilities for doing and using long-range social planning. For each of these organization-initiated activities, there is an increasing number of organizations and publications ready to service these desires — and to stimulate them by generating an imagery that everybody else is busily and innovatively doing even more of the same, and that long-range social planning is the pragmatic and farsighted thing to do.

For the most part results that go beyond such initial involvements seem meager. Certainly they fall far short of long-range social planning in the sense argued for here. While some corporations buy or do in-house future studies, there is usually no commitment to or effective means for using them. Generally the study ends with itself. If it is used, it is because it is compatible with what the organization sees itself as doing now. In a few organizations a preferred vision of the future becomes doctrine. Not surprisingly, the tendency is to emphasize those aspects of the conjectured future that can be faced within the existing social and structural context of the organization, rather than to pay attention to those aspects that an outsider (with a different bias) would see as part of their relevant future. By facing only a future compatible with their present, they avoid the pains of uncertainty over whether technological and social developments will in fact turn out to be compatible with their intentions. (One apparently widespread version of compatible future expectations: "We're not worried about environmental protection chewing up our profits. New technologies will solve the pollution problem one way or another.")

Into it are pumped activities that reinforce it and screen out appreciation of its status as only one among several conjectures. Sometimes this preferred future is also used to screen out and select younger personnel according to their ability to contribute ideas and activities supportive of the accepted future. Some executives and planners acknowledge that there are macro-problems at the societal level that their activities could exacerbate or ameliorate, but they see *doing* something about them as the government's responsibility. They still tend to pass on to government the ethical dilemmas around the societal consequences of their activities. At the same time, however, they seem to expect that it will be in the interest of the government to act on these dilemmas compatibly with the traditional interests of the corporations. Clearly, there are unresolved issues about the allocation of ethical responsibility, issues that were always complicated if not obfuscated, but which are beginning to surface anew under the impact of the developing societal condition. [17]

In-house planning staffs are usually encapsulated, their outputs able to influence only the executives to whom they are responsible, executives who are usually much more influenced by the needs, actions, and purposes of their line management who in turn have little, if any, interest in future studies except those that further what they already are doing or want to do. After all, *their* futures are dependent on exploiting the rewarding characteristics of the present. As D. Ewing observes:

Reward systems generally favor the man who turns in a good current showing, whether measured in terms of profitability, sales volume, reduction of employee turnover, or some other way. Salary, bonus, and promotion rewards tend to be based on this month's, this season's, this year's performance — not contributions to goals three, four, or more years off. [18]

Most large organizations reward their middle management for extracting maximum present payoff because in divisionalized firms — 85 percent of *Fortune's* 500— accounting data are the only means for judging division performance available to corporate officers who otherwise understand very little about the multiple businesses they are in. But rewarding *present* payoff makes it impossible by any known means to simultaneously reward concern with a future that would interfere with immediate payoff.

What few attempts there seem to be to move toward long-range social planning have produced multiple problems and possibilities. Issues arise around what *values* are to take priority and how to reconcile them; what *planning technologies* to use; how to *reorganize sub-units* to meet corporate-level planning purposes; how to develop *skills and motivations* at the divisional or group level to plan compatibly with corporate planning; how to *make the future the major input*, rather than the past or present,; what to do with *people*, especially senior people, who are unable or unwilling to move in these directions; how to establish *feedback systems* that truly evaluate programs undertaken in furtherance of planning objectives.

Since the most advanced efforts at corporate long-range planning are at most a year or two old, goal setting and plan readjustment via feedback evaluation have been incomplete and inadequately evaluated. In sum, there are a very few corporations beginning to face the valuing, conceptualizing, operating, and evaluating issues that seem inherent in long-range social planning. At this early date these corporations show evidence that they will face the kinds of social psychological problems and these episodic, unarticulated, opportunities conjectured in other chapters of this book.

The eventual impact, of these new, episodic, and unarticulated activities on changing toward long-range social planning for the public interest is unclear, especially given the changing roles of corporations and attitudes toward them. Corporations may yet experiment more quickly and effectively than government agencies with learning how to change toward long-range social planning. This possibility arises from the greater control that corporation executives can have over organizational boundaries and resources; the growing corporate interest in and experiments with participative management and organizational development; and the opportunities in areas traditionally considered to be dependent on government services, for demonstrating successful new approaches to long-range social planning through successful market development.

But the present role of private enterprise most certainly is not the protection and fulfillment of the public interest, and its norms and structures are decidedly different from those of government.[19] Whatever successes or failures corporations experience in trying to move toward long-range social planning, it does not follow that governments will experience the same. The important point of this chapter is that, as of now, corporations appear not to have overcome the social psychological resistances we shall be examining.

1. At their request, the names of some of those interviewed do not appear in the List of Respondents included in this Appendix.

2. Shonfield, A. Modern Capitalism: The Changing Balance of Public and Private Power. New York: Oxford University Press, 1965, pp. 358, 362.

3. Ewing, D. The Human Side of Planning: Tool or Tyrant? New York: Macmillan, 1969, pp. 50-51.

4. See Bower, J. Managing the Resource Allocation Process: A Study in Corporate Planning and Investment. Boston: Harvard Business School, 1970.

5. Martino, J. "Forecasting the Survival of the Forecaster." The Futurist (1971) p. 33.

6. Shonfield, op. cit., p. 221. See also Steiner, G. Top Management Planning. Toronto: Collier-Macmillan, 1969, p. 23.

7. Hall, W. "Strategic Planning Models . . . Are Top Managers Really Finding Them Useful?" Graduate School of Business Administration, University of Michigan, 1972, p. c.

8. Ibid, p. 3.

9. Di Bona, C. "Where Is System Analysis?" CNA 451-67, revised. Washington, D.C.: Center for Naval Analysis, 1967, p. 3.

10. See Brooks, H. "Science and the Allocation of Resources." American Psychologist, 22 (March 1967), p. 200.

11. Schon, D. Technology and Change: The Impact of Invention and Innovation on American Social and Economic Development. New York: Dell, 1967.

12. Mockler, R. "Theory and Practice of Planning." Harvard Business Review, 48(2) (1970), pp. 156-158.

13. Ewing, D. The Human Side of Planning: Tool or Tyrant? New York: Macmillan, 1969, p. 42.

14. Butkis, A. "The New Youth Movement." Dunn's, 98(2) (1971).

15. Steiner, G. Top Management Planning. Toronto: Collier-Macmillan, 1969, p 7. References within the quote are to Drucker, P. The Practice of Management. New York: Harper and Row, 1954, p.351 and Gross, B. The Managing of Organizations. New York: The Free Press, 1964, p. 760.

16. Stabler, C. "Changing Times: For Many Corporations, Social Responsibility Is Now a Major Concern." Wall Street Journal (October 29, 1971), p. 1.

17. Miller, A. "Business Morality: Some Unanswered (and Perhaps Unanswerable) Questions." The Annals of the American Academy, 363 (1966).

18. Ewing, op. cit., p. 47.

19. Bernstein, M. The Job of the Federal Executive. Washington, D.C.: The Brookings Institution, 1958.

★ List of Respondents ★

(Affiliations as of the time of the interview. Some respondents chose to remain anonymous.)

Joseph F. Abely, Jr.
Controller
General Foods Corp.
White Plains, N.Y.

David Ackerman
Senior Behavioral Scientist
Stanford Research Institute
Menlo Park, California

Marvin Adelson
Professor, School of Architecture &
    Urban Planning
University of California at Los
Angeles

Chris Argyris
Professor
Department of Administrative
    Sciences
Yale University

Herbert Auerbach
Vice President
Descon-Concordia Ltd.
Montreal, Canada

Paul Baran
Vice President
Institute for the Future
Palo Alto, California

Arthur Barber
President
Institute of Politics and Planning
Arlington, Virginia

Richard Barber
Director
Transportation Planning Study
National Academy of Sciences

Russell Bartels
Office of the Mayor
Bureau of the Budget
New York City

Raymond Bauer
Professor
Graduate School of Business
    Administration
Harvard University

Warren G. Bennis
Vice President for
    Academic Development
State University of New York
    at Buffalo

Robert Biller
Professor
Graduate School of Public Policy
University of California at Berkeley

Gordon Binder
Graduate Student (and ex-Staff
    Intern Environmental
    Protection Agency)
University of Michigan

John Brandel
Deputy Assistant Secretary for
    Program Evaluation
U.S. Department of Health,
    Education, and Welfare

William C. Bryant
Associate Executive Editor
U.S. News and World Report
Washington, D.C.

Robert Burco
Public Policy Analyst
Berkeley, California

David S. Bushnell
Research Director
Project Focus
Washington, D.C.

William Byron
Associate Commissioner
Administration and Fiscal
  Management
N.Y. State Department of
  Mental Hygiene

John Caffrey
Director
Commission on Administrative Affairs
American Council on Education

Lynton Caldwell
Professor
Department of Political Science
University of Indiana

Donald Campbell
Professor
Department of Psychology
Northwestern University

Nathan Caplan
CRUSK, Institute for Social
  Research
University of Michigan
Bayard Catron
Graduate Student
University of California at Berkeley

Bernard Cazes
Commissariat General du Plan
  d'Equipement et de La
  Productivité
Paris, France

C. West Churchman
Research Philosopher and
  Professor of Business
  Administration
University of California at Berkeley

Matthew Coffee
Special Assistant to the
  Director
Corporation for Public
  Broadcasting
Washington, D.C.

Timothy Costello
Deputy Mayor
New York City

Douglas Costle
Woodrow Wilson Fellow
Smithsonian Institution

Arch D. Crouch
Principal City Planner
Los Angeles, California

James Crowfoot
Consultant
Organizational Development Group
Lutheran Synod of Illinois

Michel Crozier
Director
Centre de Sociologie des
  Organisations
Paris, France

James Dator
Professor
Department of Political Science
University of Hawaii

Henry David
Executive Secretary
Division of Behavioral Sciences
National Academy of Sciences

Paul Davidoff
Director
Suburban Action Institute
White Plains, N.Y.

John Dixon
Director
Center for a Voluntary Society
Washington, D.C.

Gilbert Donahue
Labor Management Services
  Administration
U.S. Department of Labor

Charles Dresher
Manager
Information Systems
Los Angeles Technical Services Corp.

Yehezkel Dror
Rand Corporation
Santa Monica, California

Leonard Duhl
Associate Director
Program on Social Policy
College of Environmental Design
University of California at Berkeley

Richard Duke
Director
Environmental Simulation Laboratory
University of Michigan

Matthew Dumont
Director
Center for Studies of
    Metropolitan Problems
National Institute of Mental Health

Robert Ehler
Professor
Urban and Policy Sciences Program
College of Engineering
State University of New York
    at Stony Brook

Duane Elgin
Commission on Population Growth
    and the American Future
Washington, D.C.

Edward H. Erath
President
Los Angeles Technical
    Services Corporation

Martin Ernst
Vice President
Management Science Division
A. D. Little, Inc.

Carl Eugster
Head
Corporate Development
CIBA-GEIGY AO
Basel, Switzerland

Keith Evans
Budget Systems Coordinator
Office of Vice President
    for Academic Affairs
University of Michigan

Lansing Fair
Director
Developing Great Lakes
    Megalopolis Research Project

William Finley
Vice President
Community Planning & Research
The Rouse Company
Columbia, Md.

Jack Fisher
Associate Director
Center for Urban Studies
Wayne State University

John Ford
President's Commission on
    Management Improvement

John Forester
Graduate Student
University of California at Berkeley

Harley Frankel
Executive Assistant to
    the Commissioner of
    Education, HEW

Winston Franklin
Vice President, Planning
Charles F. Kettering Foundation

Louis Friedland
Associate Dean
School of Liberal Arts
Wayne State University

John Friedmann
Chairman
Urban Planning Program
University of California
    at Los Angeles

Dennis Gabor
Professor
Applied Electron Physics
Imperial College of Science and
    Technology
London, England

Sheldon Gans
Vice President
Marshall Kaplan, Gans, and Kahn
San Fransicso, California

Jack Gibbons
Director
ORNL-NSF
Environmental Program
Oak Ridge National Laboratory

Gideonse Hendrik
Staff Member
Senate Subcommittee on Executive
   Reorganization and Government
   Research
Washington, D.C.

Clifford Glover
Directorate for Scientific Affairs
OECD
Paris, France

Robert Goe
Special Assistant to the Mayor
Los Angeles, California

Theodore Gordon
President
The Futures Group
Glastenbury, Conn.

Andre Grandsard
Directeur D'Etudes
Compagnie D'Etudes Industrielles
   et D'Amenagement du Territoire
Paris, France

Bertram Gross
Professor
Department of Urban Affairs
Hunter College
New York City

Robert Grosse
Director
Health Planning Program
University of Michigan

Walter Hahn
Special Assistant for Planning
   to the Secretary of Commerce
Washington, D.C.

Calvin Hamilton
Chief of City Planning
Los Angeles, California

Wallace Hamilton
Institutional Development
The Rouse Company
Columbia, Md.

James Hardy
Associate Executive Director
YMCA National Headquarters
New York City

Willis Harman
Educational Policy Research Center
Stanford Research Institute
Menlo Park, California

Robert Heilbroner
New School for Social Research
New York City

Kurt Hellfach
General Electric Company
New York City

Dee Henderson
Associate Head
Special Programs Department
Graduate School
U.S. Department of Agriculture

David Hertz
McKinsey & Company, Inc.
New York City

Towsend Hoopes
Cresap, McCormick, and Paget
Washington, D.C.

Ida Hoose
Space Sciences Laboratory
University of California at Berkeley

Morton Hoppenfeld
Vice President
American City Corporation
Columbia, Md.

Alan Jacobs
Director of Planning
San Francisco, California

Erich Jantsch
College of Environmental Design
University of California at Berkeley

Robert Jungk
Technische Universitat
West Berlin, Germany

Alfred Kahn
Professor
Columbia University School
    of Social Work
New York City

Robert Kahn
Director
Survey Research Center
Institute for Social Research
University of Michigan

Robert Kantor
Educational Policy Research Center
Stanford Research Institute

Marshall Kaplan
President
Marshall Kaplan, Gans, and Kahn
San Francisco, California

Stephen Kaplan
Professor
Department of Psychology
University of Michigan

Marvin Kelkstein
Director
Technical Assistance Office
State University of New York
    at Stony Brook

George Kozmetsky
Dean
College of Business Administration
University of Texas
Austin, Texas

Jody Ladio
Senior
Residential College
University of Michigan

Todd La Porte
Professor
Department of Political Science
University of California at Berkeley

Kai Lee
Postdoctoral Fellow
Institute of Governmental Studies
University of California at Berkeley

Robert Levine
Assistant Director
Research Plans, Programs, and
    Evaluation
U.S. Office of Economic Opportunity

Ronald Lippitt
Program Director
CRUSK, Institute for Social Research
University of Michigan

Ralph Littlestone
Chief
Planning Branch
National Institute of Mental Health

John Maddux
Special Assistant to the President
International Bank for
    Reconstruction & Development

Floyd Mann
Director
Center for Research on Utilization
    of Scientific Knowledge, ISR
University of Michigan

Robert Marans
Past Supervisor of Environmental
    Design Studies (Transportation
    and Land Use Study)
Detroit Regional Planning
    Commission

O. W. Markley
Educational Policy Research Center
Stanford Research Institute

Joseph Margolin
Director
Educational Policy Group
Program of Policy Studies in
    Science and Technology
George Washington University

M. Benjamin Matalon
Charge de Recherches
C.E.R.A.U.
Puteaux, France

John McHale
Director
Center for Integrative Studies
State University of New York
    at Binghamton

William Medina
Director
Executive Development Program
U.S. Civil Service Commission

Dennis Medows
Research Program on Technology
and Public Policy
Dartmouth College

Richard L. Meier
Professor
College of Environmental Design
University of California at Berkeley

Daniel Metlay
Graduate Student
University of California at Berkeley

Michael Michaelis
Director
A. D. Little, Inc.
Washington, D.C.

Alan Miller
Commissioner
New York State Department of
Mental Hygiene

Arnold Mitchell
Assistant Director
Educational Policy Research Center
Stanford Research Center

Lawrence Mohr
Professor
Institute for Public Policy Studies
University of Michigan

Charles Morris
Professor
Department of Philosophy
University of Florida
Gainesville, Fla.

Claire Nader
Associate Director
ORNL-NSF
Environmental Program
Oak Ridge National Laboratory

Charlotte Neagle
Intern
Detroit City Planning Commission

Robert Newman
Corporate Headquarters
General Electric Company
New York City

Mancur Olsen
Deputy Assistant Secretary
Department of Health, Education,
and Welfare

Robert Patton
Associate Commissioner
Office of Program Planning
and Coordination
N.Y. State Department of
Mental Hygiene

Harvey Perloff
Dean
School of Architecture and
Urban Planning
University of California at Los
Angeles

Jeffrey Pressman
Department of Political Science
University of California at Berkeley

Daniel Rader
Chief, Planning Section
State Department of Mental Health
Raleigh, N.C.

Philburn Ratoosh
Professor
Department of Psychology
California State University,
San Francisco

Paul Ray
Lecturer
Urban Planning
University of Michigan

Richard Raymond
President
Portola Institute
Menlo Park, California

A. Kenneth Rice
Center for Applied Social Research
Tavistock Institute of Human
Relations
London, England

Arliss Roaden
Vice Provost and Dean, Graduate
  School
Ohio State University

Andrew Rouse
Director
Resources Planning Staff
Executive Office of the President
U.S. Bureau of the Budget

William Royce
Senior Behavioral Scientist
Stanford Research Institute

Irving Rubin
Director
Transportation and Land Use Study
Detroit Regional Planning
  Commission

Rudy Ruggles
Office of Exploratory Planning
International Business Machines
  Corporation

Bryce Russell
Corporate Planning Staff
Ford Motor Company

Donald Schon
President
Organization for Social and
  Technological Innovation
Cambridge, Mass.

Herbert Shepherd
Consultant on Group Processes
Stamford, Conn.

W. W. Simmons
Director
Exploratory Planning
International Business Machines
  Corporation

Robert Solo
Professor
Department of Economics
Michigan State University

Jay Starling
Graduate Student
University of California at Berkeley

Herbert Striner
Dean
College of Continuing Education
American University

James Sundberg
Graduate Student
Institute of Urban and
  Regional Planning
University of California at Berkeley

Michael Tate
Assistant Director,
  PPBS Training
Financial Management and
  PPBS Training Center
U.S. Civil Service Commission

Michael Timpane
Program Analyst
Office of Program Evaluation
U.S. Department of Health,
  Education, and Welfare

Jeffrey Tirengel
Graduate Student (and ex-Staff
  Intern, NIMH)
University of Michigan

Wilber Thompson
Professor
Department of Economics
Wayne State University

Geoffrey Vickers
Goering-on-Thames, England

Dwight Waldo
Professor
Department of Political Science
Syracuse University

Richard Walton
Professor
Graduate School of Business
  Administration
Harvard University

Graham Watt
City Manager
Dayton, Ohio

Melvin Webber
Director
Center for Planning and
  Development Research
University of California at Berkeley

Alan Westin
Director, Center for Research and
   Education in American Liberties
Columbia University and Teachers
   College

Charles Williams
Staff Director
National Goals Research Staff

Ian Wilson
Consultant
Business Environment Studies
General Electric Company
New York City

Langdon Winner
Graduate Student
University of California at Berkeley

Paul Ylvisaker
Director
New Jersey Department of
   Community Affairs

☆ *References* ☆

ABELSON, P. "The National Goals Research Staff Report." *Science*, 1970, *169*.

ACKOFF, R. *The Concept of Corporate Planning*. New York: Wiley-Interscience, 1970.

ALLISON, G. *Essence of Decision*. Boston: Little, Brown, 1971.

ANDERSON, S. (Ed.) *Ombudsmen for American Government?* Englewood Cliffs, N.J.: Prentice-Hall, 1968.

Annual Report. New York: Social Science Research Council, 1968-1969.

ARCHIBALD, K. "Three Views of the Expert's Role in Policymaking: Systems Analysis, Incrementalism, and the Clinical Approach." *Policy Sciences*, 1970, *1*.

ARENDT, H. *The Human Condition*. Chicago: University of Chicago Press, 1958.

ARENDT, H. *Eichmann in Jerusalem: A Report on the Banality of Evil*. New York: Viking, 1963.

ARGYRIS, C. *Interpersonal Competence and Organizational Effectiveness*. Homewood, Ill.: Dorsey Press, 1962.

ARGYRIS, C. "The Incompleteness of Social-Psychological Theory: Examples from Small Group, Cognitive Consistency, and Attribution Research." *American Psychologist*, 1969, 24(10).

ARGYRIS, C. "Resistance to Rational Management Systems." Innovation, 1970 (10). (In 1972 *Innovation* merged with *Business and Society Review*.)

ARGYRIS, C. *Applicability of Organizational Sociology*. New York: Cambridge University Press, 1972.

ARNSTEIN, S. "A Ladder of Citizen Participation." *Journal of the American Institute of Planners*, July 1969, *35*.

ARNSTEIN, S. "Maximum Feasible Manipulation." Third Conference on Crises, Conflict, and Creativity, National Academy of Public Administration, July 1970.

ARONSON, E. "The Theory of Cognitive Dissonance: A Current Perspective." In L. Berkowitz (Ed.), *Advances in Experimental Social Psychology*. New York: Academic Press, 1969. Vol. IV.

ASHBY, W. R. *An Introduction to Cybernetics*. London: Chapman and Hall, 1956.

BACHMAN, J., AND VAN DUINEN, E. *Youth Look at National Problems.* Ann Arbor: Institute for Social Research, 1971.

BALDRIDGE, J. "Images of the Future and Organizational Change: The Case of New York University." In W. Bell and J. Mau, *The Sociology of the Future.* New York: Russell Sage Foundation, 1971.

BANFIELD, E. "Ends and Means in Planning." In S. Mallick and E. Van Ness (Eds.), *Concepts and Issues in Administrative Behavior.* Englewood Cliffs, N.J.: Prentice-Hall, 1962.

BARAM, M. "Social Control of Science and Technology." Science, 1971, *172.*

BARNARD, C. *The Functions of the Executive.* Cambridge: Harvard University Press, 1938.

BARRETT, J. "Power Influence and Control In Organizations." In S. E. Seashore and R. J. McNeill, *Management of Urban Crises.* New York: The Free Press, 1971.

BART, P. "The Myth of a Value-Free Psychiatry." In W. Bell and J. Mau (Eds.), *The Sociology of the Future.* New York: Russell Sage Foundation, 1971.

BARTON, A., AND MERTON, R. *Social Organization Under Stress: A Sociological Review of Disaster Studies.* Washington, D.C.: National Academy of Sciences, National Research Council, 1963.

BAUER, R. (Ed.) *Social Indicators.* Cambridge: M.I.T. Press, 1966.

BAUER, R. "Societal Feedback." *The Annals of the American Academy of Political and Social Science,* September 1967, *373.*

BAUER, R., POOL, I. DE SOLA, AND DEXTER, L. *American Business and Public Policy.* New York: Atherton, 1963.

BAUER, R., WITH ROSENBLOOM, R., AND SHARP, L., and the assistance of others. *Second Order Consequences: A Methodological Essay on the Impact of Technology.* Cambridge: M.I.T. Press, 1969.

BAUMAN, Z. "The Limitations of 'Perfect Planning'." In B. Gross (Ed.), *Action Under Planning.* New York: McGraw-Hill, 1967.

BAZELON, D. "Psychology's Roles and Contributions in Problems of Crime, Delinquency, and Corrections." Address to the American Association of Correctional Psychologists' Conference. Washington, D.C.: Mimeographed, January 1972.

BEARD, C. *The Supreme Court and the Constitution.* Englewood Cliffs, N.J.: Prentice-Hall, 1962.

BECKHARD, R. *Organization Development: Strategies and Models.* Reading, Mass.: Addison-Wesley, 1969.

BELL, D. "Twelve Modes of Prediction—A Preliminary Sorting of Approaches in the Social Sciences." *Daedalus,* 1964, *93,*(3).

BELL, D. "The Cultural Contradictions of Capitalism." *The Public Interest,* Fall 1970, (21).

BELL, W., AND J. MAU, J. "Images of the Future: Theory and Research Strategies." In W. Bell and J. Mau, *The Sociology of the Future*. New York: Russell Sage Foundation, 1971.

BELL, W., AND MAU, J. *The Sociology of the Future*. New York: Russell Sage Foundation, 1971.

BENNIS, W. *Changing Organizations*. New York: McGraw-Hill, 1966.

BENNIS, W. *Organization Development*: Its Nature, Origins, and Prospects. Reading, Mass.: Addison-Wesley, 1969.

BENNIS, W. "A Funny Thing Happened on the Way to the Future." *American Psychologist*, 1970, 25(7).

BENNIS, W., BENNE, K., AND CHIN, R. *The Planning of Change*. New York: Holt, Rinehart and Winston, 1962 and 1969 (revised).

BENNIS, W., AND SLATER, P. *The Temporary Society*. New York: Harper and Row, 1968.

BERGER, P., AND BERGER, B. "The Eve of the Bluing of America." *The New York Times*. February 15, 1971.

BERGER, P., AND LUCKMANN, T. *The Social Construction of Reality*. Garden City, N.Y.: Anchor Books, 1966.

BERLIN, I. *The Hedgehog and the Fox*. New York: New American Library, 1957.

BERLYNE, D. *Conflict, Arousal, and Curiosity*. New York: McGraw-Hill, 1960.

BERNSTEIN, M. *The Job of the Federal Executive*. Washington, D.C.: Brookings Institution, 1958.

BILLER, R. "Converting Knowledge Into Action: The Dilemma and Opportunity of the Post Industrial Society." In J. Jun and W. Storm (Eds.), *Tomorrow's Organizations: Challenges and Strategies*. Glenview, Ill.: Scott, Foresman, 1973.

BION, W. *Experiences in Groups*. New York: Basic Books, 1959.

BIRCH, D. "The Model-Building Process and Its Interaction with Organizations: Two Exploratory Field Studies Involving Mathematical Decision Models." Thesis. Graduate School of Business Administration, Harvard University, Jan. 1966.

BLACKBURN, T. "Sensuous-Intellectual Complementarity in Science." *Science*, 1971, 172.

BLAKE, R., AND MOUTON, J. "Grid Organizational Development." *Personnel Administration*, Jan.-Feb. 1967.

BLAKE, R., AND MOUTON, J. *Corporate Excellence Through Grid Organizational Development*. Houston, Tex.: Gulf, 1968.

BLAU, P. *The Dynamics of Bureaucracy: A Study of Interpersonal Relations in Two Government Agencies*. Chicago: University of Chicago Press, 1963.

BLUMENTHAL, M., KAHN, R., ANDREWS, F., AND HEAD, K. *Justifying Violence: Attitudes of American Men.* Ann Arbor: Institute for Social Research, University of Michigan, 1972.

BLUMER, H. "Social Problems as Collective Behavior." *Social Problems*, 1971, *18*.

BOETTINGER, H. "Big Gap in Economic Theory." *Harvard Business Review*, 1967, 45(4).

BOORSTIN, D. *The Image: A Guide to Pseudo-Events in America.* New York: Harper and Row, 1964.

BORGATTA, E. "Research Problems in Evaluation of Health Service Demonstrations." *Milbank Memorial Fund Quarterly*, Oct. 1966, *44*, Part II.

BOULDING, K. *The Image.* Ann Arbor: The University of Michigan Press, 1956.

BOULDING, K. "Ethics of Rational Decision." *Management Science*, 1966, *12*(6).

BOWER, J. *Managing the Resource Allocation Process: A Study in Corporate Planning and Investment.* Boston: Harvard Business School, 1970.

BOWERS, D. "Perspectives in Organizational Development," CRUSK-ISR Working Paper, Ann Arbor: Center for Research on Utilization of Scientific Knowledge, Institute for Social Research, University of Michigan, 1971.

BRINTON, C. *Shaping of the Modern Mind.* New York: Mentor Books, 1953.

BROOKS, H. "Science and the Allocation of Resources." *American Psychologist*, March 1967, *22*.

BRZEZINSKI, Z. *Between Two Ages: America's Role in the Technetronic Era.* New York: The Viking Press, 1970.

BUCKLEY, W. (Ed.) *Sociology and Modern Systems Theory.* Englewood Cliffs, N.J.: Prentice-Hall, 1967.

BUCKLEY, W. (Ed.) *Modern Systems Research for the Behavioral Scientist.* Chicago: Aldine, 1968.

BUHLER, C. "Basic Theoretical Concepts of Humanistic Psychology." *American Psychologist*, 1971, *26*(4).

BURCO, R. "The Assessment of Technology as a Problem in the Distribution of Technical Expertise." Private paper, December 1971.

BURNS, T., AND STALKER, G. *The Management of Innovation.* London: Tavistock, 1961.

BUTKIS, A. "The New Youth Movement." *Dunn's*, 1971 *98*(2).

CAHN, E., and CAHN, J. "Citizen Participation." In H. Spiegel (Ed.), *Citizen Participation in Urban Development.* Washington, D.C.: NTL Institute for Applied Behavioral Science, 1968.

CALDWELL, L. *Environment: A Challenge for Modern Society.* Garden City, N.Y.: The Natural History Press, 1970.

CALDWELL, L. *In Defense of Earth: International Protection of the Biosphere.* Bloomington, Ind.: Indiana University Press, 1972.

CAMPBELL, D. "Methods for the Experimenting Society." Paper delivered to the American Psychological Association meetings, Washington, D.C., September 1971. To appear in the *American Psychologist.*

CAMPBELL, J. *The Hero with a Thousand Faces.* Princeton, N.J.: Bollingen Series No. 17, 1968.

CAMPBELL, J. *The Flight of the Wild Gander: Explorations in the Mythological Dimension.* New York: Viking, 1969.

CAPLAN, N. "The Impact of Social Research on Policy Decisions." Invited address to the American Society for Public Opinion Research, May 19, 1971, Pasadena, California. Ann Arbor: Center for Research on Utilization of Scientific Knowledge, Institute for Social Research, University of Michigan.

CAPLAN, N., AND NELSON, S. "On Being Useful: The Nature and Uses of Psychological Research on Social Problems." *American Psychologist,* 1973, *28*(3).

CARROLL, J. "Participatory Technology." *Science,* 1971, *171.*

CAZES, B. "The Promise and Limits of Social Indicators." *European Business,* Summer 1972, (34).

"Change in the Corporations." By the Editors. *Harvard Today,* March 1972, p. 4.

CHAPMAN, J. "Voluntary Association and the Political Theory of Pluralism." In J. Pennock and J. Chapman (Eds.), *Voluntary Associations: Nomos XI.* New York: Atherton, 1968.

CHARLESWORTH, J. (Ed.) "Ethics in America: Norms and Deviations." *The Annals of the American Academy,* 1966, *31*(3).

CHESLER, M., AND GUSKIN, A. "Intervention in High School Crises: Consultant Roles." Ann Arbor: Educational Change Team, School of Education, University of Michigan, 1970.

CHURCHMAN, C. W. *Challenge to Reason.* New York: McGraw-Hill, 1967.

CHURCHMAN, C. W. *The Systems Approach.* New York: Dell, 1968.

CHURCHMAN, C.W. "Operations Research as a Profession." *Management Science,* 1970, *17*(2).

CHURCHMAN, C.W., and EMERY, F. "On Various Approaches to the Study of Organizations." In J. Lawrence (Ed.), *Operational Research and the Social Sciences.* London: Tavistock, 1966.

CLAIBORNE, R. Review of R. Titmuss, *The Gift Relationship.* In "Book World," *The Washington Post,* May 9, 1971, p. 4.

CLARK, K. "Problems of Power and Social Change: Toward a Relevant Social Pathology." *Journal of Social Issues,* 1965, *21*(3).

CLARK, T. "The Concept of Power: Some Overemphasized and Underrecognized Dimensions—An Examination with Special Reference to the Social Community." *Social Science Quarterly*, December 1967.

CLEVELAND, H. *The Future Executive: A Guide for Tomorrow's Managers.* New York: Harper and Row, 1972.

COHEN, A., STOTLAND, E., AND WOLFE, D. "An Experimental Investigation of Need for Cognition." *Journal of Abnormal and Social Psychology*, 1959 (51).

COLM, G., AND GULICK, L. *Program Planning for National Goals.* Washington, D.C.: National Planning Association, 1968.

Concepts for Los Angeles. Los Angeles: City Planning Department, 1967.

COSER, L. *Functions of Social Conflict.* Glencoe: The Free Press, 1956.

COSER, L. *Continuities in the Study of Social Conflict.* New York: The Free Press, 1967.

COSTELLO, T. "Change in Municipal Government: A View from the Inside." *Journal of Applied Behavioral Science*, 1971, 7(2).

COTTLE, T. "Temporal Correlates of the Achievement Value and Manifest Anxiety." *Journal of Consulting* and *Clinical Psychology*, 1969, 33(5).

COTTRELL, L., AND SHELDON, E. "Problems of Collaboration Between Social Scientists and the Practicing Professions." *The Annals of the American Academy of Political and Social Science*, March 1963, 346.

CRECINE, J. *Defense Budgeting: Organizational Adaptation to External Constraints.* Prepared for the United States Air Force Project Rand. Santa Monica, Calif.: The Rand Corporation, March 1970.

CROWE, B. "The Tragedy of the Commons Revisited." *Science*, 1969, 166.

CROWFOOT, J. "Planning and Social Systems Organizations as a Special Case." Working paper, Center for Research on Utilization of Scientific Knowledge. Ann Arbor: Institute for Social Research, 1972.

CROZIER, M. *The Bureaucratic Phenomenon.* Chicago: University of Chicago Press, 1964.

CYERT, R., AND MARCH, J. *A Behavioral Theory of the Firm.* Englewood Cliffs, N.J.: Prentice-Hall, 1963.

DAHL, R. "The Concept of Power." *Behavioral Science*, 1957, (2).

DALE, E. "The 'Unfavorables'." *New York Sunday Times*, Financial Section, November 7, 1971.

DAVID, H. "Assumptions About Man and Society and Historical Constructs in Futures Research." *Futures*, 1970, 2(3).

DEARDEN, J. "Myth of Real-Time Management Information." *Harvard Business Review*, 1966, 44(3).

DE HOGHTON, C., PAGE, W., AND STREATFEILD, G. . . . *And Now the Future: A PEP Survey of Futures Studies.* London: PEP, 1971.

DE JOUVENEL, B. *The Art of Conjecture*. New York: Basic Books, 1967.

DEL GUIDICE, D. *The Potential for Developing a Local Goals-Setting Model and NGRS [National Goals Research Staff] Involvement Therein*. National Academy of Public Administration, 1970.

DEUTSCH, K. *The Nerves of Government*. New York: The Free Press, 1966.

DEUTSCH, M. "An Experimental Study of the Effects of Cooperation and Competition Upon Group Processes." *Human Relations*, 1949, 2.

DEUTSCH, M. "The Effect of Motivational Orientation Upon Trust and Suspicion." *Human Relations*, 1960, 13.

DIAL, O. *Urban Information Systems: A Bibliographic Essay*. Urban Systems Laboratory, M.I.T. Cambridge, Mass.: 1968.

DI BONA, C. "Where Is Systems Analysis?" CNA 451-67, Revised. Washington, D.C.: Center for Naval Analysis, 1967.

Diplomacy for the 70's: A Program of Management Reform for the Department of State. Department of State. Washington, D.C.: U.S. Government Printing Office, 1970.

Discussion Paper: Planning Goals for the Los Angeles Metropolis. Los Angeles: City Planning Department, 1967.

DOWNS, A. *Inside Bureaucracy*. Boston: Little, Brown, 1966.

DOWNS, A. "A Realistic Look at the Final Payoffs From Urban Data Systems." *Public Administration Review*, 1967 27(3).

DREWS, E. *Policy Implications of a Hierarchy of Values*. Menlo Park, Calif.: Educational Policy Research Center, Stanford Research Institute, 1970.

DREWS, E. AND LIPSON, L. *Values and Humanity*. New York: St. Martin's Press, 1971.

DRIVER, M., AND STREUFERT, S. The General Incongruity Adaptation Level (GIAL) Hypothesis-II. Incongruity Motivation to Affect, Cognition, and Activation-Arousal Theory. Paper No. 148. Lafayette, Ind.: Institute for Research in the Behavioral, Economic, and Management Sciences, Purdue University, 1966.

DROR, Y. "Muddling Through—'Science' or Inertia?" *Public Administration Review*, 1964, 24(3).

DROR, Y. *Public Policymaking Reexamined*. San Francisco: Chandler, 1968.

DROR, Y. "Law as a Tool of Directed Social Change." *American Behavioral Scientist*, 1970, 13(4).

DRUCKER, P. *The Practice of Management*. New York: Harper and Row, 1954.

DUHL, L. "Creation of Forecasting and Planning Mechanisms." American Academy of Arts and Sciences, Commission on the Year 2000. Unpublished paper.

DUMONT, M. *The Absurd Healer: Perspectives of a Community Psychiatrist.* New York: Science House, 1968.

DUNCAN, O. "Social Forecasting: The State of the Art." *The Public Interest,* Fall 1968 (17).

DUNN, E. *Economic and Social Development: A Process of Social Learning.* Baltimore: Johns Hopkins, 1971.

EDELMAN, M. *The Symbolic Uses of Politics.* Chicago: University of Illinois Press, 1964.

EDELSTON, H., AND KOLODNER, F. "Are the Poor Capable of Planning for Themselves?" In H. Spiegel (Ed.), *Citizen Participation in Urban Development.* Washington, D.C.: NTL Institute for Applied Behavioral Science, 1968.

EMERY, F. "The Next Thirty Years: Concepts, Methods, and Anticipations." *Human Relations,* 1967, *20.*

EMERY, F., AND TRIST, E. "The Causal Texture of Organizational Environments." *Human Relations,* 1965, *18.*

ERBER, E. (Ed.) *Urban Planning in Transition.* New York: Grossman, 1970.

"To Establish a Select Senate Committee on Technology and the Human Environment." Hearings before the Subcommittee on Intergovernmental Relations. Washington, D.C.: U.S. Government Printing Office, March 1967.

ETZIONI, A. " 'Shortcuts' to Social Change?" *The Public Interest,* Summer 1968a (12).

ETZIONI, A. *The Active Society.* New York: The Free Press, 1968.

ETZIONI, A., AND LEHMAN, E. "Some Dangers in 'Valid' Social Measurement." *The Annals of the American Academy,* September 1967, *373.*

EVAN, W. "The Organization-Set: Toward a Theory of Interorganizational Relations." In J. Thompson (Ed.), *Approaches to Organizational Design.* Pittsburgh: University of Pittsburgh Press, 1966.

EWING, D. *The Human Side of Planning: Tool or Tyrant?* New York: Macmillan, 1969.

Experimental Symposia on Cultural Futurology, American Anthropological Association, Office of Applied Social Science and the Future, University of Minnesota, 1970, 1971.

FERKISS, V. *Technological Man.* New York: Braziller, 1969.

FISCHER, R. "A Cartography of the Ecstatic and Meditative States." *Science,* 1971, *174.*

FLACKS, R. "Protest or Conform: Some Social Psychological Perspectives on Legitimacy." *Journal of Applied Behavioral Science,* 1969, 5(2).

FRAISSE, P. *The Psychology of Time.* New York: Harper and Row, 1963.

FRENCH, J., AND CAPLAN, R. "Psychosocial Factors in Coronary Heart Disease." *Industrial Medicine,* 1970, *39*(9).

FRENCH, J., AND RAVEN, B. "The Basis of Social Power." In Cartwright, D. (Ed.) *Studies in Social Power.* New York: Harper and Row, 1968.

FRIEDLANDER, F. "The Primacy of Trust as a Facilitator of Further Group Accomplishment." *Journal of Applied Behavioral Science,* 1970, *6*(4).

FRIEDMANN, J. "The Future of Comprehensive Urban Planning: A Critique." *Public Administration Review,* 1971, *31*(3).

FRIEDMANN, J. *Retracking America: A Theory of Transactive Planning.* Garden City, N.Y.: Anchor Press-Doubleday, 1973.

FRIEND, J., AND JESSOP, W. *Local Government and Strategic Choice.* London: Tavistock Publications; Sage Publications, 1969.

FROHMAN, M., AND HAVELOCK, R. "The Organizational Context of Dissemination and Utilization." In R. Havelock and others, *Planning for Innovation.* Ann Arbor: Institute for Social Research, Center on Utilization of Scientific Knowledge, 1971.

FROMM, E. *Escape from Freedom.* New York: Holt, Rinehart and Winston, 1941.

Full Opportunity and Social Accounting Act. Hearings before the Subcommittee on Government Research of the Committee on Government Operations. Washington, D.C.: U.S. Government Printing Office, 1967.

GABOR, D. *Inventing the Future.* New York: Knopf, 1964.

GAMSON, W. *Power and Discontent.* Homewood, Ill.: Dorsey Press, 1968.

GANS, H. "The Need for Planners Trained in Policy Formation." In E. Erber (Ed.), *Urban Planning in Transition.* New York: Grossman, 1970.

GARDNER, J. "America in the Twenty-Third Century. *New York Times,* Editorial Page, July 27, 1968.

GEORGE, A. "Power as a Compensatory Value for Political Leaders." *Journal of Social Issues,* 1968, *24*.

GEORGOPOULOS, B. "An Open-System Theory Model for Organizational Research." In A. Negandhi and J. Schwitter (Eds.), *Organizational Behavior Models.* Kent, Ohio: Kent State University, 1970.

GLATT, E. AND SHELLEY, M. *The Research Society,* New York: Gordon and Breach, 1969.

GOODING, J. "It Pays to Wake Up the Blue-Collar Worker." *Fortune,* September 1970.

GORDON, W. *Synectics.* New York: Harper and Row, 1961.

GORE, W. *Administrative Decision-Making: A Heuristic Model.* New York: Wiley, 1966.

GRAVES, C. "Deterioration of Work Standards." *Harvard Business Review,* 1966, *44*(5).

GRAVES, C. "Levels of Existence: An Open System Theory of Values." *Journal of Humanistic Psychology,* 1970, *10*(2).

GRINSPOON, L. "Interpersonal Constraints and the Decision Maker." In R. Fisher (Ed.), *International Conflict and Behavioral Science*. New York: Basic Books, 1964.

GROSS, B. *The Managing of Organizations*. New York: The Free Press, 1964.

GROSS, B. "Activating National Plans." In B. Gross (Ed.), *Action Under Planning*. New York: McGraw-Hill, 1967.

GROSS, B. "Friendly Fascism: A Model for America." *Social Policy*, November-December 1970, *1*.

GROSS, B. *Management Strategy for Economic and Social Development*. Working Paper prepared for the United Nations Interregional Seminar on the Use of Modern Management Techniques in the Public Administration of Developing Countries, Washington, D.C. ESA/PA/MMTS/27. New York: United Nations, 1970.

GROSS, B. "Planning in an Era of Social Revolution." *Public Administration Review*, 1971, *31*(3).

GROSS, B., AND SPAINGER, M. (Eds.) *Social Intelligence for America's Future: Explorations in Societal Problems*. Boston: Allyn and Bacon, 1969.

GUSKIN, A., MICHAEL, D., AND CROWFOOT, J. "The Implications for the Change-Over to Long-Range Planning of the Rise of the Advocate Planner." Working Paper 2. Center for Research on Utilization of Scientific Knowledge, Institute for Social Research, University of Michigan, 1970.

GUTTENTAG, M. "Models and Methods in Evaluation Research." *Journal of Theory of Social Behavior*, 1972, *1*(1).

HABERSTROH, C. "Control as an Organizational Process." In W. Buckley (Ed.), *Modern Systems Research for the Behavioral Scientist*. Chicago: Aldine, 1968.

HAGE, J., AND AIKEN, M. *Social Change in Complex Organizations*. New York: Random House, 1970.

HAHN, W. *The Department of Commerce: Its Past Present and Future*. A Task Force Report. Washington, D.C.: The Department of Commerce, December 1968.

HALL, M. "A Conversation with Harold Dwight Lasswell: The Psychology of Politics." *Psychology Today*, 1968, *2*(5).

HALL, W. "Strategic Planning Models . . . Are Top Managers Really Finding Them Useful?" Graduate School of Business Administration, University of Michigan, 1972. (Limited circulation.)

HALPERIN, M. "Why Bureaucrats Play Games." Washington, D.C.: The Brookings Institution Reprint, 1971.

HANS, H. "The Need for Planners Trained in Policy Formation." In E. Erber (Ed.), *Urban Planning in Transition*. New York: Grossman, 1970.

HARDIN, G. "The Tragedy of the Commons." *Science*, 1968, *162*.

HARMAN, W. "Nature of Our Changing Society: Implications for Schools." In P. Piele and T. Eidell (Eds.), *Social and Technological Change: Implications for Education.* Eugene, Ore.: Center for the Advanced Study of Educational Administration. University of Oregon, 1970.

HARRISON, A. *The Problem of Privacy in the Computer Age: An Annotated Bibliography.* Memorandum RM-5495-PR/RC. Santa Monica: The Rand Corporation, 1967.

HAVELOCK, R. "Specialized Knowledge Linking Models." In R. Havelock and others, *Planning for Innovation.* Ann Arbor: Institute for Social Research, Center for Research on Utilization of Scientific Knowledge, 1971.

HAVELOCK, R., with the collaboration of A. Guskin, M. Frohman, M. Havelock, M. Hill, and J. Huber. *Planning for Innovation.* Ann Arbor: Institute for Social Research, Center for Research on Utilization of Scientific Knowledge, 1971.

HEILBRONER, R. *The Future as History.* New York: Grove Press, 1959.

HEILBRONER, R. *The Making of Economic Society.* Englewood Cliffs, N.J.: Prentice-Hall, 1962.

HEILBRONER, R. "On the Limited 'Relevance' of Economics." *The Public Interest,* Fall 1970, (21).

HEILBRONER, R. "Phase II of the Capitalist System." *The New York Times Magazine,* November 28, 1971.

HENRIOT, P. "Political Implications of Social Indicators." Paper presented at the Annual Meeting of the American Political Science Association. Chicago, September 1971. Seattle: Seattle University, 1971.

HERMANN, C. "Some Consequences of Crises Which Limit the Viability of Organizations." *Administrative Science Quarterly,* 1963, *8*(1).

HERTZ, D. "Has Management Science Reached a Dead End?" *Innovation* (now *Business Society Review*), 1971 (25).

HEYDERBRAND, W. "Administration of Social Change." *Public Administration Review,* 1964, *24*(3).

HIRSCHMAN, A. *Exit, Voice, and Loyalty: Responses to Decline in Firms, Organizations, and States.* Cambridge: Harvard University Press, 1970.

HIRSCHMAN, A., AND LINDBLOM, C. "Economic Development, Research and Development, Policy Making: Some Converging Views." *Behavioral Science,* 1962, *7*(2).

HOFFER, E. *The Ordeal of Change.* New York: Harper and Row, 1963.

HOLT, J. *The Underachieving School.* New York: Dell, 1970.

HOOK, S. *The Hero in History.* Boston: Beacon Press, 1943.

HOOPES, T. *The Limits of Intervention: An Inside Account of How the Johnson Policy of Escalation in Vietnam was Reversed.* New York: David McKay, 1969.

HOOS, I. *A Critical Review of Systems Analysis: The California Experience.* NASA Report CR-61350. Berkeley: University of California, 1968.

HOOS, I. "A Realistic Look at the Systems Approach to Social Problems." *Datamation,* 1969, *15*(2). In the journal section, "The Forum."

HORNEY, K. *The Neurotic Personality of Our Time.* New York: Norton, 1937.

HUBER, B. "Studies of the Future: A Selected and Annotated Bibliography." In W. Bell and J. Mau (Eds.), *The Sociology of the Future.* New York: Russell Sage Foundation, 1971.

HUNT, R. "Technology and Organization." *Academy of Management Journal,* September 1970.

HUNT, R. "Role and Role Conflict." In Hollander, E., and Hunt R. (Eds.) *Current Perspectives in Social Psychology.* New York: Oxford University Press, 1971.

HUXLEY, A. *The Perennial Philosophy.* New York: Harper and Row, 1944.

HYMAN, H. "Reference Groups." In *International Encyclopedia of the Social Sciences.* Vol. XIII. New York: Crowell Collier and Macmillan, 1968.

Information Technology: Some Critical Implications for Decision Makers. New York: The Conference Board, Inc., 1972.

"Is There a New Man?" *The Center Magazine,* 1971, *4*(6).

JANIS, I. "Groupthink Among Policy Makers." In N. Sanford and C. Comstock (Eds.), *Sanctions for Evil.* San Francisco: Jossey-Bass, 1971a.

JANIS, I. "Groupthink." *Psychology Today,* November, 1971.

JANTSCH, E. "From Forecasting and Planning to Policy Sciences." Paper for presentation at the AAAS Annual Meeting, Boston, December 26-31, 1969.

JANTSCH, E. (Ed.) *Perspectives of Planning.* Paris: Organization for Economic Co-operation and Development, 1969a.

JANTSCH, E. *Technological Planning and Social Futures.* London: Associated Business Programs Limited, 1972.

JONES, E. *Systems Approaches to Multi-Variable Socioeconomic Problems: An Appraisal.* Staff Discussion Paper 103, Program of Policy Studies in Science and Technology. Washington, D.C.: The George Washington University, 1968.

JONES, R. "The Model as a Decision Maker's Dilemma." *Public Administration Review,* 1964, *24*(3).

JUNG, C. *Two Essays on Analytical Psychology.* Cleveland: World Publishing Co., 1956.

KAHN, A. *Theory and Practice of Social Planning.* New York: Russell Sage Foundation, 1969.

KAHN, R. "The Justification of Violence: Social Problems and Social Solutions." *Journal of the Society for the Psychological Study of Social Issues,* 1972, 28.

KAHN, R., AND BOULDING, E. (Eds.) *Power and Conflict in Organizations.* New York: Basic Books, 1964.

KAHN, R. WOLFE, D., QUINN, R., SNOEK, J. AND ROSENTHAL, R. *Organizational Stress: Studies in Role Conflict and Ambiguity.* New York: Wiley, 1964.

KANTOR, R. *Psychological Theories and Social Groupings.* Research Memorandum EPRC-6747-5. Menlo Park, Calif.: Stanford Research Institute, 1969.

KANTOR, R. "The Affective Domain and Beyond." *Journal for the Study of Consciousness,* 1970, 3(1).

KANTOR, R. *Implications of a Moral Science.* Memorandum Report EPRC 6747-14. Menlo Park, Calif.: Educational Policy Research Center, Stanford Research Institute, 1971.

KANTOR, R. "Moral Science." Menlo Park, Calif.: Stanford Research Institute, 1971.

KAPLAN, M. "The Role of the Planner in Urban Areas: Modest, Intuitive Claims for Advocacy." San Francisco: Address to the National Conference on Social Welfare, 1968.

KAPLAN, S. *Cognitive Maps in Perception and Thought.* Ann Arbor: University of Michigan, 1970.

KATZ, D., AND GEORGOPOULOS, B. "Organizations in a Changing World." *Journal of Applied Behavioral Science,* 1971, 7(3).

KATZ, D., AND KAHN, R. *The Social Psychology of Organizations.* New York: John Wiley, 1966.

KAYSEN, C. "Model-Makers and Decision-Makers: Economists and the Policy Process." *The Public Interest,* Summer 1968 (12).

KIEFER, D. "Industry Maps Tomorrow's Technology." *Chemical and Engineering News,* 1972, 50(9).

KLUCKHOHN, C., AND KELLY, W. "The Concept of Culture." In R. Linton (Ed.), *The Science of Man in the World Crisis.* New York: Columbia University Press, 1945.

KNIGHT, F. *Risk Uncertainty and Profit.* Chicago: University of Chicago Press, 1921.

KOHN, M. "Bureaucratic Man." *New Society,* October 28, 1971.

KUHN, T. *The Structure of Scientific Revolution.* Chicago: University of Chicago Press, 1970. Second Edition.

LA PORTE, T. *Organizational Response to Complexity: Research and Development as Organized Inquiry and Action—Part I.* Working Paper No. 141. Berkeley: Center for Planning and Development Research, Institute of Urban and Regional Development, University of California, 1971.

LASSWELL, H. *Power and Personality.* New York: W. W. Norton, 1948.

LASSWELL, H. "The Changing Image of Human Nature." *The American Journal of Psychoanalysis*, 1967, *26*(2).

LASSWELL, H. "A Note on 'Types' of Political Personality: Nuclear, Co-Relational, Developmental." *Journal of Social Issues*, 1968, *24*(3).

LASSWELL, H., And CLEVELAND, H. *The Ethic of Power*. New York: Harper and Row, 1962.

LASSWELL, H., AND KAPLAN, A. *Power and Society*. New Haven: Yale University Press, 1950.

LAWRENCE, J. (Ed.) *Operational Research and the Social Sciences*. London: Tavistock, 1966.

LAWRENCE, P. "The Uses of Crises: Cynamics of Ghetto Organization Development." In R. Rosenbloom and R. Marris (Eds.), *Social Innovation in the City*. Cambridge: Harvard University Press, 1969.

LAWRENCE, P., AND LORSCH, J. *Organization and Environment: Managing Differentiation and Integration*. Cambridge: Harvard University Press, 1967.

LEAVITT, H. "Applied Organizational Change in Industry: Structural Technological, and Humanistic Approaches." In March, J. (Ed.) *Handbook of Organizations*, Chicago: Rand McNally, 1965.

LEE, I. *The Language of Wisdom and Folly*. New York: Harper and Bros., 1949.

LEVINE, S., AND WHITE, P. "Exchange as a Conceptual Framework for the Study of Interorganizational Relationships." *Administrative Science Quarterly*, 1961, *5*(4).

LEVINE, S., WHITE, P., AND PAUL, B. "Community Interorganizational Problems in Providing Medical Care and Social Services." *American Journal of Public Health*, 1963 *53*(8).

LEWIN, K. "Feedback Problems of Social Diagnosis and Action." In W. Buckley (Ed.), *Modern Systems Research for the Behavioral Scientist*. Chicago: Aldine, 1968.

LICHTMAN, C., AND HUNG, R. "Personality and Organization Theory: A Review of Some Conceptual Literature." *Psychological Bulletin*, 1971, *76*.

LIKERT, R. *New Patterns of Management*. New York: McGraw-Hill, 1961.

LINDBLOM, C. "Contexts for Change and Strategy: A Reply." *Public Administration Review*, 1964, *24*(3).

LINDBLOM, C. *The Intelligence of Democracy: Decision Making Through Mutual Adjustment*. New York: The Free Press, 1965.

LINDBLOM, C. "The Science of 'Muddling Through'." IN E. Schneier (Ed.), *Policy Making in American Government*. New York: Basic Books, 1969.

LITWAK, E., AND HYLTON, L. "Interorganizational Analysis: A Hypothesis on Coordinating Agencies." *Administrative Science Quarterly*, 1962, *6*(4).

LONG, N. "The Local Community as an Ecology of Games." *American Journal of Sociology*, 1958, *64*(3).

LONG, N. "The Administrative Organization as a Political System." In S. Mallick and E. Van Ness (Eds.), *Concepts and Issues in Administrative Behavior.* Englewood Cliffs, N.J.: Prentice-Hall, 1962.

LOWI, T. *The End of Liberalism.* New York: W. W. Norton, 1969.

LOWI, T. "Government and Politics: Blurring of Sector Lines." In *Information Technology.* New York: The Conference Board, 1972.

LUBOVE, R. "Social Work and the Life of the Poor." *The Nation.* May 1966, *202.*

MAIMON, Z. "Second-Order Consequences—A Presentation of a Concept." Discussion Paper. Detroit: Center for Urban Studies, Wayne State University, May 1971.

MAIMON, Z. "Some Aspects of the Treatment of Costs and Benefits in Social Psychology." Discussion Paper. Detroit: Center for Urban Studies, Wayne State University, May 1971.

MANSFIELD, H. "Federal Executive Reorganization: Thirty Years of Experience." *Public Administration Review*, 1969, *29*(4).

MARINI, F. (Ed.) *Toward a New Public Administration.* Scranton, Pa.: Chandler, 1972.

MARKLEY, O. W., CURRY, D., AND RINK, D. "Contemporary Societal Problems." Research Report EPRC 6747-2. Educational Policy Research Center, 1971.

MARRIS, P., And REIN, M. *Dilemmas of Social Reform.* New York: Atherton, 1967.

MARROW, A., BOWERS, D., AND SEASHORE, S. *Management by Participation.* New York: Harper and Row, 1967.

MARTIN, R. "Be Kind to Your Plants or You Could Cause a Violet to Shrink." *Wall Street Journal*, February 2, 1972.

MARTINO, J. "Forecasting the Survival of the Forecaster." *The Futurist*, 1971.

MARX, F. *The Administrative State.* Chicago: University of Chicago Press, 1957.

MASLOW, A. *Toward a Psychology of Being.* Princeton: Van Nostrand, 1968.

MAY, R. *Man's Search for Himself.* New York: Norton, 1953.

MAY, R. (Ed.) *Symbolism in Religion and Literature.* New York: Braziller, 1959.

MAY, R. "Reality Beyond Rationalism." In Smith, G. Kerry (Ed.), *Agony and Promise: Current Issues in Higher Education 1969.* San Francisco: Jossey-Bass, 1969.

MAYO, E. *The Human Problems of an Industrial Civilization.* New York: Macmillan, 1933.

MC CLEERY, M. "On Remarks Taken Out of Context." *Public Administration Review*, 1964, *24*(3).

MC CLUSKY, H. "The Adult as Learner." In S. Seashore and R. McNeill (Eds.), *The Management of Urban Crisis*. New York: The Free Press, 1971.

MC HALE, J., AND CORDELL, M. *Typological Survey of Futures Research in the U.S.* Binghamton, N.Y.: Center for Integrative Studies, State University of New York, 1971.

MC KEAN, R., AND ANSHEN, M. "Problems, Limitation, and Risks." In D. Novick (Ed.), *Program Budgeting: Program Analysis and the Federal Budget*. Santa Monica, Calif.: The Rand Corporation, 1965.

MC NAMARA, R. *Address to the Board of Governors*. Washington, D.C.: International Bank for Reconstruction and Development, 1970a.

MC NAMARA, R. *Address to the Columbia University Conference on International Economic Development*. Washington, D.C.: International Bank for Reconstruction and Development, 1970.

MC QUADE, W. "What Stress Can Do to You." *Fortune*, 1972, *85*(1).

MC WHINNEY, W. "Organizational Form, Decision Modalities, and the Environment." *Human Relations*, 1968, *21*(3).

MEAD, G. *Mind, Self, and Society*. Chicago: University of Chicago Press, 1934.

MEAD, M. AND BYERS, P. *The Small Conference*. The Hague, The Netherlands: Mouton, 1968.

MEADOWS, D., MEADOWS, D., RANDERS, J., AND BEHRENS, W. *The Limits of Growth*. New York: Universe Books, 1972.

MEIER, R. "Information Input Overload." *Libri*, 1963, *13*.

MERTENS, H., AND GROSS, B. (Eds.) "Symposium on Changing Styles of Planning in Post-Industrial America." *Public Administration Review*, May-June 1971, *31*(3).

MEYER, M. "Two Authority Structures of Bureaucratic Organization." *Administrative Science Quarterly*, 1968, *13*(2).

MICHAEL, D. "Civilian Behavior Under Atomic Bombardment." *Bulletin of the Atomic Scientists*, May 1955, *11*.

MICHAEL, D. "Cybernetics and Human Behavior." Bethesda, Md.: Army Medical Service Graduate School, Walter Reed Army Medical Center, 1954.

MICHAEL, D. "Psychopathology of Nuclear War." *Bulletin of the Atomic Scientists*, May 1962, *18*.

MICHAEL, D. "Speculations on the Relation of the Computer to Individual Freedom and the Right to Privacy." *The George Washington Law Review*, 1964, *33*(1).

MICHAEL, D. "On Coping with Complexity: Planning and Politics." *Daedalus*, 1968, *97*(4).

MICHAEL, D. *The Unprepared Society: Planning for a Precarious Future*. New York: Basic Books, 1968.

MICHAEL, D. "Influencing Public Policy: The Changing Roles of Voluntary Associations." *Journal of Current Social Issues*, 1971, *9*(6).

MICHAEL, D. "The Individual: Enriched or Impoverished, Master or Servant?" *Information Technology: Some Critical Implications for Decision Makers*. New York: The Conference Board, Inc. 1972.

MILLER, A. "Business Morality: Some Unanswered (and Perhaps Unanswerable) Questions." *the Annals of the American Academy*, 1966, *363*.

MILLER, A. *The Dossier Society*. Ann Arbor: University of Michigan Press, 1971.

MILLER, E., AND RICE, A. K. *Systems of Organization*. London: Tavistock, 1967.

MILLER, J. "Information Input, Overload, and Psychopathology." *American Journal of Psychiatry*, 1960, *116*.

MILLWARD, R. "PPBS: Problems of Implementation." *Journal of the American Institute of Planners*, 1968, *34*(2).

MILSUM, J. "The Technosphere, The Biosphere, The Sociosphere." IEEE *Spectrum*, 1968, *5*(6).

MITCHELL, A., AND BAIRD, M. *American Values*. Long Range Planning Service, Report 378. Menlo Park, Calif.: Stanford Research Institute, 1969.

MOCKLER, R., "Theory and Practice of Planning." *Harvard Business Review*, 1970, *48*(2).

MOHR, L. "Determinants of Innovation in Organizations." *The American Political Science Review*, 1969, *62*(1).

MORRIS, C. *The Open Self*. New York: Prentice-Hall, 1948.

MORRIS, C., AND SMALL, L. "Changes in Conceptions of the Good Life by American College Students from 1950 to 1970." *Journal of Personality and Social Psychology*, 1971, *20*(2).

MOSHER, F. "The Public Service in the Temporary Society." *Public Administration Review*, 1971, *31*(1).

MOYNIHAN, D. *Maximum Feasible Misunderstanding*. New York: The Free Press, 1969.

MOYNIHAN, D. "Counselor's Statement." *Toward Balanced Growth: Quantity with Quality*. Report of the National Goals Research Staff. Washington, D.C.: U.S. Government Printing Office, 1970.

MOYNIHAN, D. "Eliteland." *Psychology Today*, 1970, *4*(4).

MUMFORD, L. *The Transformations of Man*. New York: Harper Bros., 1956.

MUNSINGER, H., AND KESSEN, W. "Uncertainty, Structure, and Preference." *Psychological Monographs: General and Applied*, 1964, *78*.

MYRDAL, G. "The World Poverty Problem." *Encyclopedia Britannica Annual World Book*, 1972.

NEEDLEMAN, J. *The New Religions*. New York: Simon and Schuster Pocket Books, 1972.

NELSON, R., PECK, M., AND KALACHEK, E. *Technology, Economic Growth, and Public Policy*. Washington, D.C.: The Brookings Institution, 1967.

The New York City Rand Institute: A Review, January 1968-June 1970. New York: New York City Rand Institute, 1970.

NOVAK, M. *The Experience of Nothingness*. New York: Harper and Row, 1970.

Our Future Business Environment: Developing Trends and Changing Institutions. ERM-85A. General Electric Company, 1968.

OZBEKHAN, H. "Toward a General Theory of Planning." In E. Jantsch (Ed.), *Perspectives of Planning*. Paris: Organization for Economic Co-operation and Development, 1969.

PARSONS, T. *Structure and Process in Modern Societies*. New York: The Free Press, 1960.

PEABODY, R., AND ROURKE, F. "Public Bureaucracies." In J. March (Ed.), *Handbook of Organizations*. Chicago: Rand McNally, 1965.

PECCEI, A. "How to Survive on the Planet Earth." *Successo* (International Edition). Milan, 1971, 2.

PERSICO, C., AND MC EACKRON, N. *Forces for Societal Transformation in the United States, 1950-2000*. SRI Project 6747, Vol. 1. Menlo Park, Calif.: Stanford Research Institute, 1971.

PICKERING, G. *Voluntarism and the American Way*. Occasional Paper 7. Washington, D.C.: Center for a Voluntary Society, 1970.

The Planning-Programming-Budgeting System: Progress and Potentials. Hearings before the Subcommittee on Economy in Government of the Joint Economic Committee. Washington, D.C.: U.S. Government Printing Office, 1967.

PLATT, J. "Lock-ins and Multiple Lock-ins in Collective Behavior." *American Scientist*, 19169, 57(2).

PLATT, J. "What We Must Do." *Science*, 1969, 149.

PLATT, J. *Hierarchical Restructuring*. Ann Arbor: University of Michigan, Mental Health Research Institute Communication 269, 1970.

POLAK, F. *The Image of the Future*, Vol. II. Translated by E. Boulding. The Netherlands: A. W. Sijhoff, 1961.

POLANYI, M. *The Tacit Dimension*. New York: Doubleday, 1966.

POUNDS, W. *The Process of Problem Finding*. Cambridge: Massachusetts Institute of Technology, 1965. Unpublished manuscript.

RATOOSH, P. "Experimental Studies of Implementation." In J. Lawrence (Ed.), *Operational Research and the Social Sciences*. London: Tavistock, 1966.

READ, W. *Factors Affecting Upward Communication at Middle Management Levels in Industrial Organizations*. University of Michigan, 1959. Unpublished dissertation.

READ, W. "Upward Communication in Industrial Hierarchies." *Human Relations*, 1962, *15*.

REIN, M. "Social Planning: The Search for Legitimacy." *Journal of the American Institute of Planners*, 1969, *35*.

REIN, M. "Social Policy Analysis as the Interpretation of Beliefs." *Journal of the American Institute of Planners*. September 1971, *37*.

RICE, A. K. *Learning for Leadership*. London: Tavistock, 1965.

RIESMAN, D., GLAZER, N., AND DENNEY, R. *The Lonely Crowd*. New York: Doubleday Anchor Books, 1955.

RITTEL, H., AND WEBBER, M. *Dilemmas in a General Theory of Planning*. Working Paper N. 194, Institute of Urban and Regional Development, University of California, Berkeley, 1972.

RIVLIN, A. *The Planning, Programming, and Budgeting System in the Department of Health, Education, and Welfare: Some Lessons from Experience*. Washington, D.C.: The Brookings Institution, 1969.

RIVLIN, A. *Systematic Thinking for Social Action*. Washington, D.C.: The Brookings Institution, 1971.

ROKEACH, M. *Beliefs, Attitudes, and Values*. San Francisco: Jossey-Bass, 1968.

ROETHLISBERGER, F. *Management and Morale*. Cambridge: Harvard University Press, 1941.

ROETHLISBERGER, F., AND DICKSON, W., with the assistance of Wright, H. *Management and the Worker*. Cambridge: Harvard University Press, 1946.

ROGERS, E., WITH SHOEMAKER, F. *Diffusion of Innovations*. New York: The Free Press, 1971.

ROSENTHAL, R. *Experimenter Effects in Behavioral Research*. New York: Appleton Century Crofts, 1966.

ROSENTHAL, R., AND WEISS, R. "Problems of Organizational Feedback Processes." In R. Bauer (Ed.), *Social Indicators*. Cambridge: M.I.T. Press, 1966.

ROSS, R., AND GUSKIN, A. "Advocacy and Democracy: Towards a Research Program." Working paper, Center for Research on Utilization of Scientific Knowledge. Ann Arbor: Institute for Social Research, 1972.

ROTTER, J. "Generalized Expectancies for Interpersonal Trust." *American Psychologist*, 1971, *26*(5).

SALOMEN, J. "Science Policy and Its Myths." *Futures*, 1971, *3*(1).

SCHEIN, E. *Process Consultation: Its Role in Organization Development*. Reading, Mass.: Addison-Wesley, 1969.

SCHICK, A. "Systems Politics and Systems Budgeting." *Public Administration Review*, 1969, *24*(1).

SCHICK, A. "Can the States Improve Their Budgeting?" Brookings Research Report 120. Washington, D.C.: The Brookings Institution, 1971.

SCHON, D. *Technology and Change: The Impact of Invention and Innovation on American Social and Economic Development*. New York: Dell, 1967.

SCHON, D. *Beyond the Stable State*. New York: Random House, 1971.

SCHRODER, H., DRIVER, M., AND STIEUFERT, S. *Human Information Processing*. New York: Holt, Rinehart and Winston, 1967.

SCHULTZE, C. *The Politics and Economics of Public Spending*. Washington, D.C.: The Brookings Institution, 1968.

SCODEL, A., RATOOSH, P., AND MINAS, J. *Some Personality Correlates of Decision Making Under Conditions of Risk*. Reprint 1. Berkeley: Institute of Industrial Relations, University of California, 1960.

SEASHORE, S., AND MC NEILL, R. (Eds.) *The Management of Urban Crisis*. New York: The Free Press, 1971.

SEIDMAN, H. *Politics, Position, and Power: The Dynamics of Federal Organization*. New York: Oxford University Press, 1970.

SHAPLEY, D. "Professional Societies: Identity Crisis Threatens on Bread and Butter Issues." *Science*, May 19, 1972, *176*.

SHELDON, E., AND FREEMAN, H. "Notes on Social Indicators: Promises and Potential." *Policy Sciences*, 1970, *1*(1).

SHONFIELD, A. *Modern Capitalism: The Changing Balance of Public and Private Power*. New York: Oxford University Press, 1965.

SIMON, H. "On the Concept of Organizational Goal." *Administrative Science Quarterly*, 1964, *9*(1).

SIMON, H. "Administrative Behavior." *International Encyclopedia of the Social Sciences*, Vol. I. New York: Browell Collier and Macmillan, 1968.

SLATER, P. *The Pursuit of Loneliness*. Boston: Beacon Press, 1970.

SMELSER, N. *Theory of Collective Behavior*. New York: The Free Press, 1972.

SOFER, C. *The Organization From Within*. Chicago: Quandrangle Books, 1962.

SOLO, R. *Economic Organizations and Social Systems*. New York: Bobbs-Merrill, 1967.

SOLO, R. "New Maths and Old Stabilities." *Saturday Review*, January 22, 1972.

SPERLICH, P. *Conflict and Harmony in Human Affairs: Cross-Pressures and Political Behavior*. Chicago: Rand McNally, 1971.

SPILHAUS, A. "Ecolibrium." *Science*, February 18, 1972, *175*.

STABLER, C. "Changing Times: For Many Corporations, Social Responsibility Is Now a Major Concern." *Wall Street Journal*, October 29, 1971.

STAGNER, R. "Decision-Making and Conflict Resolution." In S. Seashore and R. McNeill, *The Management of Urban Crisis*. New York: The Free Press, 1971.

STEINER, G. *Top Management Planning*. Toronto: Collier-Macmillan, 1969.

STRASSMAN, P. "Managing the Evolution to Advanced Information Systems." Presented at the Tenth American Meeting of the Institute of Management Sciences, Atlanta, Georgia. Stamford, Conn.: Xerox Corporation, 1969.

SUCHMAN, E. *Evaluative Research: Principles and Practice in Public Service and Social Action Programs*. New York: Russell Sage Foundation, 1967.

SUZUKI, D. *Zen Buddhism*. W. Barrett, Ed. Garden City, N.Y.: Doubleday and Co., 1956.

TANNENBAUM, A. *Control in Organizations*. New York: McGraw-Hill, 1968.

TART, C. *Altered States of Consciousness*. New York: Wiley, 1969.

TART, C. "States of Consciousness and State-Specific Sciences." *Science*, 1972, *176*.

TEAD, O. "The Ethical Challenge of Modern Administration." In H. Cleveland and H. Laswell (Eds.), *Ethics and Bigness*. New York: Harper and Row, 1962.

TERKEL, S. "Servants of the State." *Harper's Magazine*, 1972, *244*.

TERREBERRY, S. "The Evolution of Organizational Environments." *Administrative Science Quarterly*, 1968, *12*(4).

THANT, U. "At the United Nations." *The American Way*, 1970, *3*.

THOMAS, T., AND MC KINNEY, D. *Accountability in Education*. Research Memorandum, EPRC-6747-15. Menlo Park, Calif.: Stanford Research Institute, 1972.

THOMPSON, J. "Decision-Making, the Firm, and the Market." In W. Cooper, H. Leavit, and M. Shelly (Eds.), *New Perspectives in Organizational Research*. New York: Wiley, 1964.

THOMPSON, J. *Organizations in Action: Social Science Bases of Administrative Theory*. New York: McGraw-Hill, 1967.

THOMPSON, J., AND TUDEN, A. "Strategies, Structures, and Processes of Organizational Decision." In J. Thompson and others (Eds.), *Comparative Studies in Administration*. Pittsburgh: University of Pittsburgh Press, 1959.

THOMPSON, V. "How Scientific Management Thwarts Innovation." *Trans-action*, 1968, *5*(7).

THOMPSON, W. *A Preface to Urban Economics*. Baltimore: Johns Hopkins Paperbacks, 1965.

TRIBE, L. "Towards a New Technological Ethic: The Role of Legal Liability." *Impact of Science on Society*, 1971a, *21*(3).

TRIBE, L. "Legal Frameworks for the Assessment and Control of Technology." *Minerva*, 1961, *9*(2).

TRIPATHI, R. *A Review of Conceptualizations of Organizational Environment and Studies of Environment-Organization Relationships.* Manuscript prepared for the University of Michigan's Organizational Psychology Program, December 1971.

TUGWELL, R. "Drafting a Model Constitution." *The Center Magazine,* 1970, *3*(5).

Urban and Regional Information Systems: Support for Planning in Metropolitan Areas, M/MP-71, U.S. Department of Housing and Urban Development. Washington, D.C.: U.S. Government Printing Office, 1968.

The Urban Detroit Area Effort: The Substance of Findings of the UDA Research Project. Athens, Greece: Doxiadis Associates, 1969.

VANDIVER, K. "The Aircraft Brake Scandal." *Harpers Magazine,* 1972, *244.*

VICKERS, G. *The Art of Judgment.* New York: Basic Books, 1965.

VICKERS, G. "The Multi-Valued Choice." In L. Thayer (Ed.), *Communication Concepts and Perspectives.* New York: Spartan Books, 1967.

VICKERS, G. *Freedom in a Rocking Boat.* Middlesex, England: Penguin Books, 1970.

VICKERS, G. "The Management of Conflict." *Futures,* 1972, *4*(2).

WADE, N. "Freedom of Information: Officials Thwart Public Right to Know." *Science,* Feb. 4, 1972, *175.*

WALTON, R. "Theory of Conflict in Lateral Organizational Relationships." In J. Lawrence (Ed.), *Operational Research and the Social Sciences.* London: Tavistock, 1966.

WALTON, R. *Interpersonal Peacemaking: Confrontations and Third-Party Consultation.* Reading, Mass.: Addison-Wesley, 1969.

WARREN, R. "Interorganizational Field as a Focus of Investigation." Waltham, Mass.: Brandeis University, 1968.

WARWICK, D. "Socialization and Personality." In S. Seashore and R. McNeill (Eds.), *The Management of Urban Crisis.* New York: The Free Press, 1971.

WEBB, E. *Individual and Organizational Forces Influencing the Interpretation of Indicators.* Research Paper P-488. Arlington, Va.: Institute for Defense Analyses, Science and Technology Division, 1969.

WEBBER, M. "The Roles of Intelligence Systems in Urban-Systems Planning." *Journal of the American Institute of Planners,* 1965, *31*(4).

WEBBER, M. "Planning in an Environment of Change." *The Town Planning Review,* 1968, *39*(3).

WESTIN, A. (Ed.) *Information Technology in a Democracy.* Cambridge: Harvard University Press, 1971.

WESTIN, A. "Introduction." In C. Beard, *The Supreme Court and the Constitution.* Englewood Cliffs, N.J.: Prentice-Hall, 1962.

WESTIN, A. *Privacy and Freedom.* New York: Atheneum, 1967.

WESTIN, A. "Information Technology and Public Decision-Making." In *Harvard University Program on Technology and Society, 1964-1972, A Final Review.* Cambridge: Harvard University Press, 1972.

"What Goals?" New York Times, July 21, 1970, p. 34.

WHEELIS, A. *Quest for Identity.* New York: Norton, 1958.

WIELAND, G. "The Determinants of Clarity in Organization Goals." *Human Relations,* 1969, *22(2).*

WILDAVSKY, A. *The Politics of the Budgetary Process.* Boston: Little, Brown, 1964.

WILENSKY, H. *Organizational Intelligence: Knowledge and Policy in Government and Industry.* New York: Basic Books, 1967.

WILKINS, L., AND GITCHOFF, T. "Trends and Projections in Social Control Systems." *The Annals of the American Academy of Political an Social Science,* 1969, *381.*

WILSON, D., AND WILSON, A. *Toward the Institutionalization of Change.* Working Paper 11. Middletown, Conn.: Institute for the Future, 1970.

WOHLSTETTER, R. *Pearl Harbor: Warning and Decision.* Stanford: Stanford University Press, 1962.

ZIMBARDO, P., AND EABESEN, E. *Influencing Attitudes and Changing Behavior, A Basic Introduction to Relevant Methodology, Theory and Applications.* Reading, Mass.: Addison-Wesley, 1969.

☆ *Index* ☆

Disaster, as situation of acute
uncertainty, 135; *also see*
Behavior; disaster
"Dissociation," as means for coping
with turbulence, 50-51
Distributive equity, and long-range
social planning, 92
Dominant mode of appreciation, 331
Downs, Anthony, 280, 293
Dror, Yehezkel, 90, 105-106
Drucker, P., 360
Dunn, Edgar, 35-36, 68, 81-82, 327
Dynamic programming, 76

E

"Ecological ethic," 337
Economic theory, inadequacies of, 78
Economics, Establishment, 79;
Keynesian, 164
Edelman, Murray, 153-154, 157
Eichman. *See* "*petit* Eichman"
Emery, Fred, 49-52, 114, 304
Environment: components of
turbulent environment, 52;
definition, as intended herein, 86-
87; natural, 86; participation in
planning, 87-90; rational or
emotional stance toward, 123-
124; as a major source of
uncertainty, 126; "turbulent
environment" defined, 50; types
of, as differentiated by Emery and
Trist, 49-52; relationship with
organization, 86
Environmental Protection Act, 72
Environmental turbulence: *See*
Turbulence, environmental
Error embracing: and accountability,
160-164; effect of childhood
experiences on, 153, 158; as
guarantee of environmental
involvement, 152; and leadership,
153-155; as natural prerequisite
for learning, 163-164; and need
to control, 154-155; in R and D,
156; social psychological rewards

of, 158-160; reinforcement of
behavior, 152-153
Ethical considerations, in evaluation
of social experiments, 94-95
Etzioni, Amitai, 67
Europe, long-range social planning
in, 105
European Trade Community, 342
Ewing, D., 354, 358-359, 362

F

Feedback: in assessing goal
achievement, 174-176; defenses
against, 58; as generator of
turbulence, 57; as necessary for
long-range social planning, 58;
reasons for avoidance, 56; in
situations of accelerated change,
66
"Fire-fighting," 58-59
Flow concept of learning, 65
Food and Drug Administration, 314
Forecasting: as essential feature of
"new" planning, 66; technological,
79-80
Forrester, J.W., 146
Fortune, 354, 362
Fraisse, P., 181-182
"Fractionation," as means for coping
with turbulence, 50-51
Friedmann, John, 64-65
Friend, J., 66-67, 129-130
"Friendly fascism," 64
Fromm, Erich, 59, 329
Future-conjecture: and goal setting,
171-172; methods, 76; reflecting
obsolescence, 173
Future studies: avoidance of, 314-
315; as contributing to
turbulence, 58; as generator of
feedback, 316; and latent
uncertainties, 187; as source of
myths, 187-189 weaknesses of,
83
Futures, alternative, 66

Interpersonal competence, 211-217;
  Burns and Stalker on, 216-217;
  and establishing trust, 225-227;
  and expressing feelings, 218-220;
  and intuition, 222. *Also see*
  Interpersonal relations
"Inventing the future," 188

J

James, William, 329
Janis, Irving, 249-250,253
Jantsch, Erik, 66
Jessop, William, 66-67, 129-130
Johnson, Mark, 17
Jung, Carl, 329

K

Kahn, Alfred, 67-68, 88-89, 278-279
Kahn, Robert, 116-118, 334
Kantor, Robert, 337
Kelly, William, 47
Kluckhohn, Clyde, 47
Knight, Frank, 123
Kuhn, Thomas, 331, 348

L

La Porte, Todd, 122, 125-127, 132,
  135, 146
Laing, J.D., 329
Lakoff, George, 17
Lawrence, Paul, 259, 265, 267
Leadership: and anxiety, 340-341;
  requirement for accepting
  uncertainty, 144-145
Lichtman, C., 191-192
Likert, Rensis, 243, 253
Lindblom, Charles, 91, 157
Linear programming, 76
Lodge, George C., 335
Long, Lewis, 158
Long, Norton, 265
Long-range social planning: activities
  that should constitute, 68-70;
  areas of application, 88-89;
  central goal of, 67; choosing to
  learn, 43; components of as
  uncertainty-reducers, 143;

concept of, 37, 63-75; cyclic
  nature of, 68-70; derivation of
  resistance to, 43-44; difficulties of
  implementation, 74; and elitism,
  63, 87-88; and evaluation of
  social experiments, 92-95;
  obstructions to learning, 42-43;
  and openness to turbulence, 57;
  phases of, as summarized by A.
  Kahn, 68; as philosophy, 84;
  political consequences of, 64; as
  prerequisite for responsible
  organizational performance, 41;
  requirements for, 38;
  requirements as summarized by
  Webber, 68-70; role of
  inadvertence in, 338; social
  psychological implications of, 71;
  social psychological reactions to,
  43; sources and support for, 89;
  as synonymous with future-
  responsive societal learning, 37-
  38; why long-range social
  planning must be a learning
  process, 39-40;
Lorsch, James, 259, 265, 267
Luckmann, Thomas, 46-47

M

Management: "by exception," 55;
  participative, 117
Management information systems
  (MIS), 75, 100, 296; Argyris on,
  145; and uncertainty, 134
Management science, 81
Managers, desirable characteristics,
  335-336
Marcuse, Henri, 329
Marris, Peter, 272
Martino, J., 354
Marx, Karl, 100
Maslow, Abraham, 329
Mau, J., 78
May, Rollo, 187, 188-189, 329
Mayo, E., 241
McGregor, Donald, 329
McWhinney, William, 56

Public agencies: *See* Government

R

Rand Corporation, 346
Ratoosh, Philborn, 140
Rein, Martin, 172-173, 197-198, 272
"Requisite variety:" requirement for in activities responding to the environment, 86-87
Research and development: and relationship of organization to environment, 86; and technological assessment, 79
Rice, A. Kenneth, 103-104, 135, 241, 242, 247, 250, 253, 266, 283
Risk: concept of as distinguished from uncertainty, 123
Rivlin, Alice, 80-81
Rogers, Carl, 329
Rogers, E., 101-103, 104
Role competence: definitions of, 200-201; in government agencies, 205-206
Role performance: moral consequences of, 57
Role stress, research on, 334
Roethlisberger, F., 241
Rosenthal, R., 305-306, 316, 317
Royal Dutch/Shell, 351

S

Salomen, J., 83
"Satisficing," as used by H. Simon, 90-91
Schein, Edgar, 30
Schick, Alan, 91
Schon, Don, 123, 128, 133, 135, 357
Shonfield, A., 352
Science, 336
"Second-order and third-order consequences," 79-80
"Segmentation," as means for coping with turbulence, 50-51
Self-image: and achievement, 181; role of past on, 181
Senge, Peter, 30
Shoemaker, F., 101-103, 104

Sierra Club, 314
Simon, Herbert, 90, 260, 304
Simulation, 76
Slater, Philip, 335
Social-change theory, 77
"Social engineering:" avoiding in long-range social planning, 64; definition, 36-37, 39; effect of assumptions on goal setting, 169-170; inhumanity of, 347; and mechanistic planning concept, 66
Social indicators: data development and testing, 82; and distributive equity, 344; to interpret feedback, 58; lack of, 81-83; as planning technology, 75; in reducing uncertainty, 135; and theory development, 309;
Social reality: as constructed by humans, 46-47, 54; Berger and Luckmann on, 46-47, 54
Social reorganization: as means for coping with turbulence, 51-52
Solo, Robert, 33, 78-79
Stabler, E., 360
Stalker, G., 134
State, Department of, 278
Steiner, G., 360
Sun Oil, 79
System design, as central subject of planning, 66
Systems approach, 76

T

Tavistock Institute, 66, 278
"Technocratic planning," 347
"Technological core," 136
Technology: preoccupation with, and emphasis on control, 123-124; as source of uncertainty, 125
Also see Planning technology
Third World, long-range social planning in, 105
Thompson, James, 126, 127, 136-137, 171-172, 265-266
Thompson Ramo Wooldridge (TRW), 245